America in Crisis

AMERICA

Perry Miller

Richard B. Morris

Richard H. Shryock

Louis Hartz

Howard Mumford Jones

C. Vann Woodward

Henry David

Richard Hofstadter

Meyer Schapiro

Dexter Perkins

Walton H. Hamilton

Paul B. Sears

Morris Janowitz

Norman Holmes Pearson

IN CRISIS

Fourteen
Crucial
Episodes
in
American
History

Edited by

Daniel Aaron

Hamden, Connecticut

Archon Books   **1971**

973.08
A113a

L. C. catalog card number: 72-131372
ISB number: 0-208-01043-2

The Shoe String Press, Inc.

Foreword

In the summer of 1949 the Carnegie Corporation of New York made a grant to Bennington College for an experimental course designed to bring out the role and operation of values in American history. The fourteen essays in this volume, first presented by their authors as public lectures during the winter of 1950–1, provided the resulting course with its thematic substance. The course, directed by Professor Daniel Aaron, was entitled "American Response to Crisis."

The theme of crisis was chosen by a committee of the Bennington College faculty not only as challenging in itself to students and teacher but as setting the problem of American beliefs and values in the dynamic context of concrete historical situations. The committee's choice of crises from some two hundred suggestions will not escape cavil, but it is worth noting that they range widely over such American interests as medicine, education, and art, as well as politics, economics, and foreign affairs. It must be admitted that the episodes dealt with were not all "crises" in a strict or conventional sense; but each entailed some degree of social dislocation and intellectual challenge that forced Americans to re-examine old values and face new ones head on.

The reader will find here fresh and penetrating interpretations of significant events in our history, as well as a basis for judgments on permanence and change in our value patterns. Indeed this book, like the course from which it derives, may be considered not an easy answer to the complicated question of American values in times of decision, but a challenge to thought in a time of crisis.

THOMAS P. BROCKWAY, *Acting President*
Bennington College
Bennington, Vermont
December 1951

Introduction

Daniel Aaron

"Every nation," said Emerson, "believes that the Divine Providence has a sneaking kindness for it." Americans have been particularly receptive to this idea, and history has confirmed them. Today, however, as they face their greatest crisis, Providence seems less benign, and the question whether or not the country is prepared for the tests that lie ahead in the ominous future is no longer impertinent.

We shall know soon enough, but in the meantime an examination of our response to past crises and an inquiry into our behavior during other crucial periods may be in order as we speculate on the nation's ability to meet and to surmount the present one. How, for example, have the Americans—in groups or as a people—responded to events or situations that seem to threaten their physical well-being and their personal values? How have they behaved when their customary habits of living and thinking are disrupted? The fourteen essays in the Bennington series contain some answers to these questions. Each in its own way brings out the defects and virtues of the American character and institutions, and reveals how American values have manifested themselves in moments of crisis.

The reader will notice that of the fourteen crises discussed here only three relate directly to foreign affairs. The limitation is deliberate. Until comparatively recently, American crises have revolved around domestic rather than international issues. The most serious emergency the nation faced between the two great crises of 1776 and 1941 was the Civil War (an event toward which two of the essays are pointed); the lesser disturbances that occurred —the strikes, riots, panics, and natural catastrophes—preoccupied public attention far more than did foreign affairs. Our geographical isolation and the demands of the huge and unexploited territory undoubtedly had much to do with national self-sufficiency, but whatever the explanation, international affairs (although momentarily exciting and even capable of provoking hysteria) were quickly subordinated to the more pressing routine of daily life. Not even the first World War seriously disturbed American buoyancy or the popular faith in our inevitable progress. Since then, however, the serious misgivings that began with the fall of France in 1940 have continued with fluctuating intensity.

Quite understandably, the American people for well over a century have been absorbed in their own private affairs; their loyalties have been personal rather than corporate. This attitude is not peculiar to Americans, and yet it may have more fateful implications for the United States than for European countries where policy-making was not and is not yet a popular prerogative. Thus, with notable exceptions, we have displayed more intelligence and inventiveness in our private enterprises than in our public, and the latter have aroused less interest. As a rule we have preferred to meet a problem when it comes, whether in diplomacy or finance or agriculture or labor, and to avoid long-term plans or policies. In dealing with such matters as flood control, public-safety measures, or the rise of Fascism or Communism, we have been traditionally opportunist, trusting in the proverbially sound common sense of the people to carry us through the unanticipated crisis.

The result has been that although we have risen magnificently to the crises often brought about or aggravated by negligence and shortsightedness, we have done little to prevent their recurrence. The characteristic American response has been to "deal with" the emergency or "fix" the machinery and then pay no further attention until another breakdown disturbs the domestic tranquillity.

Thus far our singular good fortune, our extraordinary resources, and our abounding confidence in the future have helped us to gloss over our failures and to justify a trust in "manifest destiny." But this very faith, this conviction that each generation must automatically advance over its predecessor (materially speaking, at any rate, if not morally), helps to account for the shock and chagrin, sometimes followed by despair, when progress bogs down. As a nation, we don't take our setbacks very philosophically: Korea and Yalta, economic slumps or defeats at the Olympic games, Bull Run and Kasserine Pass come very hard. We are not good losers because losing ill befits our destiny; it is somehow un-American. This belief obtains despite the warnings of our realists that the "perpetual land-boom" can't last, that as we grow rich and powerful we become fair game for envious rivals, that nations decline as swiftly as they advance, that progress is not certain, and that with world power come new responsibilities which necessitate the development of new abilities and techniques. We have never listened to these voices very long or seriously.

Nor have we ever learned to distinguish between our views of ourselves and ourselves as others see us. Instead, we have expected the outside world to take our protestations at face value (because we believe them to be true and in good faith, and because we want to be liked), but when other countries fail to do so we attribute their response to malice or base ingratitude. Hence the frequently described American pendulum of intervention and withdrawal. Tocqueville was only the first to describe the compulsive and evangelical spirit in which the Americans on occasion could "burst the bonds of matter by which they are restrained," and "soar impetuously toward Heaven." Tocqueville observed further: "An American attends to his private concerns as if he were alone in the world, and the next minute he gives himself up to the commonweal as if he had forgotten them. At one time, he seems animated by the most selfish cupidity; at another by the most lively patriotism." History bears him out. Our wars with Mexico and Spain became crusades, and the submission of thousands to a higher collective loyalty only carried over into secular experience what had already occurred in the great religious revivals like the "Great Awakening" in the eighteenth century. Just as the religious revivals were followed by backsliding into sin, so cynicism or disillusion followed the nation's outbursts of generous emotion. The war with Spain culminated with the shoddy adventures in the Philippines; the crusade to save the world for democracy in 1917 petered out in a churlish nationalism.

Until a few years ago, our deficiencies as a people seemed supremely unimportant and certainly quite removed from the question of national security. The opinion of the foreigner mattered very little. We hated the ill-tempered Mrs. Trollope and were pleased by the friendly, if not uncritical, assessments of Lord Bryce, but we considered irrelevant all European evaluations of our society, whether hostile or flattering. In the spring of 1952, the opinion of the world cannot be shrugged away. We are beginning to recognize that our treatment of minorities, our ideas on civil rights, even the books we write, the music we compose, and the films we produce can help, as much as the size of our stockpiles, to determine our future relations with Europe and the East.

To a nation hitherto self-contained and confident, the new responsibilities do not come easily. We have never bothered to understand alien ideas ("isms" were something to fear or to deride), and "selling America" has simply meant the dispensing of American largesse. Now we see the extent of our involvement and the vulnerability of our talismans: natural resources and "know-how." We see that world problems are not merely American problems writ large, that it will take more than a little common sense and a few "man to man" talks with the Russians to solve them. Finally, we can appreciate the degree to which our strengths and weaknesses as a people have been conditioned by the American past, how we have been blessed and victimized by our history. Because of our wealth and isolation and our vast inland empire, because of the advantages we have enjoyed as a result of European rivalries, we did not develop some of the qualities and abilities we now so desperately need.

Today we no longer enjoy all of these advantages which permitted us to act impatiently and emotionally, operate without plan, rely on short-term expediency. Such crises as those growing out of the abolitionist riots or the Mitchell Palmer "red scare" in 1920 passed quickly. We could exploit our immigrant groups and then, out of political considerations, submit to the pressures from these same ethnic minorities. It is doubtful if we can now indulge ourselves to the same extent, for we face a long-term emergency that won't let us relax and that demands difficult psychological and social adjustments.

If the Bennington lectures describe how Americans have acted during their most vulnerable moments, they also offer impressive documentation of national strength and resiliency. Crisis has brought out the worst and weakest in our society, but it has also brought out the strongest and best. It has produced great leaders and martyrs, and demonstrated a remarkable capacity of the Americans to act collectively for a common purpose. Our galvanic or evangelical response to crisis may be caused by the release of energies ordinarily dammed up by restraints of various kinds, but whatever its origin, it has sometimes resulted in more generosity of spirit and the demonstration of qualities less apparent in calmer times. In the crises of the future, our traditional apathy, our parochialism and emotionality will have to be reckoned with, but so must the resourcefulness and courage that we have displayed in the face of a common peril, internal or external. During the painful and uncertain years ahead, an America already tested will discover the value of its rigorous apprenticeship.

Contents

America in Crisis

I. *Jonathan Edwards and the Great Awakening*

The great revival that swept over the American colonies in the early middle decades of the eighteenth century was, in a religious sense, a crisis for a large part of the population, but it was also a social revolution that profoundly modified Colonial society. During this period of religious upheaval the revivalists challenged the orthodox and the conservative, who stood for sobriety and rationality in religious matters and for social hierarchy in political affairs. What Professor Perry Miller refers to here as the "silent democracy" found its aspirations expressed in the pronouncements of revival leaders like Jonathan Edwards. The Great Awakening, furthermore, set the pattern for a particular kind of American group experience, which continued in subsequent religious and secular ceremonies. From the eighteenth century to the present, the ritualism of national celebrations, political rallies, and the like have permitted the individual to identify himself with his fellows by joining with them in allegiance to a higher community loyalty.

I

Jonathan Edwards and the Great Awakening

Perry Miller

Professor of English, Harvard University

Although in the year 1740 some fairly flagrant scenes of emotional religion were being enacted in Boston, it was mainly in the Connecticut Valley that the frenzy raged and whence it spread like a pestilence to the civilized East. The Harvard faculty of that time would indeed have considered the Great Awakening a "crisis," because to them it threatened everything they meant by culture or religion or just common decency. It was a horrible business that should be suppressed and altogether forgotten. Certainly they would not have approved its being dignified as a starting-point in a series of great American crises.

As far as they could see, it was nothing but an orgy of the emotions. They called it—in the lexicon of the Harvard faculty this word conveyed the utmost contempt—"enthusiasm." It was not a religious persuasion: it was an excitement of overstimulated passions that understandably slopped over into activities other than the ecclesiastical and increased the number of bastards in the Valley, where already there were too many. And above all, in the Valley lived their archenemy, the deliberate instigator of this crime, who not only fomented the frenzy but was so lost to shame that he brazenly defended it as a positive advance in American culture. To add insult to injury, he justified the Awakening by employing a science and a psychological conception with which nothing they had learned at Harvard had prepared them to cope.

It was certainly a weird performance. Edwards delivered his revival sermons—for example the goriest, the one at Enfield that goes by the title "Sinners in the Hands of an Angry God" and is all that most people nowadays associate with his name—to small audiences in country churches. In these rude structures (few towns had yet prospered enough to afford the Georgian churches of the later eighteenth century which are now the charm of the landscape) the people yelled and shrieked, they rolled in the aisles, they crowded up to the pulpit and begged him to stop, they cried for mercy. One who heard him described his method of preaching: he looked all the time at the bell rope (hanging down from the roof at the other end of the church) as though he would look it in two; he did not stoop to regard the screaming mass, much less to console them.

Of course, in a short time the opinion of the Harvard faculty appeared to be vindicated. In 1740 Edwards had writhing in the churches not only his own people but every congregation he spoke to, and he dominated the entire region. Ten years later he was exiled, thrown out of his church and town after a vicious squabble (the fight against him being instigated by certain of the first citizens, some of them his cousins, who by adroit propaganda mobilized "the people" against him), and no pulpit in New England would invite this terrifying figure. He had no choice but to escape to the frontier, as did so many misfits in American history. He went to Stockbridge, where he eked out his last years as a missionary to a lot of moth-eaten Indians. Because of the works he produced under these—shall we call them untoward?—circumstances, and because he was still the acknowledged leader of the revival movement, he was invited in 1758 to become president of the College of New Jersey (the present-day Princeton), but he died a few weeks after his inauguration, so that his life really belongs to the Connecticut Valley.

One may well ask what makes such a chronicle of frenzy and defeat a crisis in American history. From the point of view of the social historian and still more from that of the sociologist it was a phenomenon of mass behavior, of which poor Mr. Edwards was the deluded victim. No sociologically trained historian will for a moment accept it on Edwards's terms—which were, simply, that it was an outpouring of the Spirit of God upon the land. And so why should we, today, mark it as a turning-point in our history, especially since thereafter religious revivals became a part of the American social pattern, while our intellectual life developed, on the whole, apart from these vulgar eruptions? The answer is that this first occurrence did actually involve all the interests of the community, and the definitions that arose out of it were profoundly decisive and meaningful. In that perspective Jonathan Edwards, being the most acute definer of the terms on which the revival was conducted and the issues on which it went astray, should be regarded—even by the social historian—as a formulator of propositions that the American society, having been shaken by this experience, was henceforth consciously to observe.

There is not space enough here to survey the Awakening through the vast reaches of the South and the Middle Colonies, nor even to list the intricate consequences for the social ordering of New England. The splintering of the churches and the increase of sectarianism suggest one way in which Americans "responded" to this crisis, and the impulse it gave to education, most notably in the founding of Princeton, is another. Such discussions, however valuable, are external and statistical. We come to a deeper understanding of what this crisis meant by examining more closely a revelation or two from the most self-conscious—not to say the most literate—theorist of the Awakening.

The theme I would here isolate is one with which Edwards dealt only by indirection. He was skilled in the art of presenting ideas not so much by expounding as by vivifying them, and he achieved his ends not only by explicit statement but more often by a subtle shift in emphasis. In this case, it is entirely a matter of divining nuances. Nevertheless, the issue was present throughout the Awakening and, after the temporary manifestations had abated, on this proposition a revolution was found to have been wrought that is one of the enduring responses of the American mind to crisis.

I mean specifically what it did to the conception of the relation of the ruler—political or ecclesiastical—to the body politic. However, before we can pin down this somewhat illusive development, we are confronted with the problem of whether the Great Awakening is properly to be viewed as a peculiarly American phenomenon at all. It would be possible to write about it—as has been done—as merely one variant of a universal occurrence in Western culture. Between about 1730 and 1760 practically all of Western Europe was swept by some kind of religious emotionalism. It was present in Germany, Holland, Switzerland, and France,

and in Catholic circles there was an analogous movement that can
be interpreted as an outcropping of the same thing, and that the
textbooks call "Quietism." And most dramatically, it was present
in England with the Wesleys, Whitefield, and Methodism.

Once this international viewpoint is assumed, the American outburst becomes merely one among many—a colonial one at that—
and one hesitates to speak about it as a crisis in a history specifically American. What was at work throughout the Western world
is fairly obvious: the upper or the educated classes were tired of
the religious squabbling of the seventeenth century, and turned
to the more pleasing and not at all contentious generalities of
eighteenth-century rationalism; the spiritual hungers of the lower
classes or of what, for shorthand purposes, we may call "ordinary"
folk were not satisfied by Newtonian demonstrations that design
in the universe proved the existence of God. Their aspirations
finally found vent in the revivals, and in each country we may
date the end of a Calvinist or scholastic or, in short, a theological
era by the appearance of these movements, and thereupon mark
what is by now called the era of Pietism or Evangelicalism.

In this frame of reference, the Great Awakening was only inci-
dentally American. It is only necessary to translate the European
language into the local terminology to have an adequate account.
In this phraseology, the Great Awakening in New England was
an uprising of the common people who declared that what Harvard and Yale graduates were teaching was too academic. This
sort of rebellion has subsequently proved so continuous that one
can hardly speak of it as a crisis. It is rather a chronic state of affairs. And in this view of it, the uprising of 1740 belongs to the
history of the eighteenth century rather than to any account of
forces at work only on this continent.

Told in this way, the story will be perfectly true. Because we
talk so much today of the unity of Western European culture,
maybe we ought to tell it in these terms, and then stop. But on the
other hand there is a curiously double aspect to the business. If we
forget about Germany and Holland and even England—if we examine in detail the local history of Virginia, Pennsylvania, and
New England—we will find that a coherent narrative can be constructed out of the cultural developments in each particular area.
The Awakening can be seen as the culmination of factors long at

work in each society, and as constituting, in that sense, a veritable crisis in the indigenous civilization.

II

The church polity established in New England was what today we call Congregational. This meant, to put it crudely, that a church was conceived as being composed of people who could certify before other people that they had a religious experience, that they were qualified to become what the founders called "visible saints." The founders were never so foolish as to suppose that everybody who pretended to be a saint *was* a saint, but they believed that a rough approximation of the membership to the Covenant of Grace could be worked out. A church was composed of the congregation, but these were only the professing Christians. The rest of the community were to be rigorously excluded; the civil magistrate would, of course, compel them to come to the church and listen to the sermon, collect from them a tax to support the preacher, but they could not be actual members. Those who qualified were supposed to have had something happen to them that made them capable—as the reprobate was not—of swearing to the covenant of the church. They were able, as the others were not, *physically* to perform the act.

The basic contention of the founders was that a church is based upon the covenant. Isolated individuals might be Christians in their heart of hearts, but a corporate body could not come into being unless there was this preliminary clasping of hands, this taking of the official oath in the open and before all the community, saying, in effect: "We abide by this faith, by this covenant." In scholastic language, the congregation were the "matter" but the covenant was the "form" of the church. They objected above all things to the practice in England whereby churches were made by geography; that a lot of people, merely because they resided in Little Willingdon, should make the church of Little Willingdon, seemed to them blasphemy. That principle was mechanical and unreal; there was no spiritual participation in it—no covenant.

That was why they (or at any rate the leaders and the theorists) came to New England. On the voyage over, in 1630, John

Winthrop said to them: "For wee must Consider that wee shall be as a Citty vppon a Hill, the eies of all people are vppon us." They had been attempting in England to lead a revolution; after the king's dismissal of Parliament in 1629 it looked as though there was no longer any hope of revolution there, and so they migrated to New England, to build the revolutionary city, where they could exhibit to Englishmen an England that would be as all England should be.

The essence of their conception was the covenant. As soon as they were disembarked, as soon as they could collect in one spot enough people to examine each other and acknowledge that each seemed visibly capable of taking the oath, they incorporated churches—in Boston, Charlestown, and Watertown, and, even in the first decade, in the Connecticut Valley. But we must always remember that even in those first days, when conviction was at its height, and among so highly selected and dedicated numbers as made up the Great Migration, only about one fifth of the population were found able, or could find themselves able, to take the covenant. The rest of them—with astonishingly few exceptions—accepted their exclusion from the churches, knowing that they were not "enabled" and praying for the grace that might yet empower them.

From that point on, the story may seem somewhat peculiar, but after a little scrutiny it becomes an old and a familiar one: it is what happens to a successful revolution. The New Englanders did not have to fight on the barricades or at Marston Moor; by the act of migrating, they *had* their revolution. Obeying the Biblical command to increase and multiply, they had children—hordes of them. Despite the high rate of infant mortality, these children grew up in New England knowing nothing, except by hearsay and rumor, of the struggles in Europe, never having lived amid the tensions of England. This second generation were, for the most part, good people; but they simply did not have—they could not have—the kind of emotional experience that made them ready to stand up before the whole community and say: "On Friday the 19th, I was smitten while plowing Deacon Jones's meadow; I fell to the earth, and I knew that the grace of God was upon me." They were honest people, and they found it difficult to romanticize about themselves—even when they desperately wanted to.

In 1662 the churches of New England convoked a synod and announced that the children of the primitive church members were included in the covenant by the promise of God to Abraham. This solution was called at the time the Halfway Covenant, and the very phrase itself is an instructive demonstration of the New Englanders' awareness that their revolution was no longer revolutionary. These children, they decided, must be treated as members of the church, although they had not had the kind of experience that qualified their fathers. They must be subject to discipline and censures, because the body of the saints must be preserved. But just in case the authorities might be mistaken, they compromised by giving to these children only a "halfway" status, which made them members but did not admit them to the Lord's Supper.

This provision can easily be described as a pathetic, where it is not a ridiculous, device. It becomes more comprehensible when we realize that it was an accommodation to the successful revolution. Second and third generations grow up inheritors of a revolution, but are not themselves revolutionaries.

For the moment, in the 1660's and 1670's, the compromise worked, but the situation got worse. For one thing, New England suffered in King Philip's War, when the male population was decimated. Then, in 1684, the charter of Massachusetts was revoked, and after 1691 the colony had to adjust itself to the notion that its governor was imposed by the royal whim, not by the election of the saints. Furthermore, after 1715 all the colonies were prospering economically; inevitably they became more and more concerned with earthly things—rum, land, furs. On the whole they remained a pious people. Could one go back to Boston of 1710 or 1720—when the ministers were asserting that it was as profligate as Babylon—I am sure that one would find it, compared with modern Hollywood, a strict and moral community. Nevertheless, everybody was convinced that the cause of religion had declined. Something had to be done.

As early as the 1670's the ministers had found something they could do: they could work upon the halfway members. They could say to these hesitants: "You were baptized in this church, and if you will now come before the body and 'own' the covenant, then your children can in turn be baptized." Gradually a whole segment of doctrine was formulated that was not in the original theory—which made it possible to address these citizens who were neither outside the pale nor yet snugly inside, which told them that however dubious they might be as saints, visible or invisible, they yet had sufficient will power to perform the public act of "owning the covenant."

With the increasing pressures of the late seventeenth and early eighteenth centuries, the practice of owning the covenant gradually became a communal rite. It was not enough that the minister labored separately with John or Elizabeth to make an acknowledgement the next Sunday: a day was appointed when all the Johns and Elizabeths would come to church and do it in unison, the whole town looking on. It is not difficult to trace through the increasing re-enactments of this ceremony a mounting crescendo of communal action that was, to say the least, wholly foreign to the original Puritanism. The theology of the founders conceived of man as single and alone, apart in a corner or in an empty field, wrestling with his sins; only after he had survived this experience in solitude could he walk into the church and by telling about it prove his right to the covenant. But this communal confession— with everybody doing it together, under the urgencies of an organized moment—this was something new, emerging so imperceptibly that nobody recognized it as an innovation (or rather I should say that some did, but they were shouted down) that by the turn of the century was rapidly becoming the focus for the ordering of the spiritual life of the town.

The grandfather of Jonathan Edwards, Solomon Stoddard of Northampton, was the first man who openly extended the practice of renewal of covenant to those who had never been in it at all. In short, when these occasions arose, or when he could precipitate them, he simply took into the church and up to the Lord's Supper everyone who would or could come. He called the periods when the community responded *en masse* his "harvests," of which he had five: 1679, 1683, 1696, 1712, 1718. The Mathers attacked him for so completely letting down the bars, but in the Connecticut Valley his success was envied and imitated.

The Great Awakening of 1740, seen in the light of this development, was nothing more than the culmination of the process. It was the point at which the method of owning the covenant became most widely and exultingly extended, in which the momentum of the appeal got out of hand, and the ministers, led by Jonathan Edwards, were forced by the logic of evolution not only to admit all those who would come, but to excite and to drive as many as possible, by such rhetorical stimulations as "Sinners in the Hands of an Angry God," into demanding entrance.

All of this, traced historically, seems natural enough. What 1740 did was present a number of leading citizens, like the Harvard faculty, with the results of a process that had been going on for decades but of which they were utterly ignorant until the explosion. Then they found themselves trying to control it or censure it by standards that had in fact been out of date for a century, although they had all that while professed them in filial piety. In this sense—which I regret to state has generally eluded the social historian—the Great Awakening was a crisis in the New England society.

Professional patriots, especially those of New England descent, are fond of celebrating the Puritans as the founders of the American tradition of rugged individualism, freedom of conscience, popular education, and democracy. The Puritans were not rugged individualists; they did indeed believe in education of a sort, but not in the "progressive" sense; they abhorred freedom of conscience; and they did not believe at all in democracy. They advertised again and again that their church polity was not democratic. The fact that a church was founded on a covenant and that the minister happened to be elected by the mass of the church—this emphatically did not constitute a democracy. John Cotton made the position of the founders crystal clear when he told Lord Say and Seal that God never ordained democracy as a fit government for either church or commonwealth; although at first sight one might suppose that a congregational church was one, in that the people chose their governors, the truth was that "the government is not a democracy, if it be administered, not by the people, but by the governors." He meant, in short, that even though the people did select the person, the office was prescribed; they did not define its functions, nor was it responsible to the will or the whim of the electors. "In which respect it is, that church government is iustly denied . . . to be democratical, though the people choose their owne officers and rulers."

The conception ran through every department of the social thinking of New England in the seventeenth century, and persisted in the eighteenth up to the very outbreak of the Awakening. The essence of it always was that though officers may come into their office by the choice of the people, or a number of people, nevertheless the definition of the function, dignity, and prerogatives of the position does not depend upon the intentions or wishes of the electorate, but upon an abstract, divinely given, absolute prescription, which has nothing—in theory—to do with such practical or utilitarian considerations as may, at the moment of the election, be at work among the people.

The divine and immutable pattern of church government was set, once and for all, in the New Testament; likewise, the principles of political justice were given in an eternal and definitive form. The machinery by which a particular man was chosen to fulfill these directives (as the minister was elected by the vote of a congregation, or as John Winthrop was made governor of the Massachusetts Bay Company by a vote of the stockholders) was irrelevant. The existence of such machinery did not mean that the elected officer was in any sense responsible to the electorate. He knew what was expected of him from an entirely other source than their temporary passions; he knew what he, upon becoming such a being, should do—as such!

The classic statement, as is widely known, was the speech that John Winthrop delivered before the General Court on July 3, 1645. He had been accused by the democracy of overstepping the limits of his power as a magistrate, and was actually impeached on the accusation. He was acquitted, and thereupon made this truly great declaration. He informed the people that the liberty of the subject may sometimes include, as happily it did in Massachusetts, the privilege of selecting this or that person for office, but that it did not therefore mean the right to tell the officer what he should do once he was installed. The liberty that men enjoy in civil society, he said, "is the proper end and object of authority, and cannot subsist without it." It is not a liberty to do what you will, or to require the authority to do what you want: "It is a liberty to do that only which is good, just, and honest." Who defines the good, the just, and the honest? Obviously, the authority does.

In other words, the theory of early New England was basically medieval. Behind it lay the conception of an authoritative scheme of things, in which basic principles are set down once and for all, entirely before, and utterly without regard for, political experience. The formulation of social wisdom had nothing to do with the specific problems of any one society. It was not devised by a committee on ways and means. Policy was not to be arrived at by a discussion of strategy—for example (in modern terms), shouldn't we use the atomic bomb now? This sort of argument was unavailing, because the function of government was to maintain by authority that which was inherently—and definably—the true, just, and honest.

In Hartford, Connecticut, a colleague of the great Thomas Hooker, the most comprehensive theorist of the Congregational system, summarized the argument by declaring that Congregationalism meant a silent democracy in the face of a speaking aristocracy. There might be something which we call democracy in the form of the church, but the congregation had to keep silent when the minister spoke. And yet, for a hundred years after the death of Hooker, this strange process went on inside the institution. The official theory remained, down to the time of Edwards, that the spokesman for the society—be he governor or minister— told the society, by right divine, what it should or should not do, without any regard to its immediate interests, whether emotional or economic. He had laid upon him, in fact, the duty of forgetting such wisdom as he might have accumulated by living as a particular person in that very community or having shared the hopes and qualities of precisely these people.

What actually came about, through the device of renewing the covenant, was something that in fact completely contradicted the theory. (We must remember that the church was, during this century, not merely something "spiritual," but the institutional center of the organized life.) Instead of the minister standing in his pulpit, saying: "I speak; you keep quiet," he found himself, bit by bit, assuming the posture of pleading with the people: "Come, and speak up." He did not know what was happening. He began to find out only in the Great Awakening, when the people at last and multitudinously spoke up.

III

The greatness of Jonathan Edwards is that he understood what had happened. But note this carefully. He was not Thomas Jefferson; he did not preach democracy, and he had no interest whatsoever in any social revolution. He was the child of this aristocratic, medieval system; he was born to the purple, to ecclesiastical authority. But he was the man who hammered it home to the people that they *had* to speak up, or else they were lost.

Edwards was a Puritan and a Calvinist. He believed in predestination and original sin and all those dogmas which college students hold to be outworn stuff until they get excited about them as slightly disguised by Franz Kafka. Edwards did not submit these doctrines to majority vote, and he did not put his theology to the test of utility. But none of this was, in his existing situation, an issue. Granting all that, the question he had to decide was: What does a man do who leads the people? Does he, in 1740, say with the Winthrop of 1645 that they submit to what he as an ontologist tells them is good, just, and honest?

What he realized (lesser leaders of the Awakening, like Gilbert Tennent, also grasped the point, but none with the fine precision of Edwards) was that a leader could no longer stand before the people giving them mathematically or logically impregnable postulates of the eternally good, just, and honest. That might work in 1640, or in Europe (where to an astonishing extent it still works), but it would not work in Northampton. By 1740 the leader had to get down amongst them, and bring them by actual participation into an experience that was no longer private and privileged, but social and communal.

In other words, he carried to its ultimate implication—this constitutes his "relation to his times," which no purely social historian can begin to diagnose—that slowly forming tendency which had been steadily pressing through enlargements of the ceremonial owning of the covenant. He carried it so far that at last everybody could see what it really did mean. Then the Harvard faculty lifted its hands in horror—because this ritual, which they had thought was a segment of the cosmology of John Winthrop, was proved by Edwards's use to flow from entirely alien principles. For this reason, his own Yale disowned him.

IV

In the year 1748 Edwards's revolutionary effort—his leadership of the Awakening must be seen as a resumption of the revolutionary thrust that had been allowed to dwindle in the Halfway Covenant—was almost at an end. The opposition was mobilizing, and he knew, even before they did, that they would force him out. When the fight had only begun, his patron and friend, his one bulwark in the civil society, Colonel John Stoddard, chief of the militia and warden of the marches, died. There was now no civil power that could protect him against the hatred of the "river gods." Out of all New England, Stoddard had been really *the* outstanding magistrate in that tradition of aristocratic leadership which had begun with Winthrop and had been sustained through a massive succession. As was the custom in New England, the minister gave a funeral sermon; Edwards preached over the corpse of the town's greatest citizen—who happened, in this case, to be also his uncle and his protector. Those who were now certain, with Colonel Stoddard in the ground, that they could get Edwards's scalp were in the audience.

Edwards delivered a discourse that at first sight seems merely one more Puritan eulogy. He told the people that when great and good men like Stoddard are taken away, this is a frown of God's displeasure, which indicates that they ought to reform their vices. This much was sheer convention. But before he came, at the end, to the traditional berating of the populace, Edwards devoted the major part of his oration to an analysis of the function and meaning of authority.

It should be remembered that Winthrop had commenced the New England tradition by telling the people that they had the liberty to do only that which is in itself good, just, and honest; that their liberty was the proper end and object of authority thus defined; that the approbation of the people is no more than the machinery by which God calls certain people to the exercise of the designated powers. And it should also be borne in mind that these powers are given apart from any consideration of the social welfare, that they derive from ethical, theological—*a priori*—considerations.

Jonathan Edwards says that the supreme qualification of a ruler is that he be a man of "great ability for the management of public affairs." This is his first and basic definition! Let us follow his very words, underlining those which carry revolutionary significance. Rulers are men "of great *natural* abilities" who are versed in discerning "those things wherein the *public welfare or calamity consists*, and the proper *means* to avoid the one and promote the other." They must have lived among men long enough to learn how the mass of them disguise their motives, to "unravel the false, subtle arguments and cunning sophistry that is often made use of to defend *iniquity*." They must be men who have improved their talents by—here are his great criteria—*study, learning, observation,* and *experience.* By these means they must have acquired "skill" in public affairs, "a great understanding of *men and things,* a great *knowledge of human nature,* and of the way of *accommodating* themselves to it." Men are qualified to be rulers if and when they have this "very extensive knowledge of men with whom they are concerned," and when also they have a full and particular understanding "of the *state and circumstances* of the country or people that they have the care of." These are the things—not scholastical articles—that make those in authority "fit" to be rulers!

Look closely at those words and phrases: skill, observation, men and things, state and circumstances—above all, experience! Is this the great Puritan revivalist? It is. And what is he saying, out of the revival? He is telling what in political terms the revival really meant: that the leader has the job of accommodating himself to the realities of human and, in any particular situation, of social, experience. No matter what he may have as an assured creed, as a dogma—no matter what he may be able to pronounce, in the terms of abstract theology, concerning predestination and original sin—as a public leader he must adapt himself to public welfare and calamity. He cannot trust himself to *a priori* rules of an eternal and uncircumstanced good, just, and honest. There are requirements imposed by the office; authority does indeed consist of propositions that pertain to it, but what are they? They are the need for knowing the people, the knack of properly manipulating and operating them, the wit to estimate their welfare, and the cunning to foresee what may become their calamity.

When we are dealing with so highly conscious an artist as Edwards, we not only are justified in submitting so crucial a paragraph to close analysis, we are criminally obtuse if we do not.

Most of my effort in my recent studies of him comes down to persuading people to read him. So it becomes significant to note what Edwards does immediately after his radically new definition of the ruler. Following his own logic, he is prepared at once to attack what, in the state and circumstances of the Connecticut Valley, constituted the primary iniquity, from which the greatest social calamity might be expected.

He does it without, as we might say, pulling punches: a ruler must, on these considerations of welfare, be unalterably opposed to all persons of "a mean spirit," to those "of a narrow, private spirit that may be found in little tricks and intrigues to promote their private interest, [who] will shamefully defile their hands to gain a few pounds, are not ashamed to hip and bite others, grind the faces of the poor, and screw upon their neighbors; and will take advantage of their authority or commission to line their own pockets with what is fraudulently taken or withheld from others." At the time he spoke, there sat before him the merchants, the sharp traders, the land speculators of Northampton; with the prompt publication of the sermon, his words reached similar gentlemen in the neighboring towns. Within two years, they hounded him out of his pulpit.

The more one studies Edwards, the more one finds that much of his preaching is his condemnation, in this language of welfare and calamity rather than of "morality," of the rising and now rampant businessmen of the Valley. It was Edwards's great perception—and possibly his greatest value for us today is precisely here—that the get-rich-quick schemes of his contemporaries were wrong not from the point of view of the eternal values but from that of the public welfare. The ruler, he said, must know the "theory" of government in such a way that it becomes "natural" to him, and he must apply the knowledge he has obtained by study and observation "to that business, so as to perform it most advantageously and effectually." Here he was, at the moment his protector was gone, and he knew that he was lost, telling those about to destroy him that the great man is he who leads the people by skill and experiential wisdom, and not by making money.

It is further revealing that, after Edwards had portrayed the ruler in this frame of utility and calculation, when he came to his fourth point he then for the first time said that the authority ought to be a pious man, and only in his fifth and last did he suggest the desirability of a good family. For Winthrop these qualifications had been essentials of the office; for Edwards they were radically submitted to a criterion of utility. "It also contributes to the strength of a man in authority . . . when he is in such circumstances as give him advantage for the exercise of his strength, for the public good; as his being a person of honorable descent, of a distinguished education, his being a man of estate." But note— these are all "useful" because they "add to his strength, and increase his ability and advantage to serve his generation." They serve "in some respect" to make him more effective. It had never occurred to John Winthrop that the silent democracy should imagine for a moment that the elected ruler, in church or state, should be anyone but a pious, educated, honorably descended person, of adequate economic substance. Edwards (who was pious, educated, and very well descended, but not wealthy) says that in some respect these advantages are helps to efficiency.

From one point of view, then, this was what actually was at work inside the hysterical agonies of the Great Awakening. This is one thing they meant: the end of the reign over the New England and American mind of a European and scholastical conception of an authority put over men for the good of men who were incapable of recognizing their own welfare. This insight may assist us somewhat in comprehending why the pundits of Boston and Cambridge, all of whom were rational and tolerant and decent, shuddered with a horror that was deeper than mere dislike of the antics of the yokels. To some extent, they sensed that the religious screaming had implications in the realm of society, and those implications they—being businessmen and speculators, as were the plutocracy of Northampton—did not like.

Again, I would not claim too much for Edwards, and I have no design of inscribing him among the prophets of democracy or the New Deal. What he marks—and what he alone could make clear—is the crisis from which all the others (or most of them) dealt with in this book depend, that in which the social problem was taken out of the arcana of abstract morality and put into the arena of skill, observation, and accommodation. In this episode, the Americans were indeed participating in an international movement; even so, they came—or Edwards brought them—to sharper formulations of American experience. What the Awakening really meant for Americans was not that they too were behaving like

Dutchmen or Germans or Lancashire workmen, but that in the ecstasy of the revival they were discovering, especially on the frontier, where life was the toughest, that they rejected imported European philosophies of society. They were now of themselves prepared to contend that the guiding rule of this society will be its welfare, and the most valuable knowledge will be that which can say what threatens calamity for the state.

II. *Insurrection in Massachusetts*

Shortly after the American Revolution, Massachusetts went through a crisis in public and private finance. Angered by the unwillingness of the state government to relieve the crushing debt burden, an aroused yeomanry, under the dubious leadership of Captain Daniel Shays, defied the authorities. This rural incident reverberated throughout the states and frightened the conservative leaders already inclined to identify democracy with mobocracy. The consequences of this episode, described by Professor Richard B. Morris, were soon forgotten, but the issues remained. Whole campaigns were fought by the dissatisfied descendants of the "rebels" over the question of banks and currency, and America was not to hear the last from her outraged agrarians. The Populists attacked the "moneycrats" a century later; grim farmers flouted the courts during the early years of the Great Depression.

II

Insurrection in Massachusetts

Richard B. Morris
Professor of History, Columbia University

Only a few weeks after Lexington and Concord, John Adams, that forthright revolutionist, wrote to James Sullivan: "Such a levelling spirit prevails, even in men called the first among mighty, that I fear we shall be obliged to call in a military force to do that which our civil government was originally designed for." Eleven years later, and long after the dust of Revolutionary battles had settled, George Washington, writing as a civilian from his estate at Mount Vernon, declared, in a letter to James Madison dated November 5, 1786: "We are fast verging to anarchy and confusion." He followed up this prediction with a quotation from a communication he had only just received from General Knox concerning the Shaysites: "Their creed is, that the property of the United States, has been protected from confiscation of Britain by the joint exertions of *all*, and therefore ought to be the *common property* of all."

In their references to the radical notions entertained in western Massachusetts at the time, Washington and Knox were not referring to the red flag that floated over many a Berkshire settlement in those days. That banner did not signify revolutionary leveling. It was the trademark of the auctioneer, raised with tragic frequency to announce foreclosure sales. To folks who saw their worldly possessions sold for pitifully small sums at such proceedings the only leveling was a grinding down of the poor, not a leveling down of the rich.

In fact, had the American War for Independence been a real

social revolution, Shays' Rebellion would never have occurred. Following oversimplified formulas, some modern students of the period view the civil war of the Revolution as a class struggle, whereas in fact such tension as had existed between classes and sections was in considerable measure suspended during the military conflict. The war did not array capitalists against proletarians, and refuses to be fitted into a neat Marxian pattern. Small tenant-farmers in New York and Regulators in the up-country Carolinas favored the Tory cause against rich landlords and Tidewater aristocrats, many of whom chose the side of rebellion. Although in Virginia many planters, as Jefferson attests, were heavily in debt to Scottish and British businessmen, the war in America was not fought between creditors on one side and debtors on the other, between hard-money men and paper-money men, between democrats who wanted the suffrage enlarged and conservatives who wanted the restrictions maintained. On the floor of the Continental Congress signers of the Declaration of Independence who were wedded to laissez-faire economics wrangled with signers who advocated planned economy. In the southern states the planters actually sought the aid of the Revolutionary military authorities against a British government bent on freeing their slaves in reprisal.

What American Whigs were united upon was not *freedom*, but *political independence*, and even here the objectives of the federalists or nationalists differed sharply from the aims of the states' righters or sectionalists. In the long run the attainment of freedom from external restraint was liberalizing in its political effects, but, aside from independence, American Whigs were sharply divided on most other objectives. Since diverse interests forged the Whig alliance, it was only to be expected that the victory of the patriots would settle no single social or economic issue except freedom from British mercantilistic controls. Therefore, in appraising the social reforms frequently attributed to the Revolution, we must move with caution. Many of the Loyalist estates that were broken up went to large Whig speculators, and the purpose of confiscation was not leveling, but fiscal aid to replenish empty state treasuries. Although primogeniture and entails were largely terminated in this period, these feudal devices to monopolize landed property had been largely ignored in practice in the Colonies long before this time. Slavery was ended or modified in areas where it had no significance, but white servitude, imprisonment for debt, and other substantial social evils stood uncorrected.

In short, at the end of the War for Independence the great internal social reforms lay ahead. This fact was appreciated by Harrison Gray Otis, who once wrote to a friend of Revolutionary days: "You and I did not imagine when the first war with Britain was over, that revolution was just begun."

During the years of the Revolution Massachusetts had strenuously resisted political and social upheaval. In the Bay state the very towns that rallied to the relief of Boston in '74, now, six years later, ratified a constitution, drafted by John Adams, that was a creditors' and property owners' document. The only popular wing of the government was the House of Representatives, apportionment in which favored the bigger eastern towns—the commercial interests—while the Senate, which allotted representation on the basis of taxes paid, constituted an even more formidable bulwark of property. The strong executive provided by the constitution and the independent judiciary appointed for good behavior, rather than elective, constituted a political mechanism that seemed to assure to the conservatives control of the state for many years to come.

Although John Fiske may have overplayed the chaos and confusion of the postwar period, exigent problems of reconstruction confronted every state. In Massachusetts the problems were especially formidable. The economic depression of the postwar years hit New England hardest. The cessation of legal trade with the British West Indies (considerable illegal trade persisted), the collapse of the distilling industry, and the decline of the whale fisheries resulted in unemployment in the seacoast areas. While war profiteers and ex-privateers managed to ride out hard times, and the mercantile interests continued to accumulate considerable quantities of specie, far greater economic deterioration prevailed in the interior of the state. Here mortgages were foreclosed, and debtors were imprisoned and even sold for servitude. The reasons for this blight of indebtedness are near at hand. After 1782, farm prices slowly declined, and the wages of farm laborers had shrunk to a low of forty cents a day by 1787.[1] In addition to poor mar-

---

[1] Massachusetts Bureau of Statistics and Labor: 16th Annual Report (Boston: 1885), pp. 160–449.

keting conditions in disposal of his crop, the Massachusetts farmer had to eke out a livelihood on a relatively small homestead.

Court and jail records reveal the extent of the economic crisis in central and western Massachusetts. In the year 1785–6 there were four thousand suits for debt in Worcester County alone. My own examination of the common-pleas records of Hampshire and Berkshire indicates a mounting total of judgments in debt in the years 1786–7. Unable to pay for seed and stock and tools, farmers were thrown into jail or sold out to service. Except for the clothes on the debtor's back, no property was exempt from seizure on execution. There was no homestead exemption, and property at execution sales brought nothing approaching its real value. The number of debtors in Worcester jail alone had risen from seven in 1786 to some seventy-two persons for the period from March to December 1786, out of a total of ninety-four jailed. Some were jailed for debts as low as six shillings.

These jails rivaled any description in Dickens. The one in Worcester was a small three-story building. The lower story was assigned to serious criminals, the second story to minor offenders and debtors, who had liberty of the yard. It was in this jail that Colonel Timothy Bigelow, Worcester's most famous soldier of the Revolution, spent his declining years, while war profiteers like Stephen Salisbury, who had kept far from the sound of cannon, waxed fat on mortgage foreclosures. One of the memorable passages in Bellamy's *Duke of Stockbridge* is his picture of the tavern-jail at Great Barrington, small, cramped, its walls and floors mildewed and spotted with mold—a dark, noisome spot where Perez Hamlin, the veteran returned from wars, first laid eyes upon his debtor brother, the emaciated Reuben.

But imprisonment for debt is only part of the story. The records disclose case after case of debtors sold off for sizable terms to work off their debts to their creditors—peonage lacking only the Mexican title. As the tight-faced tavern jailor, Bement, told Hamlin: "I dunno 'baout slavery exactly, but there's plenty o' that sort o' thing, fer sartin. Creditors mostly would rather dew that way, 'cause they kin git suthin' aout of a feller, an' ef they send 'em tew jail it's a dead loss." [2]

[2] For the problem of servitude for debt, see R. B. Morris: *Government and Labor in Early America* (New York: 1946), pp. 354–63. For servitude in lieu of restitution for larceny in this period, see, e.g.: *Martin's Case, Suffolk Gen. Sess.* (Unbound, April 18, 1780).

In terms of the thinking of the time, it was natural that the debtors should have sought relief through liberal doses of inflation—printing-press money—and at the same time should have retaliated against the chief instruments of their creditors, the courts and the lawyers. Seeking judgments against debtors, creditors crowded the offices of the attorneys. Popular indignation found vent in letters to the newspapers attacking the bar and in petitions from the towns "to restrain that order of gentlemen denominated lawyers." Massachusetts had a long tradition of hostility to a paid bar. Thomas Lechford, the Bay colony's first attorney, was disbarred for an illegal attempt to influence the jury out of court, and the first code of laws adopted in Massachusetts, the Body of Liberties of 1641, generously consented to have attorneys plead causes other than their own, but disallowed all fees or rewards. This restriction seems to have been relaxed, and the eighteenth century witnessed the rise to eminence of the American lawyer. In New England names like John Read, Jeremiah Gridley, Judge Edmund Trowbridge, and John Adams signified both technical competence and public recognition.[3] While the bar had remained a small, select group, trained legal scholars were outnumbered by parasitic pettifoggers, encouraged by the practice of filling writs by sheriffs and their deputies. Shoemakers, wigmakers, and masons procured deputations from the sheriffs and stirred up petty and contemptible litigation. John Adams himself declaimed against "the dirty dabblers in the law." In 1742 and again in 1758 it was necessary for the Colony to enact laws forbidding sheriffs and their deputies from filling writs or giving legal advice. As a result, the legal profession was purified, but the process rendered the bar more exclusive than formerly, its numbers now severely restricted, and for a good many years the bar held an unchallenged monopolistic position. In the main the influence exercised by the legal profession on economic and social trends in the Revolution generally was a conservative one. Not the bar but the church seems to have been the repository of the spirit of leveling. For, despite the fact that perhaps half of the members of the bar in Massachusetts supported the Revolutionary cause, the lawyers in their attitude toward property rights were far from being revolutionaries. As Jefferson attests, the attorneys in New England,

[3] See R. B. Morris: *Studies in the History of American Law* (New York: 1930), pp. 41–4, 65–7.

like others throughout the colonies, "seduced by the honeyed Mansfieldism of Blackstone, began to slide into Toryism." In the years immediately following the War for Independence, the legal profession, which had hailed the common law as the guardian of constitutional rights, now defended it as the protector of creditor's privilege. The decision of the well-known Rhode Island case of *Trevett v. Weeden* (1786), handed down at the peak of debtor unrest in New England and effectually preventing paper money from being passed to settle private debts, represented the sentiment of the New England bar as a whole.

Perhaps the idea was a little too naïve, but the insurgents felt that if judges were elected by the people they might be more sympathetic with popular grievances. Until that eventuality it was thought expedient to keep the lawyers from appearing in behalf of creditors and to prevent the courts of common pleas, chief tribunals in matters of debt, from sitting altogether. Since such actions were riotous, if not subversive, the insurgents soon found it expedient to prevent the courts of general sessions and the supreme court as well from sitting, in order that criminal proceedings might not be taken against them for their contumacy. As a long-range program, a reduction of court fees was urged on all sides.

But it was not only private debts that provided a critical issue. Public debt—state and local—was proving an intolerable burden to the taxpayers. Town after town followed Coxhall, which announced: "We are almost ready to cry out under the burden of our taxes as the children of Israel did in Egypt when they were required to make brick without straw," for "we cannot find that there is money enough in the town to pay." Recent historians who see in the "critical period" significant evidences of reconstruction all point to the rapid amortization of state debts as an evidence of the ability of the states to put their financial houses in order without much help from a central government.[4] There is no doubt that the states had now assumed the debt funding function that the federal government had proven incapable of shouldering. But, in terms of more recent ideas of a planned economy, it would now seem that states like Massachusetts made the mistake of a too rapid amortization of the state debt—thereby initiating a sharp deflationary thrust. Even a conservative like Governor Bowdoin

4 Merrill Jensen: *The New Nation* (New York: 1950), pp. 388–98.

urged in 1786 a more gradual plan of amortization than that which the property-conscious legislature had enacted.

For the times the public debt seemed staggering. Before the war the state debt was under a hundred thousand pounds. At war's end it had risen to approximately three million pounds, about one half of which was the state's share of the federal debt. In addition, every town was embarrassed by having, on its own credit, to meet state requisitions during the war for men and supplies. These debts had to be paid off by taxes, and the principal taxes levied in the state were on polls and estates. In addition, an impost and excise were adopted in Massachusetts for the discharge of the interest on the debt.

Now, the agrarian interests felt that the tax burden had been disproportionately shifted upon their shoulders by the commercial interest. In fact, the taxes did fall more heavily on the western counties than upon the seaboard. While in 1781 the seaport towns were assessed for the same kinds of property as ten years earlier, the assessors reached out to the farming centers for new sources of revenue, and now listed barns, neat cattle under two years, and swine under one year, which had not been itemized in previous returns. Before the constitution of 1780 went into effect, it has been estimated by one investigator, one third of the state tax was levied on polls and two thirds on real estate. But the new legislature began to increase the proportion paid by polls by raising the poll tax, which in 1785 reached a high for this period of one pound per poll. In 1778, polls amounted to 30 per cent of the entire levy; in 1781, 32.1 per cent; in 1784, 36.3 per cent of the state tax; and by 1786 they had been increased to 40 per cent. This tax hit hardest the interior counties, which were the least wealthy. Thus in the 1784 levy Worcester actually paid 32.3 per cent on polls, and Suffolk, Boston's county, only 22.8 per cent. These statistics, perhaps more convincingly than any amount of rhetoric, highlight the grievances of the central and western counties.

Both personal and town tax delinquencies were alarmingly high. To a people squeezed between their government and their creditors it is no small wonder that on the one hand they should have cried out against the cost of government, demanding a reduction in the salary of the governor particularly, and insisting on general economies, and on the other constantly urged more paper money for the payment of both public and private debts. The state had already found it necessary to issue the rough equivalent of tax-anticipation warrants, which, accumulating at an accelerated pace, came to serve as a kind of currency, changing hands at depreciated value, before being returned to the treasury. But the towns favored paper money that would not be redeemed over too short a term, and among the many impractical proposals offered was the proposition that such paper depreciate at fixed rates at certain stated periods until at a suitable time all should be extinguished. Of course, were such depreciation tables set there would have been a wild scramble to unload the money at once, but the theorists avoided painful economic realities.

A study of petitions and votes shows the clean-cut character of sectional alignments in the critical years of 1785-6. On file in the Massachusetts Archives for the three-week period ending February 6, 1786, are petitions for paper money from fourteen towns, chiefly from the interior part of the country. While support was found in the coastal areas, the seaboard interests in the legislature (notably Suffolk) were strongly opposed to altering the laws for the collection of private debts. Even in seafaring Essex the representatives were about evenly divided on this question, but when one examines the votes of legislators coming from merely thirty miles west of Boston, from Worcester County, for instance, one finds complete opposition to Suffolk on virtually all the social and economic issues that came before the General Court.

In considering the machinery of protest used by the disaffected elements in the state, it should be noted that the principal types had been in wide use during the entire Revolutionary period. I refer, first, to the lawful, or, some might prefer, extra-legal, practice of drafting protests through local conventions; secondly, to the less peaceful course of blocking action by the courts; and thirdly, to recourse to military action. All three were in the good tradition of the Revolutionary generation, for the initial drive to independence was through the local machinery of Committees of Correspondence, which encouraged direct action and ultimately forcible resistance. Massachusetts had initiated the practice of adopting wage and price schedules through local and interstate conventions. Aimed to check wartime inflation, such conventions appear as early as 1776 and cease their activities in 1780, by which time the futility of price-fixing was apparent to all. The conventions to redress common grievances which mushroomed throughout western Massachusetts as early as 1781 mark a virtual continuity with the wage- and price-fixing meetings of the years 1774–80. There was nothing novel about these procedures.[5] The element of innovation, however, lay in the relation between these extra-legal, but orderly, bodies and the more lawless course of mobs and troops. In the early eighties there is no question that these conventions were against lawlessness, but as time goes on, despite avowals of peaceful intentions, it is no longer clear that the leaders of the conventions were not in many cases the chief supporters of the Shaysites.

The forcible stoppage of court sessions represents another illustration of the continuation of Revolutionary techniques of protest. In September 1774 a crowd of some six thousand, at the instigation of the committee of correspondence, had blocked passage to the courthouse at Worcester, and that court did not resume its functions until July of '76, and then under the Revolutionary state government. In Berkshire and Hampshire courts were held from '74 to '78 or '79, and an enormous backlog of litigation piled up to be dealt with when the courts once more opened for business. Here, again, the Shaysites continued a familiar technique.

In dealing with the third form of protest, organized military action, it must be borne in mind that both the leadership and the rank and file in the movement of insurgency were recruited from among the veterans of the late war. Not only did the ex-soldiers share with other citizens the economic heartaches common to most debtors, but they faced formidable problems of readjustment from military to civilian life. This accounts for the special intensity of their feeling on current issues. The ex-officers had one set of grievances; the common soldiers another. In the fall of '82 the Bay state's commissioned officers sent a delegation to Boston to get action from the legislature on the matter of back pay. In December their grievances were presented to Congress. In March came the Newburgh Address. Though unsigned, it was written by an arrivist, Major John Armstrong, aide-de-camp to Horatio Gates. This was an appeal from "the justice to the fears of government" and pointedly suggested coercing Congress. With charac-

[5] R. B. Morris: *Government and Labor*, pp. 94–113.

teristic firmness Washington then intervened, called a meeting of representatives among the officers, and advised patience and confidence in the good faith of Congress. Thus a threat of a military coup, secretly backed by such property-conscious conservatives as Robert Morris and his brilliant aide, Gouverneur Morris, was temporarily checked.

To contrast the well-planned G.I. Bill of Rights passed during the recent war with the financial assistance provided for veterans at the end of the Revolution is to bring into sharp relief the haphazard and inadequate nature of the latter. The assistance was too little and came too late. To induce officers to remain for the duration, Congress in 1780 promised them half pay for life. In March 1783 the federal government, fearful of saber-rattling at Newburgh, commuted the half pay to a lump sum of five years' full pay in the form of six-per-cent certificates. But a storm of protest arose from the taxpayers, many of whom concealed their self-interest behind the disingenuous argument that this measure discriminated against the private soldier.

But any idea that the officers would become a money aristocracy soon dissipated as the six-per-cent certificates rapidly depreciated. Within two or three years the majority of the officers had sold them to speculators at rates as low as $12\frac{1}{2}\phi$ on the dollar. In fact, few were able to hold on to the certificates until 1790, when the public debt was funded under the new Constitution.

Hearkening to the clamor against class legislation, Congress in May 1785 decreed that all commissioned officers should get half pay during disability, and that noncommissioned officers and privates should receive a pension of five dollars a month. Not until March 1818 were needy officers and men granted a minimum of eight dollars a month, but since that date federal largesse to old army men has burgeoned incredibly.[6]

In the light of the special difficulties that faced the returning soldier it is understandable why the leadership of Shays' Rebellion was so heavily recruited, with one exception, from among the former officers of the American Revolution and why the rank and file followed them without question.

Let us turn the spotlight on the leadership for a moment. None came forward possessing the fiery and magnetic qualities of a Sam

[6] See W. H. Glasson: *Federal Military Pensions in the United States* (1919), pp. 85 ff.

Adams, or the precise intellect of his cousin, John. There was none among the insurgents who had the eloquence of a Danton or the iron will of a Robespierre or a Lenin. These were average men —little men, neither wedded to a revolutionary ideology nor willing to gain the kind of immortality that the Christian martyrs won in the Roman arenas. When the heat was on, their resolve melted. But for the better part of a year they enjoyed the support of a substantial segment of the whole commonwealth. Their personalities and personal problems epitomized the dissatisfactions and disillusionments of the average man of the day.

Shays himself has earned a certain tarnished immortality by having the revolt named in his behalf, but he cannot be credited with launching the movement of insurgency, nor does he appear at any stage to outdistance measurably some of his co-leaders. First to kindle the embers of discontent was a cast-off preacher named Samuel Ely. Forced out of his parish in Somers, Connecticut, by factional quarrels he is credited with having promoted, he moved across the border and settled in Hampshire County. He first came to public attention by promoting the calling of the conventions in 1782, going so far as to raise a mob to prevent the holding of the courts at Northampton in April of that year. Ely was promptly tried for sedition and accused of having urged that we must throw up our constitution, for, he is said to have insisted, "the constitution is broke already, the governor has too much salary, the judges of the superior court have too much salary. We can get men that will ride the circuit for half the money." Finally, he warned that "the General Court should not sit. We will pay no more respect to them than to puppies." Condemned to a term in prison, he was released by action of a mob. When the ringleaders in the prison break were captured and held as hostages, the commander of the militia agreed, under threats, to release them on their parole. Everyone but Ely was pardoned. He fled the state, and in September was reported to be in Vermont, that refuge of Yankee malcontents. From all the evidence at hand it appears that this uneducated, crude, frustrated leader of the premature insurgency was in fact more of a true revolutionary in temper than those who donned the mantle of leadership.

While Ely had started the pot simmering at Northampton, Luke Day assumed military direction of the insurgency in the vicinity of Springfield. Day appears to have been something of a demagogue and declaimer of the Nazi beer-*stube* type. He was in bad economic straits, and for some reasons was passed over by his father in favor of a younger brother in the inheritance of a sizable landed estate. A veteran of seven years' service in the army, breveted a major, he was Shays's senior in years by four and in military ability at least his equal. Day raised his own men, and drilled and paraded them. In lieu of uniforms they wore a spring of hemlock in their hats, and, in the absence of enough guns, carried hickory clubs. But after sufficient arms were procured, he talked of opposing the state militia at Springfield, and, if necessary, of spilling "the last drop of blood that ran in his veins." This extreme sacrifice, however, he forebore at a critical moment in the revolt.

At the time of the outbreak of the rebellion Daniel Shays, its titular leader, was thirty-nine years old. Born into poverty in Middlesex County, he had worked as a farm laborer, then moved west to Great Barrington, finally settling at Pelham, where he had a farm of his own. Shays enlisted on May 1, 1775, and quickly won a promotion to sergeant for bravery at Bunker Hill. He was later assigned to the recruiting service, raised a company in Massachusetts that he took with him to West Point, but failed to obtain the captain's commission that he had been promised, until 1779. He fought with Arnold and Gates at Saratoga and, with Mad Anthony Wayne, stormed Stony Point. Mustered out in 1780, he bore at least one wound to remind him of his five years of war service. "I served in the company of Shays," commented one who later fought against him. "I knew him to be a brave and a good soldier." [7]

Shays, on quitting the service, returned to Pelham. He was elected to the Committee of Safety in 1781 and 1782, was a delegate to the county conventions held at Hatfield and Hadley in the latter year, and, though he did not attend, was chosen for the Hadley Convention in October. Although he enjoyed good repute among his neighbors, the specter of debtors' jail always hovered close by. In February 1784 he was sued in common pleas at Hadley for a debt of twelve dollars that he was unable to pay,

---

[7] Park Holland: "Narrative of the Shays' Rebellion," MS transcribed as an appendix to Joseph P. Warren: "Shays' Rebellion, a Study in the History of Massachusetts," Ph.D. Thesis, MS, Harvard University Archives.

and as late as September 1, 1786, he signed a note for 18s. 6d., payable January 1 next, but the impending military disasters prevented him from meeting the note, and it was never paid.

Shays was quickly recognized as an exceptional drillmaster and, captured by the oratory of radical associates who met and harangued in Conkey's Tavern, not far from his farm, he soon was thrust into the forefront of the movement. By October '86 he appears to have been in supreme command of the insurgent troops.

But behind the demagogues and the discontented veterans were a host of others. Joseph Hawley warned Caleb Strong: "You would be astonished to know with what amazing rapidity the spirit of the insurgents propagates. Many are infected with it of whom you would never have the least suspicion. We are not certain who besides the Devil sprang Ely at first. But we are not at a loss who ventilates the flame, for the fire is now become such a flame as I cannot describe to you. The General Court have not had any affair of greater magnitude before them since the Revolution." [8]

With men like Hawley it was an obsession that Tories and British agents were behind the revolt,[9] but there is not a particle of evidence to substantiate the charge of British intervention. Numbered among the Shaysites were some ex-Loyalists, but they stood behind Shays not as Tories but as co-sharers in the economic misfortunes of the time. It was widely feared that the Shaysites were levelers who wanted a social revolution. This kind of attack has a contemporary ring. Ever since the first World War it has become the fashion to drag out the red herring—often a very smelly one—whenever any social reform is proposed. This is not to exclude the possibility that *agents provocateurs* were at work among the Shaysites. But if so, they were more likely financed by conservative businessmen than by British gold. A good rebellion was what was needed, some reactionaries felt, to force the people to recognize the need for a strong central government with power to act in emergencies. These were the same people who had on a number of occasions favored setting up Washington with the powers of a dictator.

---

[8] Hawley Papers, Box II (New York Public Library).
[9] Hawley to Strong, June 24, 1782, Hawley Papers, Box II (New York Public Library).

Take the case of General von Steuben, Prussian drillmaster of the Continental army. The rioting did not faze him. Describing the Worcester clash, he wrote his friend, Major "Billy" North, with some relish: "They say that the senior Judge Ward, who is also a general, received some light pricks of the bayonette in the stern and the belly." On September 17, 1786, he wrote again to North: "When a whole people complains . . . something must be wrong." Then he added: "Lycurgus declared that citizen infamous who did not take a decided part in cases of division. But in this case I beg Monsieur Lycurgus to have a little patience with me, for in truth, I do not yet know which side to take."

When Steuben learned of Knox's scheme to send federal troops to put down the uprising, he wrote an article for a New York newspaper under the pseudonym of "Belisarius," exposing the subterfuge that the troops were going to be used to fight Indians on the frontier as "only a stratagem to fix the public attention." He closed with a question: "If, however, the numerous militia should coincide in sentiment with the malcontents, and a very small number of *respectable gentlemen* only, should be interested in keeping up the present system of administration, would Congress dare to support such an abominable oligarchy?" These grievances are the responsibility of the state legislature to correct, Steuben insisted. They were not the business of the federal government.[1] It was only natural that Rufus King should immediately turn upon the Prussian and denounce him as a Cataline prepared to lead the discontented and the ignorant in an attack upon property and privilege.

But Steuben's remedy seemed curious, coming from one who so openly avowed his sympathy with the lower classes. The day after the publication of the "Belisarius" article, he wrote to his friend, Prince Henry of Prussia, transmitting another letter written by a prominent American statesman, probably Nathaniel Gorham, the Bay state merchant and land speculator, president of the Continental Congress at that time, asking whether he would accept the throne in the event that a limited monarchy were tendered him.[2] While Steuben was publicizing his support for the

---

[1] New York *Daily Advertiser*, November 1, 1786.

[2] Richard Kranel: "Prince Henry of Prussia and the Regency of the United States," *American Historical Review*, Vol. XVII (1911), pp. 44-51.

insurgents and, for whatever motive, seeking to undermine federal armed resistance, his closest friend, Major "Billy" North, was at that very moment engaged, as an aide of Knox, in recruiting troops to put down the uprising. All this prompted Mercy Warren's comment to John Adams: "Time will make curious disclosures, and you, Sir, may be astonished to find the incendiaries who fomented the discontents among the miserable insurgents of the Massachusetts, in a class of men least suspected." [3] Minot, the contemporary historian of the rebellion, who was clerk of the house, reinforced Mrs. Warren's insinuations by identifying one element among the insurgents as consisting of persons "who wish to carry popular measures to such extremes as to shew their absurdity, and demonstrate the necessity of lessening the democratick principles of the constitution."

The leaders of the counterrevolution were drawn from the conservatives who, by the latter part of the War for Independence, had wrested political power from the hands of the radicals. John Dickinson, Charles Carroll, Robert Morris, James Wilson, Alexander Hamilton, and Gouverneur Morris had their counterparts in Massachusetts. The titular leader of the forces of law and order was the merchant James Bowdoin, the state's chief executive. Temperate in politics, he sat on the fence during the late war until, to borrow a phrase from the author of the *Biglow Papers*, "Prov'dence pinted how to jump." But Bowdoin's own excuse for his relative inactivity was ill health. In 1785 he had won the governorship as the choice of the conservative mercantile interests in a bitter and close fight with Thomas Cushing, regarded as the "popular" candidate. Lacking a popular majority, the election was put up to the legislature, where the disproportionately strong commercial and propertied interests in the Senate threw their weight behind Bowdoin enthusiastically, and the lower chamber reluctantly yielded. A moderate nationalist, Bowdoin sought to check the revolt with as little bloodshed as possible, but he urged action on the part of a supine legislature. He himself contributed to the twenty-thousand-dollar fund that General Benjamin Lincoln, who headed the state's armed forces, personally raised from Boston businessmen to put down the uprising. "Vigour, decision, energy will soon terminate this unnatural, this unprovoked insur-

[3] Massachusetts Historical Society, *Proceedings*, Vol. XLIV, p. 160.

rection, and prevent the effusion of blood," he declared in an address to the legislature in February 1787. But by then blood had already been shed.

Bowdoin's ideas of meeting the crisis with a blend of firmness and moderation were shared by General Lincoln. A veteran of the fighting against Burgoyne, Lincoln allowed himself and his whole army to be captured by Clinton in Charleston. Notwithstanding this debacle, he had been named Secretary of War under the Congress of the Confederation, preceding Henry Knox. After demonstrating considerable ability as a tactician in quelling the rebellion and capturing the Shaysite remnant, he proved his statesmanship by urging the legislature to be lenient toward the rebels.

Representative of the more extreme nationalist wing of the conservative party was the ex-Boston bookseller, Henry Knox. Eyewitness of the Boston Massacre, he soon distinguished himself as an artillerist in the War for Independence. The fortification of Dorchester Heights, which forced Howe to evacuate Boston, was in large measure the result of Knox's resourcefulness in dragging artillery pieces over the snows from Fort Ticonderoga. At the time of the mutiny of the Pennsylvania line in 1780 he was chosen by Washington to present to the New England states the grievances of the army and to secure monetary relief from Massachusetts and New Hampshire. Organizer of the Society of Cincinnati, composed of ex-Revolutionary officers, Knox was a leader of a military clique of ardent nationalists. Despite his bulk of three hundred pounds and his "Bacchanalian figure," he showed astounding speed when, as Secretary of War, he was confronted with insurrection in Massachusetts. Knox spread alarming reports about the character of the uprising, which he depicted as a social revolution, and sought financial support for secret measures to put down the rioters with federal troops, on the ground that Congressional property was threatened.

The Boston businessmen perceived the crisis as first-rate propaganda for a strong federal government. On October 22, 1786, Knox reminded Stephen Higginson that "exertions must be made and something must be hazarded by the rich." He replied that "the present moment is very favorable to the forming further and necessary arrangements for increasing the dignity and energy of government." Hence, conservatives hoped that the insurgency would seem sufficiently threatening to cause a strong military force to be raised. "I am afraid the Insurgents will be conquered too soon," Colonel Benjamin Hickborn wrote Knox on December 14, 1786, and doubtless he was not alone in that fear.

Intelligent and poised conservatives like George Washington were needled by the alarming reports received from Knox and others. From Mount Vernon Washington wrote to David Humphreys, on October 22, 1786:

> But for God's sake tell me what is the cause of all these commotions? Do they proceed from licentiousness, British-influence disseminated by the tories, or real grievances which admit of redress? If the latter, why were they delayed 'till the public mind had been so much agitated? If the former, why are not the powers of Government tried at once? It is as well to be without, as not to live under their exercise. Commotions of this sort, like snow-balls, gather strength as they roll, if there is no opposition in the way to divide and crumble them. Do write me fully, I beseech you, on these matters, not only with respect to facts, but as to opinions of their tendency and issue. I am mortified beyond expression that in the moment of our acknowledged independence we should by our conduct verify the predictions of our trans-atlantic foe, and render ourselves ridiculous and contemptible in the eyes of all Europe.

Nine days later he wrote to Henry Lee, and, after observing pessimistically that " mankind when left to themselves are unfit for their own Government," advised: "Know what the insurgents aim at. If they have *real* grievances, redress them if possible; or acknowledge the justice of them, and your inability to do it in the present moment. If they have not, employ the force of government against them at once." By the following week his anxiety had soared still higher, and in a letter to his old war comrade, Benjamin Lincoln, he asked pointedly: "Are your people getting mad?" The author of "The Anarchiad" warned: "For so Faction waves her flaming hand,/And discord riots o'er the ungrateful land."

In short, the reaction of the conservative nationalists to Shays' Rebellion lends some substantiation to J. Allen Smith's charge that "from all the evidence which we have, the conclusion is irresistible that they [the framers] sought to establish a form of government which would effectually curb and restrain democracy,"⁴ democracy being synonymous in their minds with mobism and "unruly passion."

It would not be quite fair to end this sampling of public opinion without considering the special position of such professional radicals as Sam Adams and John Hancock. At the beginning of the riots in September, Adams addressed a Fanueil Hall meeting and insisted upon the forced submission of the minority to the will of the majority. To Adams the Revolution of '76 was justified, but the insurgency of '86 was indefensible, as the minority must look to the legislature for their relief. Adams dishonestly ignored the fact that property qualifications for voting left many citizens unenfranchised and airily waved aside the substantial grievances of the malcontents, countering with the baseless charge that the trouble came solely from British emissaries and from "wicked and unprincipled men" who sought only their own profit. Hancock, that idol of the people, was conveniently sick and out of public life during the height of the rebellion, but staged a miraculous recovery as soon as it was suppressed.

Our chief concern is with the causes, impact, and reaction to the crisis rather than with the hectic sequence of events that crowded upon each other from the early fall of '86 to the spring of the following year. The actual account of the rebellion is well known. Restiveness went back at least to the winter of 1782. The Hatfield Convention in February of that year alarmed that Northampton delegate, James Hawley, who commented: " Government seems to be endangered by the noise of people in debt." After the riots under Samuel Ely had abated, the ardor of the protestants seems to have been drained off by town conventions at Deerfied and Hatfield. These conventions were renewed in significant number the very next year. But the actual crisis may be said to date from midsummer of 1786. Not only were economic conditions close to the lowest ebb at that time, but the remedies enacted by the legislature were entirely ineffectual. On July 1 the legislature adjourned until January 31 of the following year.

---

⁴ *The Spirit of American Government* (New York: 1907), a work, written in the spirit of Bellamy, that foreshadowed interpretations of the Confederation interlude by Charles A. Beard, Vernon L. Parrington, and Merrill Jensen.

This pusillanimous refusal of the General Court to look the facts in the face really precipitated the crisis.

Hardly had the legislature adjourned when town conventions began to meet. One at Worcester on August 15 was followed by a meeting at Hatfield a week later at which some fifty towns of Hampshire County were represented. After carefully affirming the constitutionality of the meeting, the convention prepared a long list of grievances. While directing that the proceedings be transmitted to conventions at Worcester and Berkshire, the Hatfield meeting significantly went on record declaring "that this convention recommend it to the inhabitants of this county that they abstain from all mobs and unlawful assemblies until a constitutional method of redress can be obtained."

But the dikes hurriedly put up by the more temperate leaders could not hold back the flood tide of violent feeling that soon swept the countryside. Four days after the Hatfield convention had ended, a mob, variously estimated at from four hundred to fifteen hundred, stopped the Northampton court from sitting. The adjournment of the court was "without day," and it is recorded that one of the more literal-minded of the rioters was not satisfied with the court's phraseology as, under it, "the Court might sit in the night." Back east, and under the lead of Job Shattuck, the people of Middlesex broke up the sessions of the court of common pleas at Concord the next month. Shattuck addressed a threatening memorial to the court in which he declared "that it was the voice of the people of the county that the court of general sessions of the peace and common pleas shall not sit in this county until such time as the people shall have a redress of a number of grievances they labor under at present, which will be set forth in a petition . . . to the next general court." Three hundred insurgents posted themselves in front of the Worcester courthouse and denied the judges admittance.

The governor and his advisers decided to make Concord a test of strength. But the orders of the common-pleas justices for calling out the militia were countermanded in that town, and a mob held the courthouse. The insurrectionary spirit soon spread to the Berkshires and north into New Hampshire. On September 20 there was a riot at Exeter and only by a *ruse de guerre* were the mobbers quieted.

When it was learned that the insurgents planned to move

against the courts at Springfield, the governor ordered the court-house to be taken by six hundred militiamen under the command of Major General William Shephard. The courts deemed it prudent to adjourn without delay and Shays marched his forces right past Shephard's troops. Shephard then moved to protect the federal arsenal and to make sure that this cache of arms was not seized by the rebels. Even when the court did sit, as at Taunton and Cambridge, the towns in those counties joined with the western protestants in asking measures of relief.

By October it was clear to all that a large-scale rebellion might very well be in the making. In the middle of September, Knox, then Secretary of War, had rushed to Springfield to check on the safety of the federal arsenal. Deluging Congress, Washington, and other leading statesmen with alarming reports, he succeeded in getting Congress in secret session to adopt a report recommending the requisitioning of federal troops ostensibly to be used against the Indians in the northwest but chiefly to be stationed in Massachusetts against the rebels. The speculator, James Swan, let the cat out of the bag in a letter to Knox on October 26, when he informed him: "I am agreeably saluted with the news of war being declared against the Indians. I hope in this declaration 'Indians' is meant all who oppose the dignity, honour, and happiness of the United States or either of the states." Swan's indiscreet remark indicates that Knox's plans were considered rather disingenuous. As Gerry commented, "some of the county members laugh and say the Indian War is only a political one to obtain a standing army." Major North, Knox's recruiting officer, was quite outspoken. "The people here smell a rat, that the troops about to be raised are more for the insurgents than the Indians."

In his study of the role of the federal government in the crisis, Joseph P. Warren has stressed the fact that the report of the committee of Congress that endorsed the Knox recommendation contained no reference to the crisis in Massachusetts, but did give a highly colored account of the impending danger from the Indians of the Ohio;[5] reference to the Massachusetts situation is found in a secret report, unanimously approved by Congress. Therein the point was made that "it would undoubtedly defeat the object of the federal interposition should a formal applica-

[5] "The Confederation and the Shays Rebellion," *American Historical Review*, Vol. XI (1905), pp. 41–67.

tion" for such be made by the legislature. Nevertheless, it was felt "that the aid of the federal government is necessary to stop the progress of the insurgents," and that the seizure of the Springfield Arsenal would "not only reduce that commonwealth to a state of anarchy and confusion, but probably involve the United States in the calamities of a civil war." Hence, it was recommended that the troops be raised "chiefly in the eastern states" in order that they might "effect these salutary purposes before they are moved to the western country." [6] Despite the deviousness of Congress's resolution, the insurgency never reached that stage where the intervention of federal troops was really needed.

Since Shays and his armed followers moved about the countryside almost at will, intimidating judges and sheriffs, it was deemed advisable to adjourn courts until January 23. Although the revolt in the eastern counties had been crushed at the end of November when the government forces, after a severe fight, captured Job Shattuck and arrested four other insurgent leaders of Groton and Shirley, the Shaysites were at their zenith in the interior of the state. In the first week of December several hundred Shaysites appeared in Worcester, and increased their recruits to the number of perhaps a thousand, only to retire to Rutland on December 9.

From an interview that Shays had with General Rufus Putnam over a fortnight before the attack on the Springfield Arsenal, it is clear that the leaders at this stage were more concerned about saving their own necks than about pressing forward with revolutionary objectives. Putnam, who hoped that the problems of the ex-army officer could be solved by western lands, and who acted as a front for the Ohio Company Associates, perhaps as skillful a group of Congressional lobbyists as ever operated in this country, reported his talk to Governor Bowdoin. Although Shays hardly emerges as a heroic figure, he certainly seems free of treasonable intent.

> PUTNAM: It is absurd to expect that another general pardon should be ever granted.
>
> SHAYS: No! Then we must fight it out.
>
> PUTNAM: That as you please, but it's impossible you should succeed, and the event will be that you must either run

[6] *Secret Journals of the Acts and Proceedings of Congress,* Vol. I (Domestic Affairs), (Boston: 1821), pp. 267–70.

your country or hang, unless you are fortunate enough to bleed.

SHAYS: By God I'll never run my country!

PUTNAM: Why not? It's more honorable than to fight in a bad cause, and be the means of involving your country in a civil war. You owned to me at Holden the week before you stopped Worcester court, that it was wrong in the people ever to take up arms as they had.

SHAYS: So I did, and so I say now, and I told you then, and tell you now, that the sole motive with me in taking the command at Springfield, was to prevent the shedding of blood, which would absolutely have been the cause, if I had not; and I am so far from considering it as a crime, that I look upon it that the government are indebted to me for what I did there.

PUTNAM: If that was the case, how came you to pursue the matter? Why did you not stop there?

SHAYS: I did not pursue the matter; it was noised about that the warrants were out after me, and I was determined not to be taken.

PUTNAM: This won't do. How came you to write letters to several towns in the county of Hampshire, to choose officers and furnish themselves with arms and 60 rounds of ammunition?

SHAYS: I never did. It was a cursed falsehood.

And more of these denials of leadership. Shays insisted that Putnam was "deceived," that he "never had half so much to do with the" disturbances as was believed. Putnam patiently explained to Shays that since the rebel had refused an offer of mercy and resumed his recalcitrant course, the government could not "with any kind of honor and safety" overlook it "without hanging somebody; and as you are at the head of the insurgents, and the person who directs all their movements, I cannot see you have any chance to escape." "I at their head!" Shays answered, with characteristic deviousness. "I am not." He steadfastly denied that he had ever assumed command of any but county forces. But when asked what course he would pursue if he was denied a pardon, he replied: "Why, then, I will collect all the force I can and fight it out; and, I swear, so would you or anybody else, rather than be hanged." Putnam summarizes the concluding exchange, an especially revealing one:

PUTNAM: I will ask you one question more, you may answer it or not, as you please. It is this: Had you an opportunity, would you accept of a pardon, and leave these people to themselves?

SHAYS: Yes—in a moment.

PUTNAM: Then I advise you to set off this night to Boston, and throw yourself upon the mercy and under the protection of Government.

SHAYS: No, that is too great a risk, unless I was first assured of a pardon.

PUTNAM: There is no risk in the matter, you never heard of a man who voluntarily did this, whose submission was not accepted; and if your submission is refused, I will venture to be hanged in your room.

SHAYS: In the first place, I don't want you to be hanged, and in the next place, they would not accept of you.

In conclusion, Putnam told the governor, "the only observation I shall make is, that I fully believe he may be brought off, and no doubt he is able to inform Government more of the bottom of this plan that they know at present." [7]

The Putnam interview came as the crisis was approaching its greatest intensity. Already, on December 26, Shays had marched into Springfield and forced the courts to cease business. When General Lincoln, who was now acting as head of the expedition against the insurgents, learned that Shays was situated six miles south of Springfield and that Luke Day and his followers were holding West Springfield, he set off for the relief of General Shephard, who was defending the arsenal. Upon Lincoln's "attempts to restore system and order" Governor Bowdoin, in his orders of January 19, wished "the smiles of heaven." Had Luke Day executed his part of the plan agreed upon by the two rebel leaders, and joined forces with Shays, the results might have been quite different. But Day sent a message to Shays informing him that he could not join him for the planned attack on January 25, but needed an extra day. This message was intercepted by Shephard's men. Shays went ahead with his attack on the scheduled

[7] C. O. Parmenter: *History of Pelham, Mass.* (Boston: 1898), pp. 395-8.

date, mistakenly assuming that Day would join him. Marching his men up to the arsenal, he defied a command by Shephard not to come nearer "at his peril." Two warning salvos of artillery were ignored. A third, through the center of the column, caused the attackers to hesitate; a fourth and fifth caused a complete rout. Had Shephard been disposed to charge upon their rear and flanks he could have cut them to pieces, but he forbore further action in his anxiety to avoid unnecessary bloodshed.

Lincoln came up on the 27th and crossed the river upon the ice, to come between Shays and Day and cut off Day's retreat. A surprised guard at the ferry house fled their post, and after a "little shew of force" Day's contingent retired in disorder and took to the woods.[8]

Shays now took up fortified positions on a hilltop in Pelham and, when urged by Lincoln to surrender and throw himself upon the state for mercy, agreed to lay down arms "on condition of a general pardon." But Lincoln had not been authorized to make such conditions, and the negotiations fell through. Washington could not understand why Shays continued to resist. "Surely," he wrote Knox around this time, "Shays must be either a weak man, the dupe of some characters who are yet behind the curtain, or has been deceived by his followers." The General Court now declared the Shaysites in a state of rebellion and authorized the governor to pardon privates and noncommissioned officers, but not the leaders.

During the negotiations the main body of Shaysites withdrew from Pelham and marched to Petersham. But Lincoln was alert and, in a memorable forced march through the deep winter snows in a subzero night, advanced his forces some thirty miles in thirteen hours. Their front reached Petersham at nine o'clock in the morning, and the complacent insurgents were thrown into complete confusion by this seemingly impossible feat. Some hundred and fifty were taken prisoner, others retired to their homes, and their chief officers fled to Vermont, New Hampshire, or New York. Henceforward the insurgents confined themselves to guerrilla operations such as those engaged in by Captain Hamlin's band, who, using New York as a base of operations, raided

---

[8] Lincoln to Bowdoin, *American Historical Review*, Vol. II (1897), pp. 693–8; Journal of Capt. Phineas Hardy, *New England Historical and Genealogical Register*, Vol. VII (1853), p. 352.

the border and plundered Stockbridge, unlocking the jail cells of that town—a scene made memorable in Bellamy's novel. Even though Eli Parsons, as late as February 13, called upon the people of Berkshire to rise and "to Burgoyne" Lincoln and his army, the rebellion was now at an end.

Toward his erstwhile adversaries Lincoln favored a magnanimous course, but, as James Truslow Adams in a brilliant comment on the rebellion, remarks, "it is notorious that men who have fought an enemy show magnanimity afterward, whereas the splenetic vindictiveness of the stay-at-homes is apt to rise as the danger diminishes." On February 16 the legislature passed an act refusing pardon to all former rebels above the grade of noncommissioned officers, to citizens of other states, to anyone who had ever sat in the legislature, or who had ever held any civil or military commission, or who had ever attended any state or county convention—thus indiscriminately bulking the more lawful protestants, including some of the most solid citizens of the interior of the state, with the hotheads. Even the remainder to whom amnesty might be given were to be forbidden to vote, hold office, serve on a jury, teach school, keep an inn, or retail liquor, for three years. While Lincoln favored singling out a few of the leaders of the rebellion, he disapproved of the large-scale disfranchisement this piece of legislation involved. In a letter to Washington he argued that this action gave the people a basis for complaining that no constitutional way had been left them to redress their grievances. Washington thoroughly agreed with him. He wrote Knox urging that "punishments . . . ought to be light on principle," and remonstrated to Lincoln "that measures more generally lenient might have produced equally as good an effect without entirely alienating the affections of the people from the government. As it now stands," Washington pointed out, "it affects a large body of men, some of them, perhaps, it deprives of the means of gaining a livelihood; the friends and connections of these people will feel themselves wounded in a degree, and I think it will rob the state of a number of its inhabitants, if it produces nothing worse"—a strikingly accurate prediction.

Perhaps realizing the impractical and rigid position they had adopted, the legislature the following month appointed a committee of three persons, consisting of General Lincoln, Samuel

Philips, Jr., and Samuel A. Otis, to receive applications from the western rebels and pardon them unconditionally. Some 790 ex-Shaysites availed themselves of this opportunity for pardon by the commission. But Shays, Parsons, Day, and Wheeler were specifically excepted.[9]

In the first week of April, the Supreme Court condemned six men to death in Berkshire County, and two more were given like sentences in May. The cases are significant because they are probably the first trials brought in America for treason against a state—foreshadowing the Dorr Rebellion trial in Rhode Island and John Brown's trial in Virginia on the eve of the Civil War. Meantime, a new election had produced an overturn of the old legislature, and pro-Shaysite forces appeared in the General Court in sufficient number to effect the passage of a more liberal amnesty act granting complete pardon to all who would take the oath of allegiance. On June 16 some of those convicted were reprieved until August 2, but, in the sadistic fashion of the day, the Hampshire sheriff was ordered not to open his directions until the criminals had arrived at the gallows. Parmenter and Shattuck were pardoned on September 12. In February 1788 Shays and Parsons admitted their error, denied that they had ever combined with secret enemies of America, "if any such there were," to subvert her independence, and promised good behavior. They, too, were pardoned the following summer, but on condition they should never hold civil or military office in Massachusetts. Thus, as in the later cases of the Whisky Rebellion and the Chartist uprising in England, a policy of forbearance was wisely adopted and those condemned to death were never executed.

While the rebellion created a panic among conservatives, more temperate folk believed that the legislature had bungled the entire affair. Had a serious attempt been made to deal with these grievances there would have been no rebellion. But when it was suppressed, the vindictiveness of the legislature left the public astounded. Had Herbert Hoover carefully studied this episode he might not have made the fatal blunder of his political career, the routing of the Bonus Army, which General Douglas MacArthur, with that characteristic hyperbole we have since come to expect from him, stigmatized as "a bad-looking mob animated by the

[9] Day was taken in New Hampshire in January 1788, but Shays and Parsons escaped capture.

spirit of revolution." The voters of Massachusetts went on record in no uncertain terms. In the election held in the spring of '87, John Hancock, running on the popular party platform of amnesty for the rebels, defeated Bowdoin for the governorship by a vote of three to one. Only one fourth of the members of the new House of Representatives had been in the former one. This sensational overturn sent a number of prominent Shaysites to the legislature. In the upper house two thirds of the membership consisted of entirely new faces. Minot saw the election as a "revolution in the public mind," and twentieth-century Americans may see in that event a striking parallel to the overturn in 1932, when the Republicans were swept out of office following the administration's notable victory at Anacostia Flats.

Defeated on the field of battle, the insurgents had the satisfaction of seeing many of their recommendations carried out by the new legislature. Laws were enacted exempting clothing, household goods, or tools of trade from debt process, allowing personal or real estate to be used in payment of debts, and providing that imprisoned debtors might obtain their freedom by taking the pauper's oath. A new fee bill was passed, lessening court charges. The number of terms of holding the courts of common pleas and general sessions were reduced. No direct tax whatsoever was enacted for 1787, and in the years following the tax burden was much lighter than it had been at the time of the crisis. Lastly, Hancock made an appeasement gesture to those who felt that the governor was overpaid by voluntarily reducing his salary for the year by three hundred pounds, once again demonstrating what John Quincy Adams called his "peculiar talent of pleasing the multitude." But James Madison, less charitably inclined, observed that Hancock's merits were "not a little tainted by a dishonorable obsequiousness to popular follies."

On the local scene the Shaysites, though routed, had won a number of their main objectives. On the national scene the rebellion may have been the greatest single spur to the reconciliation of differences at the Federal Convention. Writing on March 25, 1787, to Lafayette, Washington, after commenting on the suppression of the uprising, told the marquis about the Philadelphia meeting scheduled for May. "What may be the result of this meeting is hardly within the scan of human wisdom to predict," he added. Madison, with Shays' Rebellion very much on his mind, confessed: "The nearer the crisis approaches the more I tremble for the issue." At the Philadelphia Convention the ghost of Shaysism was not easily laid. John Langdon of New Hampshire went so far as to favor the use of federal troops to put down insurrections within a state without application of the state legislature, a more extreme position than that which was finally taken. In opposing the grant to the states of power to emit bills of credit, Langdon is reputed to have declared that "rather than the states should have the power of emitting paper money he would consent to make General Washington despot of America." [1]

Never again were the leaders of the insurgency to exercise sway over the emotions of Americans. They were broken and discredited. Shays, who had fled to New Hampshire after the rout at Petersham, hid for a time in Vermont as an outlaw. As late as 1791 he is known to have been in Bennington County. Then he moved west to Sparta, New York, but never prospered. In filing an application for an army pension in 1820 he listed his meager personal effects as totaling a mere $40.62. He died in poverty at the age of seventy-eight, managing to live for the last seven years on a twenty-dollar monthly army pension. But Shaysism did not die with Shays. It was spread by restless New Englanders who formed the Yankee exodus to Maine and Vermont, and to New York and the West. [2] That Yankee insistence upon social justice was behind the anti-rent agitation in New York, behind the abolition movement, behind the Homestead Act, and behind the Populist movement. It inspired much of the farm program and the emergency relief measures of the New Deal.

Lastly, Shays' Rebellion raises an issue of transcendent importance to Americans today. How patient should a democracy be when confronted with overt acts aimed at bringing about social reform by force? The Colonial period offered a number of examples of resort to force where the governmental authorities

[1] Max Farrand (ed.): *The Records of the Federal Convention* (New Haven: 1911), Vol. II, p. 310; Vol. III, p. 305. See also Thomas W. Nazro: "John Langdon of New Hampshire," M.A. Thesis, Columbia University (1950).

[2] Perhaps 100,000 people moved out of the four older states of New England in the eighties. The population of Vermont increased from 30,000 in 1784 to 85,000 by 1790, and Maine's population was a fourth that of Massachusetts by the latter date.

seemed indifferent to the demands of sectional or class interests. Bacon's Rebellion in 1676, the large-scale tenant riots in New York and New Jersey in the middle of the eighteenth century, and the Regulator movement in the Carolinas are concrete manifestations of that tendency of the colonials, under conditions of extreme stress, to take up arms to redress grievances. The American Revolution was the culminating demonstration of popular resistance to governmental authority when a more peaceable course had failed. Even Alexander Hamilton, hardly an apostle of revolution in the postwar period, expressed the view in *The Federalist* that "if the representatives of the People betray their constituents, there is then no resource left but in the exertion of that original right of self-defense which is paramount to all positive forms of government," and that in single states where the subdivisions had no distinct government to oppose a usurper, "the citizens must rush tumultuously to arms, without concert, without system, without resource, except in their courage and despair." This is as succinct a description as will be found anywhere of what actually happened in Shays' Rebellion.

The lesson seems patent to a generation now staggering from crisis to crisis. We must continue to achieve the ends of democracy under the rule of law. The attempts of minorities, whether bearing the banners of Fascism or of Communism, to achieve their objectives by force or to subordinate our national interest to those of a foreign power cannot be tolerated today any more than in Washington's time. Nevertheless, if we wish minority groups to accept majority rule we must give them reason to feel that they are a part of the whole, that under democracy they will not be reduced to a status of second-class citizens, that no groups may enjoy special privileges, and that *all* the people of the United States are working together "to form a more perfect Union, establish justice, insure domestic tranquillity, provide for the common defence, promote the general welfare, and secure the blessings of liberty to ourselves and our posterity." As in 1787, the price of liberty is still eternal vigilance.

III. *The Yellow Fever Epidemics,*
1793–1905

According to Professor Richard H. Shryock, the yellow fever epidemic of 1793 was "perhaps the most devastating natural disaster that has ever befallen a single American city." The story of Philadelphia's complete disintegration makes grisly reading in an age of atomic bombs and bacteriological warfare, but the story of that city's response and recovery is heartening. Out of complete chaos and hysteria, a leadership developed that brought confidence to the stricken capital. A handful of prominent men and a score of their now forgotten assistants maintained the city services, transformed a pesthouse into a hospital, and saved many from death. Although epidemics, aggravated by apathy and negligence, occurred with regularity throughout the nineteenth century, the Philadelphia experience suggests a pattern of response that could be counted upon under the most trying of conditions: powerful collective action and unsuspected capacities of leadership in the "kingly commons."

III

The Yellow Fever Epidemics, 1793–1905

Richard H. Shryock

Director, Institute of the History of Medicine,
The Johns Hopkins University

The summer of 1793 was uncommonly hot and dry in Philadel-phia, then the national capital and also the economic and cultural center of the new nation. The citizens, no less than fifty-five thousand of them, sweltered day after day in the intense heat and endured the dust of the streets and the mounting stench of the waterfront. To make matters worse, everyone was plagued by swarms of flies and mosquitoes; and unusual forms of illness ap-peared. There was something ominous in the breathless air: men pondered with dread what the sickly autumnal season might have in store for them.

The answer was soon forthcoming. Early in August Dr. Ben-jamin Rush, signer of the Declaration of Independence and physi-cian extraordinary, saw several cases of a fatal fever accom-panied by jaundice and other acute symptoms. On August 19 he announced that it was the true "Black Vomit" or Yellow Fever, and that the city was threatened by disaster. This terrible dis-ease was known to have visited the city on four previous occa-sions between 1699 and 1762, and the outbreak of the latter year was still recalled when Rush made his announcement. Al-though the doctor was criticized as an alarmist, his diagnosis was soon confirmed by the College of Physicians. Any lingering doubts were dispelled by the rapid spread of the disease. Within a week the popular anxiety was succeeded by alarm, and alarm then deepened into terror.

During the next two months Philadelphia experienced the worst epidemic—perhaps the most devastating natural disaster—that has ever befallen a single American city. Business was abandoned while thousands fled the city; and of those who remained, many died without medical care or even the simplest human ministrations. About ten per cent of the total population succumbed. If Philadelphia were to endure a similar visitation next year, with the same proportionate mortality, it would suffer a loss of almost two hundred thousand lives within a single season!

Several observers left accounts of the disaster of 1793, written during or soon after that fateful year. Here are a few word pictures of the epidemic, as penned by Dr. Rush:

> Fear or terror now sat upon every countenance. The disease appeared in many parts of the town . . . [and] this set the city in motion. The streets . . . were crowded with families fleeing in every direction for safety to the country. Business began to languish.
>
> The contagion . . . spared no rank of citizens. Whole families were confined by it. There was a deficiency of nurses . . . [and] of physicians from the desertion of some and the sickness and death of others. At one time there were only three physicians . . . able to do business outside their houses, and . . . no less than six thousand persons ill with the fever. . . .
>
> I seldom went into a house for the first time without meeting the parents or children of the sick in tears. Grief, after awhile descended below weeping . . . many persons submitted to the loss of relatives and friends, without manifesting any . . . of the common signs of grief.

Rush adds that more than half the houses in the city were shut up, and that the streets were almost deserted except for those seeking doctors or nurses. Even the formality of funerals was abandoned; except that when coffins were carted away, a few relatives might follow on foot at what they considered a safe distance. Keenly aware of psychological aspects of the crisis, he noted that the rumbling of these cart wheels over cobblestones "kept alive anguish and fear, in the sick and well, every hour of the night." [1]

[1] Benjamin Rush: *An Account of the Bilious remitting Yellow Fever . . . of Philadelphia in the Year 1793* (Philadelphia: 1794), pp. 122–5.

Much of the behavior noted here could be ascribed to simple, almost instinctive, fear. We now know that yellow fever did not pass directly from person to person; but the terror it aroused was certainly contagious, and accounted for mass flight and other symptoms of demoralization. There was nevertheless another side to the picture. While many of the prosperous fled, including President Washington and other founding fathers, there were some who stayed. The poor had no choice in any case, and a few leaders remained with them in an effort to save the situation. Heroism also appeared in humble places, as when unknown shopkeepers or artisans gave unstintingly of their services. Such conduct not only exhibited courage but involved some co-ordination, some social planning, and is to be balanced against the less admirable aspects of the story.

What resources did an American city of 1793 have at its command for meeting a crisis of this magnitude? What of the churches, the government, the hospitals, and the medical profession? It may be said at once that the churches, as such, played little part in the epidemic. Clergymen doubtless presided at the earlier funerals, but none of them stood out as community leaders. The bells were rung and there were requests for public prayers; but if any parishes conducted organized relief work, it seems to have escaped the notice of the chroniclers. In contrast to the pattern of earlier centuries, there was little disposition to ascribe the disaster to divine wrath or to turn primarily to religious intercessions. This was the age of The Enlightenment, even though there was—unfortunately—so little enlightenment concerning yellow fever.

Under ordinary conditions the health of the community was left to individuals and their respective physicians, but the yellow fever emergency demanded public measures. Dr. Rush therefore called on Mayor Clarkson in order to urge civic precautions. But the mayor, in turn, had to depend on medical opinions. One must know how the plague spread before deciding what could stop it. Rush replied that the disease was of local origin, that it was spread by some subtle atmospheric poison (miasma) that arose from decaying substances, and that it could be checked by sanitary measures. The mayor therefore ordered that the streets be cleaned with dispatch.

As a tough-minded official, however, Clarkson wanted the ad-

vice of more than one doctor. Since there was then no board of
health to provide expert opinion, he appealed to the College of
Physicians.[2] This was probably the first time in American history
that a private medical organization was requested to guide government action. The College promptly held several meetings in
order to suggest measures for the public safety, thus acting in the
same capacity as would boards of health in subsequent years. This
pattern was to be repeated many times in later American experience: a private body initiating a role which later would be taken
over by official agencies.

When the College convened in response to the mayor's appeal,
it soon appeared that the medical profession had its limitations as
a community asset. These gentlemen represented medical science.
What did this science have to say about the causes, spread, and
means of checking epidemics? Unfortunately, it spoke with many
tongues. Ever since classical days some physicians had held that
epidemics had their origin, as Rush declared, in atmospheric poi-
sons arising from decaying materials. These "noxious miasmas"
could be eliminated by measures for clearing the air. Sanitary precautions were called for—cleaning streets and homes, supplying
pure water, carrying a pungent scent on one's person, and so on
—as well as such dramatic gestures as building bonfires and ex-
ploding gunpowder.

Another school, however, had insisted that epidemics were
spread by contagion and therefore could be checked by a different procedure: all those harboring the disease should be avoided.
Notification, isolation of cases, and quarantines were indicated.
There were minor controversies within each of these schools
which need not detain us here. Those who believed in miasmata,
for example, often held that these were of local origin; but at
other times said that some mysterious poison pervaded the atmosphere over large areas. This was a so-called "epidemic constitution" of the air.

Common opinion, among both doctors and laymen, favored
the contagion hypothesis. This view prevailed because of long
and bitter experience with such apparently contagious diseases as
leprosy, bubonic plague, and smallpox. Indeed, few denied con-

---

[2] The College, founded only seven years before this epidemic, was the
first medical academy in the country. It represented the elite of the local
profession.

tagion in these particular infections. But in yellow fever one encountered a baffling phenomenon. Here was a disease that acted in some ways as if it were contagious, and in other respects as if it were not. The contagionists could show that in Philadelphia, as in other epidemics, the outbreak began with the arrival of ships harboring yellow fever. The original foci of the disease, moreover, were in neighborhoods to which sailors from these ships resorted when they went ashore. All this looked like contagion. But it was also true that those tending the sick frequently did not "catch it"; whereas others who had avoided all contacts *were* brought down by the malady. This suggested that the infection was literally "in the air."

The controversy was more than an academic one among the doctors. The application of one theory led to practices quite different from those indicated by the other. These differences related to individual conduct as well as to governmental policy. The miasmatists, for example, were bitter because the contagion thesis led men to avoid and thus to neglect the sick. Few would volunteer as nurses, and patients were sometimes abandoned even by their friends and relatives. The measures advocated by the miasmatists, such as clean-ups and bonfires, did no such harm; but they also did no good and were a waste of time and effort. At best, they only met that psychological need *to do something* which was deeply implanted in everyone.

When the Fellows of the College of Physicians convened on August 25, 1793, there was a sharp division of opinion between contagionists who declared the yellow fever had been imported, and miasmatists who insisted it had a local origin in the contaminated atmosphere. The Fellows finally compromised by urging precautions indicated by one theory as well as the other. Men should avoid infected persons, and at the same time the streets must be cleaned. Citizens were also advised to watch their personal hygiene—to avoid fatigue or intemperance—in much the manner that health authorities advise today when they are still faced with some mysterious malady. The College did, in addition, make some constructive suggestions. Stop tolling the church bells, for this only alarmed the public. Stop building fires but by all means burn gunpowder. And provide a large hospital for the poor who could not otherwise be attended.

This report was conveyed to the mayor and duly published in

the newspapers. The press was already informing the people of the lurking danger, and printing various precautions or remedies suggested by their readers. People began staying indoors, white-washing their houses, and burning gunpowder. Those who went abroad carried camphor bags or chewed garlic to purify the air about them. Druggists advertised sure remedies, from Peruvian bark to patent elixirs. So disturbing did the situation become that the governor of Pennsylvania took notice and demanded advice from the health officer and the port physician, who were the only public-health officials then provided in public administration. Since these gentlemen were confused, the governor next brought the situation before the legislature. Philadelphia was then the state capital, and state and local jurisdiction overlapped in this crisis.

Governor Mifflin, in addressing the legislature, refused to admit that the epidemic was caused by miasmas arising from local filth. This view would hurt trade and damage the reputation of the city. The governor implied, rather, that the disease was con-tagious and had been imported by French refugees then crowd-ing the city. Here one observes a commercial motive intruding itself into a scientific controversy—a pattern often repeated in subsequent epidemics. The governor went on to urge the im-portance of the city health officer, stating that his function "be-comes daily more important to the well being of our metrop-olis." Effective health legislation must be provided. In a word, yellow fever was arousing a demand for permanent health agen-cies and administration.

The legislature, in reply, granted the governor emergency powers for the duration of the plague; and then hurriedly ad-journed until December. The members wanted to get out of town. Mifflin used his powers to enforce quarantines against ships in port, and then he too left town. What, meanwhile, of the fed-eral government, which was also located in the city? Such offi-cials as Washington and Jefferson watched the epidemic with concern, but no official action was taken other than the moving of federal offices to the suburbs. The national authorities appar-ently viewed health control as one of those "states' rights" which they were only too glad to avoid. But the state government had meantime disintegrated, and the whole machinery of government was thus left in the hands of the local authorities.

Unfortunately, local government was also disintegrating. The city council hurried away and only the devoted mayor remained to carry on. Clarkson did his best to enforce sanitary regulations, but it became almost impossible to find workers who would clean up the streets, the wharves, and the markets. The most immediate problem was to find some means for caring for the sick poor. Ordinarily these people would have been sent to the large almshouse or to the Pennsylvania hospital, two institutions of which the city was justly proud. But the directors of each, anxious to protect their inmates from infection, absolutely forbade the admission of yellow fever patients.

At this point the Guardians of the Poor, another municipal office, came into operation. People lay dying in deserted homes and even in the doorways and alleys: something must be done. Since there was nothing else to do, the guardians took over an unused circus-building in town and moved in some dying paupers. But no one would care for them and the neighbors, alarmed by their presence, threatened to burn the place down. Thereupon, the guardians seized a vacant mansion at Bush Hill outside the city and transported to it the few surviving paupers from the circus. They had no legal authority to do this; law as well as government was breaking down. But the guardians now had what they hoped would be the "large and airy hospital" originally requested by the College of Physicians.

By mid-September the city was threatened with chaos. Not only was business abandoned, but newspapers ceased to publish and the mails were no longer distributed. It was estimated that almost half the population had fled. Federal, state, and the greater part of local government had disappeared. Mayor Clarkson, in desperation, organized a special Citizens' Committee; and this courageous group of volunteers—skilled workers, shopkeepers, and merchants—composed the only real governing authority during the ensuing weeks. It was an extra-legal body but it worked! Society had reverted to a primitive level of organization.

The Committee, headed by the mayor and including about fifteen active members, had innumerable things to do. How were the sick poor and the doctors to be transported, orphans cared for, and burials to be conducted? But most of all, what to do about Bush Hill? As soon as it was opened, this so-called hospital became merely a charnel house. Patients died untended, while nondescript women employed as nurses consumed the supplies of food and wine. The sick poor dreaded to go near the place but were forced into it because of the prevailing fear. Two heroic volunteers, a cooper named Peter Helm and the merchant Stephen Girard, finally agreed to act as superintendents; and they gradually introduced discipline into the establishment. Better employees were found, new rooms opened up, and some attention given to the inmates. Girard nursed the sick with his own hands, and served as attorney for the dying. By October 1 he and Helm directed a well-ordered hospital. All this took money, and members of the Citizens' Committee put up bonds for a loan secured from the Bank of North America.

One of the most troublesome problems faced by Girard was the provision of medical attention. Several young physicians were paid by the Committee to drive out to the hospital at intervals, but this provided only sporadic attention for the hundred or more patients. There was, moreover, a bitter controversy about the type of treatments that should be employed. Here the medical profession again came into the picture. Theoretically, if the epidemic could not be checked, it might at least be ameliorated by effective therapy. But doctors who differed on the causes of yellow fever were likewise divided over its proper treatment. Rush, having found various remedies useless, retired into his study in order to find a solution in the older literature. He emerged with the doctrine that only heroic practice could combat the virulent poison of this fever: patients should be given the most violent purges and bled to extremity. In some cases, they must be relieved of four fifths of all the blood in their bodies!

Rush was formulating what he proudly believed was a new and basic theory: all fevers were but manifestations of a single, underlying pathologic state. This was identified as one of "excessive action" (hypertension?) in the blood vessels, and one could cure this by relieving tension through bleeding. Anyone who saw a feverish patient could observe that if bled long enough he did relax—sooner or later! What better proof could there be that the theory was correct? Rush and his followers proceeded to bleed and purge with abandon.

Certain physicians condemned this practice as too heroic. They advocated, instead, a mild regimen of "bark," tonics, and cold baths. Rush, they said, was killing his patients instead of curing them. But Rush, distraught by overwork and illness, retorted bitterly that these doctors were murdering their patients by neglect. He refused to consult with such colleagues, and both he and his opponents appealed to the public through the press. Laymen took sides, and this therapeutic controversy only added to the general confusion. Plainly needed was the confidence united professional opinion might have afforded, but the medical science of the day was quite inadequate for the occasion.

Girard, at Bush Hill, was an intelligent layman who distrusted extreme procedures. Of French origin, he had more confidence in the cautious treatments advocated by French refugee doctors. But when he urged that one of these men, Dr. Dévèze, be appointed resident at the hospital, he found that native physicians distrusted the foreigners. French medicine would later acquire great prestige in the United States; but in 1793 the British-trained Americans knew little about it. A crisis, they felt, was no time to turn to the unfamiliar. Hence it was only by the most clever manipulations that Girard finally secured the appointment for Dévèze. This able doctor introduced a moderate type of treatment. He also performed autopsies, and reported the ravages caused in some bodies by excessive purging. One can now see that his methods, although without specific value, had the merit of not interfering with the healing powers of nature. While Rush weakened his patients, Dévèze permitted them to recover of their own accord.

By early October, with the plague still at its height, the Citizens' Committee had reduced chaos to some order. More money was borrowed and, encouraged by the Committee's example, more volunteer workers appeared. The city was divided into ten districts, watched over by forty-six assistants, who reported cases to be removed to Bush Hill and provided relief to stranded families. Soon they were aiding some twelve hundred people with money and provisions. Help arrived at this point from other cities. There had originally been much fear that the epidemic would spread to distant towns, which indeed would have been the case had there been an "epidemic constitution" in the country's atmosphere. But as this fear subsided, money and food were sent in by relief committees of Wilmington, Boston, and New York. Actual need in the homes of Philadelphia, thus generously provided for, began to decline.

The Committee, of course, could not at once overcome wide-spread demoralization. As always, there were those who took advantage of the situation for their own ends. Side by side with the heroism of the Committee was the conduct of men who looted vacant houses, and of landlords who evicted tenants no longer able to pay. The sick also exhibited unusual behavior, born perhaps of a desperate fatalism. Some prearranged their funerals and even lay down to be measured for their coffins. Jones, Gray, and Allen—colored men who courageously volunteered to seek out the sick—found them "in various situations, some lying on the floor, as bloody as if they had been dipped in it, without any appearance of having even a drink of water for their relief; . . . some appeared, as if they had fallen dead on the floor, from the position they died in." [3] Such distress could be overcome only by a decline in the disease itself.

It was confidently expected that, with the advent of cold weather, the fever would disappear as it had in previous epidemics. Heavy rains fell on October 12 and the residents hoped for relief. But one hundred and eleven died that day. On October 18 the mercury dipped as low as forty-one degrees and the deaths fell to sixty-six. The mortality rose again fitfully; but after the 25th, with really cool weather, it declined steadily. Fewer cases appeared, and residents began returning to town. Early in November the epidemic had practically ceased, and the city resumed its customary activity with a universal sigh of relief. Shops re-opened, newspapers appeared, and the city council again took over. President Washington, who had wondered whether the Constitution authorized him to convene Congress in some other town, had the problem solved for him. The members now had no objection to returning to the capital.

By December the city once again exhibited a normal appearance; although there lingered, beneath the surface, a widespread sense of personal losses and a heightened anxiety about recurrences of the fever. So ended the worst localized epidemic in the nation's history. The experience had solved nothing; no one knew why the epidemic had ceased, any more than he understood how it had begun. So far as human nature was concerned, the visitation had only shown what contrasts between heroism and de-

[3] Quoted in J. H. Powell: *Bring Out Your Dead* (Philadelphia: 1949), p. 253.

moralization were to be expected. The need for medical progress and for public-health controls was certainly made apparent, but there was nothing new in this. Earlier epidemics, some of which had swept over entire countries and caused far greater total mortality, had demonstrated these needs on many previous occasions.

Certain circumstances, nevertheless, lent unusual significance to the yellow fever of 1793. Its high mortality rate, the peculiar terror it aroused, and the fact that it occurred in the capital city, all dramatized the threat of epidemics on a national scale. This dramatization was made especially effective by the availability of improved media of communication. Newspapers reported the crisis throughout the country, and various observers subsequently published reports on the outbreak which were widely circulated at home and abroad. No such publicity would have been possible a century before.

The timing of the epidemic, moreover, had an even larger significance. It was in this era that the great increase in urban populations was just getting under way. Philadelphia's population was destined to double within the next two decades, while that of New York would expand at an even faster rate. If epidemics of similar mortality were to be expected in such cities, their whole future was in jeopardy. This was realized at the time, and some observers concluded that further urban growth would only invite disaster. The epidemic, wrote Ebenezer Hazard, should teach this lesson. It ought to check the "prevailing taste for enlarging Philadelphia, and crowding so many human beings together on so small a part of the earth." America should reject the "fashions of the Old World in building great cities." [4] This view, so consistent with Jeffersonian attitudes, may evoke a sympathetic response even among modern readers; although the disasters now feared are the manmade rather than the natural.

Other critics believed that urban growth could continue, if only adequate measures were taken against the menace of disease. But for them also, the warning of 1793 was more timely than it would have been in the medieval era of stationary populations. If cities did not bestir themselves, yellow fever might yet prove to be the fateful writing on the wall.

[4] Ibid., p. 276.

❋   ❋   ❋

So, at least, thought Benjamin Rush and other observers when the disease returned in 1794 and in subsequent years. There were repeated epidemics up and down the coast, indeed, over the next thirty years—in Charleston, Baltimore, New York, and New Haven. Outbreaks occurred as far north as Boston. None of these were as terrifying as that of 1793, but all were serious enough to arouse widespread alarm. Striving to combat them, cities tightened quarantine regulations in deference to the contagionists; and also introduced sanitary improvements in response to the miasmatic theory. Philadelphia, as the chief sufferer, led the way by providing the first municipal water-supply early in the 1800's. This was done by using steam engines for the pumping of water throughout the town—thus calling modern technology to the assistance of health control. The same city also set up tent hospital facilities in anticipation of later outbreaks, and was thus better prepared to meet social emergencies than it had been in 1793.

As the epidemics recurred, moreover, the larger centers organized permanent boards of health. The duties of these bodies were to advise on sanitation and other precautions, as well as to oversee quarantines. In 1833 a cholera pandemic reached the United States from India via Europe, and fear of this scourge reinforced that already aroused by yellow fever. Certain cities responded by providing wardens who were to report all cases of epidemic diseases, and to warn the public against them by some sort of notification. Such a system, as was shown in New York in the 1850's, was anything but efficient; but it at least represented a beginning.

After 1830, yellow fever ceased to visit the Northern ports, for reasons that are still difficult to explain; but it continued to devastate the South. New Orleans, Charleston, Savannah, and Norfolk all experienced serious outbreaks after 1830; indeed, there were only three years between 1800 and 1880 when no American city was visited by this plague. The phenomena observed were very similar to those in Philadelphia in 1793, albeit upon a less extreme scale. Only New Orleans, "the graveyard of the Southwest," could compete with the Quaker City for the dubious honor of the highest mortality. Yet doctors as well as laymen fled from even the smaller ports, and varying degrees of demoralization ensued.

The letters of Dr. Richard Arnold, commenting on the Savannah outbreak of 1854, were reminiscent of Rush. "Such a panic as exists here," he wrote his daughter, "is hard to describe."

> The city is almost deserted. Quackery is rife. Dr. Wildman flourishes with Tincture of Iron. Dr. M. Scheley had the fever they say & has *vamoosed* to Augusta. . . . Dr. Freeman Schley went up the road this morning in hot haste. I call this the *Stampede* fever.

Subsequently, Arnold added that both the medical students living with him had died: their "cases were awfully severe and rapid." As for Dr. Wildman, "his specific did not save him. I considered it a humbug while he was living & his death affords no reason why I should change my opinion." [5]

It will be noted that the doctors of 1854 continued to disagree on treatments. Arnold was still using Rush's method—in a less extreme manner—but by this time there was popular opposition to it. Encouraged by homeopathy and other sects, the people were becoming suspicious of bleeding; and Arnold encountered more trouble than Rush ever had on this score. "The wiseacres," he wrote, "abused me at the corners of the Streets (I'll assure you this was literally the fact) for being old-fashioned and prejudiced and for killing all my patients with the Lancet and calomel. . . ." [6]

The doctors also continued to debate the causes of yellow fever and the measures needed to prevent it. Although the ineffectiveness of health measures was partly the result of political conditions, it was even more a product of medical confusion. Had science been able to indicate clearly whence the disease came, more effective precautions might have been taken. It was primarily science, rather than administration, that was still unequal to these emergencies.

It is true that the contagionists were losing ground to the miasmatists, and to this extent Rush's thesis was being vindicated. ". . . am . . . a decided *Non Contagionist*," wrote Arnold in '54. "The *importation* of the disease by any vessel is the *sheerest*

---

[5] R. H. Shryock (ed.): *The Arnold Letters*, Papers of the Trinity College (Duke University) Historical Society, Vols. XVIII, XIX (1929), pp. 69 ff.
[6] *Ibid.*, 71.

nonsense." [7] The miasmatic view seems to have been increasingly adopted between 1800 and 1860 because it called for sanitary improvements; and these were clearly needed by the crowded and dirty cities of the industrial age—for more reasons than one. Quarantines, in any case, had been long employed and found wanting: why not try sanitary reform?

Such views were not peculiar to the United States. Indeed, they were inspired here as much by contemporary British efforts as they were by national experience. Up to the 1840's, American attempts to control public health had been limited to local activities; but a national movement was under way in Britain and this stimulated a similar effort in the United States. The threat of epidemics was common to all cities throughout the country. The federal system, however, proved an obstacle to any unified action. Congress continued to view the whole matter as pertaining to "states' rights," and declined to set up a national health board on the British model. Nor, prior to 1870, did the states themselves display any concern. This was a problem of the cities. Let them handle it.

Left to their own resources, urban officials decided that they might at least co-operate with one another. They therefore organized a series of national but unofficial health conventions, which met from 1857 to 1860, and which really constituted the first American public health association. The mayors, health officers, and other physicians who attended were primarily concerned with the persistent enigma of yellow fever. In the proceedings of the New York sessions of 1859, some seventy-five pages were devoted at one point in the discussions to this subject alone. The pressing questions continued to be: is the fever imported and contagious, or is it of local (miasmatic) origin and noncontagious? The contagionists, although now outnumbered, continued to hold their ground. The argument still stood just where it had in 1793.

As a matter of fact, confusion continued until the end of the century—to within the memory of many still living. This was true despite the fact that much progress was made in the administrative aspects of the health program. After 1870, many states set up health boards; and the cities gradually introduced

[7] R. H. Shryock (ed.): "Selections from the Letters of Richard D. Arnold," *Bulletin of the Johns Hopkins Hospital,* Vol. XLII (1928), p. 183

improved sanitary regulations and facilities. But all this was of no avail against yellow fever. At the end of the Spanish-American War in 1899, the United States Army feared a yellow fever epidemic in occupied Havana; and that city was therefore "cleaned up" in terms of the traditional miasmatic theory. Dr. Rush would have approved of this thoroughly. Yet the fever returned the next year despite all these precautions. In a word, sanitation—even as quarantines before it—was unable to prevent this plague. Was there no answer to the mystery?

One can hardly maintain suspense today about yellow fever. There is little current fear of the disease in this country; and even as far as the earlier experience is concerned, we all know the answers. We have read the end of the mystery story in advance. It is easy now to see that there was some missing factor in the whole picture which explained why the disease seemed contagious in some respects, noncontagious in others. As early as 1795, indeed, one Dr. E. H. Smith of New York suggested that there must be such an x-factor—something less direct than personal contacts, yet more tangible than the all-pervading air. But he had no means for identifying this x. It does seem curious, in retrospect, that neither he nor others thought of equating it with insect vectors; for theories about such possibilities had been expressed from time to time, and were not entirely unknown to Dr. Rush and his contemporaries. But this speculation doubtless seemed fanciful, in comparison with the more obvious theories about contacts and miasmas.

Before the theory of insect carriers could be taken seriously, it had to find some rational basis in medical science. The clue here, we now know, lay in a special theory concerning causal factors in disease; that is, in the thesis of a living contagion. This concept had been clearly presented as early as the seventeenth century, and had been boldly announced in America by none other than the Reverend Mr. Cotton Mather in a forgotten work of 1722. But for a number of reasons, interest in a *contagium animatum*—in the "germ theory"—lagged for nearly two centuries. It was not even partially aroused until after 1820, when an improvement in microscopes made possible extensive studies of micro-organisms.

Various physicians, between 1820 and 1850, re-examined known disease phenomena in order to see if the "animalcular" (germ) theory could explain them. Several prominent American doctors, for example, then concluded that certain epidemics behaved *as if* spread by living organisms. This was not "mere speculation"; for these men examined the epidemiologic evidence with care. Unfortunately, this evidence was not enough. Only laboratory checks could provide final confirmation, and few Americans then indulged in studies of that nature. Early advocates of the germ theory were therefore ignored by their colleagues who were actually battling with the yellow fever. It remained for Europeans, more devoted to basic research, to prove the germ theory by laboratory experiments.

This proof was finally presented by Pasteur, Koch, and others, between 1860 and 1885 for a whole series of infectious diseases. Although no yellow fever organisms were then found, it was assumed by analogy that these must exist. Hence an impetus was given to research on the mode of their transmission; for if this could be discovered, the disease could be checked without ever seeing the hidden germs themselves. Recalling ancient speculations, research men began to search for insect or other animal carriers of mysterious infections. Insect transmission was proved in the case of a tropical disease, filariasis, in 1879; and the same process was found during the next two decades to be involved in malaria and several other scourges. Following up such leads, Dr. Carlos Finlay of Cuba ascribed yellow fever transmission to mosquitoes and even identified the particular species concerned. Only when a United States Army board led by Walter Reed performed controlled experiments at Havana in 1899, however, was the validity of Finlay's view finally confirmed.

The mosquito carrier thus proved to be the x-factor in medicine's great detective story. Once it was understood, all the other parts to the puzzle fell nicely into place. Yellow fever was indeed carried through the air, but by insects rather than by miasmas. It was indeed transmitted by contacts, but contacts via insects rather than through direct contagion. The contagionists had been right in saying that the disease was imported to American cities and then spread by infected crews, but they had been wrong in thinking that this transmission had occurred through ordinary contagion. All the efforts to avoid contacts, which led to such a neglect of the sick in 1793, had been—as Rush claimed—of no avail. In accepting a partly erroneous scientific theory, urban societies had not only failed to solve their problem but had actually made matters worse than was necessary.

By the same token, the scientific explanation made available in 1900 thereafter enabled American cities to avoid this plague and all its secondary consequences. Both quarantines of infected vessels *and* sanitary measures (mosquito controls) could now be intelligently employed by local, state, and national health authorities.[8] Only one American city was so careless as to permit another yellow fever epidemic. And in this one case, New Orleans in 1905, a program of mosquito elimination proved the new view by checking the disease in mid-course. Since that time, no yellow fever has invaded the United States, although the disease is still endemic in Africa and in parts of South America. It is of concern within this country chiefly because rapid air transit might introduce infected mosquitoes from tropical areas. And against this possibility health authorities are on guard.

One may conclude this story with certain reflections on the nature of these yellow fever epidemics, and on the manner in which American society reacted to them. It is now clear that they involved three primary factors; namely, man, the mosquito vector, and the causative organisms or virus.[9] Man must be considered, first, as an animal; and second, in relation to his social behavior. As an animal, he could conceivably have evolved increasing resistance to yellow fever through a "survival of the fittest" of his kind; but the period 1793 to 1905 was too short for such a process. The Negro, however, had presumably lived with this plague for many centuries in Africa, and thus might have developed some racial immunity. The evidence on this seems conflicting. Several hundred Negroes died in the outbreak of 1793; but in that of 1854 Dr. Arnold insisted that Negroes suffered far less than did the whites. He might have added that there was nothing in their living conditions, as distinct from their heredity, that could account for this contrast. The white mortality rate in Savannah for that year was reported as more than twice the rate among Negroes.

[8] After 1900, the U.S. Marine Hospital Service increasingly took on the functions of a national health office.
[9] This last factor was finally isolated during the virus research of the last two decades. This made it possible during World War II to develop an anti-yellow-fever vaccine, which is believed to provide some immunity for those who are infected despite all precautions.

In terms of social behavior, man was just as responsible for the epidemics as were the mosquitoes. For it was commercial expansion that imported the disease from the tropics to the temperate zones. Negro slaves from Africa were probably first responsible for infecting the hitherto innocent mosquitoes of the New World; that is, from the mosquitoes' viewpoint, man was the vector! When Europeans, Africans, and Indians came together in America, they engaged in a free exchange of their respective infections; and the yellow fever record indicates what tragic results followed this continental interchange.

Man, then, was a variable in the picture. Whether this was true of the other factors is difficult to say. Mosquito populations may have waxed and waned in particular localities, but there is no evidence on this before the time of eradication programs. It seems more likely that it was the yellow fever virus that played a varying role. Viruses are known to change in virulency through mutations or other obscure biologic processes. The onset of a series of vicious epidemics beginning in 1793 could possibly be explained by the rush of French West-Indian refugees to the United States in the 1790's. But it could also be accounted for by the emergence of an especially potent virus in those years. The influx of refugees largely ceased after 1800, but the yellow fever did not. Certainly the virus was then in "an epidemic mood." Over this aspect of the matter, man still has little control.

It is of some interest to place the yellow fever crises in a comparative perspective by contrasting the response they aroused with that elicited by other diseases. These contrasts are quite striking. Many of us, for example, still recall the influenza pandemic of 1918, which inflicted a greater total mortality than did all the yellow fever epidemics combined. The latter were highly localized, and rarely visited more than two or three cities within a single year; while influenza swept the country and indeed the world. Yet "the flu" aroused no such fear as did "Yellow Jack." Why this contrast?

The truth is that each serious disease arouses its own particular response—has its own social psychology. This is compounded of various elements of apprehension, repugnance, sympathy, and so on. It also involves the consideration of what can be done about the menace: if there is nothing to do, the reaction is likely to be a passive, fatalistic one. Hence the public indifference today to nephritis, one of the most deadly of conditions. Epidemics usually arouse more concern than do endemic conditions; partly because of fear of the unusual, partly because it is natural to assume that the unusual is more preventable. Within the epidemic category diseases that kill suddenly, that present repulsive or long-persisting symptoms, and that one can supposedly avoid in some way, arouse the greatest anxiety.

Yellow fever met most of these specifications—it was repulsive, it killed quickly, and *one could avoid it by running away*. One recalls the James theory of the emotions: the very act of running probably increased the terror. This suggests that social psychologists as well as public-health men might well study behavior associated with various diseases. Where this involves panic, unusual or pathologic types of conduct can be observed. It may be added that the modern health movement owed much to yellow fever just because it did inspire such fear. Wherever it passed, this disease—like the plague and cholera—left in its wake a demand for action, for protection. Perhaps health officers should raise a statue to "Yellow Jack" in appreciation of its public services.

Moving on in these comparisons, one may contrast public reactions to epidemics with those precipitated by other natural disasters. Earthquakes and even floods are usually sudden in onset and termination: it is all over before the victims have time to think. But men had to live with yellow fever week after week, distraught by the loss of loved ones and fearful for their own lives. Fear is the greater in epidemics because it is cumulative.

Natural disasters as a whole elicit different responses than do crises that are primarily manmade in origin. The latter, such as a John Brown's raid, usually produce varying degrees of bitterness toward other men—against opponents or enemies. One can hardly be as bitter against an earthquake or a disease. Resentment will be aroused against other men during an epidemic, however, just in so far as certain persons are accused of being responsible for it. Hence Dr. Rush's feeling against the doctors who opposed his cure-all. He excused all his bitterness, years after 1793, by declaring: "I was contending with the most criminal ignorance, and the object of the contest was the preservation of a city."[1]

Reactions to natural disasters are likely to be more uniform in

[1] George W. Corner (ed.): *The Autobiography of Benjamin Rush* (Princeton: 1948), p. 97.

various times and places than are responses to manmade crises. The earthquake or the disease, as such, provides a common factor that is lacking in the more complex circumstances of human antagonisms. Many of the reactions to the yellow fever of Philadelphia in 1793 had already appeared in the West Indies during the seventeenth century, and would reappear in Savannah in 1854. Only when the societies involved were radically different in cultural outlook can one observe marked contrasts. A primitive people would have resorted to incantations (who knows how many still did this in 1793?), and medieval folk would have crowded the local shrines. Americans, living in a different intellectual climate, turned primarily to science; and this confidence—at long last—was vindicated.

This suggests, however, that in so far as there were minor differences between American outlooks and those in other western countries, there may have been subtle differences in the American response to the yellow fever crises. No final opinion can be expressed on this until more careful comparative studies have been made. Obvious contrasts are lacking, and one should guard against the nationalistic urge to find something distinctive about one's own country, at any cost. Yet the subtle differences may have existed. One wonders, for example, whether the response of other cities to the plight of Philadelphia in 1793—a pattern repeated in later epidemics—was more marked than were similar reactions in West Indian or Mediterranean outbreaks? Perhaps one has here the beginning of an American tradition of public generosity.

On the debt side, however, it seems unlikely that the national governments of France or Britain would have been so inactive in crises affecting their capital cities as was the federal government in Philadelphia in 1793. This inaction may be ascribed, at least in part, to the federal system, which was peculiar to this country.

Other distinctively American reactions to the yellow fever crises may suggest themselves upon further study. The United States was visited by yellow fever more frequently than was Europe, but it is doubtful if mere repetition modified the response in any essential manner. On the whole, the reaction to this disease reflected man's struggle against nature, and nature itself laid down many of the rules.

IV. *South Carolina vs. the United States*

Since the practical issues that lay behind South Carolina's attempted nullification in 1832 have long been decided, one is tempted to dismiss it as an exciting episode in American history, important chiefly as a prelude to more momentous events. No state would now attempt to nullify a federal law or deny the sovereignty of the federal courts. But as Professor Louis Hartz here demonstrates, the moral and philosophical considerations that almost precipitated a rebellion and made the Civil War inevitable have their counterparts today. We are still preoccupied with the dialectic of minority vs. majority rights, and we have seen in our own time how the ostensible points of difference between nations are often mere camouflages for completely antithetical notions of what constitutes the good society.

IV

South Carolina vs. the United States

Louis Hartz

*Associate Professor of Government,
Harvard University*

In the summer of 1832 a bitterly contested election was held in South Carolina. Voters were bribed and kidnapped, street violence was on the verge of breaking out, and both sides were secretly collecting arms in the event of civil war. The issue was whether the "sovereign" state of South Carolina should take it upon itself to nullify the tariff legislation of the federal government. Few South Carolinians supported the tariff, but the state had had a vigorous tradition of nationalism, and there were many who looked with horror on the "revolutionary" policy of nullification. The election went against them. Spurred on by the legal logic of Calhoun and the wild oratory of McDuffie, a strange but effective pair of influences, the Nullifiers swept the state and achieved an objective they had failed to achieve two years before: a legislative majority sufficiently large to call a constituent convention. After that there was no stopping the headlong rush toward nullification. Governor Hamilton called a special session of the legislature, the legislature immediately called a convention, and by November South Carolina's famous Ordinance of Nullification had been issued. The Tariff Acts of 1828 and 1832 were "null, void, and no law."

The Nullifiers, however, had rushed into a situation they did not quite foresee. If you had asked them before nullification what was going to happen afterward, you would not have received a very clear answer, except possibly from Calhoun. The reason was that they were relying on such overwhelming support from other Southern states and even from President Jackson himself that they did not believe that their action would seriously be challenged by the federal government. As it turned out, however, this was precisely the support they did not get. Every Southern state condemned the Ordinance of Nullification. Jackson denounced it as "treason." A force bill was introduced in Congress to put its provisions down. Wherever they turned the Nullifiers faced the bitter pill that passionate men again and again have to swallow in politics: the realization that even their friends are not as passionate as they. Instead of putting South Carolina at the head of a glorious movement against "consolidation," they had isolated it from the Union, and left it facing alone the imminent threat of civil war.

It has been said of a certain French politician of the nineteenth century that he followed the formula of Danton except for one variation: he believed in audacity, audacity, and then *no* more audacity. One might say the same thing, if it were not a bit too cruel, about the South Carolina Nullifiers. Of course, when they saw the drift of events, they began to drill a volunteer army, and to set up arsenals throughout the state, but in the process they silently searched their souls. Eleven days before the Ordinance of Nullification was supposed to go into effect, on the very day that the Force Bill was reported in the Senate, that search came to a spectacular end. A large meeting of Nullifiers gathered at the Circus in Charleston and, saying that reform of the tariff was imminent, they virtually suspended the Nullification Ordinance. Nothing could hide the panic that went into this assembly. It was composed of private citizens, not of legislators or members of a constituent convention. The setting aside of the action of a sovereign state by such a body must surely be ranked as one of the hastiest forms of "nullification" that has ever been devised.

But the Nullifiers were right in one thing: action was being taken to reform the tariff. Jackson and Clay, while determined that the Force Bill should make no concession to nullification, were ready to compromise on the tariff itself. Clay introduced a measure, later replaced by one originating in the House, that modified the Act of 1832. Both this bill and the Force Bill were signed by Jackson on the same day, with the result that, as William Graham Sumner once put it, "the olive branch and the rod were bound up together." The Nullifiers hailed the reduction in the tariff as a victory they had won, and though the episode ended in a complete defeat for the legal principles they put forth, they had a chance of saving face. Jonathan Trumbull said: "We have driven the enemy from his moorings, and compelled him to slip his cables and put to sea." [1] The nullification crisis, on the surface at least, had ended in a draw.

II

This essay will concern itself with the theory of nullification, and after the events just described, the point I intend to make about it is bound to seem perverse. I intend to agree with Calhoun that the theory was a "conservative" theory. It is a tribute to Calhoun's gloomy genius as a political prophet that it is possible to stress his view again today. For it is, of course, in light of the Civil War that came after Calhoun died that the nullification idea takes on conservative significance. In the perspective of the Civil War the Harpers and McDuffies of 1832 cease to be "revolutionaries," cease to be "jacobins." They become men of peace, trying to solve by legal means the only problem in American history that has shattered completely the framework of our legal institutions.

In that perspective, too, our traditional approach to the theory of nullification has to be turned around a bit. What becomes even more important than the way the Nullifiers tried to limit the national government is the way they tried to limit themselves. It is easy to overlook this second matter. The Nullifiers could have chosen the path of secession, and indeed some of their opponents in South Carolina, like William Drayton and Langdon Chaves, would have gone along with them if they had. They could have appealed to a Jeffersonian right of revolution, as the violent McDuffie came close to doing on many occasions. But they did not want to secede and they did not want to revolt. The whole purpose of their philosophy was to construct a legal framework within which the battle between North and South could be contained, a peaceful "preservative," as Calhoun put it, of the

[1] Quoted in Frederic Bancroft: *Calhoun and the South Carolina Nullification Movement* (Johns Hopkins Press; 1928), p. 167.

American federal system. If their action symbolizes a trigger-happy impulse on the part of Americans to resist oppression, it symbolizes also something else that has been its curious counterpart: perhaps the most sensitive legal conscience in the world.

Here indeed, was the root of their philosophic troubles. They would not have had to agonize themselves to justify secession or revolution. The premise of state "sovereignty" from which they began led directly to the most radical conclusions. What actually bothered them was how to bring a state conceived as supreme and uncontrollable into any sort of binding relationship with other states that, of course, were as supreme and uncontrollable as it was. It was this question that inspired the elaborate apologetics in which they engaged, the labyrinthine subtleties that few men outside of Calhoun and Chancellor Harper, even in South Carolina, were able to follow. If South Carolina was sovereign, why bother with the tariff at all? Why trouble yourself over 'the opinion of other states? The Nullifiers were astride the wild horse of Bodin and Hobbes, and it was not their radicalism that was illogical but their conservatism.

The North, however, was not quite in a position to make the most of this embarrassment. The Nullifiers argued that in 1787 South Carolina had entered into a "compact" with other "sovereign" American states for the purpose of creating a federal government that was the "joint agent" of them all. Now the real problem in this argument is that when you impose a binding compact on sovereign states you have bound them *too much:* technically they cannot be bound at all. But what troubled Daniel Webster was that South Carolina had not been bound *enough,* and so instead of pointing out that the conclusions of the Nullifiers did not match their premises, he assailed both as empirically false. This reduced the argument to a historical plane where, because the evidence was sufficiently vague, an endless stream of charge and countercharge became the order of the day. Webster denied that the Constitution was a " compact"; they asserted it. He asserted that a compact could create a vital American nation; they denied it. He insisted that the nation had acted in 1787; they insisted that the states had acted. The central logical flaw of nullification, its attempt to limit at all an illimitable sovereign, was removed from the spotlight of controversy.

Calhoun saved his logic, but in the process he virtually lost his constitutional "preservative." It has been said of Calhoun that he is the most rigorous thinker in American political thought; but his rigor, I suggest, was the rigor of John Stuart Mill: he tried to unite antitheses as logically as any man could. In a letter to Governor Hamilton, in which he insisted on the "total dissimilarity" between secession and nullification, he outlined the course a sovereign state should take after it had nullified an act of the "joint agent." Solemnly obeying legal process, it would wait for the issue to be submitted to the other sovereign states, but three quarters of them would be required for a decision against it, since that is the number needed for amending the Constitution. It is shocking to think what would happen to the federal government under such a procedure, but it is puzzling to see why a sovereign state should bother to embark upon it. What if three quarters of the states actually do go against it? Is it any less sovereign then? Calhoun is too honest to evade this question. And so he tells Governor Hamilton, quite by the way: "Nullification may, indeed, be succeeded by secession." [2] In other words, two things that are "totally dissimilar" on one page blend into another on the next as if nothing at all has happened.

The truth is, nothing has happened. The state was sovereign to begin with and it was sovereign to end with. What is curious is the elaborate ritual of legalism that has intervened in the middle. But there is no use laboring this point further. It would be possible to follow the struggle with "sovereignty" out at length in the nullification literature, and to show how it finally mastered its verbal limitations in the claim for independence that came with the Civil War. But the Civil War was not brought about because the sixteenth century had fashioned a concept that the American Southerners insisted on using in the nineteenth. If we want to get at some of the deeper causes of the breakdown of Calhoun's constitutional conservatism, it would be well to turn to the social alignments of the age, and to Calhoun's attempt to deal with them.

[2] Calhoun: *Works* (Cralle, ed.), Vol. VI (D. Appleton & Co.; 1883), p. 169. *Cf.* A. C. McLaughlin: *A Constitutional History of the United States* (D. Appleton-Century Co.; 1936), p. 444.

III

It is a commonplace of American history that the theory of states' rights has followed the course of economic interest. What makes the process bizarre is that at the same time the theory has been developed with infinite logical labor, so that one gets the odd impression that Hegel is proving himself on the American scene while Marx is doing so too. If the pure metaphysical passion is to be found in American political thought at all, where would we place it if not in the men who have struggled so heroically with the categories of state and nation? And yet everyone knows that Jefferson tended to forget his metaphysics at the time of the Louisiana Purchase and that the New England Federalists tended to discover theirs at the time of the Embargo. The same principle holds true of the South Carolina Nullifiers. Before Calhoun became concerned over the tariff and slavery, he had denounced the notion of strict constitutional construction, and McDuffie, who joined the nullification movement late, had said things that were even worse. He had said that politicians who exalted the states were inferior men who did so because they could not win a place on the national scene.

The fact that the Nullifiers misunderstood their economic ills does not alter the fact that we are dealing here with a genuine problem in the politics of economic interest. Basically the troubles of South Carolina did not come from the tariff: they came from concentration on the production of cotton at a time when the settlement of new lands in the Southwest was forcing the price of that commodity down. But whatever might be said about cotton, or the slave economy on which it rested, South Carolina was pretty well destined to be an agricultural state, and above all it would be absurd to insist on a classical pattern of perfect rationality in the behavior of economic interests. If such a pattern were the normal thing, the record of American history would read a good deal differently from the way it does. It would read a good deal differently on the score of the tariff itself, and not because of the kind of enlightenment South Carolina needed. It is reasonable to suspect that more economic mistakes have been made in the process of supporting the American tariff than have been made in the process of opposing it.

Calhoun's defense of the South as an economic interest represents the same failure of conservatism that we find in his defense of the South as a collection of states. In terms of theory, to be sure, this is not entirely true. When in his political speeches and in the *Disquisition on Government* Calhoun substitutes "minorities" and "interests" for "states" and gives them the power of nullifying national policy, he releases himself from the wild theoretical horse he' is trying to ride on the legal plane. Minorities and interests can hardly be called "sovereign," and Calhoun does not call them that. But all that Calhoun really accomplishes by this is to remove his problem from the realm of logic and put it in the realm of social fact. In social fact the Southern minority that Calhoun starts with has been torn away from the rest of the American nation as effectively as the concept of sovereignty would ever tear it away. It is a grim and isolated group, engaged in a war it cannot win, whose secession he actually predicted before he died. Under such circumstances preserving the Union by the simple technique of the "concurrent majority," if not legally illogical, is at any rate practically impossible.

Calhoun's method was to shatter the fabric of American community and then to attempt to restore it by a purely mechanical device. But this was to overlook a very important truth: mechanical devices are only as strong as the sense of community that underlies them. And yet his error was not unprecedented in American thought. The Founding Fathers had made it too. In the minds of many of them, Adams and Hamilton and Morris for example, the American scheme of checks and balances was designed to control a destructive war between proletarians on the one hand and aristocrats on the other. This war, which in the case of Adams was deduced largely from the irrelevant experience of ancient Greece and the Renaissance city-states, would surely have shattered the American Constitution as quickly as the struggles of France after the Restoration shattered the Charter of 1814. Happily such war has not been a general characteristic of American life, which has been permeated by a sense of social agreement that has been the wonder of foreign critics since the time of Tocqueville, and so the wrongness of the premises of the Founding Fathers has been obscured by what seems to be the "rightness" of their conclusions. But the case of Calhoun, alas, was somewhat different. The desperate struggle that he was describing was actu-

ally becoming a fact. He was making the mistake of the Founding Fathers at the only time in our history when it could readily
be exposed. Of course, the "concurrent majority" was not
adopted, and neither was his scheme of a dual executive, which
embodied it. But if it had been, is it fair to assume that the North
would have found it tolerable?

Notice, however, that Calhoun does not merely accept the
scheme of Adams: the "concurrent majority" goes beyond it and
supplements political checks with economic-interest checks. A
threefold division of the functions of government on the national
plane is not enough, because a single party can gain control of
them simultaneously. Calhoun, in other words, is busily piling up
checks in face of the very situation that is going to explode them
all. This seems strange but, given the premises of the eighteenth
century, is it? Once you concede that mechanical devices can
serve as a substitute for the spirit of community which permits
them to function, are you not automatically embarked on such a
course? There is logic here, even if of a rather inverted kind:
the more conflict you have, the more checks you need, and the
more certain it is that no checks will work. Calhoun, like some
tragic hero, was fated to bring the tradition of Adams to a climax
in American thought at the moment it collapsed completely.

This is just another version of the paradox that Mr. Peter
Drucker should recently rediscover Calhoun as the chief philosopher of our free and easy system of pressure politics—Calhoun
who wrote on the eve of the Civil War. It is possible, I think, to
carry Mr. Drucker's point too far. Weak as party discipline is in
America, single interests do not have a veto on public policy, as
real estate knows in connection with rent control and labor in
connection with the Taft-Hartley Act. But the relevance of the
"concurrent majority" principle to the pulling and hauling of interests on the American political scene is striking enough, and it
reveals again the strange tragedy of Calhoun's nullification conservatism. The system of American logrolling is a system of
"checks and balances" that bears a curious resemblance to the one
our Founding Fathers had in mind, but instead of being imposed
on the fabric of the American community, it has largely risen out
of it. It has had many causes, one of which is the constitutional
scheme itself, but no one can doubt that the social unity of American life has been among the most important. Societies frozen by

deep and permanent conflict have never inspired the easy barter of individual interests.

But what Calhoun was doing, if he is to be considered a philosopher of our interest-group system, was offering it as a substitute for the social unity on which it rests. Of course, if we were to agree with what he often implies, that the struggle between the North and South were simply the result of using the device of the "numerical majority," there would be nothing fantastic about this procedure. Legislating the logrolling technique into existence would be a perfectly reasonable act. But the sectional struggle obviously came from deeper sources, as he himself practically admits when he declares the South to be a permanent and hopeless minority. Minorities cannot be permanent unless there is some profound division of interest to make them so. And under such circumstances not even legislation can produce the spirit of pressure-group adjustment. For that spirit is ordinarily possible precisely because the nation is not split into warring social camps, because majorities and minorities are *fluid* and the groups that make them up know that they can easily exchange places on another issue or at another time. Calhoun said that the "concurrent majority" produced the spirit of compromise. What was actually the case, however, was that the spirit of compromise produced the "concurrent majority."

Nothing shows up the anguish of the man more clearly than this perpetual putting of the cart before the horse. Looked at from one angle, his mood is the authentic mood of irrational desperation: not merely because he clings to the form of compromise while its substance is disappearing, but because he has convinced himself that an exaggeration of its form will somehow compensate for a loss of its substance. Mr. Drucker's point, as I have said, ought not to be taken too literally: we have never had the "concurrent majority" in American politics. The spirit of compromise Calhoun calls for outdoes in amiability even the spirit that pervades a Congressional cloakroom in a time of high profits and high wages. As he himself puts it, each interest will "promote its own prosperity by conciliating the good will, and promoting the prosperity of others." There will be a "rivalry to promote the interests of each other." There will be "patriotism, nationality, harmony, and a struggle only for supremacy in promoting the common good of the whole." All of this when the country is on the brink of civil war, and simply by extending a notch the logic of John Adams! One is tempted to wonder whether the keenest pathos of the compromise spirit before the Civil War lies in the speeches of Henry Clay, or whether it lies right here, in Calhoun, dreaming up out of the South's own bitterness a mirage of social peace the like of which even a peaceful nation has never experienced.

At the time in which Calhoun was writing, however, neither South Carolina nor the South as a whole was quite in the position he made it out to be. There is one problem that Calhoun and other Nullifiers were careful to avoid: the problem of the minority within the minority—the problem, in other words, of the Unionists in South Carolina. It is not strange, given the treatment the Unionists received, that they should blast the Ordinance of Nullification with the very language the Nullifiers used to defend it, that they should call it "the mad edict of a despotic majority." How were the Calhounians to meet this charge? It would have been suicidal for the Nullifiers to give their opponents a veto, but let us suppose, out of passion for logic, that they did. There was also a minority within the Unionist minority, and a minority within that. Were these minorities to be given a veto too? The point I am making is the fairly obvious one that if the minority principle is carried to its logical conclusion it unravels itself out into Locke's state of nature where separate individuals execute the law of nature for themselves. Locke's acceptance of majority rule was by no means ill considered.

But this is merely a logical victory over Calhoun, and it is likely to lead us away from rather than closer to the central problem to be faced. In politics most principles break down when carried to their "logical conclusion," and if a man is brave enough to match his mind against reality, provided he does not use concepts like "sovereignty," which make it impossible, he ought to be given the privilege of silently drawing a few lines. The real significance of the Unionist minority lies in another place. It lies not in the fact that it was a minority but in the fact that it was *Unionist*. And the reason why this is important is that it reveals an important mechanism by which groups are held together in a political community: the mechanism of crisscrossing allegiances. Had the South Carolinians been one hundred per cent in favor of Nullification, or had the Unionist minority simply been indifferent to the question, they would hardly have given up so quickly their challenge to the federal government. But Jackson was in direct negotiation with the Unionist minority—he had promised them all the aid they needed—and this was a very sobering piece of knowledge for the Nullifiers to have. In other words, the fact that South Carolina was not a monolithic entity, as the Calhounian terms of "state" or "interest" or "minority" might imply, had a lot to do with uniting it to the rest of the nation.

If Calhoun's concern with a national "preservative" had transcended everything else, he would have welcomed this empirical defect in his premises. And as a matter of fact, there is a certain amount of evidence, on the wider plane of the struggle between North and South, to suggest that he actually did. With a number of other Southerners, as the Civil War approached, he suggested an alliance between Northern capitalists and Southern planters to keep both the slaves and the free working-class down. This alliance presumably would have helped to save the Union by exploiting common tensions within the sectional interests he usually described in monolithic terms. But Calhoun was in general no philosopher of intrasectional conflict, for the obvious reason that he was too embittered a Southerner. Instead of welcoming this imperfection in his premises, he glossed it over. Which, of course, made it harder than ever for him to reach his conservative conclusions.

History, as usual, was on the side of his premises. The drift toward civil war was a drift toward the consolidation of North and South into increasingly monolithic interests. Intersectional allegiances, one by one, began to disappear. America approached what is probably the most dangerous moment in the political life of any community: the moment of the almost perfect *rationalization* of its internal conflict. This made Calhoun's simplistic antithesis of majority and minority a real one, but what it did for the mechanical approach to politics is a matter of the obvious record. Once again, as in the case of his states'-rights legalism, Calhoun had laid a foundation that exploded the structure he tried to build upon it.

IV

I have discussed nullification as a legal issue and as an issue of social interest. There was also a moral question in the crisis of 1832, the question of slavery, which already, at the hands of Harper and Senator Smith, had begun to produce that massive defense of a stratified society which flowered in the South before the Civil War. As this argument evolved, fed by the attack of Northern abolitionism, it did as much as anything else to produce the sectional intransigence that shattered Calhoun's nullification conservatism, but it challenged nullification in another way as well: philosophically. For the doctrine of nullification was, as I I have shown, an exaggerated version of the mechanical rationalism of the eighteenth century, while the theory of slavery was a romantic revolt against it. Even if they had not had Burke, Disraeli, and Carlyle to read, the logic of their attack on Jefferson would have impelled the Southerners to discover that the Social Contract was a myth, that governments were divinely inspired, and that coercion was a law of life. But if this was so, how could the Constitution be a "compact," and why should minorities be so diligently defended? The philosophy of slavery struck hammer-blows at the finespun rationalism of nullification, and because Calhoun contributed to it he found himself caught in the most painful contradiction of his strange career, more painful even than the conflict between "sovereignty" and "preservative" or, on the plane of practice, between the war of the sections and the "concurrent majority."

Interestingly enough, it is this devotion of Calhoun to the theory of slavery that has given him his familiar reputation as a "conservative." In terms of what I have been saying, it is precisely this devotion that is "radical," that challenges his clinging to the Union. One is tempted now to give up Calhoun's own Nullification Act terminology. For while a case can be made for abolishing the term "conservative" from the study of American thought as a whole, it is precisely in connection with the theory of slavery that it has its most legitimate use. That theory, with its predominantly feudal image, comes as close to the authentic mood of the Western reaction as anything America has ever turned up. But though it does not pay to quibble over terms, provided the substance of an issue is clear, a word can still be said for Calhoun's claim that the rationalist theory of nullification was "conservative," and not merely in the obvious political sense that it sought to preserve the Union, but in the philosophic sense as well. For the "reaction" that the defense of slavery inspired in Southern thought was strangely enough an Enlightenment, since the philosophy of Jefferson was the vested theoretical interest that men like Bledsoe and Harper were forced to assail. This miraculous inversion of the European pattern, which gave to the Southern disciples of Burke the spirit of iconoclastic discovery we might expect to find in Diderot, confounds the issue of terminology so badly that we can even call rationalism reactionary. We can say, at any rate, that it was an older thing than the "feudal conservatism" it confronted.

Mixing nullification with "feudal conservatism" was like mixing water with oil. Things could not have been worse. What is inevitably the *bête noire* of any reactionary attack is precisely what the Nullifiers had to advance: the idea of the manmade constitution. Fitzhugh branded it as "absurd." Calhoun, courageous to the end, drew a distinction between "constitution" and "government," as if by keeping Sieyes and Maistre in watertight compartments he might be able to enjoy them both. Governments were natural and divinely inspired, but constitutions, which controlled them, were not. It was a tenuous enough distinction. Can it reasonably be argued that what governs government is any less governmental than government itself?

The clash between the Enlightenment and the reaction became even more vivid when the question of "rights" came up. There is a happily unconscious paradox in a lot of Southern oratory: slavery is excellent, but Southerners will die rather than be "slaves" of the North. Of course, as long as the defense of slavery grounds itself in racial theory concerning the Negro, this is a paradox easily resolved. But Southern thought, as in the case of men like Hughes, Holmes, and Fitzhugh, refused to stop at the color line, insisting that slavery or something like it was the ideal system of life for whites as well as blacks. Even here, to be sure, the "slavery" of the South is not automatically justified, since slaves ought to be inferior men and Southern gentlemen are certainly not in that class. But once again the bottom falls out of the Southern position. The definition of justifiable slavery is the mysterious status quo ordained by a mysterious Providence, and only wild Jeffersonian "metaphysicians" would dare to overturn it. If this is true, the enslavement of the South by the tariff would seem to be just as valid as the enslavement of the slave by the lash. The Hegelian type of conservatism, which young Thomas Dew brought back to Virginia from Germany, has burnt many fingers in the history of social thought.

One of the reasons the Southerners would not stop their defense of slavery at the racial line was that they wanted to belabor the "wage-slavery" of the North and to insist that their own system of labor, suitably defined by Henry Hughes and others as a kind of feudal "warranteeism," was actually superior to it. There was a movement of thought, partially inspired by the Young England philosophy of Disraeli, in which iron laws of capitalist oppression and proletarian revolt were contrasted with sentimental laws of paternal care and social peace. Calhoun himself contributed something to this movement, which gave him a curious resemblance to the European "feudal socialists" whom Marx so bitterly derided. But the main point for us to grasp is the striking way in which this philosophy clashed with the rational mechanics of nullification. If the corporate ideal of the plantation is to be maintained, how can one also maintain a theory of minority rights which logically unravels itself out into Locke's state of nature? An anonymous critic of the "concurrent majority" in *DeBow's Review* assailed Calhoun for deserting the great slave truth that the best type of rule was the "natural" rule of the "despot." [3] He was, alas, on solid ground.

These contradictions were bad enough, but what was even worse, from the angle of Calhoun's nullification conservatism, was that the romantic theory of slavery itself threatened to resolve them. Men who have read Burke and Scott do not need to rely on constitutional apologetics in order to defend their sectional life. They are led automatically to another type of claim: the blood-and-soil claim of any ancient culture. This claim solved Calhoun's problem at a single stroke. It absorbed into the organicism of his defense of slavery the very sectional plea that had impelled him to repudiate it. It made Burke do the job of Adams as well. And as time passed, and the cult of "Southernism" defined itself in contrast to the commercialism of Yankeedom, it grew

[3] Vol. 23 (1857), p. 170.

enormously in the Southern mind. Mr. Rollin Osterweiss has documented it brilliantly in a recent study.[4] But the question is, what did it do to Calhoun's "preservative" of the nation? Didn't it pack even more explosive power than the concept of "sovereignty" itself?

It is strange that this idea should begin to evolve in the South and not the North, for it was of course the basic idea of modern nationalism—in its liberal form, the passionate thesis of Rousseau and Mazzini. Webster could surely have used it. A charge of Burkian or Rousseauian romanticism would have lifted his concept of the American "people" to a high ground where the constitutional exegesis of the Nullifiers could not have undermined it. But Webster, the great philosopher of American "nationalism," remains as dry and legalistic as Marshall. The ironic fact was that the liberal romanticism of the North did not lead to the nationalism of Rousseau as the conservative romanticism of the South led to the nationalism of Burke or Scott. With the exception of a few men like Barlow and perhaps Emerson, it led in other directions: radical individualism, as in Thoreau, or radical cosmopolitanism, as in Garrison. The South, the home of "particularism," became in a curious sense the originator of romatic nationalism in American political theory.

It is not hard to see that the idea of blood-and-soil nationalism was more explosive than either the idea of "sovereignty" or the idea of "minority." Sovereignty was an uncontrollable concept, but it was at any rate a concept, a rational abstraction, something you could argue about. So was "minority." But there was really no arguing with the spirit of Southern culture, for by definition its ethos was irrational and its claim divine. As the romantic philosophy of slavery swept forward it not only corroded the mechanical premises of nullification but it advanced in their place a sectional plea colored with the most frightening overtones. Fitzhugh, with his "organic nationality," with his bitter attack on the "Calhoun school," was the great philosopher of this movement. He is the man, I suggest, who ought to have the reputation for theoretical consistency which Calhoun has attained. Flamboyant, reckless, a Maistre without reading Maistre, he nevertheless sought in almost everything he wrote to unify the Southern

    [4] *Romanticism and Nationalism in the Old South* (Yale University Press; 1949).

mind around the authentic principles of the Western reaction. He had Maistre's love of violence, which came to him from his attack on the humanitarians, and he did not hesitate to fuse it with "organic nationality." When war came, he hailed it as a veritable boon to the Southern soul.

This was the end of Calhoun's constitutional conservatism, this swallowing up of the Southern argument into the romantic logic of reactionary thought. Of course, the South was never as logical as Fitzhugh wanted it to be. It continued to divide its time between the world of Burke and the world of Jefferson, as indeed it still does. Even in 1861, after all of Fitzhugh's lessons, it appealed to a Jeffersonian right of revolution. But there is no doubt that the rise of the naturalistic authoritarianism that Fitzhugh represented did as much as anything else in the South to discredit the reasoning of Calhoun. And the irony of it, as usual, was that Calhoun himself had helped its rise along.

V

Many of the crises discussed in this book could easily happen again. We could have another great religious awakening, or another debtor revolt, or another imperial adventure. But it seems extremely unlikely that in the twentieth century the delegates of any "sovereign" state in the Union will ever gather, as the South Carolina delegates gathered in the fall of 1832, to hold an act of Congress "null, void, and no law." In the perspective of a hundred years of steady centralization the nullification movement has about it a quality as antique as the florid language and the swallowtail coats of the Southern orators who defended it. But if what I have said here is at all correct, the antiquity of its significance is superficial enough. Beneath its concern with the sovereign rights of South Carolina and the South lies an issue that is not only permanent but is perhaps the deepest issue that any society, internally or externally, has to face: the issue of law and force, of war and compromise.

Calhoun's approach to this issue was a failure because he started with the premises of force and after that tried to arrive at the conclusions of law. He started with the uncontrollable concept of sovereignty, and then he tried to control it. He started with a condition of the deepest conflict, and then he tried to resolve it with mechanical devices it was bound to destroy. He started with the romantic notion of the divinity and inscrutability of power, and then he tried to erect upon it the rationalism by which it might be limited. He was forever slamming the door in his own face, shutting out the very "preservative" he wanted to create. But how, in the last analysis, are we to judge his effort? We can say the obvious thing: he should have modified his premises, should have laid the basis for law before he attempted to attain it. But Calhoun was a crusader as well as a conservative, which is not necessarily bad. What is a man to do when his honest sense of oppression matches perfectly his love of peace? Here we have one of the mysterious and tragic dilemmas of political life, and because we in our own time have experienced it, we have no right to smile at the agony it caused Calhoun. I do not know what the solution to it is. Perhaps it is right that men should prepare to fight when they find their freedoms at stake, and right also that they should cherish the dream of peace that their preparation destroys.

V. *Horace Mann's Crusade*

"Knowledge is power" was an expression frequently on the lips of Fourth of July orators in the 1840's, but the popular faith in education as an indispensable training for a democratic society did not necessarily imply an unqualified support for a free public-school system. In Massachusetts, as Professor Howard Mumford Jones illustrates in his essay, a "portentous social cleavage" divided the children of the rich and poor, and the stubborn opposition to the common school from special interest groups indicated that many who approved of education in theory were not prepared for the drastic reforms of Horace Mann. By skillful appeals to the interests and prejudices of all groups in the community, Mann carried out his program and perhaps more than any other public figure was responsible for the national acceptance of the free-school principle. His great series of educational reports are a part of the history of the public-school movement, but they also have a direct bearing on the touchy questions that continue to plague us.

V

Horace Mann's Crusade

Howard Mumford Jones
Professor of English, Harvard University

Perhaps the most difficult imaginative feat we can perform is to try to envision what history would have been, had it been different from what it was. Suppose Wellington had not stuck it out when he murmured: "Blücher or night"—! Suppose Washington's gamble in crossing the Delaware had failed and Trenton had proved a disaster—! Suppose F.D.R. had not been elected for a third term—! An analogous effort of the imagination is necessary if we are to understand Horace Mann. Suppose there were no American public schools, or at least no public schools as we understand them today!

The public school is so much a part of the American order that it is almost impossible to think it away. When you go on an extended automobile trip in this republic, you see without surprise on the outskirts of a town or in its center a modern high-school building, of which the citizens are understandably proud because they paid for it. When you leave city A and drive towards city B, you take for granted another modern school-building, this time in the country—the new consolidated school, to which the children of farmers are brought by bus at public expense. We take it as a matter of course in many states that it is possible to proceed from the kindergarten to a Ph.D. without stepping outside an institution supported by tax money. Our system, if it be a system, is the admiration of other countries and has profoundly influenced the educational systems, if they are systems, of nations as different as China, Russia, Germany, and Japan.

On closer view, however, we find imperfections. In great cities I shall not name, the school board, spending as it does millions of dollars of public money, is an irresistible attraction to the politician. In commonwealths I shall not enumerate, there is tension between the public schools and systems of private schools supported by this or that church. In still other states, there is a painful disharmony between the quality of schools maintained for white children and the quality of schools maintained for children not so white—a disharmony so great that the courts have had to intervene to compel equality of opportunity. One state—New York —annually spends $256.90 on the education of each child in the public schools; another state—Mississippi, for years at the bottom of the list—spends only $71.42. The Americans believe in education, but they do not believe in it sufficiently to pay salaries that will attract first-rate young people into the profession, or keep them in it once they are accredited. There is alarm about the shortage of teachers. Moreover, the institutions, usually public institutions, in which teachers are trained do not awaken universal enthusiasm. A total expenditure for public-school purposes of over three billion one hundred million dollars in 1947 looks impressive until you put it beside expenditures of more than six billion for the army and air force and five and one-half billion for the navy in 1947—over eleven billion in all. An enrollment of over twenty million in the public schools of 1947 looks like success until you discover that out of 106 million Americans fourteen years of age or more in 1947, about three million could neither read nor write English or any other language, and that out of eighty-two and one-half million Americans who were twenty-five years old or more in April 1947, twenty-five million, or thirty per cent of them, never got beyond the eighth grade. Maintaining the public-school system has been a battle and a march, and anything that shows what previous battles have been is relevant to modern life.

I have spoken of the American public-school system as if it were a single system. That it is not, and what principally puzzles the foreigner come to inspect it is its curious contradictions. There is no national system, though surprising uniformity is created by public opinion and by imitation.

In virtually every other country in the world the national government includes a minister of education. But the American Constitution never mentions the word "education," and no minister of culture or education sits in the Presidential Cabinet. Almost the sole federal agency directly concerned with pedagogy is the Office of Education, which was not created until 1867 and which has floated about Washington ever since, being sometimes an independent office and sometimes an attachment to this or that bureau or department. Latterly it has come to rest in the Federal Security Agency. There is a quality of drift in the life of this bureau, and its duties are also vague. It had originally no powers except to collect and disseminate information, and in more than fourscore years those powers have not been much increased. The only direct responsibility of the federal government for schools is the District of Columbia, though in a sense it has some responsibility for schools in the territories, and for educational provisions written into state constitutions when new commonwealths are admitted into the union. Otherwise its influence is indirect, as when it appropriates money to send veterans to school or matches federal and state dollars to encourage domestic science. Of course there is perennial debate over direct federal support of the public schools.

When the foreigner compares this queer situation with the clear responsibility of a minister of education in Europe for the national pedagogy, he may wonder how the Americans manage. They manage, of course, by throwing responsibility elsewhere; and we have, counting the District of Columbia, not one but forty-nine systems of public education in the country. But though the responsibility is commonly placed upon the legislature by the state constitution to support and encourage education, and although every state has a state superintendent or commissioner of education, American practice is again unique. In Bavaria, which is to Germany what an American state is here, the minister of education has centralized responsibility. He appoints the teachers, he directs the expenditure of public money, he approves what is taught, he has final authority. But his American counterpart has no such importance and no such powers. The state superintendent with us may partially enforce laws passed by the legislature, he and his board may have some control over the licensing of teachers and some control over curricula and textbooks, and he may be the agent for dispersing the state school-fund. But he seldom controls the institutions in which teachers are trained, he cannot commonly force a local school-board to hire this teacher and fire that one, and he cannot in most cases—at least, he commonly does not—suspend a teacher. His relations to the country schools are one thing, his relations to city school-boards are another. He cannot even compel parents to send their offspring to the schools of which he is the theoretical head, since, if parents desire to send their children to private schools or to educate them at home, the law has been fulfilled.

All this may or may not be familiar, and all this may seem to be a long way round to the solemn, crotchety radical, Horace Mann. What I am saying is that the American public schools are primarily matters of local concern rather than of national uniformity. They have developed in, and their life has come from, the locality, not from the state capitol or from Washington. By and large, the local public school mirrors the local community. What is taught is what the community allows to be taught, and what is paid for, despite state school-funds and other aids, is usually measured by what the community is willing to pay. If this seems commonplace, it is a commonplace that is readily forgotten. It is part of the insight of Horace Mann to have seen the significance of this commonplace. The locality had been dragging the schools downhill in Massachusetts for half a century, and he set himself the task of reversing the tide of local opinion. Unless we understand that it is precisely because he worked in a limited field—Massachusetts is forty-fourth in area among the states today and was no larger in 1837—unless, I say, we understand that precisely because his work was limited it was successful, we cannot comprehend his problem. Until the people of a community could be persuaded that a state school-system was necessary and good, the people of no community, be it state or national, could be so persuaded. The unique achievement of Horace Mann was to realize that until the local battle could be won, the national battle could not be even fought.

When, on the last day of June 1837, Horace Mann was made secretary to the newly created Massachusetts state board of education, most American commonwealths had provided on paper for the state support of education. But the laws, whether constitutional or statutory, were oftener permissive than mandatory, and even when mandatory were not always enforced. There was no agreement as to what was meant by a public school, public tax-money sometimes going to private sectarian institutions. A state like Ohio, though it benefited from having been part of the Northwest Territory and though it became a state in 1803, did nothing to establish a public-school system until 1821, and even then it merely permitted, it did not require, the districts dividing a township to maintain schools. The constitution of Pennsylvania, adopted in 1790, declared that the legislature should, as soon as conveniently might be, provide by law for the establishment of schools throughout the state in such manner that the poor might be taught gratis, but not until 1834 did this commonwealth pass beyond the concept of the pauper school to something resembling the public school. In South Carolina, a state commonly paired by opposition with Massachusetts, a law passed in 1811 established public schools that any white child might attend, but in fact these schools were, like those in Pennsylvania, pauper schools, the act was ignored, a supplementary act of 1835 was equally ineffective, and it remained for the carpet-bag legislatures of 1868–70 to lay the foundation of the present system. By virtue of age and educational achievement, Massachusetts was looked upon as more advanced than other states, but in Massachusetts the church-state system of the seventeenth century had given way to the more secularized state of the eighteenth century, which in turn had been transformed into the more democratic commonwealth of the nineteenth century; and one aspect of this democratic devolution of power had been the creation of the school district as an autonomous educational unit. The school district created the district school, and the district school, as constituted in the thirties of the last century, was, according to the unanimous opinion of historians of education, the low-water mark of the American school system. Although the towns (townships) theoretically determined the school tax, and although no school-teacher could be legally hired until a committee representing the town approved him, in fact the districts did as they pleased. As late as 1844 some districts spent less than ten dollars a year to provide schooling for a child. The plot of ground on which the primitive district-school building was erected was commonly chosen because the land was valueless, the teacher was "boarded round," and since the cheaper the teacher, the longer the school term, there was a tendency to hire more and more mediocre teachers, commonly persons without culture or education. When Mann took office the average wage of male schoolteachers was $15.44 a month, exclusive of board, and a female's $5.38, and he said there was a complete want of competent candidates for the job of teaching. A series of legislative enactments had ended the responsibility of the towns to maintain grammar schools (that is, schools whose original character had been college preparatory) except in seven instances, so that an important educational tradition had virtually disappeared from most of Massachusetts.

When the general schools were reduced to this level of ignorance, they could not be satisfactory for the children of the well-born and the cultivated. These were characteristically educated in academies, the earliest of which dated from 1761 and the existence of which had been recognized by a law of 1797 permitting the creation of new academies in areas having thirty or forty thousand persons not accommodated by any existing academy. State aid could be, and was, given in certain circumstances to such schools, some of them obviously sectarian, so that by 1840 one hundred and twelve acts of incorporation had opened academies in eighty-eight towns. The academies were in fact private preparatory schools, although as early as 1795 Sam Adams had prophesied that, since the academies were patronized by the wealthy, the common schools must become the sign of poverty. The more flourishing the academy, the worse the district school. A portentous social cleavage was developing in the commonwealth between the children of the rich and the children of the poor. Into this social crisis stepped Horace Mann, not the first, but the most notable, of a group of reformers who wished to reshape the commonwealth. The situation seems so obviously intolerable, we wonder anybody opposed him, and it is not until we study both the man and the elements of his problem that we see why the twelve years during which Mann held his post were years of conflict. Some of the actual disputes—for example, that between Mann and the Boston schoolmasters over the question of corporal punishment—were petty in themselves, and it is not until we look into the implications of these disputes that the real issues emerge.

At forty-one Horace Mann had become that most uncomfortable of human beings, a dedicated spirit. When he took on his new duties, he instantly rented his law office and sold his books because, as he said, he had been called "to a larger sphere of mind and morals." He never understood why everybody asked him what his new salary was: "No man," he confided to his diary in amazement, "seems to recognize its possible usefulness, or the dignity and elevation . . . inwrought into beneficent action"—no man, that is, except the radical Channing. His childhood was thoroughly unhappy—he seems never to have played, and at the age of ten he was only too vividly aware of the probability that his mother, his sister, his brother, and himself were damned to all eternity, a prospect over which, he says, he "wept and sobbed until Nature found . . . counterfeit repose in exhaustion." The most terrible experience of his life came when he was twelve years old: his brother, a charming boy, was drowned, and at the funeral service the minister devoted himself to the horrors of "dying unconverted," whereupon young Horace, in emotional revolt, defied the Omnipotent, yet was never sure that his break with Calvinism was not inspired by the devil. He says with regrettable pride: "I was never intoxicated in my life . . . I never swore; indeed, profanity was always most disgusting and repulsive to me. And [I consider it always a climax] I never used the 'vile weed' in any form."

His wife tells us that he was full of sparkling wit, and we must believe her, but his educational papers are totally without humor, and he seems to have been incapable of the drollery by which Lincoln relaxed the tensions of public debate. He suffered all his life from ill health, probably the sequel to the psychic trauma of his unnatural childhood. For that reason he always pushed himself too hard. He lost all sense of proportion and became portentous, hortatory, and orotund. A dreadful footnote in his *Ninth Annual Report* shows how little he knew about children. It runs:

During the last year, while I was passing by a school, the children came out to take their forenoon recess. They were boys, in appearance, but between eight and ten or eleven years of age. As they rushed into the street, one of the largest boys turned and cried out, "Now let's play robber!" Whereupon he drew a pine dagger from under his coat, seized one of his fellows, and exclaimed, "Your money, or your life!" This scene, thus enacted in sport, was doubtless drawn from some of the novels of the day, whose guilty authors receive the patronage, if not the homage of society;

while the comparatively innocent felon, who only steals a horse or burns a house, is sentenced to the penitentiary. Was that school doing its duty, or building up character after a Christian model?

This is appalling, but what else is to be expected from a man who had written, without a smile, six years earlier: "In the reports of some of the French hospitals for lunatics, the *reading of romances* is set down as one of the standing causes of insanity"? He wanted to throw Scott and Bulwer-Lytton into the fire. Pleasure frightened him; he did not understand it, just as he did not understand the psychology of art, for he was a fanatic, a crusader, a zealot for education, for temperance, for abolitionism, for phrenology, for Antioch College, for the innumerable reforms of the forties and fifties—a man who, seriously afraid that itinerant book-peddlers might corrupt country youth, found the central function of education to be that it cultivated the moral nature of the child. In his blindness towards child psychology Mann is unique among educational statesmen. But the blindness did not matter, because his audiences were adult audiences, themselves convinced that in life as in education the moral issue is the central one. All of Mann's appeal is implicit in two lines of Emerson's:

> *When duty whispers low, "Thou must!"*
> *The Youth replies, "I can."*

Mann's hearers might not understand transcendentalism, but they understood this simple emotional imperative. They were descended from men who had lived exemplary lives, and of whom Mann wrote: "What we call the enlightened nations of Christendom are approaching, by slow degrees, to the moral elevation which our ancestors reached at a single bound." Such complacency did not endear New England to the rest of the country, but it measured the identification of speaker and audience, it measured the appeal of Horace Mann to the inherited conscience of Massachusetts.

Mann's demand for rehabilitating the schools of the state touched on many issues, of course: on the hurt pride of working-men, who would not patronize pauper schools; on the pocketbook nerve of the wealthy, who could see no good reason for paying for the education of the poor; on the self-interest of the industrialists, who had to be persuaded that through public education Yankee ingenuity could be released and Yankee profits swell; on the defensive response of the cultured, timid before the lower orders whose education somehow threatened the supremacy of Protestant humanism in the Boston Latin School. The politics, the economics, the social history of Mann's educational crusade have been analyzed with subtlety and insight in special studies. But the strength of the man, and the greatness of his annual reports and of his *Common School Journal*, lay in an ethical appeal that could not be denied. Others—Barnard, Harris, Francis Parker, John Dewey—made public education a problem of statesmanship or of psychology or of philosophy, but with Mann it was first, last, and all the time a moral issue. That was his greatness. But it was precisely the basis and quality of his moral appeal that created the enormous difficulties he encountered. These difficulties arose out of the threefold relation of morality, religion, and the state.

In the purely theocratic state such difficulties are less likely to occur. When, as in seventeenth-century Massachusetts, church and state were two sides of the same shield, the school had theoretically the simple job of teaching an official program geared to an official creed. Again, in any system of schools completely under the control of a given church, difficulties will diminish, since whatever is taught must *a priori* be satisfactory to the church that establishes the teaching. Finally, in a purely secular state, if voters and administrators will but agree for school purposes never to allow sectarian motives to influence their judgment, when difficulties arise about teaching in the schools they can be settled by rational compromise. In matters of morality and religion this compromise commonly means arriving at some general principle satisfactory to everybody, or at least not violently unsatisfactory to the various creeds, this general principle then governing whatever ethical or religious training is offered in the school. (This last was Horace Mann's theory.) But I have sketched theoretical situations that seldom occur in pure form. In the theocratic state there is bound to be division of opinion between those who belong to the official church and those who do not. In the church-controlled school system there is bound to be tension between the clerical party and the laity. In the secular, or public-school system, local values condition teaching. I repeat that the American public school draws its life from the community. As Mann put it: "The people will sustain no better schools, and have no better education, than they personally see the need of."

Horace Mann was one of a group in New England that regarded itself as progressive and that its enemies regarded as radical. He had distinctive views about the morality of property. If a Protestant Christian republic was to be maintained, universal education must be paid for. But universal education meant taxation, and taxation is both a practical and a formal problem. Why is it, asked Mann in his *Tenth Annual Report* (1846), that wealthy Christians are reluctant to be taxed for the support of the common schools? Why this "dereliction from duty"? It is because of "the false notions which men entertain respecting the nature of their right to property." Property, he argued, is not an absolute right but a transient possession. Riches "were created for the race collectively . . . to be possessed and enjoyed in succession." Nature "ordains a perpetual entail and transfer, from one generation to another, of all property . . . and no man, nor any one generation of men, has any such title to or ownership in these ingredients and substantials of all wealth, that his right is invaded when a portion of them is taken for the benefit of posterity. . . . Is not the inference irresistible," he continues, "that no man, by whatever means he may have come into possession of his property, has any natural right, any more than he has a moral one, to hold it, or to dispose of it, irrespective of the needs and claims of those who, in the august procession of the generations, are to be his successors on the stage of existence?" Wealthy men must cease to argue that taxation for school purposes is confiscation. The common-school system is postulated upon these three propositions: first, "the successive generations of men, taken collectively, constitute one great commonwealth"; second, "the property of this commonwealth is pledged for the education of all its youth, up to such a point as will save them from poverty and vice, and prepare them for the adequate performance of their social and civil duties"; and third, "the successive holders of this property are trustees, bound to the faithful execution of their trust by the most sacred obligations; and embezzlement and pillage from children and descendants have not less of criminality, and have more of meanness, than the same offences when perpetrated against contemporaries."

Nobody likes to be accused of embezzling and pillaging from children, of course, but Mann's argument goes beyond this question-begging statement and neatly pins his opponents between the horns of a dilemma. In one sense, all Mann is doing is elaborating the theory on which, from the beginning, Massachusetts had taxed its citizens for the support of schools. In another sense, he is merely spelling out the Christian doctrine that we bring nothing into this world and it is certain we can carry nothing out. In a third sense, he is applying to the school tax the American doctrines of progress and usefulness. Even the crustiest of State Street bankers could not argue that posterity should not be better off than the present generation. Even the most reactionary industrialist could not deny that an educated citizenry, particularly a trained working-class, was preferable to an ignorant one—something Mann pointed out in his *Fifth Annual Report* (1841), when he wrote: "Amongst a people who must gain their subsistence by their labor, what can be so economical . . . and wise . . . as to . . . endow and sustain the most efficient system of universal education for their children," especially in New England, which, lacking natural resources, must depend for "comfort and competency and independence" upon awaking the "dormant powers of the human intellect." This was good business sense.

But on the other hand, there was a general flavor of radicalism about the whole thing. Property merely a transient possession? Property something that was not a "natural right"? Property a mere matter of moral trusteeship for posterity? You could not deny these easy assumptions without being either unpatriotic or un-Christian—and yet—and yet—what did the fellow want? Look at the people who approved him—Theodore Parker, Charles Sumner, Robert Rantoul, Dr. Channing, the Reverend Mr. Bartol —Unitarians, abolitionists, dangerous spirits all. They were not governed by the admirable doctrine of President Francis Wayland of Brown University, who in his *Elements of Political Economy* proved that the accumulation of property was simply God's reward to the deserving Christian. They did not understand that sin and evil were inescapable ingredients of human nature. They had weak and sentimental views not only about this life but about a future state. For example, Mann's report for 1840 concluded:

Experience is yet to develop the grandeur and the glory, which, through the exhaustless capabilities of this institution, may be wrought out for mankind, when by the united labors of the wise and the good, its elastic nature shall be so expanded as to become capacious of the millions of immortal beings, who from the recesses of Infinite Power, are evoked into this life as a place of preparation for a higher state of existence, and whom, like a nursing mother, it shall receive and cherish, and shall instruct and train in the knowledge and the observance and the love of those divine laws and commandments upon which the Creator, both of the body and the soul has made their highest happiness depend.

Highest happiness . . . love . . . millions of immortal beings . . . exhaustless possibilities, indeed! Sheer pantheism, sheer infidelity, sheer unitarianism, smuggled into the schools in the guise of a nonsectarian system of morality! The man was a danger, not orthodox; a dreamer who, brought up to the law, knew nothing about schoolteaching, a theorist who indecently wanted to put physiology into the grades and thus encourage children to explore their own vile bodies! The best way to get rid of him was to show him up for an unbeliever, a disciple of Paine and Voltaire, no Christian, a man who, in the guise of nonsectarianism, was driving religion out of the lives of the younger generation.

Against Mann's philosophy of universal benevolism the orthodox accordingly rallied their forces to protect property by insisting that education must be founded upon the traditional interpretation of the nature of man. Thus in 1844 thirty-one Boston schoolmasters united to write a pamphlet of 144 pages defending the existing order, the climax of their argument turning upon a theory of school discipline which, in turn, depends upon the orthodox view of human nature. Mann had deprecated corporal punishment in the schools. The Boston schoolmasters defended it. School order, they said, like that of the family and of society, must be established upon the basis of acknowledged authority, enforced by an appeal to "the most appropriate motives," including the "fear of physical pain . . . for we believe," they said, "that that, low as it is, will have its place . . . not for a limited period merely, till teachers become better qualified, and society more morally refined, but while men and children continue to be human; that is, so long as schools and schoolmasters and government and laws are needed. . . . A wholesome application of the rod in youth" may "save their pupils from the dungeon and the halter in maturer life," and they gloried in the tradition of the "stern virtue, and inflexible justice, and scorn-despising firmness of the Puritan founders of our free schools." "The fear of the law," they said roundly, is "the beginning of political wisdom," and "implicit obedience to rightful authority must be inculcated and enforced upon children." And this they backed up by quoting St. Paul and the Reverend Jacob Abbott, and they cited a recent schoolboy riot in Philadelphia to show that wicked human nature must be whipped.

Philadelphia was much in the news as a warning to Massachusetts. There Stephen Girard had created his college, from which all religious instruction was to be forever excluded. Daniel Webster in 1844 argued the case for outraged citizens desiring to break this will, and now Edward A. Newton of Pittsfield asserted in another pamphlet that there was no essential difference between the irreligion of Girard and the irreligion of Horace Mann. Girard had "laid the axe at the root of Christianity itself," and Horace Mann, when he said that the Bible might be read in the public schools but not interpreted, was doing the same thing. Both excluded Christianity as an essential element of education, since, said Newton, "all teaching of what Orthodox men hold to be the doctrines of grace is excluded in the books furnished [the child] to read," and therefore "he may not, if the child of wicked, or indifferent, or ignorant parents, or guardians, ever truly know what is necessary to his salvation."

And then there was the Reverend M. H. Smith of Boston, who in 1847 preached a sermon picturesquely entitled, "The Ark of God on a New Cart." Juvenile delinquency has been, he thought, on the increase, and crime is so common that few citizens of Boston "leave their homes at dark without some fear." What is the cause of this moral deterioration? In the course of a long pamphlet-war the Reverend Mr. Smith stuck gamely to these propositions: You, Horace Mann, have in fact taken the Bible out of the public schools because you do not believe the whole Bible to be the inspired Word of God and therefore do not want the whole Bible to be read by the young. You won't have corporal punishment in the schools because, contrary to religion, "you assume the native purity of children" though the Bible says that our race are "by nature, children of wrath." Falsely interpreting the constitution of the state, you do not make religion part of public instruction, and you have put into the school libraries books that are in fact infidel writings. A paragraph from one of the Reverend Mr. Smith's pamphlets is especially illuminating. He wrote: "We ask that the principles of piety be taught in schools, and not the principles of infidelity—we ask that, blended with intellectual culture, our children shall be taught the fear of God, their accountability to him, and the great truth that lies at the base of warning and promise in the Bible, that life is a season of preparation; that in the next, men will be rewarded according to their works. You [Horace Mann] respond, that we are 'intolerant and persistent'; that we will have sectarianism, or 'scatter our common schools to the winds.' But who originated common schools? The very class of men whom you, in your official capacity, denounce as intolerant; those very dogmatists, men of the same principles of those whom you accuse, on account of those principles, of attempting to scatter those schools to the wind. The clergy and religious men, in the hands of God, did this great work. . . . But for the influence of those truths, which you reject as unfit to be taught to our children—truths in which the old Commonwealth of Massachusetts has stood firmly for more than two hundred years—neither you nor I might have been able to read. . . . If you say that teaching future retribution is sectarianism, I answer that you use terms to mislead." And the Reverend Mr. Smith pointed out with some cogency that the Thanksgiving Day proclamation of the head of the state, Governor Briggs, was guilty of "sectarianism," since it referred to the grace of Christ.

I am afraid that Mann's replies to this type of attack were confused and not altogether candid. He asserted that as secretary of the board of education he had no power whatsoever, which was true enough, but inasmuch as he was the eyes and ears of a board that almost always adopted his recommendations, this was not quite candid. He insisted that orthodox Christian sects no longer formed the overwhelming majority of the population of the state, but that "Liberal Christians" formed between a third and a fourth of the population and that, since the law forbade sectarian teaching in the public schools, the reading of the Bible without comment was the highest common denominator he could find among the sects and still insure nonsectarian teaching. In the same paragraph, however, he estimated the Catholics of Boston as thirty thousand, and he overlooked the embarrassing fact that if the reading of the Protestant Bible might conceivably be agreeable to all the Protestants, it could never be agreeable to the Catholics, and that the result must be—what in fact it came to be—a tremendous sectarian controversy. He declared that the orthodox members of the board had joined the liberal members of the board in supporting him and in approving the school libraries he recommended, but this was to evade the issue, since books having no trace of religious interpretation of man were as sectarian *ipso facto* as books that set forth a Unitarian or an orthodox or a Catholic interpretation of human nature. But finally and, as it proved in the end, most effectually, he asserted that among the best European schools and among the most enlightened European theorists and teachers, the old view of boys and girls as children of wrath had long since been abandoned and that, if the United States was to keep step with, or surpass, France and Germany, it would have to assume, for purposes of education, at least, that human nature was indefinitely malleable and that by good teaching little Americans could become improved versions of what Americans ought to be. The Calvinistic theory of childhood was static, it was outmoded in the age of progress, it must be replaced by a dynamic, an expansive theory of human nature and of what education could do, not merely for the offspring of the governing classes, but for any and every American child.

Here, then, was the real clash, an eternal conflict between two views of human nature, the Rousseauistic and the Augustinian. The benevolism of Mann and his followers held that human nature was not under a curse, that it could be improved to an indefinite degree, and that the state, or secular society, was not only the best instrument for this improvement but in all probability the sole instrument proper for shaping future citizens, inasmuch as the state knew what it wanted for the state. If religious training is an appropriate part of state-supported education, then religious training should be confined to a bare minimum satisfactory to all Christian sects: and in Protestant Massachusetts before the great Irish migration, Mann thought he had found that common denominator in the reading of the King James Bible without comment—that is, without sectarian interpretation.

But Mann's opponents had an older view of human nature. They clung to the doctrine that the children of men are rebellious little animals who stand in need of discipline because they are both weak and wicked. No state can survive, they said, unless the principle of authority survives. The first essential of education is to maintain discipline. Discipline has two branches—the secular arm and the sacred arm. The secular arm, symbolized by the schoolmaster's rod, finds its support in Paul's Epistle to the Romans: "Let every soul be subject unto the higher powers. For there is no power but of God; the powers that be are ordained of God. Whosoever therefore resisteth the power, resisteth the ordinance of God." Discipline is to be wisely administered, but administered it must be.

But the ordinance of God, they argued, as later, in the parochial-school problem, the Roman Catholics were to argue, should not be known indirectly and through incompetent channels, but directly and competently. Therefore the church school, which was in fact the only school Massachusetts had originally known. The school must be governed by the church, guardian of eternal truth and a far wiser and more experienced schoolmaster than the state. The state might, indeed, be required to support secular education for the ordinary concerns of life, but, unfortunately, education is indivisible, and the state must therefore also support religious education, either by admitting it into the secular schools or by supporting religious schools—that is, the kind of school the Atlantic community had always known up to the French Revolution. Only thus could republican virtue be maintained in the sinful generations of men. Only thus could the constitutional provision be fulfilled that requires the state of Massachusetts to diffuse wisdom, knowledge, and virtue among the body of the people. What does the constitution say? It requires the state to "countenance and inculcate the principles of humanity and general benevolence, public and private charity, industry and frugality, honesty and punctuality . . . sincerity, good humor, and all social affections and generous sentiments among the people." But these are moral virtues, to be imposed upon sinful man, and you cannot create moral virtues, the conservatives said, by ignoring or minimizing the church.

The argument is still going on. Probably it will never be settled. The immediate victory lay with Horace Mann, who, in a wonderful campaign of propaganda, persuaded the people at the grass roots to support the common schools. A century later there are increasing complaints about the failure of common-school education to create the moral discipline demanded by the constitution, and an increasing invention of ingenious ways by which to circumvent the separation of church and state in the common schools as that separation has hitherto been observed. The irresistible argument of those who do not wish to alter the present situation is that in a country which has about two hundred and seventy different religious sects, not to speak of a large body of atheists, and persons not belonging to any church, the state cannot favor any church but must remain neutral. The immovable argument of those who wish to modify the system of public education is that to have no religious training is in effect to take sides —in this case, to take sides with the agnostics, and skeptics, the unbelievers who, when they say that there may be some truth in any and all religions, say in effect also that all religions are equally faulty. Perhaps the dilemma is insoluble. But whatever solution is found in a particular place will be, I suggest, the solution satisfactory to the local community, no matter what the general laws or the constitutional provisions may be.

VI. *John Brown's Private War*

When John Brown, not yet a legend, failed in his quixotic
attempt to capture the arsenal at Harper's Ferry and
launch a slave revolt, extremists in both North and South
magnified the implications of his exploit. Southerners saw
him as a villainous fanatic, a murderer who would arm the
slaves to commit more crimes; his friends and supporters
in the North regarded him as a God-inspired prophet. In
1859 the moderate position in both sections was difficult
to maintain. Brown's execution accomplished what his
audacious raid had failed to do, and his canonization pre-
luded, if it did not initiate, a bloody war that a few farsighted Americans had anticipated more than a generation
before. Professor C. Vann Woodward in his account of
this episode illustrates what has often occurred during
other crises in our history: the crushing of the middle between the two single-minded and belligerent extremes.

VI

John Brown's Private War

C. Vann Woodward

Professor of American History,
The Johns Hopkins University

In some respects Harper's Ferry bears closer resemblance to the
crisis of our own time than do the other American crises under
consideration. For one thing, it has more of the characteristics of
an international than of a domestic crisis. It was a clash between
two Americas, each struggling for dominance. Each of the antagonistic systems had its own set of interests, institutions, and
values, and in the long perspective of nearly a century the clash
between them takes on aspects typical of other historic struggles
for power. In the mid-nineteenth century, however, the differences were usually expressed in terms of moral or ideological
conflict.

In the 1850's as in the 1950's the issue was dramatized as a
conflict between labor systems—free labor versus slave labor. Confident of the superiority of its system of wage labor, the North
attacked the South's system of slave labor as wasteful, immoral,
and inhuman. The South replied with many of the arguments
later used by Marxians against capitalism, one being that free labor was really wage slavery minus the security enjoyed by the
slave. Since world opinion regarded slavery as incompatible with
advanced civilization, the moral advantage naturally lay entirely
with the North in the labor dispute. It was therefore to the
North's interest to make the labor issue the symbol of the whole
conflict and at the same time to play down the issues of tariff,
money, banks, subsidies, and other economic privileges, in which
the North enjoyed no special moral advantage.

In a crisis as great as that which led to the American Civil War the importance of the Harper's Ferry raid should not be overestimated. It was but one of a series of violent border incidents that occurred between 1856 and 1861—from "bleeding Kansas" to Fort Sumter. They constituted a continuation of a longer war of propaganda and served as the prelude of formal war following Fort Sumter.

For present purposes, the significant thing about Harper's Ferry is the light it throws upon the American mind in the midst of crisis. Among the aspects illuminated by the incident are several that claim attention because of their relevance to our own time. It is well to remember in comparing two crises a century apart that analogies are never perfect and that there are important differences between the two eras. With this *caveat* in mind it is possible to speak of the revolutionary mentality of the 1850's and the psychology of the fellow traveler, the intellectual and his involvement in conspiracy, subversive groups and their relation to the Bill of Rights, loyalty and the problem of treason. Rarely have Americans been more sharply torn between conflicting values—between the "higher law" and the statutory law, between principles and the Constitution, between home and country. Rarely has the traditional code of American political ethics been challenged more openly by the doctrine that the end justifies the means. And perhaps there has never been in our history a clearer instance of an insecurity complex, with its attendant hysteria and bellicosity, than that offered by the South; nor a better example of how rival powers infect each other with aggression in a war crisis.

After ninety years the figure of John Brown is still wrapped in obscurity and myth. Of the fourteen biographies of Brown published since 1859 not one has been written by a professional historian. The myth and legend makers have done their part, but much of the difficulty is inherent in the nature of Brown's life and character. His fifty-nine years were divided sharply into two periods. The obscurity of his first fifty-five years was of the sort natural to a humble life unassociated with events of importance. The obscurity of his last four years, filled with conspiratorial activities, was in large part the deliberate work of Brown and his fellow conspirators and their admirers.

Poverty and failure haunted the first fifty-five years of John

Brown's life. The father of twenty children, he was compelled to see his family drag along in want and at times something approaching destitution. In thirty-five years he was engaged in more than twenty different business ventures in six states. Most of them ended in failure, some in bankruptcy, and at least two in crime. Brown was involved for years as defendant in one litigation after another brought against him for failure to meet his financial obligations. "Several of the cases in question leave no doubt of flagrant dishonesty on his part in both business and family relations," concludes Professor James C. Malin. The historian suggests that "this record of unreliability proven in court" might serve as "an index to the reliability of John Brown as a witness after he became a public character." The remarkable thing about this record is that it seems to have interfered in no way with the second of his careers. After 1855 John Brown abandoned his unprofitable business career when he was almost penniless and for the rest of his life was without remunerative employment. He depended for support upon donations from people whom he convinced of his integrity and reliability. Here and elsewhere there is strong evidence that Brown was somehow able to inspire confidence and intense personal loyalty.

The Kansas phase of Brown's guerrilla warfare has given rise to the "Legend of Fifty-six," a fabric of myth that has been subjected to a more rigorous examination than any other phase of Brown's life has ever received. Malin establishes beyond question that "John Brown did not appear to have had much influence either in making or marring Kansas history," that his exploits "brought tragedy to innocent settlers," but that "in no place did he appear as a major factor." He also establishes a close correlation between the struggle over freedom and slavery and local clashes over conflicting land titles on the Kansas frontier, and points out that "the business of stealing horses under the cloak of fighting for freedom and running them off to the Nebraska-Iowa border for sale" is a neglected aspect of the struggle for "Bleeding Kansas." John Brown and his men engaged freely and profitably in this business and justified their plunder as the spoils of war. Two covenants that Brown drew up for his followers contained a clause specifically providing for the division of captured property among the members of his guerrilla band.

It would be a gross distortion, however, to dismiss John Brown as a frontier horse-thief. He was much too passionately and fanatically in earnest about his war on slavery to permit of any such oversimplification. His utter fearlessness, courage, and devotion to the cause were greatly admired by respectable antislavery men who saw in the old Puritan an ideal revolutionary leader.

One exploit of Brown in Kansas, however, would seem to have put him forever beyond the pale of association with intelligent opponents of slavery. This was the famous Pottawatomie massacre of May 24, 1856. John Brown, leading four of his sons, a son-in-law, and two other men, descended by night upon an unsuspecting settlement of four proslavery families. Proceeding from one home to another the raiders took five men out, murdered them, and left their bodies horribly mutilated. None of the victims was a slaveholder, and two of them were born in Germany and had no contact with the South. By way of explanation Brown said the murders had been "decreed by Almighty God, ordained from Eternity." He later denied responsibility for the act, and some of the Eastern capitalists and intellectuals who supported him refused to believe him guilty. In view of the report of the murders that was laid before the country on July 11, 1856, in the form of a committee report in the House of Representatives, it is somewhat difficult to excuse such ignorance among intelligent men.

It was shortly after this report was published, however, that Brown enjoyed his most striking success in soliciting contributions and making friends for his war on slavery among men of wealth and intellectual distinction in Boston and other Eastern cities. In the first four months of 1858 he succeeded in raising twenty-three thousand dollars in cash, supplies, and credit to support his guerrilla activities.

In the spring of 1858 plans for the raid on Virginia began to take definite shape. To a convention of fellow conspirators in Chatham, Canada, in May, John Brown presented his remarkable "Provisional Constitution and Ordinances for the People of the United States." It represented the form of government he proposed by force of arms to establish with a handful of conspirators and an armed insurrection of slaves. Complete with legislative, executive, and judicial branches, Brown's revolutionary government was in effect a military dictatorship, since all acts of his congress had to be approved by the commander-in-chief of the army in order to become valid. Needless to say, John Brown was elected commander-in-chief.

By July 1859, Commander-in-Chief Brown had established himself at a farm on the Maryland side of the Potomac River, four miles north of Harper's Ferry. There he assembled twenty-one followers and accumulated ammunition and other supplies, including two hundred revolvers, two hundred rifles, and nine hundred and fifty pikes specially manufactured for the slaves he expected to rise up in insurrection. On Sunday night, October 16, after posting a guard of three men at the farm, he set forth with eighteen followers, five of them Negroes, and all of them young men, to start his war of liberation and found his abolitionist republic. Brown's first objective, to capture the United States arsenal at Harper's Ferry, was easily accomplished since it was without military guard. In the federal armory and the rifle works, also captured, were sufficient arms to start the bloodiest slave insurrection in history.

The commander-in-chief appears to have launched his invasion without any definite plan of campaign and then proceeded to violate every military principle in the book. He cut himself off from his base of supplies, failed to keep open his only avenues of retreat, dispersed his small force, and bottled the bulk of them up in a trap where defeat was inevitable. "In fact, it was so absurd," remarked Abraham Lincoln, "that the slaves, with all their ignorance, saw plainly enough it could not succeed." Not one of them joined Brown voluntarily, and those he impressed quickly departed. The insurrectionists killed one United States Marine and four inhabitants of Harper's Ferry, including the mayor and a Negro freeman. Ten of their own number, including two of Brown's sons, were killed, five were taken prisoners by a small force of Marines commanded by Robert E. Lee, and seven escaped, though two of them were later arrested. John Brown's insurrection ended in a tragic and dismal failure.

When news of the invasion was first flashed across the country the commonest reaction was that this was obviously the act of a madman, that John Brown was insane. This explanation was particularly attractive to Republican politicians and editors, whose party suffered the keenest embarrassment from the incident. Fall elections were on, and the new Congress was about to convene. Democrats immediately charged that John Brown's raid was the inevitable consequence of the "irresistible-conflict" and "higher-law" abolitionism preached by Republican leaders Seward and Chase. "Brown's invasion," wrote Senator Henry Wilson of Massachusetts, "has thrown us, who were in a splendid position, into a defensive position. . . . If we are defeated next year we shall owe it to that foolish and insane movement of Brown's."[1] The emphasis on insanity was taken up widely by Wilson's contemporaries and later adopted by historians.

It seems best to deal with the insanity question promptly, for it is likely to confuse the issue and miss the meaning of Harper's Ferry. In dealing with the problem it is important not to blink at the evidence, as many of Brown's biographers have done, of John Brown's close association with insanity in both his heredity and his environment. In the Brown Papers at the Library of Congress are nineteen affidavits signed by relatives and friends attesting the record of insanity in the Brown family. John Brown's maternal grandmother and his mother both died insane. His three aunts and two uncles, sisters and brothers of his mother, were intermittently insane, and so was his only sister, her daughter, and one of his brothers. Of six first cousins, all more or less mad, two were deranged from time to time, two had been repeatedly committed to the state insane asylum, and two were still confined at the time. Of John Brown's immediate family, his first wife and one of his sons died insane, and a second son was insane at intervals. On these matters the affidavits, whose signers include John Brown's uncle, a half-brother, a brother-in-law, and three first cousins, are in substantial agreement. On the sanity of John Brown himself, however, opinion varied. Several believed that he was a "monomaniac," one that he was insane on subjects of religion and slavery, and an uncle thought his nephew had been "subject to periods of insanity" for twenty years.[2]

John Brown himself, of course, stoutly maintained that he was perfectly sane, and he was certainly able to convince many intelligent people, both friend and foe, that he was sane. He firmly

---

[1] Henry Wilson to S. E. Sewell, December 10, 1859. Norcross Papers (Massachusetts Historical Society, Boston).

[2] The nineteen affidavits were submitted by Samuel Chilton, counsel for John Brown, to Governor Wise, "with the object of praying you to grant a postponement of the execution of the prisoner." Chilton to Wise, November 21, 1859, John Brown Papers (Division of Manuscripts, Library of Congress).

refused to plead insanity at his trial. Governor Henry A. Wise of Virginia went so far as to write out orders to the superintendent of the state insane asylum to examine Brown, but endorsed the orders, "countermanded upon reflection." On the other hand, John Brown pronounced Governor Wise mad. "Hard to tell who's mad," jested Wendell Phillips to a laughing congregation in Henry Ward Beecher's church. "The world says one man's mad. John Brown said the same of the Governor. . . . I appeal from Philip drunk to Philip sober." He meant future generations when, he said, "the light of civilization has had more time to penetrate." Then it would be plain that not Brown, but his enemies were mad.

We, the Philips sober of the future, with some misgivings about how far "the light of civilization" has penetrated, do think we know a little more about insanity than did our great-grandfathers. We at least know that it is a loose expression for a variety of mental disorders, and that it is a relative term. What seems sane to some people at some times seems insane to other people at other times. In our own time we have witnessed what we consider psychopathic personalities rise to power over millions of people and plunge the world into war. Yet to the millions who followed them these leaders appeared sublime in their wisdom.

"John Brown may be a lunatic," observed the Boston *Post*, but if so, "then one-fourth of the people of Massachusetts are madmen," and perhaps three-fourths of the ministers of religion. Begging that Brown's life be spared, Amos A. Lawrence wrote Governor Wise: "Brown is a Puritan whose mind has become disordered by hardship and illness. He has the qualities wh. endear him to our people." [3] The association of ideas was doubtless unintentional, but to the Virginian it must have seemed that Lawrence was saying that in New England a disordered mind was an endearing quality. The Reverend J. M. Manning of Old South Church, Boston, pronounced Harper's Ferry "an unlawful, a foolhardy, a suicidal act," and declared: "I stand before it wondering and admiring." Horace Greeley called it "the work of a madman" for which he had not "one reproachful word," and for the "grandeur and nobility" of which he was "reverently grateful." And

[3] Lawrence had supported Brown earlier but had grown skeptical of his methods by this time. Lawrence to Wise, October 26, 1859, John Brown Papers (Virginia State Library, Richmond).

the New York *Independent* declared that while "Harper's Ferry was insane, the controlling motive of this demonstration was sublime." It was both foolhardy and godly, insane and sublime, treasonous and admirable.

The prestige and character of the men who lent John Brown active, if sometimes secret, support likewise suggest caution in dismissing Harper's Ferry as merely the work of a madman. Among Brown's fellow conspirators the most notable were the so-called Secret Six. Far from being horse-thieves and petty traders, the Secret Six came of the cream of Northern society. Capitalist, philanthropist, philosopher, surgeon, professor, minister, they were men of reputability and learning, four of them with Harvard degrees. With a Harvard Divinity School degree, a knowledge of twenty languages, and a library of sixteen thousand volumes, Theodore Parker was perhaps the most prodigiously learned American of his times. In constant correspondence with the leading Republican politicians, he has been called "the Conscience of a Party." What Gerrit Smith, the very wealthy philanthropist and one-time congressman of Peterboro, New York, lacked in mental endowments he made up in good works—earnest efforts to improve the habits of his fellowmen. These included not only crusades against alcohol and tobacco in all forms, but also coffee, tea, meat, and spices—"almost everything which gave pleasure," according to his biographer. Generous with donations to dietary reform, dress reform, woman's rights, educational, and "non-resistance" movements, Smith took no interest whatever in factory and labor reform, but was passionately absorbed in the antislavery movement and a liberal contributor to John Brown. Dr. Samuel G. Howe, of Boston, husband of the famous Julia Ward Howe, was justly renowned for his humanitarian work for the blind and mentally defective. In his youth he had gone on a Byronic crusade in Greece against the Turk. These experiences contributed greatly to his moral prestige, if little to his political sophistication. The most generous man of wealth among the conspirators was George L. Stearns of Boston, a prosperous manufacturer of lead pipe. In the opinion of this revolutionary capitalist John Brown was "the representative man of this century, as Washington was of the last." Finally there were two younger men, fledgling conspirators. The son of a prosperous Boston merchant who was bursar of Harvard, Thomas Wentworth Higginson became pastor of a church in Worcester after taking his divinity degree at Harvard. Young Franklin B. Sanborn was an apostle of Parker and a protégé of Emerson, who persuaded Sanborn to take charge of a school in Concord.

The most tangible service the Secret Six rendered the conspiracy lay in secretly diverting to John Brown, for use at Harper's Ferry, money and arms that had been contributed to the Massachusetts Kansas Aid Committee for use in "Bleeding Kansas." This dubious transaction was accomplished by George L. Stearns, chairman of the committee, exercising as a private individual an option he held of foreclosing upon the property of the committee, then promptly transferring the arms to Brown and notifying only the conspirators. By this means the Kansas Committee was converted into a respectable front for subversive purposes, and thousands of innocent contributors to what appeared to be a patriotic organization discovered later that they had furnished rifles for a treasonous attack on a federal arsenal. Even Sanborn admitted in 1885 that "it is still a little difficult to explain this transaction concerning the arms without leaving the suspicion that there was somewhere a breach of trust." It still is.

The Secret Six appear to have been fascinated by the drama of conspiratorial activity. There were assumed names, coded messages, furtive committee meetings, dissembling of motives, and secret caches of arms. And over all the romance and glamor of a noble cause—the liberation of man. Although they knew perfectly well the general purpose of Brown, the Secret Six were careful to request him not to tell them the precise time and place of the invasion. The wily old revolutionist could have told them much that they did not know about the psychology of fellow travelers. Brown had earlier laid down this strategy for conspirators who were hard pressed: "go into the houses of your most prominent and influential white friends with your wives; and that will effectually fasten upon them the suspicion of being connected with you, and will compel them to make a common cause with you, whether they would otherwise live up to their professions or not." The same strategy is suggested in Brown's leaving behind in the Maryland farmhouse where they would inevitably be captured all his private papers, hundreds of letters of himself and followers, implicating nobody knew how many respectable fellow-travelers.

When the news of the captured documents arrived there occurred a most unheroic panic among the Secret Six, who saw stark ruin and an indictment for treason facing them. Stearns, Sanborn, and Howe fled to Canada. Parker was already abroad. Gerrit Smith's secretary did not stop until he reached England. Smith himself issued pitiable and panicky denials of his guilt, then found refuge in insanity and was confined in an asylum. Howe published a denial unworthy of respect. Higginson alone stood his ground. Stearns and Howe denied any knowledge of the attack before a congressional committee, and both of them told Sanborn they "found the question of the Senate Committee so unskillfully framed that they could, without literal falsehood, answer as they did."

The assistance that the Secret Six conspirators were able to give John Brown and his Legend was as nothing compared with that rendered by other Northern intellectuals. Among them were the cultural and moral aristocracy of America in the period that has been called a "Renaissance." Some of these men, Emerson and Thoreau among them, had met and admired Brown and even made small contributions to his cause. But they were safely beyond reproach of the law, and were never taken into his confidence in the way that the Secret Six were. Their service was rendered after the event in justifying and glorifying Brown and his invasion.

In this work the intellectuals were ably assisted by a genius, a genius at self-justification—John Brown himself. From his prison cell he poured out a stream of letters, serene and restrained, filled with Biblical language, and fired with overpowering conviction that his will and God's were one and the same. These letters and his famous speech at the trial constructed for the hero a new set of motives and plans and a new role. For Brown had changed roles. In October he invaded Virginia as a conqueror armed for conquest, carrying with him guns and pikes for the army he expected to rally to his standard, and a new constitution to replace the one he overthrew. In that role he was a miserable failure. Then in November he declared at his trial: "I never did intend murder, or treason, or the destruction of property, or to excite or incite slaves to rebellion, or to make an insurrection." He only intended to liberate slaves without bloodshed, as he falsely declared he had done in Missouri the year before. How these statements can be reconciled with the hundreds of pikes, revolvers, and rifles, the capture of an armory, the taking of hostages, the killing of unarmed civilians, the destruction of government property, and the arming of slaves is difficult to see. Nor is it possible to believe that Brown thought he could seize a federal arsenal, shoot down United States Marines, and overthrow a government without committing treason. "It was all so thin," as Robert Penn Warren has observed of the trial speech, "that it should not have deceived a child, but it deceived a generation." At Lincoln's funeral Emerson compared it with the Gettysburg Address.

Emerson seemed hesitant in his first private reactions to Harper's Ferry. Thoreau, on the other hand, never hesitated a moment. On the day after Brown's capture he compared the hero's inevitable execution with the crucifixion of Christ. Harper's Ferry was "the best news that America ever had"; Brown "the bravest and humanest man in all the country," "a Transcendentalist above all," and he declared: "I rejoice that I live in this age, that I was his contemporary." Emerson quickly fell into line with Thoreau, and in his November 8 lecture on "Courage" described Brown as "The saint, whose fate yet hangs in suspense, but whose martyrdom, if it shall be perfected, will make the gallows as glorious as the cross." [4] Within a few weeks Emerson gave three important lectures, in all of which he glorified John Brown.

With the Sage of Concord and his major prophet in accord on the martyr, the majority of the transcendental hierarchy sooner or later joined in—Channing, Bronson and Louisa May Alcott, Longfellow, Bryant, and Lowell, and of course Wendell Phillips and Theodore Parker. Parker pronounced Brown "not only a martyr . . . but also a SAINT." Thoreau and Henry Ward Beecher frankly admitted they hoped Brown would hang. To spare a life would be to spoil a martyr. They were interested in him not as a man but as a symbol, a moral ideal, and a saint for a crusade. In the rituals of canonization the gallows replaced the cross as a fetish. Louisa May Alcott called the gallows "a stepping-stone to

---

[4] There are at least three different versions of this famous passage in print. Emerson struck it out of the lecture in his published work. I have accepted the version of the passages used by Ralph L. Rusk: *The Life of Ralph Waldo Emerson* (New York: 1949), p. 402.

heaven," Parker "the road to heaven," Theodore Tilton "a throne greater than a king's," and Phillips concluded that "henceforth it is sacred forever." [5]

Among Western antislavery men there were fewer intellectuals of fame or notoriety, but abolitionist preachers, teachers, and orators joined in apotheozing Brown. Citizens of Oberlin erected a monument to three Negroes who gave their lives in Brown's raid. And Theodore D. Weld, once the genius of Western abolitionism, though now in retirement, permitted the burial of two of the Harper's Ferry raiders at his school in New Jersey. Not all of the Northern intellectuals became members of the Brown cult. Hawthorne and Whitman were two notable dissenters. Devotees of the cult showed little tolerance for dissent. Emerson declared that "all people, in proportion to their sensibility and self-respect, sympathize with him [Brown]," and Thoreau carried intolerance to the point of moral snobbery. "When a noble deed is done, who is likely to appreciate it? They who are noble themselves," answered Thoreau. "I was not surprised that certain of my neighbors spoke of John Brown as an ordinary felon, for who are they? They have either much flesh, or much office, or much coarseness of some kind. They are not ethereal natures in any sense. The dark qualities predominate in them. . . . For the children of the light to contend with them is as if there should be a contest between eagles and owls."

The task to which the intellectuals of the cult dedicated themselves was the idealizing of John Brown as a symbol of the moral order and the social purpose of the Northern cause. Wendell Phillips expressed this best when he declared in the Boston Music Hall: " 'Law' and 'order' are only means for the halting ignorance of the last generation. John Brown is the impersonation of God's order and God's law, moulding a better future, and setting for it an example." In substituting the new revolutionary law and order for traditional law and order, the intellectuals encountered some tough problems in morals and values. It was essential for them to justify a code of political methods and morals that was at odds with the Anglo-American tradition.

John Brown's own solution to this problem was quite simple.

---

[5] A convenient collection of the public tributes to the martyr, more than 500 pages of them, is James Redpath: *Echoes of Harper's Ferry* (Boston: 1860).

It is set forth in the preamble of his Provisional Constitution of the United States, which declares that in reality slavery is an "unjustifiable War of one portion of its citizens upon another." War, in which all is fair, amounted to a suspension of ethical restraints. This type of reasoning is identical with that of the revolutionaries who hold that the class struggle is in reality a class war. The assumption naturally facilitates the justification of deeds otherwise unjustifiable. These might include the dissembling of motives, systematic deception, theft, murder, or the liquidation of an enemy class.

It is clear that certain enthusiasts found in Brown's reasoning a satisfactory solution to their moral problem, but it was equally clear that the mass of people were not yet ready to accept this solution and that some other rationalization was required. The doctrine of the "Higher Law" and the doctrine of "Civil Disobedience" had already done much to prepare the way for acceptance of the revolutionary ethics. They had justified conduct in defiance of the Constitution and the government by appeal to higher moral ends. Transcendental doctrine was now used to extend the defiance of tradition even further. Thoreau's reply to attacks upon John Brown's methods was: "The method is nothing; the spirit is all." This was the Transcendentalist way of saying that means are justified by the ends. The old theologians would have spotted this instantly as the antinomian heresy. According to this doctrine, if the end is sufficiently noble—as noble as the emancipation of the slave—any means used to attain the end is justified.

The crisis of Harper's Ferry was a crisis of means, not of ends. John Brown did not raise the question of whether slavery should be abolished or tolerated. That question had been raised in scores of ways and debated for a generation. Millions held strong convictions on the subject. Upon abolition, as an *end*, there was no difference between John Brown and the American and Foreign Anti-Slavery Society. But upon the *means* to attain abolition there was as much difference between them, so far as the record goes, as there is between the modern British Labour Party and the government of Soviet Russia on the means of abolishing capitalism. The Anti-Slavery Society was solemnly committed to the position of nonviolent means. In the very petition that Lewis Tappan, secretary of the society, addressed to Governor Wise in behalf of Brown he repeated the rubric about "the use of all carnal weapons for deliverance from bondage." [6] But in their rapture over Brown as martyr and saint the abolitionists lost sight of their differences with him over the point of means and ended by totally compromising their creed of nonviolence.

But what of those who clung to the democratic principle that differences should be settled by ballots and that the will of the majority should prevail? Phillips pointed out that: "In God's world there are no majorities, no minorities; one, on God's side, is a majority." And Thoreau asked: "When were the good and the brave ever in a majority?" So much for majority rule. What of the issue of treason? The Reverend Fales H. Newhall of Roxbury declared that the word "treason" had been "made holy in the American language"; and the Reverend Edwin M. Wheelock of Boston blessed "the sacred, the radiant 'treason' of John Brown."

No aversion to bloodshed seemed to impede the spread of the Brown cult. Garrison thought that "every slaveholder has forfeited his right to live" if he impeded emancipation. The Reverend Theodore Parker predicted a slave insurrection in which "The Fire of Vengeance" would run "from man to man, from town to town" through the South. "What shall put it out?" he asked. "The White Man's blood." The Reverend Edwin M. Wheelock thought that Brown's "mission was to inaugurate slave insurrection as the divine weapon of the antislavery cause." He asked: "Do we shrink from the bloodshed that would follow?" and answered: "No such wrong [as slavery] was ever cleansed by rose-water." Rather than see slavery continued the Reverend George B. Cheever of New York declared: "It were infinitely better that three hundred thousand slaveholders were abolished, struck out of existence." In these pronouncements the doctrine that the end justifies the means had arrived pretty close to justifying the liquidation of an enemy class.

The reactions of the extremists have been stressed in part because it was the extremist view that eventually prevailed in the apotheosis of John Brown, and in part because by this stage of the crisis each section tended to judge the other by the excesses of a few. "Republicans were all John Browns to the Southerners,"

[6] Lewis Tappan to Wise, November 6, 1859, John Brown Papers (Virginia State Library).

as Professor Dwight L. Dumond has observed, "and slaveholders were all Simon Legrees to the Northerners." As a matter of fact Northern conservatives and unionists staged huge anti-Brown demonstrations that equaled or outdid those staged by the Brown partisans. Nathan Appleton wrote a Virginian: "I have never in my long life seen a fuller or more enthusiastic demonstration" than the anti-Brown meeting in Faneuil Hall in Boston. The Republican press described a similar meeting in New York as "the largest and most enthusiastic" ever held in that city. Northern politicians of high rank, including Lincoln, Douglas, Seward, Everett, and Wilson, spoke out against John Brown and his methods. The Republican party registered its official position by a plank in the 1860 platform denouncing the Harper's Ferry raid. Lincoln approved of Brown's execution, "even though he agreed with us in thinking slavery wrong." Agreement on ends did not mean agreement on means. "That cannot excuse violence, bloodshed, and treason," said Lincoln.

Republican papers of the Western states as well as of the East took pains to dissociate themselves from Harper's Ferry, and several denounced the raid roundly. At first conservative Southern papers, for example the *Arkansas State Gazette*, rejoiced that "the leading papers, and men, among the Black Republicans, are open . . . in their condemnation of the course of Brown." As the canonization of Brown advanced, however, the Republican papers gradually began to draw a distinction between their condemnation of Brown's raid and their high regard for the man himself—his courage, his integrity, and his noble motives. They also tended to find in the wrongs Brown and his men had suffered at the hands of slaveholders in Kansas much justification for his attack upon Virginia. From that it was an easy step to pronounce the raid a just retribution for the South's violence in Kansas. There was enough ambiguity about Republican disavowal of Brown to leave doubts in many minds. If Lincoln deplored Brown, there was his partner Billy Herndon, who worshipped Brown. If there was one editor who condemned the raid, there were a half dozen who admired its leader. To Southerners the distinction was elusive or entirely unimportant.

Northern businessmen were foremost in deprecating Harper's Ferry and reassuring the South. Some of them linked their denunciation of Brown with a defense of slavery, however, so that in the logic that usually prevails in time of crisis all critics of Brown risked being smeared with the charge of defending slavery. Radicals called them mossbacks, doughfaces, appeasers, and sought to jeer them out of countenance. "If they cannot be converted, [they] may yet be scared," was Parker's doctrine.

Among the Brown partisans not one has been found but who believed that Harper's Ferry had resulted in great gain for the extremist cause. So profoundly were they convinced of this that they worried little over the conservative dissent. "How vast the change in men's hearts!" exclaimed Phillips. "Insurrection was a harsh, horrid word to millions a month ago." Now it was "the lesson of the hour." Garrison rejoiced that thousands who could not listen to his gentlest rebuke ten years before "now easily swallow John Brown whole, and his rifle in the bargain." "They all called him crazy then," wrote Thoreau; "who calls him crazy now?" To the poet it seemed that "The North is suddenly all Transcendentalist." On the day John Brown was hanged church bells were tolled in commemoration in New England towns, out along the Mohawk Valley, in Cleveland and the Western Reserve, in Chicago and northern Illinois. In Albany one hundred rounds were fired from a cannon. Writing to his daughter the following day, Joshua Giddings of Ohio said: "I find the hatred of slavery greatly intensified by the fate of Brown and men are ready to march to Virginia and dispose of her despotism at once." [7] It was not long before they *were* marching to Virginia, and marching to the tune of "John Brown's Body."

The Harper's Ferry crisis on the other side of the Potomac was a faithful reflection of the crisis in the North, and can therefore be quickly sketched. It was the reflection, with the image reversed in the mirror, that antagonistic powers present to each other in a war crisis. To the South John Brown also appeared as a true symbol of Northern purpose, but instead of the "angel of light" Thoreau pictured, the South saw an angel of destruction. The South did not seriously question Brown's sanity either, for he seemed only the rational embodiment of purposes that Southern extremists had long taught were universal in the North. The crisis helped propagandists falsely identify the whole North with John Brownism. For Harper's Ferry strengthened the hand of ex-

---

[7] Joshua Giddings to Molly Giddings, December 3, 1859, Giddings-Julian Papers (Library of Congress).

tremists and revolutionists in the South as it did in the North, and it likewise discredited and weakened moderates and their influence.

The risk one runs in describing the reaction to Harper's Ferry is the risk of attributing to that event tendencies long manifest. The South had been living in a crisis atmosphere for a long time. It was a society in the grip of an insecurity complex, a tension resulting from both rational and irrational fears. One cause of it was the steady, invincible expansion of the free-state system in size and power, after the Southern system had reached the limits of its own expansion. The South therefore felt itself to be menaced through encirclement by a power containing elements unfriendly to its interests, elements that were growing strong enough to capture the government. The South's insecurity was heightened by having to defend against constant attack an institution it knew to be discredited throughout the civilized world and of which Southerners had once been among the severest critics. Its reaction was to withdraw increasingly from contact with the offending world, to retreat into an isolationism of spirit, and to attempt by curtailing freedom of speech to avoid criticism.

One of the South's tensions sprang from a lack of internal security—the fear of servile insurrection. By the nature of things a slave uprising had to be secret, sudden, and extremely bloody, sparing neither men, women, nor children. The few occurrences of this kind had left a deep trauma in the mind of the people. The pathological character of this tension was manifested in periodic waves of panic based largely on rumor. It is significant that two of the most severe panics of this sort occurred in the election years 1856 and 1860, and were accompanied by charges that abolitionists from the North were fomenting uprisings. Harper's Ferry was therefore a blow at the most sensitive area of Southern consciousness.

The first reaction to the raid, outside Virginia, was surprisingly mild. The newspapers, particularly in the Lower South, pointed out that after all the slaves had remained loyal, that Brown's invasion was a complete failure, and that it was quickly suppressed. This mood did not last long, however. The hundreds of captured documents belonging to Brown and his men persuaded Virginia authorities that the conspiracy was widespread and that the Harper's Ferry strike, had it been successful, was intended to be merely the signal for uprisings throughout the South. Among the documents were maps of seven Southern states with certain widely scattered areas and localities marked with symbols. The symbols may have indicated nothing at all, of course, but they were enough to grip the localities concerned with fear.

Another document that inspired terror was a long letter from one of Brown's emissaries reporting, two weeks before the raid, on a tour of the South. Written from Memphis, the letter suggests the presence of an extensive "fifth column" established in the South by Brown's organization. In Tennessee and Arkansas there were reported to be "an immense number of slaves ripe and ready at the very first intimation to strike a decided blow," and the writer was amazed to find "so large a number of whites ready to aid us" in Memphis. A "thorough scouring" of Arkansas convinced him that the readiness of the slaves was such that "a bold stroke of one day will overthrow the whole state." In Brownsville, Tennessee, a subversive white schoolteacher urged that "we must send out more well qualified men to the south as school teachers, and work them in everywhere," that there was "no avocation in which a man can do so much good for our cause" since the people had "so much confidence in a school teacher." The writer of the letter assured John Brown that "Southern people are easy gulled." His report reveals the man as a wishful thinker and a naïve enthusiast, but after Harper's Ferry the Southern mind was in no state to distinguish between responsible and irresponsible sources of evidence.[8]

Letters from all parts of the South deluged Governor Wise's mail with reports that Brown conspirators had been seized or punished. These, and the Southern newspapers of the time, portray a society in the throes of panic. Convinced that the South was honeycombed with subversives, Southerners tended to see an abolitionist behind every bush and a slave insurrection brewing in the arrival of any stranger. Victims of vigilante and mob action ranged from aged eccentrics and itinerant piano-tuners to substantial citizens of long residence. The mob spirit was no respecter of person or class. A sixty-year-old minister in Texas,

---

[8] Lawrence Thatcher to John Brown, October 3, 1859, John Brown Papers (Virginia State Library). "Thatcher" was evidently an assumed name for one of the conspirators close to Brown. A rather extensive search of Brown manuscripts, with Professor Malin's generous assistance, has so far not identified the handwriting.

who was a believer in the Biblical sanction of slavery and a Democrat of Kentucky birth, made the mistake of criticizing the treatment of slaves in a sermon and was given seventy lashes on his back. A schoolteacher who had lived in Louisiana and Arkansas for ten years was given thirty-six hours to leave the latter state. The newly arrived president of an Alabama college, who came from New York, was forced to give up his job and flee for his life. In December 1859, twelve families, including thirty-nine people associated with antislavery schools and churches of Berea, Kentucky, were forcibly expelled from the state for abolitionism.

Southern fire-eaters swore that no Northerner could be trusted and that all should be expelled. Even the humblest workmen from the North were in danger of insult, violence, or lynching. An Irish stonecutter in Columbia, South Carolina, was beaten, tarred and feathered, and expelled from the state by a mob. Three members of the crew of a brig from Maine were brutally flogged in Georgia, and a New England mechanic was driven out of a village in the same state because he was found to have a clean shirt wrapped in a New York paper containing one of Beecher's sermons. Two Connecticut book-peddlers were roughly handled in Charleston when lists of slaves were found in their bags, and two printers were ridden out of Kingstree, South Carolina, on rails. Four men "suspected of being abolition emissaries" were arrested in two days in Columbus, Georgia, and ten peddlers were driven out of the village of Abbeville, Mississippi. Four months after Harper's Ferry a man was lynched in South Carolina as "one of Brown's associates." Not only Northerners but associates of Northerners were subject to persecution, for guilt by association was an accepted principle in the crisis.

Then there was the Southern enemy within the gates to be dealt with. Hinton R. Helper of North Carolina had written an antislavery book, quantities of which were burned in public ceremonies at High Point in his own state, at Greenville, South Carolina, and Mayesville, Kentucky. Other public book-burning ceremonies took place at Enterprise, Mississippi, and at Montgomery, Alabama, while at Palestine, Texas, the citizens appointed a committee "to collect all said dangerous books for destruction by public burning." Thought control extended to the suppression and seizure of newspapers, a method long practiced, and in Alabama a resolution was introduced in the legislature prohibiting the licensing of teachers with less than ten years' residence, "to protect the state against abolition teachers." Not content with cutting off intellectual commerce with the North, extremists organized to end economic intercourse as well. They published blacklists of Northern firms suspected of abolitionist tendencies, organized boycotts, and promoted nonintercourse agreements. The Richmond *Enquirer* advocated a law "that will keep out of our borders every article of Northern manufacture or importation." On December 8, 1859, thirty-two business agents of New York and Boston arrived in Washington from the South reporting "indignation so great against Northerners that they were compelled to return and abandon their business."

Southern zealots of secession had no better ally than John Brown. Rhett, Ruffin, and Yancey all rejoiced over the effect of Harper's Ferry. Non-slaveholders saw dramatized before them the menace of a slave uprising and readily concluded that their wives and children, as much as the home of the planter, were threatened with the horror of insurrection. They frequently became more fanatical secessionists than the planters. In face of the Northern apotheosis of Brown there was little that Southern moderates could say in answer to such pronouncements as that of the New Orleans *Picayune* of December 2: "Crime becomes godliness, and criminals, red from the slaughter of innocent, are exalted to eminence beside the divine gospel of Peace." The Charleston *Mercury* of November 29 rejoiced that Harper's Ferry, "like a slap in the face," had roused Virginia from her hesitant neutrality and started her on the road to secession. "I have never before seen the public mind of Va. so deeply moved," wrote a Virginian sadly. "The people are far in advance of the politicians, and would most cheerfully follow the extremist counsels. Volunteer companies, horse & foot, are springing up everywhere." [9]

The crisis psychology of 1859 persisted and deepened in the fateful year of 1860 into a pathological condition of mind in which delusions of persecution and impending disaster flourished. Out of Texas came wild rumors of incendiary fires, abolitionists plotting with slaves, and impending insurrection on a vast scale. Rumors of large stocks of strychnine in the possession of slaves

[9] John C. Rutherford to W. C. Rives, Jr., December 18, 1859, W. C. Rives Papers (Division of Manuscripts, Library of Congress).

and of plans for well-poisoning were widely believed, though unproved. One scholar has aptly compared the tension of the South in 1860 with the "Great Fear" that seized the rural provinces of France in the summer of 1789 when panic spread the word that "the brigands are coming." In that atmosphere the South made the momentous decision that split the Democratic Party at Charleston in April, and before the mood was gone it was debating secession.

In the course of the crisis each of the antagonists, according to the immemorial pattern, had become convinced of the depravity and diabolism of the other. Each believed itself persecuted, menaced. "Let the 'higher law' of abolitionism be met by the 'higher law' of self-preservation," demanded the Richmond *Enquirer*. Lynch law was the only answer to pikes. "What additional insults and outrages *will* arouse it [the North] to assert its rights?" demanded Garrison. And Garrison's opposite number in Mississippi, Albert Gallatin Brown, cried: "Oh, God! To what depths of infamy are we sinking in the South if we allow these things to pass." Paranoia continued to induce counterparanoia, each antagonist infecting the other reciprocally, until the vicious spiral ended in war.

"John Brown's Body" was one of the most popular war songs America ever sang. In singing it millions of people hitherto untouched by the Brown cult became involved in the rites of apotheosis. In joining the worship of the hero, as Professor Malin has said, the victors "partook vicariously in his martyrdom" and furthered the rationalization of their conquest as a holy cause. "It is easy to see what a favorite he will be with history," declared Emerson of John Brown. And Thoreau wrote: "I foresee the time when the painter will paint the scene, the poet will sing it, the historian record it." Never did Transcendentalists utter more inspired prophecy. The poets, the painters, and the historians have been prolific. One scholar, who apologizes for an incomplete task, has studied two hundred and fifty-five poems on John Brown, together with fourteen biographies of the hero and thirty-one plays, eleven short stories, and fifty-eight novels in which he figures. This does not embrace the harvest of the last decade.[1]

Recantations were rare among the original Brown cult. A half

[1] Joy K. Talbert: "John Brown in American Literature," 2 vols., Ph.D. dissertation, University of Kansas (1941).

century after Harper's Ferry, however, William Dean Howells, who said he was one of those who had given the martyr "unqualified reverence and affection," confessed to some misgivings. He reflected that in 1910 there was "a large and largely increasing number of conscientious Americans who regard the prevalent system of capitalism with the abhorrence that Brown felt for the system of Southern slavery." He speculated on what might happen if a "latter-day John Brown" would get into "a mood to go, say, to Pittsburgh, as John Brown of fifty years ago went to Harper's Ferry," arm the proletariat, seize the steel mills, and kidnap or liquidate the millionaires. Recalling what had happened to the anarchists of Haymarket Square, he had his doubts about the experiment.

But Howells did not shake the hero's pedestal. The conservative classes of the North have been remarkably steadfast in their devotion in spite of certain implications of the legend. The Marxian revolutionaries and their fellow travelers, on the other hand, have not overlooked the potentialities of the John Brown heritage. That heritage, as a matter of fact, could be appealed to as readily by conservatives to justify some new antinomian heresy of preventive war or diabolical weapon in a world crusade for capitalism as it could by revolutionaries to justify treason in a crusade for Communism. And the tradition still remains intact, "at once a sacred, a solemn and an inspiring American heritage," according to Oswald Garrison Villard. It is likely to remain unshaken a long time, for it is buttressed by words of some of the most admired of American poets and philosophers.

VII. *Upheaval at Homestead*

In 1886 Andrew Carnegie, with his characteristic optimism, outlined the gains of labor since the eighteenth century. "Now the poorest laborer in America or England," he wrote, "or indeed throughout the civilized world, who can handle a pick or a shovel, stands upon equal terms with the purchaser of his labor." Six years later, at the Carnegie-owned steel mills in Homestead, Pennsylvania, occurred one of the bloodiest strikes in American labor history. It began with a pitched battle between strikers and Pinkerton guards and reached its climax with an attempted assassination. To many Americans who looked with disfavor upon the industrial elite that Tocqueville had warned against many years earlier, the breaking of the strike was an act of capitalistic arrogance. To others the affair at Homestead was the work of anarchists and incendiaries. In Professor Henry David's essay, the strike is presented not only as a crucial event in our industrial history but also as a drama that reflects the deepening conflicts in American life and the tensions and anxieties of the period.

Upheaval at Homestead

Henry David
Professor of History, Queens College

The bitter, exhausting steel strike at Homestead, Pennsylvania, in
1892 is one of the most traumatic episodes in the industrial history
of the United States—a history studded with severe and violent
labor conflicts.

Homestead shocked and dismayed Americans, and won comment abroad. Debated in Congress, it was the subject of House
and Senate investigations. It was discussed in the churches. It was
an issue in the Presidential election of 1892. The strike destroyed
lives and homes, and produced fears, anger, and an unprecedented
sense of unity in the ranks of organized labor. It shattered the
most powerful trade union in the country, and shaped the character of industrial relations in steel for more than four decades.

Among the men in steel, the mortifying memory of Homestead has had a long life. Over two thousand steel workers and
miners, attending a memorial meeting in Homestead itself in
1936, stood with bowed heads in honor of the strikers who died
there forty-four years earlier. Speakers recalled the violence of
the "battle of the barges," and prayed for success in the new
attempt to organize steel. "Let the blood of those labor pioneers
who were massacred here," cried the chairman of the gathering,
"be the seed of this new organization in 1936, may the souls of
the martyrs rest in peace. Amen." This memorial meeting, addressed by the lieutenant governor of the state among others,
marked the first time since the days of the great 1919 steel strike
that a public labor-gathering was permitted in Homestead.

When the struggle was finally called off, after five wearing months, *The New Nation*, journal of Edward Bellamy's Nationalist movement, declared: "The Homestead Strike is dead, but its soul goes marching on. The shots fired that July morning at the Pinkerton barges, like the shots fired at Lexington . . . were 'heard around the world.' The dramatic series of events at [Homestead] . . . roused millions of American citizens, as no amount of books or lectures could have done, to realize that there is an industrial problem which, if it be not soon solved by ballots, will be settled by bullets."

II

The protagonists of the Homestead drama, a great corporation and a powerful union, were products of the tremendous expansion of the iron and steel industry after 1870. Within twenty years, the United States became the world's leading producer of iron and steel. In 1892, a year marked by extended strikes, almost five million tons of steel were manufactured in the United States. Constant innovations in the techniques of production, substantial changes in the character of the labor force, the influence of government policy, and transformations in business organization marked the breathtaking growth of the industries. Technological changes, occurring more rapidly in the younger steel industry than in iron, resulted in increased productivity per worker, the displacement of manual labor, and a decline in the importance of the highly skilled workers, whose strong strategic position had been consistently reflected in the spread between their earnings and those of the unskilled and semiskilled.

Tariff legislation, which rendered competition from abroad ineffective, and pools and price agreements among manufacturers prevented the consequences of declining world production-costs from being felt in American prices. The emergence of large corporations and massive combinations in iron and steel were widely ascribed to the protective tariff. Well before 1890, there were great individual enterprises and combinations of once rival producers in the older manufacturing centers east of the Alleghenies. The formation of the Illinois Steel Company in 1889 produced a giant combination in the Chicago district. Capitalized at twenty-five million dollars, it could claim to be the world's largest steel company in 1890. Its leading rival, shortly to be superior, was the Carnegie enterprise in the Pittsburgh district.

Carnegie Brothers was a leading enterprise in iron manufacturing before it participated in establishing, in 1875, the first Bessemer steel plant in the Pittsburgh district, the Edgar Thomson Steel Company. When Carnegie Brothers & Co., Limited, was organized in 1881 with a capital of five million dollars, it controlled iron and coal deposits in Pennsylvania, the Lucy Furnaces, the Edgar Thomson Steel Works, and the Union Iron Mills. A Bessemer steel plant, built two years earlier by a Pittsburgh group near that city in the little town of Homestead, was acquired by the Carnegie group in October 1883. Business and labor difficulties forced the sale of the Homestead mill, one of the best equipped in the country, to the Carnegies at a price covering only the original cost of the plant and the current value of its land. The notes with which it was purchased were paid off, out of profits, in two years. In 1882, Carnegie bought into the coke enterprise of Henry Clay Frick, who controlled about four fifths of the coal business in the Connellsville district. This move ultimately brought into the Carnegie fold not only an essential raw material, but also the unusual managerial talents of the young, ambitious, and singleminded Frick. Carnegie increased his interest in the coke venture, and soon became the majority stockholder. In 1889, when the H. C. Frick Coke Company boosted its capital to five million dollars, it had almost two thirds of the coking ovens in the Connellsville district.

Significant improvements and additions were made at the Homestead works before its ownership was taken over in 1886 by a separate company, Carnegie, Phipps & Co., comprising the individuals making up Carnegie Brothers. Three years later, Frick became manager of Homestead and chairman of the Carnegie firm. His first major achievement was the purchase, for one million dollars in Carnegie Brothers bonds, of the most advanced steel-rail plant in the country, the Duquesne Steel Works. After 1889, production at the Homestead works rose rapidly. Between the close of that year and May 1892, the gain in output of the works' 32-inch slabbing mill came to 20.6 per cent, of the 119-inch plate mill to 52.3 per cent, and of the open-hearth furnaces, per turn, to 17.5 per cent.

The Carnegie enterprises were brought into a single limited partnership with the formation of the Carnegie Steel Company, Ltd., in July 1892. This was capitalized at twenty-five million dollars and embraced, in addition to iron ore, coal, and coke properties, the Edgar Thomson Works at Braddock and the Edgar Thomson blast furnaces at Bessemer; the Duquesne Steel Works; the Homestead Steel Works; the Beaver Fall Mills (formerly the Hartman Steel Works); and the Lucy Furnaces, the Keystone Bridge Company, and the Upper and Lower Union Mills, all in Pittsburgh. The new consolidation, the largest coke and one of the greatest steel companies in the world, employed thirty thousand workers, with thirteen thousand of these in its iron and steel plants.

Andrew Carnegie, who held 55.3 per cent of the shares of the new limited partnership, placed the direction of its affairs in the hands of the forty-one-year-old Frick, its chairman. The Carnegie enterprises had been lucrative in the past, and Frick's abilities were reflected in increased profits after 1889. In the first year of existence—a year marked by the six-month strike at Homestead and stoppage in other mills—Carnegie Steel produced 877,602 tons of steel, not far from one fifth of the nation's output, and the new consolidation registered four million dollars in profits.

III

In 1892, when Carnegie Steel was formed, the Amalgamated Association of Iron and Steel Workers of America was the dominant labor organization in the industry. Its membership, its financial resources, and its collective agreements gave it a claim to recognition as the strongest union in the country. At its peak at the close of 1891, its two hundred and ninety lodges had over twenty-four thousand taxable members, exclusive of those holding traveling cards. This was roughly one tenth of the total number of workers in unions in the American Federation of Labor, with which the Amalgamated Association affiliated at the close of 1887. Its treasury closed 1891 with a balance of almost $150,000, and its total receipts the following year, out of which it disbursed all but $75,000, topped a quarter of a million.

By 1890, the Amalgamated had probably won greater gains

in collective bargaining than any other union. At its height, it accounted for about one fourth of the one hundred thousand eligible workers in iron and steel. The larger group in its membership consisted of iron workers. In the Pittsburgh district its rolls included nearly half of the eligible steel workers. In steel, the union had made greater gains where the mills had first been organized in their iron-producing days. Where plants began their existence as steel mills, the Amalgamated found organization far more difficult. Thus, of the three major works in the Carnegie domain which were built as steel mills, only one, Homestead, was controlled by the Amalgamated. Duquesne had never been organized at the time of its acquisition in 1890, and the Edgar Thomson works had experienced two brief periods of unionization. West of the Alleghenies, the Amalgamated had secured wage and conditions-of-work agreements of a uniform character for most of the occupations represented by its membership [1] through discussions with an employers' association, the Western Iron Conference. These regional agreements, which pointed toward uniform national wage-scales, constituted a measure of the union's unusual power.

When the Amalgamated Association was formed, in August 1876, roughly a quarter of a century after the first ephemeral organizations appeared among iron workers, a movement to bring the existing national unions of craft workers into a single body had been under way for several years. The oldest and largest of the unions that helped bring the Amalgamated into existence and that provided the core of its membership was the United Sons of Vulcan. Made up of iron puddlers, it had become a national organization in 1862, and it had won union recognition and a sliding-scale contract in Pittsburgh as early as 1865. The impulses to organization in the iron industry which marked the 1860's and '70's produced national unions in the Associated Brotherhood of Iron and Steel Heaters, Rollers and Roughers (1872), and the Iron and Steel Roll Hands of the United States (1873). These and the Sons of Vulcan created the Amalgamated Association. In 1877, the new organization had only 111 lodges and 3,755 members, almost all in iron. Membership grew rapidly up to 1882,

[1] The tin workers were admitted to membership in 1881, and in 1897 the organization's name was changed to the Amalgamated Association of Iron, Steel and Tin Workers.

when the loss of an extended strike resulted in a sharp drop. Four years later, the union entered a five-year period of steady expansion.

The strategic position in the manufacturing process occupied by its highly skilled members, who could not be rapidly replaced, constituted the union's initial source of strength. With the steady changes in technology, it would have been suicidal to restrict membership to the highly skilled alone, and the union admitted four classes of semiskilled workers in 1877. Twelve years later, after the leadership had attempted to open the organization to "all branches of labor directly interested in the manufacture of iron and steel," all workers except common laborers were made eligible for membership. All the lodges, however, did not open their doors. Some resisted the inclusion of semiskilled workers and helpers, even though membership was a function of the national body. Many also discriminated against foreign-born workers and against Negroes, who were made eligible for membership in 1881.

The unwillingness to organize the common laborers arose from a desire to maintain substantial wage differences between the unskilled and the skilled workers and to avoid wage disputes involving easily replaceable workers. The Amalgamated's jurisdictional boundaries excluded large numbers of workers in iron and steel for whom other trade unions existed, such as engineers, bricklayers, carpenters, firemen, and the like. The organized iron and steel workers not in the Amalgamated belonged, for the most part, to the Knights of Labor, which recruited without reference to skill or color. Conflicting jurisdictions invited conflicts between the organizations in the 1880's. In 1888, the Amalgamated prohibited co-membership in the Knights, while the latter established a National Trade District, No. 217, for Iron, Steel and Blast Furnacemen. Jurisdictional rivalry was exacerbated by wage factors, for the members of the K. of L. overwhelmingly worked for hourly and daily rates, while the wages of Amalgamated workers were based on tonnage. The special tax that the Amalgamated imposed to finance the Homestead strike encouraged a dissident group, made up of finishers in Pittsburgh and Youngstown plants, which left to found a rival union. Although the new organization had a very short life, its presence injured the Amalgamated at a critical juncture.

Its membership, the tradition of the earlier organizations, and the character of the industries contributed to the Amalgamated's conservative position with respect to social and economic theory and to its militant concern with wages, hours, conditions of work, and job control. The preamble to its constitution did not quarrel with capitalism or the tendency toward consolidation and combination, and offered organization as the means of maintaining a decent life for the workers in iron and steel. The constitution itself urged the members to protect "the business of all employers" who signed agreements with the union, but warned against construing this to mean permission to depart from the wage scale adopted or from the "established rules [and] customs" governing the work of the various occupations. A "fair remuneration" for labor, said William Weihe, who served nine terms as President of the Amalgamated, was one of its key purposes, and it "watched the [steel] market as closely as" possible in order "to be ready and prepared to meet" employers upon wage issues. It sought the same wage rates for its members, wherever the job and the work were the same. In line with protecting the advantageous position of its skilled workers and their comparatively high earnings, the Amalgamated tried to set limits on output, and resisted, for many occupations, reductions in the length of the working day. It feared that a three-shift day would cut earnings and lead new workers to enter the job market. Wage considerations also made the union reluctant to abandon a seven-day week. On the other hand, because wages were based on tonnage rates, it did not oppose the introduction of improved methods and machinery.

The Amalgamated was the first American union to develop a regular system of annual wage-conferences with employers, resulting in agreements covering wages, working conditions, and limitations on output. The last were justified on the ground that they protected the health of the workers and prevented reductions in wages and the number of workers. All the lodges participated in formulating the piece-rate wage scales, and, when these were finally fixed by the annual convention, they were presented to the leading employers in printed form. In 1890, the scales in steel made up a thirty-four page pamphlet, and those in iron occupied almost as much space. While wages and the related questions of job definition, output standards, and hours were the chief concerns of the Amalgamated, agreements also dealt with grievance procedures and arbitration and conciliation machinery.

Through the job definitions specified in the Amalgamated's collective agreements, the union exercised some control over the number of workers employed. In some instances, and this is reported of Homestead as well as other mills, local lodges were strong enough to determine employment and discharge policies, and even to press grievance cases of little substance. Where the lodges were powerful, they tried to maintain old tonnage wage-rates, even though technological innovations brought sizable increases in output. Employers were irritated by such limitations on managerial prerogative, but they also saw benefits in the union's encouragement of uniform wages, rules, and working conditions. The sliding-scale wage structure and the standardized rates resulting from the collective agreements were stabilizing factors. Employers also found advantages in the regular conferences with the union and the machinery that developed for adjusting disputes. Before 1900, employers did not seriously object to output restrictions.

Until 1892, the Amalgamated observed its contracts with great fidelity. Although it was careful to build substantial strike-fund reserves, and paid strike benefits of four dollars a week, it was responsible for few work stoppages. After 1890, developments in the industry, the power wielded by the union, and the desire of management to control without qualification the conditions and terms of employment, particularly in the case of Carnegie Steel, brought a significant change in employer attitudes.

IV

Early in April 1892, two months before the three-year contract with the Amalgamated covering the Homestead plant was due to expire and before the final launching of Carnegie Steel, Andrew Carnegie drafted a notice addressed to its workers, which he submitted to Frick. This notice stated that the formation of the new consolidation forced the management to adopt a uniform policy toward union recognition. "As the vast majority of our employees are Non-Union," wrote Carnegie, "the firm has decided that the minority must give way to the majority. These works will necessarily be Non-Union after the expiration of the present agreement." No reduction of wages would follow, for Carnegie represented the rates at the non-union Edgar Thomson and Duquesne works as more advantageous than at unionized Homestead, but he did admit that improvements at the latter plant would bring temporary reductions in the number employed. He closed with the pious observation that the refusal to deal with the union was "not taken in any spirit of hostility to labor organizations, but every man will see that the firm cannot run Union and Non-Union. It must be one or the other." Carnegie also proposed, if Frick agreed to announce that Homestead would no longer be a union mill, that it would be wise to "roll a large lot of plates ahead, which can be finished" in the event of a strike. Wage discussions with the union had been initiated early in the year, and Frick disregarded Carnegie's suggestion.

Had Andrew Carnegie, whom Mark Twain described as "the Human Being Unconcealed," never publicized the sympathetic attitudes he struck on the labor question and unionism, this proposed notice would have trivial significance. But his tender concern for humanity, his philanthropies, and his desire to improve the lot of the laboring classes had not been kept secret. He had spoken warmly of the glory and importance of manual toil, and urged that workers be given a larger share of the wealth they helped create. He had preached the ideal of copartnership between employees and employers. Two widely publicized articles in *The Forum* in April and August of 1886 had been exceptional in their sympathy with unionism and collective bargaining. Declaring that there were few offenses as heinous as strikebreaking, Carnegie proposed to amend the Decalogue by adding the injunction, "Thou Shalt Not Take Thy Neighbor's Job!"

In his *Autobiography*, Carnegie later asserted that he had never employed a strikebreaker, and described his method for settling disputes: "My idea is that the Company should be known as determined to let the men at the works stop work; that it will confer freely with them and wait patiently until they decide to return to work, never thinking of trying new men—never." Up to the Homestead strike, declared Carnegie, his companies had never had a "serious" labor dispute, and he took great pride in the friendly and understanding "relations between ourselves and our men" for which he had been responsible for twenty-six years. There was, he observed, more than "the reward that comes from feeling that you and your employees are friends. . . . I believe that higher wages to men who respect their employers and are happy and content is a good investment, yielding, indeed, big dividends."

Carnegie's ambiguity makes it uncertain whether he really approved of unions which reached beyond the local plant. He showed little sympathy for organizations of larger scope, such as the Knights of Labor or the national affiliates of the A.F.L., but was, perhaps, prepared to live with a fragmented unionism. The history of industrial relations in the Carnegie enterprises before 1892 certainly is at odds with his pronouncements on labor questions.

As early as 1867, Carnegie joined with other iron manufacturers to import foreign workers when iron puddlers struck against wage cuts. Unionism was discouraged at the Edgar Thomson works, where organization first appeared in 1882. At the Beaver Fall mills two years later, the Amalgamated was defeated in a sharp struggle during which scabs from outside the district were used.

At Edgar Thomson, preceding the installation of new machinery early in 1885, Carnegie's famous superintendent, Captain William R. Jones, dismissed virtually the whole work force. When operations were resumed, the men were faced with a heavy cut in wages and a return to a twelve-hour shift. K. of L. and Amalgamated membership was slight, and the workers were forced to accept the company's terms. Captain Jones's refusal to bargain led to the disappearance of the Amalgamated lodges at Braddock. Early in 1886, another dispute there led to the discharge of seven hundred workers and their replacement by non-union labor. Further improvements at Edgar Thomson in 1887 were followed by discharges and a cut in wages. Four local assemblies of the Knights attempted unsuccessfully to negotiate a wage scale. Carnegie capped a display of seeming willingness to compromise with the declaration that the mill would operate on a non-union basis, and that the signing of a non-union pledge would be a condition of employment. Offers of conferences by the Knights were rejected, and Captain Jones resumed operations with scabs. The Knights finally, in May 1888, called off their strike, which began early in the year. This conflict terminated unionism at Braddock.

During the bitter strike against the Frick and other coke companies in the Connellsville district in 1887, which saw the use of Pinkerton guards as well as strikebreakers, Carnegie intervened from Scotland. He directed Frick to settle on the strikers' terms. Piqued, Frick offered to resign from the firm. The other operators won their battle with the K. of L. assemblies and the Miners' and Mine Laborers' Amalgamated Association. Carnegie's move was not prompted by sympathy with the strikers. His concern was with a supply of coke to keep the furnaces going. When the wage scale, higher for their workers than for others, came up for renewal in 1891, Carnegie and Frick followed a different course. The demand for steel was poor, and there was enough coke on hand to risk a showdown. Fully protected by the sheriff, and employing scabs, the H. C. Frick Coke Company won the bitter strike that ensued.

At the Homestead plant the Amalgamated made substantial gains after 1881, and had eight lodges a decade later. Wages had been cut severely in 1884, but there was no dispute until five years later, when the introduction of new machinery was followed by the offer of a new agreement by Carnegie, Phipps & Co. This reduced wages for all classes of workers (roughly to the tune of twenty-five per cent), set January 1, 1892, as the termination date of the new three-year scale, and required that each worker sign an individual agreement. The company's offer, made in May 1889, not only departed drastically from the agreement in effect, but also meant the repudiation of collective bargaining. The proposed scale based wages upon the selling price of 4 x 4 steel billets, with the proviso that rates were not to be affected if the price of steel fell below the minimum of twenty-five dollars per ton. The six Amalgamated lodges then in existence at Homestead rejected the proposal, and in June carried the issue before the union's convention, which designated a bargaining committee. Conferences with the company proved fruitless, and, when July 1 arrived without agreement on a new scale, the Homestead workers struck.

Carnegie was in Scotland during the strike, but, before leaving the United States, he had planned the company's course. Conduct of the strike fell to William L. Abbott, chairman of the company. Detectives were employed to report on the actions of the Homestead workers, and the company tried to bring strike-breakers into the plant under protection of the sheriff. Mass picketing prevented this move as well as a subsequent attempt by deputies to occupy the mill. This display of resolute resistance was free of violence. Reports of sympathetic strike votes against other Carnegie plants and of strike preparations by employees of the H. C. Frick Coke Company and of the railroads handling Carnegie products probably encouraged the reopening of negotiations. These issued in a settlement, before the last week in July, that constituted a substantial victory for the Amalgamated.

The new three-year agreement embodied the sliding scale suggested by the company, but it permitted wage reductions in only three departments of the mill, and set June 30, 1892, as the termination date. It also provided for standard union rules, grievance procedures, and a crude seniority system. Carnegie signified his displeasure with the conduct of the strike and its outcome to Abbott, bemoaning the fact that they had settled with "law breakers." Homestead operated under this agreement until the issues that had been contested in 1889 were reopened three years later.

V

Homestead, some ten miles east of Pittsburgh on the left bank of the Monongahela River and about a mile below Braddock's crossing, had been founded in 1820. Containing less than six hundred people as late as 1879, it was the creation of the steel plant located there. By 1892 its population had climbed to between eleven and twelve thousand, and it displayed the characteristic ugliness and vitality of the steel town. The plant, with its normal output of twenty-five thousand tons a month, and almost four thousand workers, most of whom were foreign-born, set the terms of life for Homestead. Its workers did not regard themselves as badly off. Many owned their own homes. Labor in the mills was exhausting, reported one worker, but it enabled most of the workers to maintain a decent physical existence. He also spoke of those who were reduced to a life of grim "misfortune" by the many mill accidents. On June 1, 1892, there were employee savings amounting to $140,000 deposited with the company. Visitors were struck by the town's drabness and by its many saloons.

In January 1892, the management requested the eight lodges of the Amalgamated Association to prepare a new wage-scale. Several fruitless conferences followed the lodge's proposal to maintain the existing schedules, and at the end of May, Frick directed the superintendent of the Homestead works, John A. Potter, to present scales similar to those in effect at Edgar Thomson and Duquesne. These would have substantially reduced the earnings of the Homestead tonnage workers. Frick required a reply by June 24, and stated that after that the management would bargain individually and not collectively with the members of the Amalgamated, which opened its convention in Pittsburgh June 7. The convention approved a schedule of steel-mill scales and appointed a committee to negotiate with the Carnegie Company. On June 23, that committee conferred with Frick and Potter.

While Frick had given no public intimation that he regarded union recognition as a crucial issue, Carnegie, in letters from England, indicated his desire to operate Homestead as a non-union plant and to be relieved from the union working rules. The advantage earlier gained from encouraging uniform wage scales through collective bargaining had served its purpose. Frick did not share Carnegie's eagerness for a showdown with the union, but he was quite prepared to hold out for a settlement on his own terms.

Before arranging for what turned out to be the final conference with the union committee, Frick had been assured by the Pinkerton agency, in reply to his own inquiry, that it could supply an adequate number of men to guard the Homestead plant in the event of a strike. Earlier, a three-mile-long board fence topped by barbed wire had been built around the plant. Regularly spaced three-inch holes in the fence were later described by Frick as designed for observation purposes. To the workers, they seemed suited to a different use. At the extremes of the mill there had been erected platforms on which searchlights were to be mounted.

Three issues occupied the June 23 conference: the minimum selling-price of steel upon which the quarterly sliding-scale was to be based; the termination date of the new contract; and the tonnage rates for the open-hearth plants and 32-inch and 119-inch mills, which would immediately affect the wages of 325 workers. Wage agreements with the other employees were not at issue.

Frick wanted the sliding-scale base reduced to twenty-two dollars a ton for 4 x 4 billets, arguing that steel had been selling for less than the old minimum of twenty-five dollars since February, and that wages which were not limited by a maximum should also reflect declining prices. The union reduced its minimum from twenty-five to twenty-four dollars, and Frick increased his to twenty-three dollars during the conference. Frick insisted on a December 31 termination date for the contract, contending that this would facilitate contracts with steel purchasers. The union, prepared to sign a three- to five-year agreement, but anxious to avoid midwinter strikes, held firm for a contract running to June 30, the date in effect for a dozen years.

Wages at Homestead ranged from a low of fourteen cents an hour for common labor to over fourteen dollars a day for a few highly skilled tonnage-workers. The proposed tonnage-rate reductions were justified on the ground that recent improvements had significantly increased output and that contemplated changes would boost it further. Of the 325 workers involved, 280 would be affected only by tonnage-rate changes, while the others would also suffer from the lower sliding-scale minimum. On the average, wages would be cut by eighteen per cent. A tableman estimated that his monthly wage would drop from $130 to $92. For some workers, a thirty-five per cent cut was at stake. It was widely believed that the new scales would soon be followed by wage cuts in the other departments and by reductions in the size of the work force. Frick later testified that he did not intend to reduce other rates until contemplated improvements were installed. The company's willingness to sign agreements with hourly-rate workers, its acceptance of the Amalgamated scale at a Pittsburgh mill, the building of the fence at Homestead, and other evidences persuaded the workers that Frick was preparing for a strike.

The conference on the 23rd ended in a stalemate, but the union expected that negotiations would continue. Two days later the management announced that there would be no further conferences, and Frick wrote to Robert A. Pinkerton requesting three hundred guards "for service at a Homestead mill as a measure of precaution against interference with our plan to start operation of the works on July 6, 1892." Frick asked for arms to be provided for the Pinkertons, and indicated that arrangements were being made to deputize them once they reached the plant. He patently knew that the Pinkertons were detested and feared, and that their arrival at Homestead was likely to cause trouble, for he directed that they be brought to the plant with the greatest secrecy. Frick later explained that his doubts concerning the ability of the sheriff to maintain order and protect property, based on what had happened during the 1889 strike, led him to employ the Pinkerton guards.

On July 28, the management shut down the armor-plate mill in the open-hearth department, and locked out eight hundred men. That night effigies of Frick and Potter were strung up in Homestead. On the following morning, three thousand workers turned out at the mass meeting called by the Amalgamated lodges and took a series of actions that in effect replied to the lockout by a strike of the entire work force. A secret meeting of the eight lodges established a forty-member Advisory Committee, headed by Hugh O'Donnell, to conduct the strike. Among his chief lieutenants were John McLuckie, Burgess of Homestead borough, Hugh Ross, and William T. Roberts. The Committee's tasks were eased by a remarkable display of worker solidarity. All of the workers, many of whom were non-English speaking Slavs and Hungarians, stood as one with the 325 who were directly involved in the wage and contract issues. Organizing its forces along military lines, the Advisory Committee set up an around-the-clock watch on all the approaches to Homestead to prevent strikebreakers from being brought in. By July 2, all the strikers were paid off and formally discharged. Wages were no longer the issue. Union recognition and collective bargaining were at stake. Announcing that there would be no further negotiations and that the plant would operate non-union, the management invited its former employees to sign individual contracts. This offer won no takers. When the struggle was more than two months old, only about three hundred former strikers had returned to work.

On July 4, Frick formally requested Sheriff William H. McCleary of Allegheny County "to protect" the company in its "property" and "in its free use and enjoyment." A week before the strike began, the company's attorney, Philander C. Knox, asked the sheriff whether he would deputize the Pinkertons when they arrived at the plant. McCleary refused to commit himself on his future course. The Advisory Committee's offer to the sheriff to guard the plant was rejected as a device for barring non-union men. When McCleary subsequently appeared at the mill with a group of deputies, the Advisory Committee permitted them to determine that everything was in order, but not to remain.

VI

Only the highlights of the strike, which continued until November, can be indicated. It is even impossible here to do justice to the events of July 6, which catapulted Homestead into fame. About two o'clock that morning, three hundred Pinkerton agents were loaded on two barges near Pittsburgh to be towed up the Monongahela River. Due to the strikers' warning system, the flotilla's movement was known long before it approached Homestead about 4 A.M. It was not at first known that the barges carried hated Pinkertons. The news flew through the town that scabs were arriving, and strikers, accompanied by their wives and children, raced out in the foggy morning to prevent them from entering the plant by the landing at its rear. The barges tied up there before the townspeople broke through the fence blocking their approach to the wharf. The Pinkertons' attempt to land, which made known the cargo of the barges, was resisted. In the exchange of shots both sides suffered casualties. After the tug steamed off to carry several wounded Pinkertons back to Pittsburgh, the barges were in effect trapped off the landing. Another attempt to land before eight o'clock set off an exchange of gunfire lasting several hours. As the hours passed, recruits came into Homestead to strengthen the strikers, as did firearms and ammunition from Pittsburgh. Workers elsewhere wired offers of assistance, and from Texas there came a proffer of artillery.

The strikers early brought into play a twenty-pound brass breechloader, used by the town in holiday celebrations, and later employed a smaller cannon belonging to the Homestead Grand Army Post. Neither was effective against the barges. Sticks of dynamite hurled against them did little damage, and the attempt to set fire to the barges with a burning raft failed. The strikers set fire to oil and waste loaded on a railroad car and sent it down the tracks into the water, but it did not reach the barges. Later they unsuccessfully tried to destroy the barges with burning oil on the river.

The Pinkertons, who harassed their besiegers with rifle and revolver fire, made their first truce offer at noon. Three hours later, at a hastily called mass meeting, Weihe, other Amalgamated officials, and O'Donnell pleaded with the strikers to permit the Pinkertons to land in safety. At the same time the Pinkertons decided that they had had enough, and at four o'clock the battle terminated, with the understanding that the Pinkertons were to receive, after being disarmed, safe passage out of Homestead. After they came ashore, the barges were set on fire, and the pledge of safety was violated. As the Pinkertons were marching into town between lines of enraged strikers and their wives and children, they were violently assaulted, and about half their number suffered injuries. The battle on the riverfront brought death to three Pinkertons and ten strikers. Some thirty Pinkertons were hospitalized, and an undetermined number of strikers were wounded.

The sheriff's frantic telegrams to Governor Robert E. Pattison for assistance brought, not the militia, but criticism of the sheriff. The governor even observed that bloodshed could have been avoided if the sheriff had accepted the Advisory Committee's proposal to guard the plant. Subsequent pleas by McCleary, who was unable to raise a deputy force, reports that the Advisory Committee was in complete control of the town, and the advice of a National Guard officer, whom he had dispatched to Homestead, finally led the governor to intervene. Late in the night of July 10, Pattison ordered Major General George R. Snowden to call out the entire militia force. Twelve hours later, the eight thousand officers and men of one of the country's best National Guard divisions began to march on Homestead. The Advisory Committee planned a formal reception for the troops, which was frustrated by their sudden appearance early in the morning of the 12th. Major General Snowden, who later declared that "revolution was proclaimed and entered upon" in Homestead, curtly refused the committee's pledge of assistance in maintaining order.

Immediately after the militia invested the town, the management took possession of the plant, and prepared to resume operations with non-union men. The furnaces were lit again for the first time on July 15, but no steel was made for a long time. The company experienced great difficulty in securing skilled workers. The strikebreakers lived at first as virtual prisoners within the plant, where they were housed and fed. Only later, after the sheriff built an adequate force of deputies, did the scabs venture to leave the mill and move about in Homestead.

The struggle at Homestead set off sympathetic strikes at other Carnegie plants. The first occurred at the Union Iron Mills on July 14, where the men declared that they would not return to work until the Homestead dispute was settled. The plant shortly began to operate with the use of strikebreakers. On July 15, the men at the Beaver Fall mills refused to work until the company opened negotiations with the Homestead strikers. "I can say with the greatest emphasis," Frick had declared a week earlier, "that under no circumstances will we have any further dealings with the Amalgamated Association as an organization." He warned that unless the Beaver Fall workers returned within a week he would regard as void the contract they had just signed, and replace them with non-union men. This strike lasted four months before it was officially called off by the three Amalgamated lodges at the Beaver Fall mills.

At non-union Duquesne, the union undertook an organizing campaign. On July 23, following appeals by Homestead strikers, its members struck. Within a week the mill was operating again. After a state militia regiment was dispatched there from Homestead, following an outburst of violence that local authorities could not contain, most of the old work force returned. Before the middle of August, unionism at Duquesne died. In each of these strikes, Carnegie Steel was able to secure strikebreakers and more than adequate police protection.

On the same day that the militia invested Homestead, a special five-member subcommittee of the House Committtee on the Judiciary began to take testimony in Pittsburgh on the employment of Pinkertons and other private guards, and on the strike. Tom

Watson, Georgia's Populist Representative, had been pressing a bill since February to regulate the employment of such private police. The events of the preceding day led to the rapid adoption on July 7 of a resolution providing for the investigation. Voting was long delayed on Senate resolutions to investigate "the Homestead riot" and the use of private armed guards. Not until August 2 did the upper house provide for an inquiry by a seven-member select committee into "the employment of armed bodies of men" in labor disputes. That committee did not begin to hear witesses for another month and a half.

The House committee-hearings stimulated interest in the issues of the strike. Alexander Berkman's attempt on Frick's life on July 23 focused the nation's attention upon Homestead, but tended to obscure these issues. Berkman, a young Russian-born revolutionary anarchist who had been active in the New York movement, was inspired by the strike. Frick, a symbol of capitalist oppression, seemed to Berkman the ideal object for a terroristic act that would fulfill the theory of propaganda-by-deed. He gained access to Frick's Pittsburgh office with the excuse that he could provide strikebreakers. Before he was overpowered, Berkman inflicted two serious, but not fatal, bullet wounds upon Frick and repeatedly stabbed him with a sharpened file. While the assault was universally condemned, a number of journals pointed out that the deed had been committed by an irresponsible person wholly unconnected with the strike. Others charged that Berkman's act followed naturally from the resort to force by the Homestead strikers. The Advisory Committee promptly published a resolution condemning Berkman's "unlawful act" and extending its "sympathy" to Frick. The deed appears to have had no discernible influence on the outcome of the strike.

One of the militiamen in Homestead, W. L. Iams, was chatting with his fellows when the news of the attempted murder reached them. He shouted: "Three cheers for the man who shot Frick!" Ordered to apologize by his commanding officer, Iams, having explained that he disliked Frick, refused. He was imprisoned and, the following day, strung up by his thumbs to force an apology. This punishment failed to accomplish its purpose, for Iams fainted and was ordered cut down by the regimental surgeon. Without a trial, Iams was found by Major General Snowden to have committed "treason." Disgraced and drummed out of camp, Iams was dishonorably discharged from the militia, a punishment that involved disfranchisement. "His conduct," declared Snowden, "was that of aiding, abetting, and giving comfort to our enemy." There was a sharp outcry against the "brutal and barbaric" treatment Iams had suffered, and several journals called attention to the civil-rights issues involved in the episode. Concerned lest "this atrocious blow at personal immunity may be condoned on account of the unworthiness of the sufferer," the *Albany Law Journal* urged a court test of the authority of National Guard officers.

The spirit shown by the strikers, the support from organized labor, the degree of favorable public sentiment, and the inability of the management to secure enough skilled strikebreakers, encouraged the Advisory Committee to optimism. But by mid-October there were some two thousand men at work in the plant, about one fifth of them former employees, and it was clear that the strike was lost. A month later, the mechanics and laborers asked the union to terminate the struggle. They had stood firm up to then, but the refusal to call the strike off sent them back to the mill for jobs. Two days later, November 20, at a meeting of three hundred Amalgamated members, a resolution to declare the mill open was carried by a slight margin. The next day, the Advisory Committee disbanded.

The struggle cost three fifths of the strikers their jobs, and meant a wage loss of about $1,250,000. Without contributions of money, food, and clothing from the business people of Homestead and the Pittsburgh area, and assistance from the organized labor movement, it would have been far more difficult for the strikers to have held out as long as they did. The state met a charge of more than $440,000 to maintain the militia at Homestead for a period of ninety-five days. While the collapse of the strike was cheered in many newspapers, it was also observed that Carnegie Steel did not merit congratulations for the victory it had scored.

VII

The events of July 6 produced responses of shock and disbelief. A pitched battle between workers and Pinkertons seemed inconceivable. Sympathy with the underdog and strong distaste for the use of armed private police appeared in expressions of applause for the courage displayed by the workers. The employment of Pinkertons played a major role in the widespread criticism of management policy responsible for the conflict. The Pinkertons, said Senator Daniel W. Voorhees, were worse than "Hessians," and the strikers who had killed some of them were clearly acting under the "law of self-defense. . . . My only regret is that Carnegie had not been at their head. . . ." He spoke of the arrogance and "bloated" wealth of the members of Carnegie's "class" who believed that they were justified in employing "a private army . . . to ride over American citizens and to dispossess and unhouse men, women, and children. . . ."

The Democratic Chicago *Globe*, quick to exploit the strike politically, declared that the Pinkertons, no better than hired assassins, were not "entitled to the privileges of civilized warfare." No other country, remarked Roger A. Pryor, exposed "the lives of citizens to the murderous assaults of hireling assassins," and others protested against a system that assigned to private armed bodies a role in the preservation of order. To the Nashville *American* this was "un-American," and *Harper's Weekly*, which condemned the strikers, held that the nation could not permit the Pinkertons to operate "without confessing to a condition of things among us which we must be ashamed of. . . . A truly civilized community," it declared on July 23, "will not have to look to a Pinkerton force to do under private pay that which is obviously the business of the regularly constituted authorities." A considered review of the strike by the *New England Magazine* concluded that Carnegie Steel's decision to employ Pinkertons instead of calling upon the state authorities could not have been made in any other land, and warranted prosecution.

The Populists, who had earlier attacked Pinkertonism, sharpened their demand for the immediate abolition of such private bodies. The preamble to the 1892 Omaha platform of the People's Party referred to "a hireling standing army, unrecognized by our laws," which had been established to shoot down workers. The platform's sixth resolution, drafted early in July, condemned "the maintenance of a large standing army of mercenaries, known as the Pinkerton system, as a menace to our liberty," and called for its extinction. The *National Economist*, a major Populist journal, echoed this demand, as did state Populist conventions. In Populist-controlled Colorado the governor refused to renew the license of the Denver office of the Pinkerton agency.

Those journals of opinion which saw the strikers' lawlessness and their seizure of company property as the crucial issues hastened to defend Carnegie Steel. The New York *Sun* declared, on July 13, that the indefensible, forcible resistance offered to the Pinkertons was in violent contrast to the traditional American respect for the law. That conservative Democratic paper, together with other journals, found that foreign-born workers, alien to American ways, were responsible for the violence at Homestead, and approved Carnegie's methods "to protect his property and his rights."

Harper's Weekly was critical of Pinkertonism, but it saw in the resort to force by the strikers an assault upon property and the public order, in the course of which "murder and robbery" had been committed by the workers. Homestead, in its eyes, constituted "a crisis in which civil government and the order of society are at stake." The *Railway World* thought that it was imperative "to teach the lawless element of Homestead a lesson," regardless of the method employed, and *The Albany Law Journal* urged the state of Pennsylvania "to put down such outbreaks by the strong hand whenever they occur. . . ." The New York *Sun* called for the punishment of the "conspirators, the murderers, all the criminals who had been concerned in this outbreak. . . ."

The Nation defended the use of Pinkertons on the ground that they did not carry arms for an unlawful purpose and showed no hostility to constituted authority. An article in *The Engineering Magazine* contended: "The 'rights' arrogated by labor unions can be conceded only in so far as they do not clash with the fundamental rights of the individual. On no plea may ex-employees take possession of their late employer's works. If such a thing as human property exists, then the Carnegies own Homestead. . . ." *The Nation* found it strange that the defenders of property were assailed by the press and political demagogues, while "the rioters at Homestead" were the objects of sympathy. In no previous large-scale industrial conflict, it noted, had the workers received so much support from "the classes socially above them. . . ."

In the attacks upon the Carnegie management, Frick was charged with responsibility for the bloodletting at Homestead, and with inhuman ruthlessness. The Chicago *Herald*, linking the strike and high protection, as did a large section of the Democratic press, remarked: "Slavery had its Legrees. Protection has its Fricks." It was widely observed that had the Carnegie Company not tried to introduce the Pinkertons into the plant, the workers would not have been driven to an act of desperation. The company's avowed determination to break the union was frequently held to be adequate ground for the workers' resistance. On July 19, the New York *World* condemned Frick's ban on unionism as "the attempt of an arbitrary and tyrannical man to impose his will upon men as free as himself."

Carnegie was unkindly reminded of his pronouncements in *The Forum* and elsewhere. The Pittsburgh *Leader*, which spoke of his "baronial absenteeism," observed that the Carnegie of the *Forum* articles was "extinct like the dodo." Several other papers joined the Brooklyn *Eagle* in doubting that it was necessary for him to cut wages in order to escape the poorhouse. The St. Louis *Post-Dispatch* found Carnegie's flight to Scotland cowardly. By contrast, Frick was "a brave man." Even a minor "spasm of consistency on Carnegie's part," remarked the Detroit *Evening News*, would have avoided the difficulties at Homestead. His contention that the workers' right "to combine and to form trade unions is no less sacred than the right of the manufacturer to enter into associations and conferences," was contrasted with his company's conduct by George Gunton, editor of the *Social Economist*, and others. The organs of radical and revolutionary groups not only applauded the strikers, but also claimed that the episode demonstrated the soundness of their particular contentions. The New York *Standard*, voice of the Henry George movement, asserted that Homestead validated its view that a social upheaval was unavoidable if the exploitation of the working-class was not brought to an end. Speaking for the Bellamy Nationalists, *The New Nation* found proof in the strike that an industrial system was indefensible if it failed to provide the opportunity to work to those who were willing. Socialist papers declared that Homestead destroyed the myth of partnership between labor and capital, and revealed the ruthlessness of capitalism and the truth of the class struggle. The episode made clear, declared *Twentieth Century*, that justice and law were different, and that unlawful resistance was justifiable to prevent the second from destroying the first. Socialist organs called upon workers to learn from the Homestead strikers how to secure their rights, but warned, as did the New York *Volkszeitung*, that nothing was to be gained by destroying property. Interviewed by the New York *Tribune* on July 7, Daniel de Leon, leader of the Socialist Labor Party, pointed out that workers had also been shot down in free-trade countries, and the cause of Homestead was not high protection. It was a manifestation of "the old struggle between capital and labor, which has been carried on and will be carried on in all parts of the world for a long time."

The events of July 6 fired the tiny anarchist movement with enthusiasm. Its members, who had regarded American workers as hopelessly bourgeois, now sensed the existence of an innate revolutionary spirit. Johann Most wrote in *Freiheit* that "the *action* of the 6th of July . . . was simply glorious, epoch-making, worthy of comparison with the greatest rebel deeds of heroism of all countries and all times." To the outstanding philosophical individualist anarchist, Benjamin R. Tucker, Homestead confirmed the truth of his central contention "that social questions cannot be settled by force." Tucker's sympathies were with the strikers, but he insisted that "the annihilation of neither party can secure justice, and that the only effective sweeping will be that which clears from the statute book every restriction of the freedom of the market."

Homestead was decisive in the developing of a broad and sympathetic concern with labor problems in the Protestant churches. The majority of the religious press condemned the strikers, assailed the union, and justified the employment of Pinkertons. Yet, there was Protestant sentiment on the other side, and a few journals assumed a position of neutrality. Walter Rauschenbusch observed in 1893 that he knew of only one Baptist paper that appeared to be fair to labor. A significant number of clerics, however, were prepared to take their stand with the workers. *The Christian Advocate* lamented the nature of their sermons inspired by the Homestead episode. Among these clerics were leaders in the growing Social Gospel movement. The Reverend W. D. P. Bliss of Boston, for example, asserted that the strike "has thrilled the rank of labor with new life, courage, new manliness. Workmen have met and defeated the . . . hirelings of capital, and for their victory we need to thank God."

A Philadelphia pastor, the Reverend C. H. Woolston, declared:

"Let the guns that flashed at Homestead proclaim that in this country slavery is over for white and black." On the Sunday after July 6, the Reverend Charles G. Ames of Boston pleaded for sympathetic understanding of the workers' "causes of . . . discontent. To every man whose daily bread comes from his daily earnings, the question of employment is simply a question of life and death, and any reduction of wages seems to push them towards the brink of misery and serfdom." At a mass meeting held at Homestead on July 14, the Right Reverend Bishop Fallows of the Episcopal Diocese of Chicago counseled the workers to a course of moderation, but also declared that they had dealt the Pinkerton system a death blow. Homestead was the first strike to produce a significant division in articulate Protestant opinion on a labor dispute of national importance, and the strike stimulated serious examination in the churches of the issues involved in industrial conflicts.

VIII

The weak trade-union movement of the country, which numbered some four hundred thousand members, responded with singular vigor to developments at Homestead. The repulse of the Pinkertons electrified organized labor, which sensed the larger import of the strike, as did Henry Demarest Lloyd. He early wrote to Samuel Gompers: "This can be made the most important conflict of the history of organized labour. . . . Carnegie can be used to teach the Captains of Industry that men who treat their 'brother' labourers like sponges to be squeezed and rats to be shot cannot continue doing business in that style in this country."

A Homestead worker told the Senate investigating committee that workingmen were profoundly disturbed by the anti-unionism of large firms in the Pittsburgh area, and felt, in consequence, "that the only right they can enjoy has been taken away from them." Terence Vincent Powderly, General Master Workman of the Knights of Labor, declared: "To accept without inquiring the why or wherefore, such terms and wages as the Carnegie Steel Company saw fit to offer would stamp the brand of inferiority upon the workmen of Homestead. . . ." At a mass meeting in Homestead on August 12, Gompers honored the strikers for refusing "to bow down" before Carnegie.

Organized labor at least condoned, when it did not hail, the pitched battle with the Pinkertons. The *Journal of the Knights of Labor* asserted that "labor is everywhere and at all times justified in meeting forcible aggression by forcible resistance whenever it can do so with a reasonable hope of success." The *Iron Molders' Journal* hoped that those responsible for the brazen crime of hiring a body of armed men to shoot down workers daring "to disagree with their employers and stand out for their rights" would be suitably punished. It would have been cowardly, observed John Swinton, not to have resisted Carnegie. A Detroit worker remarked: "I consider the action of the men resorting to arms and shooting the Pinkertons was perfectly justifiable." Eugene V. Debs, then editor of the *Locomotive and Firemen's Magazine* and not yet a Socialist, declared that the offense of the Amalgamated lay in its refusal to "submit to robbery," and that Frick had planned to reduce the workers of Homestead to the condition of "serfs."

The *Journal of the Knights of Labor* reported on August 18 that it lacked the space to reprint "the scores of resolutions" adopted by labor bodies assailing "the Pinkerton organization" and condemning Frick and Carnegie. The Amalgamated was a rival organization, but the Knights, now reduced to a puny membership of eighty thousand, gave it earnest support. K. of L. bodies held picnics to raise relief funds for the strikers, and the annual General Assembly of the Knights, held in St. Louis in November, voted to issue an appeal for the relief of "the distressed people of Homestead. . . ." A circular to the membership was followed by a more public appeal. By February 1893, the Knights had received some six hundred dollars for the relief of the Homestead strikers, and for the copper-mining strikers at Coeur d'Alene, Idaho.[2]

Local labor organizations quickly responded to the news of July 6. A sizable "indignation meeting" was organized in Philadelphia for the 8th. Eleven days later, the Chicago Trades and Labor Assembly demanded that Frick and Robert Pinkerton be

---

[2] The unpublished Powderly Papers contain information on K. of L. relief activities. See, for example, D. F. Lawlor to Powderly, December 12, 1892; Powderly to J. J. O'Brien, January 6, 1893; A. W. Wright to Powderly, February 2, 1893.

arrested and charged with murder. Workers there and in Columbus, Ohio, formally protested the employment of Pinkertons. The
South Side Glassworker's Union of Pittsburgh, supported by
other organizations, unsuccessfully demanded that the city refuse
Carnegie's gift of one million dollars for a free library. The Iron
Molders, meeting in annual convention at St. Paul, adopted a resolution sympathizing with the Homestead strikers and condemning
the Carnegie company.

There was no hesitation in placing the limited resources of the
young American Federation of Labor at the disposal of the Amalgamated, one of its wealthiest and largest affiliates. The A.F.L.'s
membership stood at some 255,000, and its total receipts in 1892
barely reached sixteen thousand dollars. By comparison, the efforts of the Federation and of Samuel Gompers, its dedicated
president, to sustain the Amalgamated Association and the strikers
were prodigious. As early as June 29, Gompers directed an A.F.L.
organizer in Detroit to do what he could to prevent the Carnegie
company from securing potential strikebreakers there. During
the first week of July, he arranged to post pickets at labor agencies in New York, Brooklyn, and elsewhere to discourage workers from taking employment in Homestead. Later, he warned
William Weihe by telegram that pipefitters, bricklayers, and riv-
eters hired in New York were scheduled to leave for Homestead.
The events of July 6 led Gompers to propose a meeting of the
Federation's Executive Council in Pittsburgh on the 12th, but
Weihe thought that this was not advisable. Gompers then offered
to convene the council whenever and wherever the Amalgamated
desired, and placed himself at Weihe's disposal in supporting the
cause of the men on strike. He urged A.F.L. officials to arrange
protest meetings. He sought to prevent immigrant workers from
being brought into Homestead as strikebreakers. Outraged by the
use of the Pinkertons, Gompers asserted that the repulse of the
"gang of mercenaries" in "the noble and manly defense of their
lives and families by the strikers" had touched "the hearts and
consciences of the American people."

At the close of July, on Weihe's suggestion, the A.F.L. Executive Council promptly approved the issuance of a circular letter
appealing for assistance to the strikers. Two weeks later, the
council and officials of the Amalgamated met in Pittsburgh to
consider additional means of insuring victory. No positive action

was taken on the major move considered, an A.F.L. boycott of all Carnegie products. The Amalgamated was reluctant to take a step that would compel its members working under agreements with other firms to refuse to work on Carnegie-produced materials.

During September and October, Gompers, distressed because the length of the strike and other developments on the labor front were pushing Homestead into the background, sought to revive interest in the struggle. On November 5, 1892, the Advisory Board of the Amalgamated decided not to ask the A.F.L. council "to issue a 'boycott' order against the material manufactured by the Carnegie Steel Company," and proposed a new, joint appeal for financial aid. Gompers, who had first favored the boycott device, recognized that it might lead to an industrywide assault upon the Amalgamated, and approved this decision. Before the month was over, the A.F.L. distributed some ten thousand circulars.

The Federation supported the plan to declare December 13 "Homestead Day," and to devote it to the raising of money for legal and relief purposes. Over three hundred of its affiliated bodies contributed $7,043.66, between November 1892, and June 1893, in response to the circulars asking for aid. The largest single sum from an A.F.L. body, three hundred dollars, came from the Trade and Labor Unions of Meriden, Connecticut, and a contribution was even received from Mexico. Gompers played a key role in the decisions of the A.F.L. convention in December to provide contributions totaling $1,500 to the legal and relief committees established in Homestead and to meet, in addition, another $2,500 in legal fees incurred in the murder trials of the strike leaders. Disheartened by the loss of the strike, Gompers was delighted by the acquittals of the strike leaders. In his report to the 1893 convention, he spoke of the decision by the Pennsylvania authorities not to press the murder, riot, and treason cases still untried.[3]

---

[3] Gompers's autobiography, *Seventy Years of Life and Labor* (New York: E. P. Dutton & Company; 1925, 2 vols.), Vol. I, pp. 338-40; Vol. II, pp. 155, 240, does little justice to either his or the Federation's efforts on behalf of the strikers and the Amalgamated Association. The 1892 and 1893 A.F.L. convention proceedings supply essential information, but an adequate account can be derived only from the *Gompers Letterbooks* in the Washington, D.C., headquarters of the A.F.L.

IX

The events of July 6 precipitated a full-dress discussion of the rights and powers of the employer and of unionism. Homestead gave editorial comments on unionism a new note of passion and urgency. *The Nation* declared, on August 11: "It is high time for the public to realize the tyranny which 'Labor' is establishing in this country." Two weeks earlier, it observed that the "intolerable tyranny" established by the Amalgamated forced Frick to choose between re-establishing the company's authority and turning "the management of the mills" over to the union. An impressive segment of the American press held that the wage bargain did not give employees any claim upon their jobs or a vested interest in the business for which they worked. True liberty, explained the New York *Sun*, meant that the employer could not be coerced into hiring a worker, and that the employee could refuse to work when he did not like the price offered for his labor.

The business community viewed the right of the employer to hire any worker he pleased for wages acceptable to the employee as legal and absolute. The vital principle in the Homestead episode, according to a Chicago businessman, was "the right of a man to work in a factory where a union had ordered a strike, or, reversed, the right of an employer to hire whom he pleases to work for him." He ticked off the union as "despotic, tyrannical, lawless, desperate and un-American," and asserted that man's "inherent and inalienable right to labor . . . must not be interfered with by unions or strikers." [4]

This view was more elaborately developed by a distinguished authority on constitutional law, George Ticknor Curtis. He contended that society was responsible for guaranteeing perfect freedom for the individual worker in order to fulfill "its duty to him and to those who wish to buy his labor for a price he is willing to pay and which it is for the interest of those who are dependent upon him to have him take." When unions bound their members to collective strike-action, they deprived workers of their right to make individual employment decisions. When they barred un-

[4] Z. S. Holbrook: "The Lessons of the Homestead Troubles. Address before the Sunset Club, Chicago, November 17, 1892," pp. 3, 4, 25.

organized workers from employment, they merited punishment for violating a right guaranteed by society. In establishing the grounds for a grand-jury indictment of the strike leaders for treason against Pennsylvania, the Chief Justice of the state supreme court concluded that if the worker could "lawfully dictate to his employer the terms of his employment, and upon the refusal of the latter to accede to them, take possession of its property, and drive others away who are willing to work, we would have anarchy."

What was arresting in the debate over the relative rights of workers and employers was the criticism directed at the traditional meaning assigned to freedom of contract. In the Senate debate touched off by the battle of Homestead, virtually all the Senators who spoke on July 7 condemned the use of the Pinkertons, but John M. Palmer, Democrat from Illinois, went far beyond that issue. He argued, for the first time on the floor of the Senate, that society could properly limit the employer's freedom of action—a freedom solidly anchored in his right to do as he pleased with his property. If there were rights that workers could claim to justify resistance to the Pinkertons, then the Carnegie Company's rights in the management of its property were not unqualified. Palmer denied that the strikers were trespassing by their presence in the plant. In resorting to force to answer force they were protecting their jobs. They "had a right to employment there," he said, "they had earned the right to live there, and these large manufacturing establishments—and there is no other road out of this question—must hereafter be understood to be public establishments. . . . in which the public is deeply interested, and the owners of these properties must hereafter be regarded as holding their property subject to the correlative rights of those without whose services the property would be utterly worthless."

Palmer readily conceded employers "a right to a reasonable profit on the capital investment in their enterprises," but he argued that large-scale industrial corporations were clothed with a public interest because they worked for and employed "the public; . . . because men in their service become unfit for other services; and . . . because there are thousands dependent on them for food and nurture." Employers had the right to operate their enterprises "at their will," but, within the limits of business vicissitudes, workers could expect, with "good" conduct, continuous employment at decent pay. Claimed human rights, said Palmer, should not be sacrificed to establish property rights. Neither capital nor labor could any longer lay claim to "absolute rights."

During a second Senate debate on August 2, Senator Palmer proposed that "the organization of labor" should be promoted as a matter of public policy, "as we have heretofore encouraged the organization of capital." In this, the Senator was well in advance of his contemporaries. The first federal statute to carry out this suggestion was the Railway Labor Act of 1926, which underwrote unionism and collective bargaining for railroad workers. When Palmer first expressed his novel views, not a single Senator ventured a reply. On August 2, Senator Hawley argued that workers were never justified in preventing others from taking their places, and enjoyed no rights that inhered in their jobs. Both employer and laborer might be moved by moral obligations, but only the former possessed legal rights. "The workmen," said Hawley, "each and all may be legally discharged, evicted—driven out. . . ." Only the "law" of the employer's private conscience might inhibit him from engaging in these lawful acts.

Dismay and surprise contended with withering criticism and censure in the dominant responses to Senator Palmer's views. To the New York *Sun*, speaking for the most conservative wing of the Democratic party, he was "an anti-Democrat of the most rabid and violent type." His willingness to sacrifice property and liberty made him worse than a Populist. "He is a Socialist and nothing else." A host of other papers found him "perilously" close to the Socialist position, and the Springfield *Republican* suggested that he might have been converted to Bellamy's Nationalism.

The characteristic arguments were that there was no "higher law" workers could invoke; that to claim a vested right to employment was to undermine the foundations of the society; and that moral rights could be underwritten only by public opinion, not by law. *The Nation*, attacking Palmer's contention concerning the right of the strikers to occupy the plant on being locked out, which anticipated the justification of the sit-down strikes of

1936–7, noted that "the right to seize other people's property and to commit an assault," if it existed at all, "must be of very recent birth."

Palmer's position was not undefended. George Gunton, in *The Social Economist,* urged recognition of unions, encouragement by the law and the courts to collective bargaining, and protection of peaceful picketing. T. V. Powderly, writing for *The North American Review,* developed a case for regarding the large corporation as a public institution on the grounds that its workers made prosperous the enterprise and the community in which it was located, and that their and the community's well-being depended on steady employment. Chauncey F. Black, writing on "The Lesson of Homestead" in *The Forum,* started with the assumption that business was invested with a public interest and was, therefore, susceptible to regulation. He pleaded for compulsory arbitration, and urged that it was better for the state to intervene in advance of a bitterly fought industrial conflict than to resort to suppression when it was under way. "No man in civilized society," declared Black, "can do what he pleases with his own." Congressman Case Broderick of Kansas admitted some merit in the conception of the big corporation as a quasi-public institution in granting that disputes of the dimensions of Homestead involved significant public as well as private interests.

X

The dimension of the Homestead episode may be read in the many facets that it touched of American life. The expressions and exchanges of views that it stimulated on key issues indicate its challenge to the social and economic thought of contemporaries. It stimulated a new awareness of the extent to which claimed human and traditional property-rights could be in conflict.

William Dean Howells, who was profoundly "excited" by the Homestead strike, shared with many contemporaries the conviction that it would bring "an end of Pinkertonism." In this they erred. Homestead made public the service rendered by Pinkertons in ninety strikes since 1874. It stimulated, in Congress and elsewhere, discussion of regulatory measures to prevent the use of private armed guards in labor disputes, just as it encouraged an eager search for ways of avoiding strikes. It brought about the passage of legislation in Pennsylvania, New York, Massachusetts, Arkansas, Colorado, Minnesota, New Mexico, and Wyoming, making it a misdemeanor to employ deputy sheriffs and private guards who were not citizens of the United States and residents of the state in which they were operating. But it did not check the employment of private detectives and guards in labor disputes.

The strike was a factor in the election of 1892, but probably a far less significant one in Grover Cleveland's victory than historians have been disposed to assert. Homestead, it has been seen, was exploited by low-tariff advocates. Democratic politicians and papers, with some exceptions, cried that the strike was the product of a high-tariff system that brought no advantages to labor. On July 7, Daniel W. Voorhees of Indiana declared on the floor of the Senate that "labor riots, battles, blood-stained fields . . . have sprung alone from the doctrine of protection," and he charged the Republicans with making "the poor people who laid down their lives yesterday on the banks of the Monongahela believe that you were protecting them." In the House the next day, Congressman Whitney of Michigan asserted that the Republicans' "pretended protection to labor" had been exposed for what it truly was. American workers, said Cleveland in his acceptance speech of July 20, "are still told the tale, oft repeated in spite of its demonstrated falsity, that the existing Protective tariff is a boon to them, and that under its beneficent operation their wages must increase, while, as they listen, scenes are enacted in the very abiding place of high Protection that mock the hopes of toil and attest the tender mercy the workingman receives from those made selfish by unjust governmental favoritism."

Low-tariff advocates maintained that Carnegie's conduct made it unlikely that labor would be taken in, as it had been in 1888, by the contention that protection was responsible for high wages and good times. It is more probable, however, that most workers who saw in Homestead compelling proof that high tariffs protected profits but not wages were initially of that opinion. Traditional party affiliations and loyalties were, of course, a function of much more than a tariff position. It is suggestive that several workers interviewed by a reporter for the Detroit *Sun*, while seeing no gain to the wage-earner in a high tariff, did not regard protection a primary cause of the strike.

Republican leaders, sensitive to the political costs of wage-cutting in good times resulting in a strike in a strongly protected industry, sought to show that there was no connection between the tariff and the Homestead episode. This contention marked two minority views that accompanied the report of the House Judiciary Committee investigation of the strike. Republican papers pointed out that the nominal rates on steel had been reduced by the much debated McKinley tariff of 1890, and that the Democrat who sought, as the Chicago *Inter Ocean* put it, for the source of "the Homestead trouble" in tariff legislation was a "crank."

Some Republican campaign strategists hoped to bring about a settlement of the strike before Election Day. It was reported that Carnegie and Frick were asked to terminate the strike, and also to increase their contributions to the Republican campaign chest. It was also asserted that Carnegie, having received the protection he needed, was, in contrast with 1888, niggardly and indifferent to pleas for campaign contributions.

The possibility of using the election to move Frick into re-opening negotiations was early considered by the Advisory Committee. Local labor and Republican leaders suggested to Hugh O'Donnell that he visit New York with the purpose of securing a prominent Republican to induce Carnegie to direct Frick to resume negotiations. With the Advisory Committee's unanimous approval, O'Donnell set off for New York on July 17. Arrangements had been made by a Pittsburgh Republican leader for an interview with John E. Milholland, member of the Republican National Committee and campaign manager for Whitelaw Reid, publisher of the New York *Tribune* and President Harrison's running-mate. There was a basis for a bargain: Republican aid in the resumption of negotiations might be exchanged for the cessation of the strike leaders' attacks upon the tariff.

Milholland arranged for O'Donnell to dictate, in the offices of the *Tribune*, a long letter to Whitelaw Reid pleading for assistance in inducing "the Carnegie company to recognize the Amalgamated Association by re-opening the conference doors," [5] and the

---

[5] For obvious reasons this letter was presumably sent from Homestead and was predated July 16.

Tribune publisher promised to communicate its gist to the absent Carnegie. Frick refused to make available Carnegie's Ranoch Lodge address in Scotland, and Reid dispatched by way of a State Department cipher cable O'Donnell's offer to settle. Carnegie's initial response was ambivalent. On July 28, he cabled Frick, recovering from the effects of Berkman's assault, that "the proposition" was worth consideration, but that he would do nothing about it and that the responsibility was Frick's.

Carnegie would have delighted in a settlement that restored his shattered reputation. At the same time, he wanted no part of an agreement committing the company to bargain with the union, whose offer to compromise he read as a sign of distress. Clearly, he had no desire to alter Frick's course. Another cable in code from Scotland on the following day declared that the whole "proposition was not worthy of consideration," and enthusiastically endorsed Frick and his conduct of the strike. In March of the following year, Carnegie used his talent for self-justification in explaining to Whitelaw Reid that he was "powerless," after the events of July 6 and the assault on Frick, to prevent the Homestead affair from injuring the Republican running-mates.

The Republican strategists made one more effort to sway Frick. John Milholland, the emissary who called upon him in Pittsburgh on July 30, learned that Frick would settle the strike only on his own terms. He was determined, Milholland reported to Reid, to fight the strike "if it takes all summer and all winter, and all next summer and all next winter. . . . I will fight this thing to the bitter end. I will never recognize the union, never, never!"

Neither the political articles that appeared during the campaign nor the post-election analyses assigned any weight to Homestead as a factor in the election. In an exchange of post-mortem letters, neither of the Republican candidates mentioned the strike. A few Republican leaders, Chauncey M. Depew and Secretary of the Treasury Charles Foster among them, cited it as a reason for Harrison's defeat. Secretary Foster had found "trouble among the laboring men" during a campaign visit to Ohio. "They were talking about Homestead," he said, "and about Carnegie being too rich, while they were poor."

The Democrats made striking gains over 1888 in the large urban centers, and did well in the industrial towns lying between Pittsburgh and Cleveland. But it has not yet been demonstrated that the strike profoundly altered voting patterns in Republican strongholds. True enough, Homestead itself, normally Republican, went Democratic, but by only 137 votes. The influence of the strike *per se* cannot be assessed. It contributed to a reaction against high protection which was also developing on other counts. It cannot be isolated from other labor disputes marked by violence and the use of troops—in the railway yards at Buffalo, New York; in the Tennessee coal and iron mining district, which witnessed a virtual uprising against the use of convict labor; and in the silver mine district at Coeur d'Alene, Idaho. Lesser strikes elsewhere, many of them bitterly fought, may have also had local significance for the election.

Cleveland ran ahead of Harrison by 400,000, but the Democratic popular vote was less than half of the twelve million cast. The Populists topped a million, and the Prohibition vote was over 262,000. Cleveland's victory did not depend upon a sweep of major industrial states. Pennsylvania and Ohio went Republican, but by smaller margins than in 1888. New York, which Cleveland had barely carried in 1884, returned to the Democratic column in 1892. Illinois, normally Republican, was also carried by Cleveland in 1892. Massachusetts remained Republican over these three elections, and Connecticut remained in the Democratic fold. Apart from California, which barely fell into the Cleveland column in 1892, other significant Republican losses occurred in predominantly agrarian or mining states, where the Populists displayed maximum strength.

The law cases spawned by the strike were of more than passing interest. During the third week of July, Frick took action to have warrants issued for the arrest of the strike leaders for murder. Members of the Advisory Committee retaliated with similar moves against Frick and his associates, including Potter, Phipps, and Francis T. F. Lovejoy, and several Pinkertons. On September 19, grand-jury true bills charging murder, aggravated riot, and conspiracy were returned against 167 strikers. Three were brought to trial—Sylvester Critchlow in November 1892, and Jack Clifford and Hugh O'Donnell in February 1893. All three were acquitted, and the Carnegie attorneys, who had shared actively in their prosecution, arranged to have the cases pending against both sides dropped.

Of frightening import was the indictment, for treason against the state of Pennsylvania, of thirty-three members of the Advisory Committee. Major General Snowden had first broached the possibility of taking such an action against the strikers to the Carnegie attorneys. No one had ever been prosecuted under the 1860 treason statute. The chief justice of the supreme court of Pennsylvania, Edward A. Paxson, who presided over the grand jury, was directly responsible for the indictments it handed down on October 10. Ten days earlier he had issued warrants for the arrest, on the charge of treason, of the Advisory Committee members. In his charge to the grand jury Paxson declared that "when a large number of men arm and organize themselves by divisions and companies, appoint officers, and engage in a common purpose to defy the law; to resist its officers, and to deprive any portion of their fellow citizens of the right to which they are entitled under the Constitution and laws, it is a levying of war against the State; and the offense is treason."

More significant than the measure of approval the chief justice's reasoning and the treason indictments won was the outburst of criticism they inspired. This was sharp and widespread enough to play a part in the decision of the state authorities not to prosecute any of the treason cases. The *American Law Review* found the indictment "a mass of stale, medieval verbiage, drawn seemingly from some old precedent not dating later than the reign of William and Mary," and declared that it could not comprehend how the events at Homestead could be "dignified into the crime of treason. . . . " The *Albany Law Journal,* which reviewed earlier state treason-trials, stated that there was no legal basis for treason indictments.

These legal developments constituted a drain upon the resources of the Advisory Committee. Those involving Berkman and Iams did not. The first, who refused to be defended, was found guilty after a four-hour trial on September 19. Sentenced to one year in the workhouse (for carrying concealed and murderous weapons) and to twenty-one years in the penitentiary (for his assault upon Frick), Berkman was released from jail in 1906. Two anarchist comrades, with whom he had stayed in the Pittsburgh area but who were not implicated in his act, were successfully prosecuted for conspiracy. The National Guard officers sued by Iams for damages were acquitted in consequence of the judge's charge that they could not "be held accountable in any civil court" if they believed that the punishment which they imposed was essential "to maintain discipline and good order. . . ." Still another case had no effect on the course of the strike. In mid-January 1893, Hugh Dempsey, a leading K. of L. official in the Pittsburgh area, and three others were found guilty of having conspired to poison, during September and October, a number of non-union men who were then housed inside the Homestead plant. All were found guilty, and Dempsey, having failed to secure a new trial, was sentenced in February to seven years' imprisonment.

The strike's consequences for unionism, at Homestead and in iron and steel generally, were costly and enduring. The Amalgamated Association's treasury suffered severely, and its membership was reduced by almost five thousand by the close of 1892. It lost about seven thousand during the following year, and by 1894 its membership had fallen to ten thousand, well under half of its peak strength in 1891. In the Carnegie enterprise, the union was virtually dead, and the management was committed to a vigorous anti-union policy. Wage scales were now kept secret, extra pay for Sunday work ceased, and grievance procedures disappeared. Union membership became a ground for discharge. When U.S. Steel absorbed Carnegie Steel in 1901, it also acquired a group of executives whose anti-unionism had been hammered out on the anvil of the strike, and a body of workers who knew the meaning of industrial absolutism. In Homestead itself, where the anguish and the glory of the great strike were recalled with pride, the very air seemed charged with bitterness, hopelessness, and fear.

VIII. *Manifest Destiny and the Philippines*

The Congressional debate on Philippine annexation, which took place after the defeat of Spain, did not provoke as much popular excitement as the currency question, but the decision to annex the Philippines was one of the most fateful in our history; one that profoundly altered the character of our traditional foreign policy. The spectacle of an American succumbing to jingoism—"that curious reaction against peaceful and industrial civilization, as well as against international morality," to quote one contemporary—was a shocking or an exhilarating experience, depending upon the philosophy of the contemporary observer. The roots of the debate, its relation to other events in the turbulent decade of the nineties, and the agonies and rationalizations it engendered in the American conscience are part of what Professor Richard Hofstadter writes about in this essay.

VIII

Manifest Destiny and the Philippines

Richard Hofstadter

Associate Professor of History, Columbia University

The taking of the Philippine Islands from Spain in 1899 marked a major historical departure for the American people. It was a breach in their traditions and a shock to their established values. To be sure, from their national beginnings they had constantly engaged in expansion, but almost entirely into contiguous territory. Now they were extending themselves to distant extra-hemispheric colonies; they were abandoning a strategy of defense hitherto limited to the continent and its appurtenances, in favor of a major strategic commitment in the Far East; and they were now supplementing the spread of a relatively homogeneous population into territories destined from the beginning for self-government with a far different procedure in which control was imposed by force on millions of ethnic aliens. The acquisition of the islands, therefore, was understood by contemporaries on both sides of the debate, as it is readily understood today, to be a turning-point in our history.

To discuss the debate in isolation from other events, however, would be to deprive it of its full significance. American entrance into the Philippine Islands was a by-product of the Spanish-American War. The Philippine crisis is inseparable from the war crisis, and the war crisis itself is inseparable from a larger constellation that might be called "the psychic crisis of the 1890's." [1]

Central in the background of the psychic crisis was the great

---

[1] A more substantial analysis of this crisis will be made in the opening chapter of the writer's forthcoming study of the American mind since 1890.

depression that broke in 1893 and was still very acute when the agitation over the war in Cuba began. Severe depression, by itself, does not always generate an emotional crisis as intense as that of the nineties. In the 1870's the country had been swept by a depression of comparable acuteness and duration which, however, did not give rise to all the phenomena that appeared in the 1890's or to very many of them with comparable intensity and impact. It is often said that the 1890's, unlike the 1870's, form some kind of a "watershed" in American history. The difference between the emotional and intellectual impact of these two depressions can be measured, I believe, not by any difference in severity, but rather by reference to a number of singular events that in the 1890's converged with the depression to heighten its impact upon the public mind.

First in importance was the Populist movement, the free-silver agitation, the heated campaign of 1896. For the first time in our history a depression had created an allegedly "radical" movement strong enough to capture a major party and raise the specter, however unreal, of drastic social convulsion. Second was the maturation and bureaucratization of American business, the completion of its essential industrial plant, and the development of trusts on a scale sufficient to stir the anxiety that the old order of competitive opportunities was approaching an eclipse. Third, and of immense symbolic importance, was the apparent filling up of the continent and disappearance of the frontier line. We now know how much land had not yet been taken up and how great were the remaining possibilities of internal expansion both in business and on the land; but to the mind of the 1890's it seemed that the resource that had engaged the energies of the people for three centuries had been used up; the frightening possibility suggested itself that a serious juncture in the nation's history had come. As Frederick Jackson Turner expressed it in his famous paper of 1893: "Now, four centuries from the discovery of America, at the end of one hundred years of life under the Constitution, the frontier has gone, and with its going has closed the first period of American history."

To middle-class citizens who had been brought up to think in terms of the nineteenth-century order, things looked bad. Farmers in the staple-growing region seemed to have gone mad over silver and Bryan; workers were stirring in bloody struggles like the Homestead and Pullman strikes; the supply of new land seemed at an end; the trust threatened the spirit of business enterprise; civic corruption was at a high point in the large cities; great waves of seemingly unassimilable immigrants arrived yearly and settled in hideous slums. To many historically conscious writers, the nation seemed overripe, like an empire ready for collapse through a stroke from outside or through internal upheaval. Acute as the situation was for all those who lived by the symbols of national power—for the governing and thinking classes—it was especially poignant for young people, who would have to make their careers in the dark world that seemed to be emerging.

The symptomatology of the crisis might record several tendencies in popular thought and behavior that had not been observable before or had existed only in pale and tenuous form. These symptoms fall into two basic moods. The key to one of them is an intensification of protest and humanitarian reform. Populism, Utopianism, the rise of the Christian Social gospel, the growing intellectual interest in Socialism, the social settlement movement that appealed so strongly to the college generation of the nineties, the quickening of protest in the realistic novel—all these are expressions of this mood. The other is one of national self-assertion, aggression, expansion. The tone of the first was sympathy, of the second, power. During the 1890's far more patriotic groups were founded than in any other decade of our history; the naval theories of Captain Mahan were gaining in influence; naval construction was booming; there was an immense quickening of the American cult of Napoleon and a vogue of the virile and martial writings of Rudyard Kipling; young Theodore Roosevelt became the exemplar of the vigorous, masterful, out-of-doors man; the revival of European imperialism stirred speculation over what America's place would be in the world of renewed colonial rivalries. But most significant was the rising tide of jingoism, a matter of constant comment among observers of American life during the decade.

Jingoism, of course, was not new in American history. But during the 1870's and '80's the American public had been notably quiescent about foreign relations. There had been expansionist statesmen, but they had been blocked by popular apathy and statecraft had been restrained.[2] Grant had failed dismally in his attempt to acquire Santo Domingo; our policy toward troubled Hawaii had been cautious; in 1877 an offer of two Haitian naval harbors had been spurned. In responding to Haiti, Secretary of State Frelinghuysen had remarked that "the policy of this Government . . . has tended toward avoidance of possessions disconnected from the main continent." [3] Henry Cabot Lodge, in his life of George Washington published in 1889, observed that foreign relations then filled "but a slight place in American politics, and excite generally only a languid interest." [4] Within a few years this comment would have seemed absurd; the history of the 1890's is the history of public agitation over expansionist issues and of quarrels with other nations.

II

Three primary incidents fired American jingoism between the spring of 1891 and the close of 1895. First came Secretary of State Blaine's tart and provocative reply to the Italian minister's protest over the lynching of eleven Italians in New Orleans. Then there was friction with Chile over a riot in Valparaiso in which two American sailors were killed and several injured by a Chilean mob. In 1895 occurred the more famous Venezuela boundary dispute with Britain. Discussion of these incidents would take us too far afield, but note that they all had these characteristics in common: in none of them was national security or the national interest vitally involved; in all three American diplomacy was

[2] See Julius W. Pratt: *America's Colonial Experiment* (New York: 1950), pp. 4–13.
[3] Albert K. Weinberg: *Manifest Destiny* (Baltimore: 1935), p. 252. There is a suggestive similarity to the conditions of the nineties in the circumstances attending the Cuban insurrection of 1868–78. The hostilities were even more bitter and exhausting than those of 1895–8; its latter phases also corresponded with an acute depression in the United States; the case of the *Virginius* offered a pretext for war almost as satisfactory as that of the *Maine*. Some public and press clamor followed. But it did not rise even near to the pitch of overwhelming pressure for war. Two things were supplied in the nineties that were missing in the seventies: a psychic crisis that generated an expansionist mood, and the techniques of yellow journalism. Cf. Samuel Flagg Bemis: *A Diplomatic History of the United States* (New York: 1936), pp. 433–5.
[4] Quoted by Samuel Flagg Bemis: Ibid., p. 432.

extraordinarily and disproportionately aggressive; in all three the possibility of war was contemplated; and in each case the American public and press response was enthusiastically nationalist. It is hard to read the history of these events without concluding that politicians were persistently using jingoism to restore their prestige, mend their party fences, and divert the public mind from grave internal discontents. It hardly seems an accident that jingoism and Populism rose together. Documentary evidence for the political exploitation of foreign crises is not overwhelmingly abundant, in part because such a motive is not necessarily conscious and where it is conscious it is not likely to be confessed or recorded.[5] The persistence of jingoism in every administration from Harrison's to Theodore Roosevelt's, however, is too suggestive to be ignored. During the nineties the press of each party was fond of accusing the other of exploiting foreign conflict. We know that Blaine was not above twisting the British lion's tail for political purposes; and there is no reason to believe that he would have exempted Italy from the same treatment. We know too that Harrison, on the eve of the Chile affair, for the acuteness of which he was primarily responsible, was being urged by prominent Republican politicians who had the coming Presidential campaign in mind to pursue a more aggressive foreign policy because it would "have the . . . effect of diverting attention from stagnant political discussions."[6] And although some Democratic papers

[5] The most notable case in our earlier history was Seward's fantastic proposal during the crisis of 1861 that Lincoln attempt to reunite the North and South by precipitating a foreign war. A classic expression of the philosophy of this kind of statecraft was made by Fisher Ames in 1802, after the Federalists had been routed by the Jeffersonians. "We need as all nations do," he wrote to Rufus King, "the compression on the outside of our circle of a formidable neighbor, whose presence shall at all times excite stronger fears than demagogues can inspire the people with towards their government." Quoted in Henry Jones Ford: *The Rise and Growth of American Politics* (New York: 1914), p. 69. One of the signal differences between the 1870's and the 1890's was that there was still a useful domestic enemy in the earlier period. "Our strong ground," wrote Rutherford B. Hayes in 1876, "is a dread of a solid South, rebel rule, etc., etc. . . . It leads people away from 'hard times' which is our deadliest foe." Quoted in J. F. Rhodes: *History of the United States* (New York: 1906), VII, p. 220.

[6] Donald M. Dozer: "Benjamin Harrison and the Presidential Campaign of 1892," *American Historical Review*, Vol. LIV (October 1948), p. 52; A. T. Volwiler: "Harrison, Blaine, and American Foreign Policy, 1889–1893," American Philosophical Society *Proceedings*, LXXIX (1938), argues plausibly that the imperial mood dawned during Harrison's administration.

charged that he was planning to run for re-election during hostilities so that he could use the "don't-swap-horses-in-the-middle-of-the-stream" appeal, many Democrats felt that it was politically necessary for them to back him against Chile so that, as one of their Congressmen remarked, the Republicans could not "run away with all the capital there is to be made in an attempt to assert national self-respect." [7] Grover Cleveland admittedly was a man of exceptional integrity whose stand against pressure for the annexation of Hawaii during 1893–4 does him much credit. But precisely for this act of abnegation his administration fell under the charge made by Republican jingoes like Lodge and by many in his own party that he was indifferent to America's position in the world. And if Cleveland was too high-minded a man to exploit a needless foreign crisis, his Secretary of State, Richard Olney, was not. The Venezuela affair, which came at a very low point in the prestige of Cleveland's administration, offered Olney a rich chance to prove to critics in both parties that the administration was, after all, capable of vigorous diplomacy. That the crisis might have partisan value was not unthinkable to members of Olney's party. He received a suggestive letter from a Texas Congressman encouraging him to "go ahead," on the ground that the Venezuela issue was a "winner" in every section of the country. "When you come to diagnose the country's internal ills," his correspondent continued, "the possibilities of 'blood and iron' loom up immediately. Why, Mr. Secretary, just think of how angry the anarchistic, socialistic, and populistic boil appears on our political surface and who knows how deep its roots extend or ramify? One cannon shot across the bow of a British boat in defense of this principle will knock more *pus* out of it than would suffice to innoculate and corrupt our people for the next two centuries." [8]

This pattern had been well established when the Cuban crisis broke out anew in 1895. It was quite in keeping that Secretary Olney should get a letter during the 1896 campaign from Fitz-

[7] Earl W. Fornell: "Historical Antecedents of the Chilean-American Crisis of 1891–92," unpublished M.A. thesis, Columbia University (1950), p. 138; see this essay, especially chapters xi and xii, for Harrison's exploitation of the war crisis and the intense public reaction.

[8] Quoted in Alfred Vagts: *Deutschland und die Vereinigten Staaten in der Weltpolitik* (New York: 1935), Vol. I, p. 511; for the domestic roots of administration policy see Nelson M. Blake: "Background of Cleveland's Venezuela Policy," *American Historical Review*, Vol. XLVII (January 1942), pp. 259–77.

hugh Lee, the American consul in Havana, advising that the conservative faction of Gold Democrats become identified with the
strong policy of mediation or intervention in Cuba. Thus, he
argued, "the 'Sound Democrats' would get, with the Executive,
the credit of stopping the wholesale atrocities daily practised
here, the acquisition of Cuba by purchase, or by fighting a successful war, if war there be. In the latter case, the enthusiasm, the
applications for service, the employment of many of the unem-
ployed, might do much towards directing the minds of the people
from imaginary ills, the relief of which is erroneously supposed to
be reached by 'Free Silver.' " [9]

When President McKinley took office he was well aware that
nationalist enthusiasm had reached a pitch that made war very
likely. A few months earlier, he had told Senator Lodge that he
might be "obliged" to go to war as soon as he entered the Presidency, and had expressed a preference that the Cuban crisis be
settled one way or another in the time between his election and
inauguration. Although he promised Carl Schurz that there would
be "no jingo nonsense under my administration," he proved to
have not quite enough strength to resist the current. Members of
his own party put a great deal of pressure on him to give the
people their war rather than endanger the Republican position.
It was held that if war was inevitable, as presumably it was, it
would be better for the President to lead than to be pushed; that
resistance to war would be ruinous to the party; that going to war
would prevent the Democrats from entering the next Presidential
campaign with "Free Cuba" and "Free Silver" as their battle cries.[1]
After Senator Proctor's speech exposing conditions in Cuba the
Chicago *Times-Herald*, a McKinley paper, declared that intervention in Cuba, peaceful or forcible, was "immediately inevitable.
Our own internal political condition will not permit its postponement. . . . Let President McKinley hesitate to rise to the just
expectation of the American people, and who can doubt that 'war
for Cuban liberty' will be the crown of thorns that Free Silver
Democrats and Populists will adopt at the elections this fall. . . .
The President would be powerless to stay any legislation, how-

---

[9] Vagts: *Ibid.*, II, p. 1266 n.
[1] Vagts: *Ibid.*, II, 1308 n; S. F. Bemis: *The Latin American Policy of
the United States* (New York: 1943), p. 407; Thomas A. Bailey: *A Diplomatic History of the American People* (New York: 1944), pp. 506-8;
C. S. Olcott: *The Life of William McKinley* (Boston: 1916), Vol. II, p. 28.

ever ruinous to every sober, honest interest of the country." [2] At the time McKinley sent his war message to Congress he knew quite well, and indeed made a passing reference to the fact, that Spain had already capitulated to the demands the United States had made upon her. This capitulation *could* have been made the basis of a peace message; instead it occupied one sentence tucked away near the end of a war message—a sentence that everyone chose to ignore. Evidently McKinley had concluded that what was wanted in the United States was not so much the freedom of Cuba as a *war* for the freedom of Cuba.

Historians say that the war was brought on by sensational newspapers. The press, spurred by the rivalry between Pulitzer and Hearst, aroused sympathy with the Cubans and hatred of Spain and catered to the bellicosity of the public. No one seems to have asked: *Why was the public so fatally receptive to war propaganda?* I believe the answer must be sought in the causes of the jingoism that had raged for seven years before the war actually broke out. The events of the nineties had brought frustration and anxiety to civically conscious Americans. On one hand, as Mark Sullivan has commented, the American during this period was disposed "to see himself as an underdog in economic situations and controversies in his own country"; [3] but the civic frustrations of the era created also a restless aggressiveness, a desire to be assured that the power and vitality of the nation were not waning. The capacity for sympathy and the need for power existed side by side. That highly typical and symptomatic American, William Allen White, recalls in his *Autobiography* how during the nineties he was "bound to my idols—Whitman, the great democrat, and Kipling, the imperialist." [4] In varying stages of solution the democrat and imperialist existed in the hearts of White's countrymen—the democrat disposed to free Cuba, the imperialist to vent his civic spleen on Spain.

I suspect that the readiness of the public to over-react to the Cuban situation can be understood in part through the displacement of feelings of sympathy or social protest generated in domestic affairs; these impulses found a safe and satisfactory dis-

---

[2] Quoted in Walter Millis: *The Martial Spirit* (New York: 1931), p. 124.

[3] Mark Sullivan: *Our Times* (New York: 1926), p. 137.

[4] William Allen White: *Autobiography* (New York: 1946), p. 195.

charge in foreign conflict. Spain was portrayed in the press as waging a heartless and inhuman war; the Cubans were portrayed as noble victims of Spanish tyranny, their situation as analogous to that of Americans in 1776.[5] When one examines the sectional and political elements that were most enthusiastic about the war, one finds them not primarily among the wealthy Eastern big-business Republicans who supported McKinley and read the conservative dignified newspapers, but in the Bryan sections of the country, in the Democratic party, and among the patrons of the yellow journals.[6] During the controversy significant charges were hurled back and forth; conservative peace-advocates claimed that many jingoists were hoping for a costly war over Cuba that could be made the occasion of a return to free silver; in return, the inflammatory press often fell into the pattern of Populist rhetoric, declaiming, for example, about "the eminently respectable porcine citizens who—for dollars in the money-grubbing sty, support 'conservative' newspapers and consider the starvation of . . . inoffensive men, women and children, and the murder of 250 American sailors . . . of less im-

[5] On the role of the press see J. E. Wisan: *The Cuban Crisis as Reflected in the New York Press* (New York: 1934); and M. M. Wilkerson: *Public Opinion and the Spanish-American War* (Baton Rouge: 1932). On the evolution of human-interest journalism see Helen M. Hughes: *News and the Human Interest Story* (Chicago: 1940); and the same author's "Human Interest Stories and Democracy," *Public Opinion Quarterly*, Vol. I (April 1937), pp. 73–83.

[6] Wisan (Ibid., p. 455) notes: "It was no mere accident that most of the leading proponents of intervention in Congress represented southern and western states where populism and silver were strongest." Cf. pp. 125–6, 283, 301. A resolution of May 20, 1897, in favor of granting belligerent rights to the Cubans was passed by the Senate, 41–14, with 33 Senators not voting. The *yeas* came from 19 Democrats, 2 Populists, 3 Maverick Republicans, and 17 regular Republicans. The *nays* came from 12 Republicans and 2 Democrats. The 17 Republican votes for recognition broke down as follows: 10 west of the Mississippi, 2 South, 3 Midwest, 2 New England. A New York *Journal* poll of the House in December 1897, on the question of recognizing Cuban belligerency, showed: *for*, 40 Republicans, 117 Democrats, and 27 Populists, total 184; *against*, 165 Republicans, 5 Democrats, and 2 Populists, total 172 (Wisan: p. 359); cf. Julius W. Pratt: *Expansionists of 1898* (Baltimore: 1936), pp. 224, 234–6, 242–3. It is noteworthy that dominant sentiment in the labor movement favored recognition of Cuban belligerency from an early date, and that Cleveland's conservative policy was considered to be another instance of the "coldness" toward the underdog that was held to characterize his labor policies. Cf. John C. Appel: "The Relationship of American Labor to United States Imperialism, 1895–1905," unpublished Ph.D. thesis, University of Wisconsin (1950), chapter ii.

portance than a fall of two points in a price of stocks." [7] Although imputations of base economic motives were made by both sides, it is also significant that the current of sympathy and agitation ran strong where a discontented constituency, politically frustrated by Bryan's defeat, was most numerous. An opportunity to discharge aggressions against "Wall Street interests" coolly indifferent to the fate of both Cuban *insurrectos* and staple farmers may have been more important than the more rationalized and abstract linkage between a war and free silver. The primary significance of the war for the psychic economy of the nineties was that it served as an outlet for aggressive impulses while presenting itself, quite truthfully, as an idealistic and humanitarian crusade. The American public was not interested in the material gains of an intervention in Cuba. It never dreamed that the war would lead to the taking of the Philippines. Starting a war for a high-minded and altruistic purpose and then transmuting it into a war for annexation was unthinkable; it would be, as McKinley put it in a phrase that later came back to haunt him, "criminal aggression." [8]

[7] Wisan: Ibid., p. 394.

[8] William James, who deplored the war fever from the beginning, correctly diagnosed the mood when he wrote to a friend in France: "The basis of it all is, or rather was, perfectly honest humanitarianism, and an absolutely disinterested desire on the part of our people to set the Cubans free. . . . Congress was entirely mad, supposing that the people was in the same condition, as it probably was, in less degree. . . . war . . . was the only possible discharge. We were winning the most extraordinary diplomatic victories, but they were of no use. We were ready (as we supposed) for war and nothing but war must come." Although he reiterated that the American disclaimer of desire for conquest was "*absolutely* sincere," he also shrewdly predicted that once the excitement of military action was aroused, "the ambition and sense of mastery which our nation has will set up new demands," and he accurately forecast that although we would never annex Cuba we might take Puerto Rico and the Philippines. Ralph Barton Perry: *The Thought and Character of William James* (Boston: 1935), Vol. II, p. 307; William James: *Letters* (Boston: 1920), Vol. II, pp. 73–4. It should be added that inhibitions against going to war were not intense. "Spain, hardly a formidable potential foe in a war whose main strategic object was in the Caribbean, had been described by the press as weak, bankrupt, degenerate, and friendless. As T. R. put it: "I do not think a war with Spain would be serious enough to cause much strain on this country. . . ." H. C. Lodge (ed.): *Selections from the Correspondence of Theodore Roosevelt and Henry Cabot Lodge* (New York: 1925), Vol. I, p. 243.

III

There is one odd paradox in the evolution of sentiment from a war over freeing Cuba to a peace treaty acquiring the Philippines by conquest. The big-business-conservative-Republican-McKinley element, overwhelmingly hostile to this romantic and sentimental war, quickly became interested in the imperialism that grew out of it.[9] The popular Populist-Democratic-Bryanite element, which had been so keen for the war, became the stronghold—although by no means resolute or unbroken—of opposition to the fruits of war. This much, however, must be said of both the populace and the business community: if the matter had been left either to public clamor or to business interests, there would have been no American entrance into the Philippines in 1898.

The dynamic element in the movement for imperialism was a small group of politicians, intellectuals, and publicists, including Senator Henry Cabot Lodge, Theodore Roosevelt, John Hay, Senator Albert J. Beveridge, Whitelaw Reid, editor of *The New York Tribune*, Albert Shaw, editor of the *Review of Reviews*, Walter Hines Page, editor of the *Atlantic Monthly*, and Henry and Brooks Adams.

Most of these men came from what are known as good families. They were well educated, cultivated, patrician in outlook, Anglo-Saxon in background, noncommercial in personal goals and standards, and conservative reformers in politics. Although living in a commercial world, they could not accept business standards for their own careers nor absorb themselves into the business community. Although they lived in a vulgar democracy, they were not democratic by instinct. They could not and did not care to succeed in politics of the corrupt sort that had become so common in America. They had tried their hands at civic reform, had found it futile, and had become bored with it. When they did not, like Henry Adams, turn away from American life in bitterness, they became interested in some large and statesmanlike theater of action, broader than American domestic policy. Although there were men of this sort in the Democratic ranks, like Walter Hines Page, they were most influential within the Republican Party,

[9] Pratt: *Expansionists of 1898*, chapter vii, is classic on the business attitude.

which during the mid-nineties had become committed to a policy of expansion.[1]

In general, this group of imperialists was inspired by the navalist theories of Mahan and by the practical example of what they sometimes referred to as Mother England. They saw that a new phase of imperialism had opened in the Western world at large, and they were fearful that if the United States did not adopt a policy of expansion and preparation for military and naval struggle, it would be left behind in what they referred to as the struggle for life or, at other times, as the march of the nations. They were much concerned that the United States expand its army and particularly its navy; that it dig an isthmian canal; that it acquire the naval bases and colonies in the Caribbean and the Pacific necessary to protect such a canal; that it annex Hawaii and Samoa. At their most aggressive, they also called for the annexation of Canada, and the expulsion of European powers from the Western hemisphere. They were much interested in the Far East as a new theater of political conflict and investment possibilities. They were, indeed, more interested than business itself in the Pacific area, particularly in China, as a potential market. As Professor Pratt has observed: "The need of American business for colonial markets and fields for investment was discovered not by businessmen but by historians and other intellectuals, by journalists and politicians." [2]

The central figure in this group was Theodore Roosevelt, who more than any other single man was responsible for our entry into the Philippines. Throughout the 1890's Roosevelt had been eager for a war, whether it be with Chile, Spain, or England. A war with Spain, he felt, would get us "a proper navy and a good system of coast defenses," would free Cuba from Spain, and would help to free America from European domination, would give "our people . . . something to think of that isn't material gain," and would try "both the army and navy in actual practice." Roosevelt

[1] The best account of the little imperialist elite is in Matthew Josephson: *The President Makers* (New York: 1940), chapters i–iii; see also Pratt: *Expansionists of 1898;* and Alfred Vagts: *Ibid.*, Vol. II, passim.

[2] Pratt: *Expansionists of 1898,* p. 22; for a succinct statement of the outlook of Republican expansionists, see Henry Cabot Lodge: "Our Blundering Foreign Policy," *Forum,* Vol. XIX (March 1895), pp. 8–17; for Mahan's position, see A. T. Mahan: *The Interest of America in Sea Power* (New York: 1898).

feared that the United States would grow heedless of its defense, take insufficient care to develop its power, and become "an easy prey for any people which still retained those most valuable of all qualities, the soldierly virtues." "All the great masterful races have been fighting races," he argued. There were higher virtues than those of peace and material comfort. "No triumph of peace is quite so great as the supreme triumphs of war." [3] Such was the philosophy of the man who secured Commodore Dewey's appointment to the Far Eastern Squadron and alerted him before the actual outbreak of hostilities to be prepared to engage the Spanish fleet at Manila.

Our first step into the Philippines presented itself to us as a "defensive" measure. Dewey's attack on the Spanish fleet in Manila Bay was made on the assumption that the Spanish fleet, if unmolested, might cross the Pacific and bombard the west coast cities of the United States. I do not know whether American officialdom was aware that this fleet was so decrepit that it could hardly have gasped its way across the ocean. Next, Dewey's fleet seemed in danger unless its security were underwritten by the dispatch of American troops to Manila. To be sure, having accomplished his mission, Dewey could have removed this "danger" simply by leaving Manila Bay. However, in war one is always tempted to hold whatever gains have been made, and at Dewey's request American troops were dispatched very promptly after the victory and arrived at Manila in July 1898. Thus our second step into the Philippines was again a "defensive" measure. The third step was the so-called "capture" of Manila, which was actually carried out in co-operation with the Spaniards, who were allowed to make a token resistance, and in exclusion of the Filipino patriots under Aguinaldo. The fourth step was an agreement, incorporated in the protocol suspending hostilities between the United States and Spain, that the United States would occupy the city, bay, and harbor of Manila pending a final settlement in the peace treaty. The fifth step came much later, on December 21, 1898, when McKinley instructed the War Department to extend the military government already in force at Manila to the entire archipelago. This began a fierce revolt by the Filipino patriots, who felt that they had been led to expect a much different

[3] See Roosevelt: *Works* (New York: 1925), Vol. XIV, pp. 182–99; H. F. Pringle: *Theodore Roosevelt* (New York: 1931), chapter xiii.

policy from the American government. Two days before the vote was taken in the Senate on the ratification of the peace treaty, the patriots and the American forces fought their first battle and American soldiers were killed, a fact that seems to have had an important influence on public discussion. Once again, administrative action had given a sharp bias to the whole process of political decision. Tyler Dennett goes so far as to say that by authorizing a campaign of conquest while the Senate was still discussing the situation, McKinley "created a situation . . . which had the effect of coercing the Senate." [4] This is a doubtful conclusion,[5] but there is some reason to believe that the hand of expansionists was strengthened by the feeling that opposition to the administration's policy would be unpatriotic.

This much can certainly be said: by the time our policy could be affected by public discussion a great deal had already been accomplished by the annexationists. The tone of the argument was already weighted towards staying in simply because we were there. As McKinley put it: "It is not a question of keeping the islands of the East, but of leaving them." [6] It is not an easy thing to persuade a people or a government during the pitch of war enthusiasm to abandon a potential gain already in hand. Moreover, a great social interest hitherto indifferent to the Philippines, the business community, quickly swung around to an expansionist position. The Protestant clergy, seeing a potential enlargement of missionary enterprise, also threw in its weight. For the first time the group of imperialists and navalists had powerful allies. Business began to talk about the Philippines as a possible gateway to the markets of eastern Asia, the potentialities of which were thought to be very large.[7] The little imperialist group itself was much heartened and, with the help of Navy officers, put increasing pressure upon a rather hesitant administration to follow through.

There seemed four possible ways of disposing of the Philippine

[4] Tyler Dennett: *Americans in Eastern Asia* (New York: 1922), p. 631.

[5] W. Stull Holt: *Treaties Defeated by the Senate* (Baltimore: 1933), 170–1, concludes that the struggle in the Philippines had no important effects on the debate; see however José S. Reyes: *Legislative History of America's Economic Policy toward the Philippines* (New York: 1923), pp. 33–4; cf. Lodge: Ibid., p. 391.

[6] *Speeches and Addresses of William McKinley from March 1, 1897 to May 30, 1900* (New York: 1900), p. 174.

[7] Pratt: *Expansionists of 1898*, pp. 233, 261–78.

problem. The first, returning the islands to Spain, found favor nowhere. The second, selling or otherwise alienating the Philippines to some other power, seemed to invite a possible general European war; and it would hardly be more justified morally than remaining in possession ourselves. Moreover, we were being encouraged by England to remain in the Philippines, for American possession of those islands was much more palatable to England than possession by any other power. The third possibility, leaving the Philippines to themselves and giving them the independence Aguinaldo's men had been fighting for, was equivalent in most American minds to leaving them to anarchy. It also seemed to be another way of encouraging a scramble among other powers interested in the Far East. The final possibility was some form of American possession, in the form of a protectorate or otherwise. In the beginning there was much sentiment for merely retaining a naval base and coaling station on the island of Luzon, or perhaps the island of Luzon itself. Second thought suggested, however, that such a base would be endangered if the rest of the islands were left open to possible occupation by other nations. The dynamics of the situation suggested an all-or-none policy, and the administration drifted rapidly towards annexation of the entire archipelago.

IV

The American public had not previously been either informed about or interested in the Philippines. In the entire eighty-year period from 1818 through May 1898, only thirty-five articles about the islands had appeared in American magazines.[8] At the moment of Dewey's victory the press, although given over to encouraging the public jubilation, did not show an immediate interest in taking the islands. However, sentiment grew with considerable rapidity. As early as July 1898, the *Literary Digest* noted that the leading Republican papers were pro-expansion. A sample of 65 newspapers taken by the magazine *Public Opinion* in August showed that 43 per cent were for permanent retention of the Philippines, 24.6 per cent were opposed, and 32.4 per cent were

[8] A. A. Greenberg: "Public Opinion and the Acquisition of the Philippine Islands," unpublished M. A. thesis, Yale University (1937), pp. 2, 18.

wavering. In this case, "wavering" usually meant formerly opposed to expansion but apparently changing views. By December 1898, when the crucial debate in the Senate was beginning, the *New York Herald* polled 498 newspapers on the subject of expansion and found that 305, or 61.3 per cent, were favorable. New England and the Middle States showed clear margins in favor of expansion, the West an overwhelming margin; the South alone, by a thin margin, was opposed. The state of press opinion does not *measure* public feeling, but probably does indicate the direction in which public opinion was moving.[9]

To President McKinley, a benign and far from aggressive man, public sentiment was of great importance. He was not a man to lead the American people in a direction in which their sympathies were not already clearly bent. There was a current joke: "Why is McKinley's mind like a bed? Because it has to be made up for him every time he wants to use it." However unjust to the President, this does characterize his response to public opinion. He was not by temperament an expansionist, but if his immediate advisers and the public at large were preponderantly for annexation, he was willing to go along, and was thoroughly capable of finding good reasons for doing so. During the fall of 1898 he left Washington for a tour of the West, and made a great many brief speeches sounding out public opinion on annexation of the Philippines, on which he seems to have tentatively been determined in his own mind. He found a warm reception for himself and an enthusiastic response to the idea of expansion. Evidently his intent was confirmed by this exposure to public opinion and also by advices concerning the state of the public mind from correspondents and advisers, and when he returned to Washington those who were opposed to expansion found him unmovable.[1] The Peace Commission negotiating the treaty in Paris was instructed to ask for all the Philippine Islands, and this provision was included in the peace treaty signed on December 10, 1898.

The debate over the retention of the Philippines then went through two phases. During the first, which lasted from December 1898 to the second week in February 1899, the question was

---

[9] For the development of press opinion, see surveys cited in *Literary Digest*: Vol. XVII (July 1898), pp. 32 ff., (September 10, 1898), pp. 307–8; *Public Opinion*: Vol. XXV (August 4, 1898), pp. 132–5, (December 29, 1898), p. 810.
[1] Greenberg: Ibid., pp. 84–6.

argued both in the Senate and in the forums of public opinion.[2]
This phase neared its end when, on February 6, the Senate narrowly voted to ratify the peace treaty; it was definitively closed
on February 14, when a resolution sponsored by Senator Bacon
of Georgia, calling for early Philippine independence, was rejected by the preciously narrow margin of one vote—the casting
vote of the Vice President, which resolved a 29–29 tie. The second
phase of the debate extended throughout 1899 and 1900, when
American policy toward the Philippines was a matter of general
public discussion and a partisan issue in the Presidential campaign
of 1900.

Who was for and who against annexation? In large measure it
was a party issue. The *New York Herald* poll showed that of 241
Republican papers 84.2 per cent were *for* expansion, and of 174
Democratic papers 71.3 per cent were *against* expansion. In some
degree it was also a young man's movement. Geographically it
extended throughout all sections of the country, and seems to
have been favored everywhere but in the South, although even
there it was strong. We do not have a clear index of public opinion
for the period, but the practical politicians, whose business it was
to gauge public sentiment in the best way they knew, concluded
that the preponderant feeling was overwhelmingly for annexation.[3]

The debate over the acquisition of the Philippines was perhaps
no more than a ceremonial assertion of the values of both sides.
The real decisions were made in the office of Theodore Roosevelt,
in the Senate cloakroom, in the sanctums of those naval officers
from whom the McKinley administration got its primary information about the Philippines during its period of doubt over annexation, and, by McKinley's own testimony, in the privacy of his
chambers late at night. The public was, by and large, faced with
a *fait accompli* that, although theoretically reversible, had the
initial impetus of its very existence to carry it along. The intensity
of the public discussion, at any rate, showed that the American

[2] For the debate in the Senate, see *Congressional Record,* 55th Congress, 3rd session, *passim;* José S. Reyes: Ibid., chapter ii; W. Stull Holt:
Ibid., chapter viii; Marion Mills Miller: *Great Debates in American History*
(New York: 1913), Vol. III, pp. 245–324; Pratt: *Expansionists of 1898,* pp.
345–60.
[3] For impressive evidence on this point see Greenberg: Ibid., pp. 35,
42–3, 46–7, 49–50, 60, 67–9, 71, 86.

conscience had really been shocked. No type of argument was neglected on either side. Those who wanted to take the Philippines pointed to the potential markets of the East, the White Man's Burden, the struggle for existence, "racial" destiny, American traditions of expansion, the dangers of a general war if the Philippines were left open to a European scramble, the almost parental duty of assuming responsibility for the allegedly child-like Filipinos, the incapacity of the Filipinos for self-government, and so on. The anti-imperialists based their essential appeal on political principle. They pointed out that the United States had come into existence pledged to the idea that man should not be governed without his consent. They suggested that the violation of these political traditions (under which the nation had prospered) was not only a gross injustice to others, of which we should feel deeply ashamed, but also a way of tempting Providence and risking degeneration and disintegration as a sort of punishment for the atrophy of one's own principles. They pointed also to the expense of overseas dominions, standing armies, and navalism, and the danger of being embroiled in imperialist wars.

Many leading anti-imperialists were men of great distinction; their ranks included by far the greater part of the eminent figures of the literary and intellectual world. Most of them were, however, in the unfortunate position of opposing the fruits of a war that they had either favored or failed to oppose. Unlike the expansionists, they did not have complete control of a major party (there were more expansionists among the Democrats than there were anti-expansionists among the Republicans). They were hopelessly heterogeneous: Gold Democrats, Bryan Democrats, New-England-conscience Republicans, and a scattering of reformers and intellectuals.[4]

They organized late—the Anti-Imperialist League grew up in the months after November 1898—and their political leadership, however ardent in sentiment, pursued a hesitant and uncertain

[4] On the anti-imperialist movement see Fred H. Harrington: "The Anti-Imperialist Movement in the United States, 1898–1900," *Mississippi Valley Historical Review*, Vol. XXII (September 1935), pp. 211–30. On the intellectual class and anti-imperialism see the same author's "Literary Aspects of American Anti-Imperialism, 1898–1902," *New England Quarterly*, Vol. X (December 1937), pp. 650–67; William Gibson: "Mark Twain and Howells: Anti-Imperialists," *New England Quarterly*, Vol. XX (December 1947), pp. 435–70.

course. Their most eminent political leaders were chiefly old men, and the strongest appeal of the anti-imperialist movement seems to have been to the old, high-principled elements in the country, while the imagination of the young was fired far more by the rhetoric of expansionism.[5] It seems clear that the main chance of this minority was to use its position in the Senate to deny the necessary two-thirds approval to the peace treaty acquiring the islands from Spain. Here the opponents of annexation might have delayed it long enough to give themselves a chance to reach the public. But William Jennings Bryan, for reasons that are not altogether clear, persuaded enough members of his party to vote for the treaty to lose the case. Bryan hoped to continue the fight, of course, and grant independence later, but over his conduct and his explanations there hangs a heavy sense of inevitable defeat, stemming from his recognition that the voice of the majority demanded the bold and aggressive policy.[6]

V

In the arguments for annexation two essential moral and psychological themes appeared over and over again. These themes were expressed in the words Duty and Destiny. According to the

[5] Harrington points out that the average age of the prominent Republican members of the Anti-Imperialist League was 71.1 years, that of the 41 Vice Presidents of the Anti-Imperialist League only 58.3. By contrast, the average age of 14 leaders of expansionism in 1898 was 51.2. The American Consul in London, William M. Osborne, wrote to McKinley: "If what I hear and what I read is true there is a tremendous party growing up for expansion of territory, *especially by the younger and more active elements in the country.*" (Italics added.) Quoted by Greenberg: Ibid., pp. 46–7.

[6] Bryan argued that the treaty should be ratified because "a victory won against the treaty would prove only temporary if the people really favor a colonial policy," and because the opponents of the treaty, if they won, "would be compelled to assume responsibility for the continuance of war conditions and for the risks which always attend negotiations with a hostile nation." A minority, he argued, could not permanently thwart annexation. His policy was to appeal to the voters in the election of 1900; but it is impossible to make a Presidential election a clear referendum on foreign policy. Bryan found, during the campaign of 1900, that anti-imperialism was not a strong talking-point. Cf. Bryan: *The Second Battle* (Chicago: 1900), pp. 126–8; *Bryan on Imperialism* (Chicago: 1900), p. 16. On the election, see Thomas A. Bailey: "Was the Presidential Election of 1900 a Mandate on Imperialism?" *Mississippi Valley Historical Review*, Vol. XXIV (June 1937), pp. 43 ff.

first, to reject annexation of the Philippines would be to fail of fulfilling a solemn obligation. According to the second, annexation of the Philippines in particular, and expansion generally, were inevitable and irresistible.

The people had entered the war for what they felt to be purely altruistic and humanitarian reasons—the relief and liberation of the Cubans. The idea that territorial gains should arise out of this pure-hearted war of liberation, and the fact that before long the Americans stood in the same relation to the Filipinos as the Spaniards had stood to the Cubans, was most uncomfortable. These things raised moral questions that the anti-imperialists did not neglect to express and exploit. The imperialists were accused of breaking our national word, of violating the pledge made by McKinley himself that by our moral code forcible annexation would be "criminal aggression." They were also accused of violating the solemn injunctions of the Founding Fathers, particularly the principles of the Declaration of Independence. The rhetoric of Duty was a reassuring answer to this attempt to stir feelings of guilt.

The feeling that one may be guilty of wrongdoing can be heightened when the questionable act is followed by adversity.[7] Conversely, it may be minimized by the successful execution of a venture. Misfortune is construed as providential punishment; but success, as in the Calvinist scheme, is taken as an outward sign of an inward state of grace. One of the most conspicuous things about the war was the remarkable successes achieved by American arms, of which the most astonishing was Dewey's destruction, without losing a single American life, of the entire Spanish Eastern fleet in Manila Bay. Victories of this sort could readily be interpreted as Providential signs, tokens of Divine approval. It was widely reported in the United States that this was Dewey's own interpretation. "If I were a religious man, and I hope I am," he said, "I should say that the hand of God was in it." [8] This was precisely the sort of reassurance that was needed. "The magnificent fleets of Spain," declared a writer in a Baptist periodical, concerning Spain's senile and decrepit navy, "have

[7] Cf. Sigmund Freud: *Civilization and Its Discontents* (London: 1930), pp. 110–11.

[8] Louis A. Coolidge: *An Old-Fashioned Senator: Orville H. Platt* (New York: 1910), p. 302.

gone down as marvelously, I had almost said, as miraculously, as the walls of Jericho went down." The victory, said an editor of the *Christian and Missionary Alliance*, "read almost like the stories of the ancient battles of the Lord in the times of Joshua, David, and Jehoshophat."

Furthermore, what might have seemed a sin became transformed into a positive obligation, a duty. The feeling was: *Providence has been so indulgent to us, by giving us so richly of success, that we would be sinful if we did not accept the responsibility it has asked us to assume.* The Protestant clergy, those tender guardians of the national conscience, did not hesitate to make lavish use of such arguments. "To give to the world the life more abundant both for here and hereafter," reasoned a writer in the *Baptist Missionary Review*, "is the duty of the American people by virtue of the call of God. This call is very plain. The hand of God in history has ever been plain." "If God has brought us to the parting of the ways," insisted a writer in the *Churchman*, "we cannot hold back without rejecting divine leadership." [9] The rhetoric of secular leaders was hardly less inspired. "We will not renounce our part in the mission of our race, trustees under God, of the civilization of the world," said Senator Albert J. Beveridge. "God has not been preparing the English-speaking and Teutonic peoples for a thousand years for nothing but vain and idle self-contemplation and self-admiration. No! He has made us the master organizers of the world to establish system where chaos reigns. He has made us adepts in government that we may administer government among savages and senile peoples." [1]

The theme of Destiny was a corollary of the theme of Duty. Repeatedly it was declared that expansion was the result of a "cosmic tendency," that "destiny always arrives," that it was in the "inexorable logic of events," and so on. The doctrine that expansion was inevitable had of course long been familiar to Americans; we all know how often Manifest Destiny was invoked throughout the nineteenth century. Albert Weinberg has pointed out, however, that this expression took on a new meaning in the nineties. Previously destiny had meant primarily that American

---

[9] The quotations are from Pratt: *Expansionists of 1898*, pp. 289–90, 294, 305.

[1] Claude G. Bowers: *Beveridge and the Progressive Era* (New York: 1932), p. 121.

expansion, *when we willed it*, could not be resisted *by others* who might wish to stand in our way. During the nineties it came to mean that expansion "could not be resisted by Americans themselves, caught, willing or unwilling," in the coils of fate.[2] A certain reluctance on our part was implied. This was not quite so much what we *wanted* to do; it was what we *had* to do. Our aggression was implicitly defined as compulsive—the product not of our own wills but of objective necessity (or the will of God).

"Duty," said President McKinley, "determines destiny." While Duty meant that we had a moral obligation, Destiny meant that we would certainly fulfill it, that the capacity to fulfill it was inherent in us. Our history had been a continuous history of expansion; it had always succeeded before, therefore it was certain to succeed in the future. Expansion was a national and "racial" inheritance, a deep and irresistible inner necessity. Here was a plausible traditionalist answer to the accusation of a grave breach of tradition.

It is not surprising that the public should have found some truth in this concept of inevitable destiny, for the acts that first involved their country with the fate of the Philippines were willed and carried out by others and were made objects for public discussion and decision only *after* the most important commitments had been made. The public will was not freely exercised upon the question, and for the citizens at large, who were in the presence of forces they could not understand or control, the rhetoric of Destiny may have been a way of softening and ennobling the *fait accompli* with which they were presented. But what of the men whose wills were really effective in the matter? If we examine their case, we find that the manufacturers of inevitability believed deeply in their own product. Indeed, while the extent to which the idea of Destiny was generally accepted is unknown, its wide prevalence among influential politicians, editors, and publicists is beyond argument. When Senator Lodge wrote to Theodore Roosevelt in 1898 that "the whole policy of annexation is growing rapidly under the irresistible pressure of events," when President McKinley remarked in private to his secretary, concerning the taking of Hawaii, "It is manifest destiny," when he declared in his private instructions to the peace commissioners that "the march of events rules and overrules human action"—

2 Weinberg, *Manifest Destiny* (Baltimore: 1935), p. 254.

what was involved was not an attempt to sell an idea to the public but a mode of communication in which the insiders felt thoroughly at home; perhaps a magical mode of thought by which they quieted their own uncertainties. It is easy to say, from the perspective of the twentieth century, that where contemporaries heard the voice of God we think we can discern the carnal larynx of Theodore Roosevelt. But if the insiders themselves imagined that they heard the voice of God, we must be careful of imputing hypocrisy. It is significant that the idea of Destiny was effective even among people who had very grave doubts about the desirability of remaining in the Philippines. Secretary of the Navy John D. Long, who was affectionately regarded by Theodore Roosevelt as an old fuddy-duddy on this score, confided to a friend in 1898 that he would really have preferred the United States to remain what it had been during the first half of the nineteenth century—"provincial," as he expressed it, and "dominated by the New England idea. But," he added, "I cannot shut my eyes to the march of events—a march which seems to be beyond human control." [3]

It would be false to give the impression that only high moral and metaphysical concepts were employed in the imperialist argument. Talk about entry into the markets of Asia was heard often after Dewey's victory; but even those who talked about material gains showed a conspicuous and symptomatic inability to distinguish between interests, rights, and duties. Charles Denby, former minister to China and a member of McKinley's commission to study the Philippines, contributed to the *Forum* two interesting articles full of this confusion. The central business of diplomacy, confessed Denby, was to advance commerce. Our right to hold the Philippines was the right of conquerors. So far, Mr. Denby was all *Realpolitik*. But he continued that he favored keeping the islands because he could not conceive any alternative to doing so except seizing territory in China, and he did not want to oppress further "the helpless Government and people of China"! Thus a rather odd scruple crept in; but Mr. Denby quickly explained that this was simply because China's strength and prosperity were in America's interest. "We are after markets," he went on, sliding back into *Realpolitik*, and "along with these markets"—sliding back into morality—"will go our

[3] Greenberg: Ibid., p. 89.

beneficent institutions; and humanity will bless us." In a second article Mr. Denby shuttled back to "the cold, hard practical question. . . . Will the possession of these islands benefit us as a nation? If it will not, set them free tomorrow, and let their people, if they please, cut each other's throats." And yet, Mr. Denby made it clear, we did come as benefactors, bringing to our cut-throat friends "the choicest gifts—liberty and hope and happiness." [4]

There was, besides the oscillatory rhetoric of Mr. Denby, a let's-be-candid school, whose views were expressed by the Washington *Post*: "All this talk about benevolent assimilation; all this hypocritical pretense of anxiety for the moral, social, and intellectual exaltation of the natives . . . deceives nobody, avails nothing. . . . We all know, down in our hearts, that these islands . . . are important to us only in the ratio of their practical possibilities, and by no other. . . . Why not be honest?" [5]

There were others who found the primary benefit of our new imperial status in the social cohesion and military spirit that would result, hoping that the energies of the country would be deflected from internal to external conflict. "Marse" Henry Watterson, the well-known editor of the Louisville *Courier-Journal*, told a New York reporter: "From a nation of shopkeepers we become a nation of warriors. We escape the menace and peril of socialism and agrarianism, as England has escaped them, by a policy of colonization and conquest. From a provincial huddle of petty sovereignties held together by a rope of sand we rise to the dignity and prowess of an imperial republic incomparably greater than Rome. It is true that we exchange domestic dangers for foreign dangers; but in every direction we multiply the opportunities of the people. We risk Caesarism, certainly; but even Caesarism is preferable to anarchism. We risk wars; but a man has but one time to die, and either in peace or war, he is not likely to die until his time comes. . . . In short, *anything is better than the pace we were going before these present forces were started into life.* Already the young manhood of the country is as a

    [4] Charles Denby: "Shall We Keep the Philippines?" *Forum*, Vol. XXVI (October 1898), pp. 279–80; "Why the Treaty Should Be Ratified," ibid., Vol. XXVI (February 1899), pp. 644, 647.
    [5] Quoted in Grayson L. Kirk: *Philippine Independence* (New York: 1936), p. 25.

goodly brand snatched from the burning, and given a perspective replete with noble deeds and elevating ideas." [6]

VI

Since Julius W. Pratt published his *Expansionists of 1898* fifteen years ago it has been obvious that any interpretation of America's entry upon the paths of imperialism in the nineties in terms of rational economic motives would not fit the facts, and that a historian who approached the event with preconceptions no more supple than those, say, of Lenin's *Imperialism* would be helpless. This is not to say that markets and investments have no bearing; they do, but there are innumerable features of the situation that they do not explain at all. In so far as the economic factor was important, it can be better studied in terms of the relation between the depression and the public mood.

The alternative explanation has been the equally simple idea that the war was a newspapers' war. This notion, once again, has some point, but it certainly does not explain the war itself, much less its expansionist result. The New Deal period showed that the press is not powerful enough to impose upon the public mind a totally uncongenial view of public events. It must operate roughly within the framework of public predispositions. Moreover, not all the papers of the nineties were yellow journals. We must inquire into the structure of journalistic power and also into the personnel of its ownership and editorship to find out what differentiated the sensational editors and publishers from those of the conservative press, and what it was about their readership that led the former to the (correct) conclusion that they could expand their circulations by resorting to jingo sensationalism.

There is still another qualification that must be placed upon the role of the press: the press itself, whatever it can do with opinion, does not have the power to precipitate opinion into action. That is something that takes place within the *political* process, and we cannot tell that part of the story without examining the state of party rivalries, the derivation and goals of the political elites, and indeed the entire political context. We must, then, supplement our story about the role of the newspapers with at least two other

[6] *Literary Digest*, Vol. XVII (July 2, 1898), p. 214; italics added.

factors: the state of the public temper upon which the newspapers worked, and the manner in which party rivalries deflected domestic clashes into foreign aggression.

When we examine the public temper, we will find that the depression, together with such other events as the approaching completion of continental settlement, the growth of trusts, and the intensification of internal social conflict, had brought to large numbers of people intense frustrations in their economic lives and their careers. To others they had brought anxiety that a period of stagnation in national wealth and power had set in. The restlessness of the frustrated classes had been heightened by the defeat of Bryan in 1896. The anxieties about the national position had been increased among statesmen and publicists by the revival of world imperialism, in particular by the feeling that the nation was threatened by the aims of Germany, Russia, and Japan. The expansionist statesmen themselves were largely drawn from a restless upper-middle-class elite that had been fighting an unrewarding battle for conservative reform in domestic politics and that looked with some eagerness toward a more spacious field of action.

It is a psychological commonplace that we tend to respond to frustration with acts of aggression, and to allay anxieties by threatening acts against others. It seems suggestive that the underdog elements in American society showed a considerably higher responsiveness to the idea of war with Spain than the groups that were more satisfied with their economic or political positions. Our entry into the Philippines then aroused the interest of conservative groups that had been indifferent to the quixotism of freeing Cuba but were alert to the idea of capturing new markets. Imperialism appealed to members of both the business and political elites as an enlargement of the sphere of American power and profits. Many of the underdog elements also responded to this new note of national self-assertion; others, however, looked upon our conduct in the Philippines as a betrayal of national principles. Anti-expansionists attempted to stir a sense of guilt and foreboding in the nation at large. But the circumstances of the period 1898–1900—the return of prosperity and the quick spectacular victories in war—made it difficult for them to impress this feeling upon the majority. The rhetoric of Duty and Destiny carried the day. The anti-expansionists had neither the numbers nor the morale of their opponents. The most conspicuous result of their lack of drive and confidence can be seen in the lamentable strategy of Bryan over the ratification of the treaty.

Clearly this attempt to see the war and expansion in the light of social history has led us onto the high and dangerous ground of social psychology. On this terrain we historians are at a great disadvantage; we are inexpert psychologists, and in any event we cannot get the kind of data for this period which would satisfactorily substantiate any psychological hypotheses. However, we have little other choice than to move into this terrain wherever simple rationalistic explanations of national behavior leave us dissatisfied. What I have attempted here is merely a preliminary sketch of a possible explanatory model that would enlarge our conception of our task. It needs further inquiry—which might make it seem more plausible at some points, more questionable at others.

A further warning is necessary: this study has been narrowly focused on a single incident. No effort has been made—and an effort should be made—to compare this crisis with other expansionist crises in our own history, which I suspect will show important differences. No effort has been made to compare American imperialism with that of other countries. No claim has been made either that the various features of our behavior are unique to our own country or that they are the same as those which will be found elsewhere. Many parallels can be found in the history of other nations to the role of the press and the parties in whipping up foreign crises. Parallels without number could be found to the role of the administration in largely committing the nation to a foreign policy before it could be made a matter of public discussion. The rhetoric and ideology of expansion also were not singular to us; duty, destiny, racism, and the other shibboleths can be found elsewhere. Only a careful comparative inquiry will tell us how our behavior in this situation compares with other instances of our own behavior, or with the behavior of other peoples in roughly comparable situations.

I cannot refrain from adding to these notes on the methods of historical understanding another note on the tragicomical procedure of history itself. It may be of some value to us to be reminded how some of the more grandiose expectations of the nineties were realized. Cuba, to be sure, which could have been freed in peace, was freed in the war—in so far as the little country of Batistas and Machados can be considered free. The sensational newspapers that had boomed the war lost money on expensive extras, costly war-news coverage, and declining advertising.[7] I do not know whether those silverites who wanted the war really expected that it would remonetize silver, but if they did they were rewarded with McKinley's renewed triumph and the Gold Standard Act of 1900. As for business, the gigantic markets of the East never materialized, and the precise value of the Philippines in getting at them is arguable. The islands themselves proved to be a mildly profitable colony that came to absorb a little over one per cent of all United States investments abroad. Yet within a generation the United States had committed itself to restoring independence to the Philippines. When this promise was enacted in 1934 many descendants of Aguinaldo's rebels were unenthusiastic about their new economic and strategic position.[8] Finally, the exact estimation that is to be put on our strategic commitment in the Far East, which began with the Philippines, is still a matter of debate. We should, however, make note of the earlier opinion of one of our most brilliant and farsighted statesmen, who declared in 1907 that the Philippines were the Achilles' heel of our strategic position and should be given "nearly complete independence" at the "earliest possible moment."[9] The author of these remarks was Theodore Roosevelt.

[7] Frank Luther Mott: *American Journalism* (New York: 1947), pp. 537–8.
[8] Julius W. Pratt: *America's Colonial Experiment*, pp. 243–4; 291–310.
[9] Pringle: *Theodore Roosevelt*, pp. 408–9.

IX. *Rebellion in Art*

In the spring of 1913, ex-President Theodore Roosevelt, who detested the lunatic fringe in art as much as he did in politics, attended the exhibit of modern painting in the New York armory and had special words of condemnation for a picture that he called "The Naked Man Going Down Stairs." T. R. only expressed the genteel view when he dismissed the Futurists as representing "only a smirking pose of retrogression," but he sensed the revolutionary import of the show and its subversive implications. Like anarchism, feminism, Freudianism, Bergsonism, and Imagism, with which it was contemporary, Post-Impressionism helped to destroy the "serenity of custom." As Professor Meyer Schapiro suggests, the attacks against modern art in 1913 have been renewed in the current assaults by the Philistines of totalitarianism, who see in the individualism of artists an affront to the state.

IX

Rebellion in Art

Meyer Schapiro

Associate Professor of Fine Arts, Columbia University

The great event, the turning-point in American art called the Armory Show, was briefly this. In December 1911, some American artists who were dissatisfied with the restricted exhibitions of the National Academy of Design formed a new society, the American Association of Painters and Sculptors, in order to exhibit on a broader basis, without jury or prizes. The members did not belong to a particular school of art; several of them had shown at the National Academy itself. They came together not simply from opposition to the æsthetic of the Academy (although there was a stirring towards modernity among them) but from a collective professional need: to create a more open market, so to speak, a means of exhibition accessible to the unacademic and not yet established men. The most active elements in the new society were the younger and more advanced artists; but not the most advanced ones, who seem to have been less concerned about exhibitions or societies at that moment.

This aim of the Association was soon overlaid by another, which none of the members perhaps foresaw. Their first exhibition, planned as a great show of American painting and sculpture at the Sixty-ninth Regiment Armory in New York—a show inspired by a new confidence of American artists in the importance of their work and of art in general—became an international show in which European paintings and sculptures far surpassed in interest and overshadowed the American. The change in the intention of the Show was due to the idea of the president, Arthur B.

Davies, to exhibit also some recent European work. But while traveling abroad for this purpose, Davies and his collaborator, Walt Kuhn, were so impressed by the new European art, which they had known only slightly, and by the great national and international shows of the newest movements in art, held in 1912 in London, Cologne, and Munich, that they borrowed much more than they had first intended. They were caught up by the tide of advancing art and carried beyond their original aims into a field where they could not maintain themselves; their own work, while unacademic, was submerged by the new art. In the great public that attended the Show in New York, Chicago, and Boston in the spring of 1913, this foreign painting and sculpture called out an extraordinary range of feelings, from enthusiasm for the new to curiosity, bewilderment, disgust, and rage. For months the newspapers and magazines were filled with caricatures, lampoons, photographs, articles, and interviews about the radical European art. Art students burned the painter Matisse in effigy, violent episodes occurred in the schools, and in Chicago the Show was investigated by the Vice Commission upon the complaint of an outraged guardian of morals. So disturbing was the exhibition to the society of artists that had sponsored it that many members repudiated the vanguard and resigned; among them were painters like Sloan and Luks, who the day before had been considered the rebels of American art. Because of the strong feelings aroused within the Association, it broke up soon after, in 1914. The Armory Show was its only exhibition. For years afterwards the Show was remembered as a historic event, a momentous example of artistic insurgence. It excited the young painters and sculptors, awakened them to fresh possibilities, and created in the public at large a new image of modernity. It forced on many an awareness that art had just undergone a revolution and that much they had admired in contemporary art during the last decades was problematic, old-fashioned, destined to die. In time the new European art disclosed at the Armory Show became the model of art in the United States.

Because of the immense excitement provoked by the foreign works, it is easy to exaggerate the effect of the Armory Show upon American art. The later course of art and public taste was undoubtedly the result of other factors besides this exhibition, although we can hardly estimate precisely how much any one of them counted in the end. It may be that, without the Armory Show, art today and our ideas about art would be much as they are. For some years before, there had been in New York a growing interest in advanced European art, supported and stimulated mainly by Alfred Stieglitz, the pioneer artist-photographer, at his gallery "291"; here were shown works by Rodin, Lautrec, Matisse, and Picasso, and by young Americans (Weber, Maurer, Marin, and Hartley) who had been abroad and absorbed the new art. American painters and sculptors had been going to Europe to study all through the last century, and the best of them had brought back the lessons of the latest European work. Paintings by several who belonged to the current of European modernism could be seen at the Armory Show. Since 1908 there had been a number of exhibitions in New York of artists who had banded together as "independents"; their work was hardly as advanced as what Stieglitz was showing, but it helped to prepare the public and the young painters for the newest art. Most important of all—although not easy to prove—the conditions that had disposed men to create a new kind of art in Europe were becoming more evident in the United States. The appeal of the new art coincided with a trend towards greater freedom in many fields. Modern art eventually came to satisfy a demand that was felt also in architecture, literature, music, and dance.

In this continuous process the Armory Show marks a point of acceleration, and it is instructive for the student of social life as well as of art to observe how a single event in a long series may acquire a crucial importance because it dramatizes or brings into the open before a greater public what is ordinarily the affair of a small group. The very scope and suddenness of this manifestation of the new art were a shock that stirred the sensitive more effectively than could have a dozen small exhibitions. The Show, coming at a moment of intense ferment in European art, lifted people out of the narrowness of a complacent provincial taste and compelled them to judge American art by a world standard. The years 1910 to 1913 were the heroic period in which the most astonishing innovations had occurred; it was then that the basic types of the art of the next forty years were created. Compared to the movement of art at that time, today's modernism seems a slackening or stagnation. About 1913 painters, writers, musicians, and architects felt themselves to be at an epochal turning-point corresponding to an equally decisive transition in philosophical thought and social life. This sentiment of imminent change inspired a general insurgence, a readiness for great events. The years just before the first World War were rich in new associations of artists, vast projects, and daring manifestoes. The world of art had never known so keen an appetite for action, a kind of militancy that gave to cultural life the quality of a revolutionary movement or the beginnings of a new religion. The convictions of the artists were transmitted to an ever larger public, and won converts for whom interest in the new art became a governing passion.

As a type of exhibition, the Armory Show was a challenging experience for the public, which was placed here in a new role. It had to consider more than ever before an unfamiliar and difficult art. Its judgments were unprepared by the selections of an authoritative jury, nor could it rely on established criteria of its own. Through the Armory Show, modern art burst upon the public like a problematic political issue that called for a definite choice. Taste as a personal decision assumed a new significance, which was to affect the meaning of art as such. Until then the idea of great art had been embodied mainly in those solemn, well certified, old European works of fabulous price, transported from the palaces of the declining European aristocracy, together with objects from the treasure chambers of kings, to the homes of the American rich. After the Armory Show—for more than one reason, but especially because of the growth of modern art—the collecting of old masters began to lose its former prestige, just as the reproduction of Renaissance villas and châteaux gave way to the design of modern homes. The cultural dignity of modern painting and sculpture was also recognized by the law; within a year of the Show, one of its most enthusiastic supporters, the collector John Quinn, persuaded the government to remove the import duty on foreign works of contemporary art.

The three hundred thousand or more visitors who saw the exhibition in the three cities were a far greater number than had attended the annual salons of the National Academy, although smaller than the public that wandered through the picture galleries at the World's Fairs. But the 1913 show was of art alone, unlike the Fairs, where art was one spectacle among many, beside machines, manufactured goods, and popular amusements. Here one came for art itself, whether one took it seriously or to satisfy curiosity about a widely advertised sensational matter. And as art it was more pointedly contemporary, in a new and radical sense—unknown to previous exhibitions, and standard from then on for shows of independent art—namely, that modernity as such was a quality, so that people looking at these works were led to consider them as belonging to the moment, to the year 1913, like the new airplanes and automobiles and the current ideas of science or the aims of the advanced political groups. Indeed, the Armory Show had something of the role in art that the Halls of Machines, with their exciting display of new inventions, had for the public feeling about technology at the World's Fairs. The contemporary in art—or living art, as it was called—did not mean simply whatever was done at the time, since the old styles and the new, the imitative and inventive, were on view together, side by side. It meant rather the progressively contemporary, that which modified the acquired past and opened the way to a still newer future. And this sense of the growing present led to a revision of the image of the past, so that one could single out in history a family of the great moderns of the past, those artists whose independence had transformed art. For them, a room had been reserved at the Armory Show; Ingres, Delacroix, Corot, Courbet and the Impressionists, artists whom the academicians acknowledged as masters, were presented beside the modern insurgents as their ancestors, a line of great innovating spirits. The plan of the Show contained then a lesson and a program of modernity. It was also a lesson of internationalism, although the emblem of the Show was the native pine, a reminder of the American revolution as well as of the eternal greenness of the tree of art. Since the awareness of modernity as the advancing historical present was forced upon the spectator by the art of Spaniards, Frenchmen, Russians, Germans, Englishmen, and Americans, of whom many were working in Paris, away from their native lands, this concept of the time was universalized; the moment belonged to the whole world, Europe and America were now united in a common cultural destiny, and people here and abroad were experiencing the same modern art that surmounted local traditions.

II

What was the nature of this new art? In what lay its novelty and its challenge to the art it came to supplant? The great variety of this rapidly developing modern art obscured its character and inspired vague or onesided interpretations. How could one enclose in a single formula the clear, bright works of Matisse and the intricate Nude of Duchamp? The creators had no ultimate common goal, but advanced from canvas to canvas, following up new ideas that arose in the course of their work, hardly imagining what would emerge in the end; they seemed to be carried along by a hidden logic that unfolded gradually, yielding forms surprising to themselves. Those artists and critics who tried in writing to anticipate the future of this art turned out to be wrong. They were contradicted in a few years by unexpected diversities and reactions. We begin only now to see the process as a whole; and it appears to us very complex, a fluctuating movement that at times negates itself. But the vaguer interpretations were perhaps not altogether bad. The more precise definitions narrowed the field and led to sectarianism and indifference at a moment when what was most in question was the artist's freedom in exploring a new realm of possibility in his art. It must be said that the Armory Show helped to maintain the loose thinking and confusion about modern art. Cubists, Expressionists, Fauves, Orphists, Neo-Impressionists, Symbolists, Classicists, and Primitivizing Realists were exhibited side by side, and the greatest artists were presented on the same plane as the imitators and the lesser men. In the selection of the Europeans, Odilon Redon, a mystical painter of poetic and allegorical themes, had the place of honor with forty-two works; there were fifteen by Puvis de Chavannes, an academic artist of the nineteenth century; the Englishman Augustus John, a quite secondary and occasional modern, received equal prominence with Matisse. By comparison, Picasso and Braque were poorly represented, and their invention, Cubism, the most important new art of the time, which was to determine much of the painting and sculpture of the next decades, was fixed in the public's mind through the pictures of Picabia and Duchamp, works that were marginal to the originators' central ideas. The European paintings had been chosen by men who had just come to modernism; their thinking had not ripened to the point of critical discrimination, and in their choice they had responded generously to the excitement of first discoveries and to suggestions from friends abroad. Yet by showing so many varied works, at the risk of presenting the new art as an incoherent chorus of odd individual voices, they set before the astonished public a boundless modernity in which an open mind could not fail to discover something to its taste. More fastidious groups, self-enclosed in their attachment to a particular ideal of art, although stimulating at first, often become ingrown and sterile; modern art required a varied audience and the enthusiasm of fresh talents in order to develop. And this need the Armory Show certainly helped to satisfy, in spite—or perhaps because—of its shapeless, uncritical modernity.

Friendly critics praised the courage and vitality and integrity of the modern artists—qualities that might have been found in the art of any time—without venturing to analyze the new styles. The hostile criticism—narrow and shortsighted as it was—in denouncing the deviations from past art, pointed more directly to the essential novelty: the image was distorted or had disappeared altogether; colors and forms were unbearably intense; and the execution was so free as to seem completely artless. It was in the advanced work of the Cubists and of Kandinsky and Matisse that these features stood out most; among the sculptors, Brancusi was the arch-modern. The nature of the new art was not sufficiently defined by these peculiarities—nor is it our purpose here to undertake a better definition—but through them we may come closer to the issues in the conflicting judgments of the Show.

1. In only a few works had representation been abandoned entirely. But in many that preserved recognizable object-forms, these were strangely distorted. It is not easy to say which was more disturbing, nature deformed or the canvas without nature. Both seemed to announce the end of painting as an art.

For millennia, painting had been an art of image-making. The painter represented imaginary religious, mythical, or historical subjects, or he imaged the world before him in landscapes, portraits, and still-lifes. The world, "picture," which literally means: "what is painted," had come to stand for any representation, even a verbal or mental one. All through the nineteenth century, how-

ever, artists and writers had proposed that the true aim of painting should not be to tell a story or to imitate a natural appearance,
but to express a state of feeling, an idea, a fancy, or, aspiring to
the condition of music, to create a harmony of colors and forms.
Yet the image remained the indispensable foundation of painting.
The coming of photography about 1840 strengthened the conviction of artists that the purely æsthetic or expressive was the
goal of art; but for sixty years afterwards image-painting continued and even became more realistic, exploring new aspects of
appearance—light, atmosphere, and movement—a fact that speaks
against the view that modern art arose as an answer to photography. In the twentieth century the ideal of an imageless art of
painting was realized for the first time, and the result was shocking—an arbitrary play with forms and colors that had only a
vague connection with visible nature. Some painters had discovered that by accenting the operative elements of art—the stroke,
the line, the patch, the surface of the canvas—and by disengag-
ing these from the familiar forms of objects, and even by elimi-
nating objects altogether, the painting assumed a more actively
processed appearance, the aspect of a thing made rather than a
scene represented, a highly ordered creation referring more to
the artist than to the world of external things. The picture also
became in this way a more powerful, direct means of conveying
feeling or, at least, the interior patterns of feeling; the strokes
and spots, in their degree of contrast, in their lightness or weight,
their energy or passivity, were unmistakably "physiognomic."
And in paintings that still preserved some representation, beside
the new self-evidence of the painter's marks with their vague in-
timations and tendencies of feeling, the image acquired an aspect
of fantasy or of some obscure region of thought. It was such positive effects rather than a search for some presumed absolute or
long-lost ideal essence of art that guided the artists in their approach to abstraction. They were neither geometers nor logicians
nor philosophers, but painters who had discovered new possibilities in the processes of their art. Much was said about purity or
form in itself, but in practice this meant a particular economy and
rigor in employing the new means.

The visitors at the Show had all seen nonrepresentational works
of art before—geometric ornament is an example—and many who
enjoyed the new art tried to justify it by the analogy of rugs and

textiles. (To which Theodore Roosevelt in a critical, though not unfriendly review of the Show, answered that he preferred the Navajo rug in his bathroom.) But this explanation was unconvincing and obscured the nature of the new art. Decoration, even in its freer forms, is servile, bound to some practical object, and bears within its patterns the trace of adaptation. Ornament embellishes its object, makes it richer, more charming or prominent; it accents the marginal or terminal parts of its carrier—the surface, the base, the border, or crown—but has no intensity and rarely invites us into itself. We can imagine the pattern of a rug continued indefinitely or enlarged, without much loss of effect; but how would we respond to a Rembrandt portrait exactly repeated several times on the same wall? In past arts of ornament, the whole was legible at once as a simple structure; a particular unit was expanded in a fairly regular way; given a part of the work, one could easily reconstruct the whole. In the new art of "abstract" painting there is no obvious nuclear motif or simple rule of design. No less than in the latest image-painting, something intimate, close to the artist himself, was projected, which required of the spectator an active engagement and response. The unpredictable character of the whole and of the details of form reflected the contingencies of life itself, with its changing complication, conflicts and occasions of freedom. (Not by chance had modern architects, who admired the new painting and sculpture, eliminated all ornament from their buildings.) Only weak imitators who failed to grasp the organic complexity of the new works, passive personalities who preferred the "decorative" in image-painting as well, interpreted Cubism or abstract art as a kind of ornament of the canvas. But for the unprepared or prejudiced observer the strongest works were chaotic and illegible, without the obvious course of an ornament; they possessed an intricacy very close to the formless, hence requiring a most tense control by the artist. A protest against formlessness and unintelligibility had been addressed in the 1870's to the Impressionist masters whose pictures of landscapes were also informal in design, offering to the spectator a turbulent surface of little brush-strokes, many of which could not be matched with a represented object. The "impression" struck people then as something arbitrary, and several decades passed before it came to be widely recognized and enjoyed as the artist's elaboration of a common experience. Impressionism was in fact the true forerunner of this art in so far as it translated on the canvas the "subjective" moment in vision (including the induced complementary colors), as well as the shapeless, diffused, unlocalized components of the landscape due to the light and atmosphere, giving at the same time a new tangibility and independence to the crust of pigment. But while the vision of an Impressionist painter was tied to a moment and place that could still be recaptured through the image of the subject (however much this subject had been transformed by the brushwork—and the image was often most faithful through this vagueness), in the new art the transformation was more radical and complete, and the starting-point often something more distinctly personal than the impression of a landscape.

Imageless painting of this kind—without objects, yet with a syntax as complex as that of an art of representation—was a revolution in the concept of art. The image had pointed to something external to the artist, an outer world to which he conformed or from which he took his most cherished values. It had not mattered whether the image was symbolical or accurate or free; whatever its style, it carried the spectator to a common sphere beyond art in nature, religion, myth, history, or everyday life. The represented objects possessed qualities that often provided a bridge to the qualities of the painting. But in the new art this kind of organizer of the observer's attention had largely disappeared. Now for the first time the content of the art was constituted by the special world of the artist, whether as personality or painter. His feelings, his operations, his most specialized and subtle perceptions, furnished the primary themes of his art. And he trained himself to perceive, feel, and design in such a way as to realize to the highest degree the freedom and self-sufficiency of his work, seeking for means that would contribute most to the desired independence and fertility of the artistic act.

The artists who abandoned the image completed a long process of dethronement of an ancient hierarchy within the subject-matter of art. In Western tradition, the greatest works had been judged to be those with the noblest subjects. Art with themes of religion, history, and myth was conceded an intrinsic superiority. By the middle of the nineteenth century, with the decline of aristocratic and religious institutions, the more intimate themes of persons, places, and things had come to be regarded as no less valid than the others; only the personal and the artistic mattered in judging a work of art. From the viewpoint of the artists who were aware of this development of the subjects, the new art was the most emancipated of all, the most advanced in the humanizing of culture, indeed the most spiritual too, since only what was immediately given in feeling and thought, unfettered by exterior objects, was admitted to the work of art.

It was objected that such an art would cut off the artist from others, that he would end by communicating only with himself. But the fact that so many painters and sculptors adopted this art and created freely within it, learning from one another and producing an astonishing variety of work, showed that abstraction had a common human basis; it was not so arbitrary and private as had seemed.

But even the artists who retained some links with the world of objects, without submitting to the strict requirement of likeness, were criticized as eccentrics; they were told that if one accepted some natural forms, a consistent representation was necessary. In time it became clear that precisely this free play of object-forms and invented forms gave to such works their peculiar expressiveness; here too the active presence of the artist was felt in the power of the operative elements of stroke, spot, and surface, and in the transformation of the world of objects.

2. Besides taking the observer into a no-man's land of imageless painting, where he had great trouble in finding his way, the new art disturbed him by the intensity of its colors and forms. To many cultivated eyes, brought up on the old masters, these works were not only meaningless, but altogether without taste. An artist like Matisse, who represented objects and was respected for the skill of his drawings, employed shockingly strong tones and abrupt contrasts, and scored his outlines emphatically in black. The brush strokes of a Kandinsky, a Rouault, or a Vlaminck were a violent assault on the canvas. The normally courteous critic, Royal Cortissoz, described a Kandinsky "improvisation" as "fragments of refuse thrown out of a butcher's shop upon a bit of canvas"; and another, more liberal writer spoke of Matisse's art as "blatantly inept" and "essentially epileptic." It is true that the qualities of intense works of art seem more drastic when first shown and in time lose their flagrancy; Romantic and Impressionist paintings that had appeared outrageous in their relative formlessness and high color today look obvious in composition and even subdued in tone. But in the art of the last sixty or seventy years, especially since Van Gogh, there has been a mounting intensity, of which the effect is not reduced by long acquaintance with the works. (At the other end of the spectrum of modern expressiveness is a kind of negative intensity, not always less difficult than the positive kind and no less striking, a search for faint nuances, for an ultimate in delicacy and bareness, that still surprises us—it appeared in Whistler, Monet, and Redon, and more recently in works of Malevitch and Klee, among others.)

In the painting of the seventeenth to the nineteenth century the elements were graded and tempered, and brought into a smooth harmony dominated by a particular color or key; the whole lay within a middle range and extremes were avoided. Light and shade softened the colors, the edges of objects were finely blurred in atmosphere and shadows, contrasts were mitigated by many qualifying tones, and objects were set back at some distance from the picture plane. Nothing was stated brusquely or loudly. The high examples of intensity of color were Titian, Rubens, and Delacroix, artists of mellowed aspect who subdued their strongest tones by light and shadow.

Beside this measured art, the new painters seemed to be coarse ruffians, and their art a reversion to barbarism. These artists were aware of their own savagery and admired the works in the ethnological museums, the most primitive remains of the Middle Ages, folk art and children's art, all that looked bold and naïve. In this love of the primitive as a stronger, purer humanity, the moderns built upon a novel taste of the nineteenth century; the realists of the 1840's and 1850's—lovers of the sincere in art and life—had discovered the beauty of children's drawings and popular imagery and the carvings of savages. But now for the first time the intensity and simplicity of primitive color and drawing were emulated seriously. Before that, even in Gauguin's art, the primitive qualities were still subject to the naturalism and the tempering devices, the atmosphere, the depth, and light and shade of civilized European art. These sophisticated means were not abandoned in the twentieth century, but they were no longer a rule. The primitive aspect was hardly a return to a savage or archaic art, as inattentive critics supposed. Comparing a Matisse or Picasso with a primitive painting, one recognizes in the moderns the sen-

sibility of a thoughtful disciplined artist, always alert to new possibilities. The simplicity of the primitive is a fixed, often rigid
style with a limited range of elements, and pervades his entire
work; in the modern it is only a quality of certain aspects. Like
the intricacy of composition already mentioned, which is not less
complex than that of the most realistic art of the nineteenth century, the color includes besides the new intensities rare chords,
off-tones, and subtle combinations—the heritage of the post-Ren-
aissance palette applied with a new freedom. For the moderns the
saturated colors, the forceful outlines, and geometrical forms
were a rediscovery of elementary potencies of the medium. They
were more than æsthetic, for through them one affirmed the value
of the feelings as essential human forces unwisely neglected or
suppressed by a utilitarian or hypocritically puritanic society.
Together with this corrective simplicity and intensity, which
seemed to revive a primitive layer of the self, like the child's and
the savage's, and which gave a new vitality to art, the painters admitted to their canvases, with much wonder, gaiety and courage,
uncensored fancies and associations of thought akin to the world
of dreams; and in this double primitivism of the poetic image and
the style they joined hands with the moralists, philosophers, and
medical psychologists who were exploring hidden regions and resources of human nature in a critical, reforming spirit. The artists'
search for a more intense expression corresponded to new values
of forthrightness, simplicity, and openness, to a joyous vitality in
everyday life.

3. A third disturbing innovation, related to the others, was the
loosening of technique. It had begun even before Impressionism,
which was attacked in the 1870's and '80's for its frightful daub-
ing of paint. The later artists outdid this freedom, enlarging and
weighting the brush-strokes and painting more sketchily, sometimes with an unconstrained fury. The old conception of painting
as a magic art, the source of a jeweled, mysteriously luminous
surface of impastos and glazes, was abandoned for simpler,
franker means. The new painters were no less sensitive to the
fabric of their work, but, concerned with immediacy of effect
and with the elementary expressiveness of colors and forms, they
found the inherited standards of facture an obstacle to their aims.
As practiced by conservative contemporaries, the old craftsmanship had become an empty, useless skill, an elaborate cookery,

that had lost its original savor. Some of the moderns adopted instead the bare coat of flat color, the house-painter's method, as better suited to their ends; or they devised still other sketchy techniques and new textures with a greater range of expression than the old. Just before the Armory Show, the Cubists, with a sublime daring or impudence, had begun to replace the sacred substance of oil paint by pasted paper, newsprint, sand, and other vulgar materials, which were applied to the canvas with a playful humor. Among the sculptors, too, the traditional marble and bronze were losing their aura of intrinsic beauty; roughly finished stone and plaster, cast stone, wood, brass, and new alloys became more frequent in this art. Most astonishing of all were the open sculptures of metal without pedestal or frame, pure constructions like industrial objects, suspended from the wall or ceiling; these first appeared shortly after the Armory Show and have transformed the character of sculpture in our time. Just as there was no longer a superior subject-matter in art, the privileged techniques and materials were brought down to a common level of substances and means, including those of modern industry and everyday use. The new materials and processes of sculpture possess within their commonplaceness a poetic appeal, like that of the vernacular in modern verse; they have also awakened the observer to the qualities of materials in their native and processed states, and to the beauty of the technical as an inventive manipulation of forms.

III

It would be surprising if such an art, introduced full-grown to an unprepared public and to artists who were bound to tradition, met with no resistance.

The modernists took this for granted; they knew that all the advanced movements of the nineteenth century, since the Romantic, had been violently attacked, and it had become a platitude of criticism that in every age innovators have had to fight against misunderstanding. This view of the original artist as a martyr, and of the development of art as a bitter struggle between partisans of opposed styles, is hardly borne out by history. The great artists of the Renaissance who created the new forms were recognized early in their careers and received important commissions—Masaccio, van Eyck, Donatello, Leonardo, Raphael, and Titian are examples. Conflicts had indeed occurred in the sixteenth century, but at no time in the past were they as acute as in the last hundred years, except perhaps in the medieval iconoclastic controversy that arose from factions in church and state, more than from artists or new styles of painting and sculpture. The hostility to novel contemporary art, the long-delayed public recognition of the most original recent artists, point rather to singularities of modern culture. Among these are the great span in the cultural levels of those who support art; the ideological value of competing styles as representative of conflicting social viewpoints; and the extraordinary variability of modern art, which requires from its audience a greater inner freedom and openness to others and to unusual feelings and perceptions than most people can achieve under modern conditions, in spite of the common desire for wider experience. But most important of all perhaps is the changed relation of culture to institutional life. Past art, attached to highly organized systems of church, aristocracy, and state, or to the relatively closed, stable world of the family, remained in all its innovations within the bounds of widely accepted values, and continued to express feelings and ideas that had emerged or were emerging within these institutions; while independent modern art, which constructs a more personal, yet unconfined world, often critical of common ideas, receives little or no support from organized groups and must find its first backers among private individuals—many of them artists and amateurs—for whom art is an altogether personal affair. The original modern art is usually far in advance of the public, which shares the artist's freedom and feeling of isolation (in both their agreeable and negative aspects), but has not discovered the sense of its new experience and aspirations still vaguely formulated within the framework of inherited and often contradictory beliefs, and must assimilate gradually—if it does so at all—and most often in a weakened, vulgarized form, the serious artistic expressions emanating from its own world. The inventions of the artist are in this respect unlike the novelties of physical science and technology. These make little claim on the feelings of lay individuals and are accepted at once as gadgets or ideas that can be utilized without personal involvement or shift in general outlook.

At the same time, the very mobility of our culture, the frequent changes of art in the nineteenth century, have weakened the resistance to new styles, although a generation or more is required for the modern forms to penetrate the originally hostile groups. In our day what is defended against the advanced art is itself something fairly recent that was at first equally difficult. The experience of the last hundred and fifty years and the historical study of art—which has its practical side in the widespread collecting of "antiques"—have accustomed people to thinking of every style as a phenomenon of its time, issuing from a unique set of conditions and ideals that were themselves possible only then and were soon to be replaced by others. Or if art was conceived as a self-generating process, its stages had their own necessity and limited tenure, unfolding new problems that the following age was to solve. To maintain in practice the art of an older period meant therefore to deny the principle that life itself is a permanent evolution, marked by occasional leaps or sudden advances; it implied a return to the outlook and circumstances of that time, and this was impossible. It was an avowal of impotence, which could only confirm the opinion of serious critics of the nineteenth century that modern society was decadent because it had produced no original style in architecture, the most social and symptomatic art. The necessary conclusion that all periods are equal in the eyes of God, provided they have their own style, dismayed many who could not easily give up in practice so much that they cherished in past art, and who found nothing of comparable nobility in their own time. What seemed to be a hopeless relativism in this eternal treadmill of stylistic invention—which appeared to some writers a cyclical motion, bringing art back to its primitive states—was surmounted, however, in the modernist's vision of the art of the last few centuries, and even of older art, as a process pointing to a goal: the progressive emancipation of the individual from authority, and the increasing depth of self-knowledge and creativeness through art. While few artists believed that there was progress in art as in science and industry or in social institutions, many were certain that there was, relative to the possibilities of the time, a reactionary and a progressive art, the latter being engaged in a constant effort of discovery, as in science, although the genius of the old painters, like that of Newton and Galileo, was not surpassed. The great artist, in this view, is essentially a revolutionary spirit who remakes his art, disclosing ever new forms. The accomplishment of the past ceases to be a closed tradition of noble content or absolute perfection, but a model of individuality, of history-making effort through continual self-transformation. Far from being the destroyers of eternal values, as their opponents said, the new artists believed themselves to be the true bearers of a great tradition of creativeness. Movement and novelty, the working out of latent possibilities, were, they supposed, the essence of history. In this, as well as in the beauty of his work, lay the artist's dignity. The movement of modern art had therefore an ethical content; artistic integrity required a permanent concern with self-development and the evolution of art. This belief in a common historical role, dramatized by the opposition of a static, conservative art, gave the artists a solidarity and collective faith, a creative morale, that sustained them at a time when they were most cut off from the public and institutional life.

Following another and unhistorical line of thought, some modernists supposed themselves to be progressive and true heirs of the great tradition because they had rediscovered a principle underlying all art, one that had been lost in the dark centuries of naturalistic painting. What was ever valid in past art, they believed, was not its skill in representation—this was merely a concession to the demands of the literal-minded, Philistine patrons before photography was available, and distracted artists from their nobler task—but its power of form and expression through which that old art still moves us today when we contemplate the old pictures and statues in ignorance of their religious or mythological sense; and in the modern search for this universal power they affirmed their continuity with a great tradition that had suffered a long decay. The fact is that the young moderns had an insatiable hunger for past art; the new movements were accompanied by a revaluation of forgotten epochs and an extraordinary expansion and deepening of historical research, often by scholars who drew from their experience of modern art a quicker sympathy for the old.

These attitudes were supported by two peculiarities of the cultural situation. In many countries, indeed in most countries outside France, the new style replaced a stagnant backward art. In France, Matisse and Braque are not greater artists than Cézanne and Renoir, but for Spaniards, Picasso and Gris mark a genuine advance after the generations of uninspired painting following the time of Goya; and for Russia Kandinsky, Chagall, Lipchitz and the whole modern school in that country were a real revival of an art that had produced nothing of international significance since the days of the old icon-painters.

A second important fact is the unique intensity of the growth of styles of painting since the 1830's, more than of literature or the other arts, unless perhaps recent music. Every great painter in that period (and many a lesser one) is an innovator in the structure of painting. In poetry and the novel the great names, Tolstoy, Dostoyevsky, Yeats, are not innovators in form; in a style or conception of their medium which hardly goes beyond that of the preceding generation, they express a new experience or outlook. The serious innovators in form, like Mallarmé and Joyce, are few. It may be that the exceptional fertility of modern painting and sculpture in new forms is connected with the restriction of their content to the perceptual, the interior, and the æsthetic-constructive, the intensity of formal invention being an indispensable sign of the artist's power and depth; while the writer is still absorbed by the representation of a world in which the extra-artistic meanings have still a considerable force.

Yet if the creation of new forms or the timeless recovery of essentials was the main task of the modern painters and sculptors, and art seemed to the public increasingly esoteric, a professional affair detached from the interests that had once furnished its subject-matter, this whole movement was felt by the artists and its defenders and even by some of its most vigorous opponents as part of a general modern outlook—a radical transformation of sensibility and thought. The individual, his freedom, his inner world, his dedication, had become primary; and the self-affirming nature of the new art, with its outspoken colors and forms and more overt operations, was a means of realizing the new values, which were collective values, for individuality is a social fact, a matter of common striving, inconceivable without the modern conditions and means. The artists' values were, in a broad sense, general values of the time, asserted in different ways by philosophers and by ethical, religious, economic, political, and pedagogical thinkers, for whom the individual's self-realization was the central problem, however limited their thought. Pervading so many fields, dominating literature too, these concepts were a developing heritage of the nineteenth century. They appeared inevitable, the necessary ones for the new century, which seemed an age of unlimited possibilities, a historical epoch as distinct and gigantic as any in the past.

Contemporary thought was made up of different and even opposed strands; but several were remarkably like the new art. Whether the artists were affected by the philosophers or had come to their ideas independently in meditating their own problems and needs, does not matter to us here. What is interesting is that the philosophers, like the artists, did not regard the mind as a passive mirror of the world, a means of simple adaptation of the organism to the environment, but affirmed its creative role in the shaping of ideas. The new philosophy investigated the ideal constructions of thought by which man imposed an order on his sensations and controlled or modified the environment. As the Cubists broke up the painting into basic operations and relationships, the logicians analyzed knowledge into formal components, elementary and irreducible operations and structures, submitted to a few rules of deduction and consistency. Opposing the older philosophers and scientists who regarded knowledge as a simple, faithful picture of an immediately given reality, they observed in scientific law a considerable part of arbitrary design or convention, and even æsthetic choices—the immense role of hypothesis. A radical empiricism, criticizing a deductive, contemplative approach, gave to the experimental a programmatic value in all fields. Still other philosophers affirmed the primacy of feeling and will, posing these as the sources of action and the clue to the creation of ideas. Psychology, splitting up into schools that investigated either the structured character of perception or the formation of personality in the course of conflicts between biological drives and social constraints, supplied theoretical bases for new interpretations of form, expression, and artistic creativeness. Certain of the philosophical ideas had been current for years, but in the period before the Armory Show they had become objects of fresh conviction and more systematic statement. No less significant than the content of philosophy and psychology was the form of science as an activity: the most impressive model of self-critical search and discovery, individual, yet co-operative, and without authority or fixed principles beside those of general method and logic. Its constantly revised picture of the world was highly imaginative, built of elements not directly given to the eye, but more adequate than older science in explaining phenomena. Its rapidity of change, its ceaseless productivity, suggested a corresponding creativeness in art and social life.

All these parallel intellectual currents, which have continued to our own time, are more or less external to art, yet produce a disposition favorable to the modern styles. It often happens that a mind radical in one field is conservative in the others, and indeed it may be questioned whether all these advanced views are compatible with each other. But where they coincide, they reinforce the common spiritual tendency, the sentiment of modernism itself as a value. They would have less effect on art, however, if they were not consistent with that individuality and intimacy of art which I have already mentioned.

Formerly tied to institutions and fixed times and places, to religion, ceremony, state, school, palace, fair, festivity, the arts are now increasingly localized in private life and subject to individual choice; they are recreations and tastes entirely detached from collective occasions. The superindividual and communal are not excluded; a looser but none the less effective bond unites people and confines their thinking and action. These common interests are approached, however, from the viewpoint of individuals who are free to explore their own beliefs, experiences, and relationships, to criticize them and transform them. The musical concert, the art exhibition, the film, the printed novel or poem, exist for a large community; but they are not bound to extra-artistic moments. Where the ancient drama was performed on a religious holiday and retained in its themes and spiritual attitude a tie with the solemn occasion, the modern film, also a collective work, is always on the screen, even when the hall is nearly empty; the film exists for distraction and is offered to the spectator as one among many films available at the same moment. After the book and the magazine, the phonograph, the radio, and television have made possible a greater privacy and self-ministration in the experience of the arts. This character of culture as a sphere of personal choices open to the individual who is conscious of his freedom and ideals, in turn affects the creation of new art, stimulating inventive minds to a fresh searching of their experience and of the resources of the art which enter into the sensory delight of the spectator and touch his heart. Among the arts, painting (and to a smaller degree, sculpture) has the unique quality of combining in a permanent state the immediately given or tangible, the material object of art, with the most evident signs of operativeness, the presence of the artist as the shaping hand and spirit. It is in this sense the most concrete art, but realizes this concreteness through forms of which the so-called "abstractness" has little to do with the abstractions of logic and mathematics.

The issues at stake in the Armory Show were not simply æsthetic problems isolated from all others. To accept the new art meant to further the outlook of modern culture as a whole. The rejection of the new art was for many an expression of an attitude to all modernism. The revolt of students against academic art was not only a break with the art of their elders, but also part of a more general desire for emancipation. People in 1913 overestimated the spiritual unity of the different examples of freedom or progress; they felt that all innovations belonged together, and made up one great advancing cause. Fewer thought, as we do today, that modernity is problematic and includes conflicting, irreconcilable elements.

IV

The new art was not received very differently here and abroad. We are observing a process that belongs to Western culture as a whole. In both the United States and Europe a few clairvoyant enthusiasts discovered quite early the little-known artists who in time became the acknowledged masters. In both continents were individuals who defended the new art on principle for its modern spirit without distinguishing original from imitative work. Attacks on the artists as madmen and charlatans, diagnoses of their styles as a symptom of social decay, were published everywhere. And in America as in Europe, compromisers or timid minds without full conviction, tried to assimilate the modern by adding some of its elements to an older style.

Yet one can discern in the common reactions differences of degree,—peculiarities that correspond to the cultural heritage and situation at the time. The English seemed more conservative and indifferent; the German collectors, museums, and writers showed an amazing enlightenment in supporting the new art, native and foreign; the Russians were perhaps the most enthusiastic of all. Germans, Russians, and Americans, even more than the French, were friends of the younger modern artists in Paris. In these comparisons, we have in mind, of course, the minority that is concerned with art.

In the reception in the United States, we are struck by a singular play of provincial backwardness and a generous disposition towards the most advanced forms. This was perhaps true in some other countries as well.

Unlike the Europeans we had no official art; there were no state museums and schools or ministers of fine arts to support an orthodoxy in art. The National Academy was a society of artists, independent of the government and centered in New York. There was nothing here like the French Salon or the annual exhibitions of the European Academies, which were patronized by an aristocracy influential in the state. In France the Academy had long ago lost the leadership in the artistic life of the nation; none of the great painters of the second half of the nineteenth century had belonged to it, and as early as the 1820's the innovators had to withstand the opposition of the academic caste. In the United States the Academy was less dogmatic and authoritative; it included the outstanding men of the older generation (Ryder, Homer, Eakins, Twachtman) and several of the younger rebels of the group of the Eight (Henri, Bellows, and Glackens). On the eve of the Armory Show, its exhibitions were of declining interest, but their weakness was that of a stagnant rather than dogmatic art. Only late in our history, when academic art had been completely discredited in Europe, was a similar pseudo-classical style promoted in the United States to satisfy the demand for symbolic decorations in the immense projects of building for the federal and state governments and the new millionaires whose sumptuous homes were designed as copies of Renaissance villas and châteaux. A school for American prize-students was founded in Rome in 1905 to enable them to study the classic and Renaissance models at the source. But this sapless academic art, though well supported, attracted no able young artists. It was at best an adjunct to the imitative architecture, which had enjoyed a vogue since the 1890's at the expense of an emerging native style of building.

The world of art here was, on the whole, more liberal than in Europe, where the antagonism of the official and the independent remained very sharp. The United States had not known the great artistic struggles of the last century in Europe; Romanticism, Realism and Impressionism were introduced from abroad with little conflict and without the accompanying political implications. The show of the French Impressionists in New York in 1886, sponsored by the National Academy, was received more warmly than the works of the same artists in Paris and London. And at the Armory Show, of the 1,600 works exhibited, about 300 were bought by visitors, a proportion that would be astounding today, when this art is better established. There was no old, native style here to defend against the foreign, and no great personality among American painters, with loyal disciples, constituting a school that would fight to maintain itself against a foreign mode. Our best painters were robust original counterparts of minor European artists. If the absence of a powerful authority made it easier for painters to consider the new in art, the lack of an intense tradition with examples of high creativeness made the acceptance of the new often shallow or passive.

We are not at all sure that this provinciality accounts for America's minor place in modern art. Countries no less backward suddenly came to the fore then. The modern movement called upon artists of many nations. Paris was the generating center, but the leaders of the new art included men from Spain, Russia, Holland, Germany, Austria, Norway, Switzerland, Belgium, Italy and Rumania. Spain, in decline, contributed Picasso and Gris, and later Miró, but the United States and Britain produced no figure of world importance. Among the Americans who adopted the new forms and developed them independently were superior artists (Prendergast, Hartley, Marin, Weber, Davis, Maurer, Demuth), but none was of the stature of the great European innovators. It is not because they are imitators of the Europeans; they are unmistakable personalities, with their own savor, but their work does not seem to us as far-reaching as that of the pioneers abroad. There is no Melville or Whitman or James among our painters. Only recently an American, the sculptor Calder, created in his "mobiles" a personal style of international interest. And in the generation of modernists born since 1900, the leading American artists stand on the same plane as the best of the Europeans—a less gifted group than their revolutionary elders.

The backwardness of American painting and sculpture relative to Europe, their failure to pursue the possibilities and to grapple with the most serious and difficult problems, is a complex affair that demands a more delicate analysis than can be given here. The conditions of life that shape culture rarely affect all the arts uniformly; painting has special requirements and possibilities that distinguish its course from that of literature and music. There is nothing in Russian art of the nineteenth century that can be set beside the great Russian novels and poems. The differences between the arts of two countries at the same moment are often a matter of a few strong individuals, even a single one.

The reaction to European art at the Armory Show was probably affected by a real lag in American art during the two decades before. Many of our painters remained confidently and even militantly realistic, committed to the spectacle of the city, of activity, and to the picturesqueness of the environment, for some thirty to fifty years after this taste had declined in Europe. The most influential new styles practiced by Americans around 1910 came out of French Impressionism; the urban realists (Henri, Luks, Sloan, Bellows) used the methods of advanced French painting of the 1860's and '70's. More secure than the Europeans, less shaken by the course of modern history, and less free in spirit, we had ignored the art of van Gogh, Gauguin, Seurat, and the later Cézanne, which belonged to the 1880's. Only a few alert young artists who had gone to Paris in the years before the Armory Show knew the works of that generation, from which the painting of the twentieth century had developed. Artists and public beheld the latter with a great amazement at the leap from Impressionism.

This lag was surely not due to the inaccessibility of the more recent art. Many Americans who traveled often to Europe were seriously devoted to painting. But while an earlier generation of travelers had brought home works of Millet, Corot, Courbet, and Manet, the collectors in the 1890's and beginning of the new century turned more often to the past, ignoring or underestimating the best contemporary art. This was true especially of the cultivated heirs of old established fortunes. Reacting against

American vulgarity, they lost touch with the vital elements in both European and American culture. Freed from practical necessities, they conceived an æsthetic paradise of old architecture, gardens, and objects of art. The more refined, those who set the standards, had absorbed something of the fervor of Ruskin and his American disciples, Jarves and Norton, and were drawn to Italian late medieval and Renaissance art, which reconciled religious and worldly ideals. Whistler's fragile art, the "æsthetic movement" of the 1880's in England, the revived Pre-Raphaelitism of their youth, and the discovery of Far Eastern art, confirmed their taste for an art detached from the problematic present. We owe to this bias the magnificent museum collections in Boston and New York, begun well before the Armory Show. The culture of these patricians was often broad, curious, and finely discerning, but it ignored the most vigorous contemporary ideas and was easily corrupted into snobbery and preciousness. Mr. Berenson, the leading American writer on Italian Renaissance painting, admiring the draftsmanship of Degas, regretted that it should be wasted on pictures of laundresses. Some might be drawn wholeheartedly to the Impressionists and Cézanne, who belonged to an older generation than themselves; very few had a sustained interest in their advancing contemporaries. For the symbolic mural decorations of the Boston Public Library, one called from Europe the fashionable portrait painter, Sargent, and the pallid Hellenist, Puvis de Chavannes. This caste of art-lovers, nowhere so much at home as in matters of decoration, supported—and perhaps was largely responsible for—the sterile vogue of historical forms in architecture at a moment when the leading European architects were moving away from it and a strong native style had arisen in the United States. The one American artist of world importance, the architect Frank Lloyd Wright, was ignored in the East during the great opportune activity of building at the time of the Armory Show, although his European colleagues had just published the first monograph about his work, which was to influence decidedly the European architecture of the new century. Fifteen years later, Wright was not even named in the history of American civilization by Charles and Mary Beard, authors who cannot be suspected of indifference to native genius, but who have been guided by academic opinion in their account of modern American architecture. This episode gives us the measure of the nostalgic taste for past art in our country.

Yet it should be said that this taste, striving to surmount the rawness of American culture, contributed to the ultimate acceptance and growth of the new art. It helped to create a serious interest in art as a sublime value, beyond skill in representation,— a self-sufficient realm of forms in which perfection was a goal.

The American collectors who were attracted early to the new art, men like John Quinn, Adolph Lewisohn, and Leo Stein, came mainly from outside the circle of that genteel æsthetic culture; a decade later, the largest museum of modern art in the world was formed by Albert Barnes, a pugnacious unsociable figure, whose modernism was indebted to the painter Glackens and to Leo Stein and John Dewey.

The introduction of modern art in this country has depended largely on the foreign-born or their immediate descendants. Its point of entry was the port of New York, which gave the Armory Show a much warmer welcome than Boston or Chicago. I have mentioned the leadership of Alfred Stieglitz in furthering the new art. Among the first artists to absorb the modern ideas were Max Weber, Abraham Walkowitz, Jacob Epstein, Joseph Stella, and Gaston Lachaise, all (except Epstein) foreign-born. The painters Marin, Demuth, and Maurer were native Americans who came from a milieu less touched by the self-conscious, backward-looking culture and close to the region of most intense mingling of peoples.

Women, it is worth noting, were among the chief friends of the new art, buying painting and sculpture with a generous hand. Art as a realm of finesse above the crudities of power appealed to the imaginative, idealistic wives and daughters of magnates occupied with their personal fortunes. But what is in question here is not simply the quicker disposition of American women to the fine arts, but their response to novel forms. At this moment of general stirring of ideas of emancipation, women were especially open to manifestations of freedom within the arts. A symbol of this period of insurgent modernism was the flamboyant personality of Isadora Duncan, an international figure who transformed the dance into a medium of ecstatic expression and release.

Modern art enjoyed also the friendliness of advanced political minds, who welcomed a reforming or revolutionary spirit in art as an ally of their own aims. The issues of art were easily translated into the language of radical politics. Academic art, the cult of the past, tradition, rigid standards and rules, represented authority and privilege; the new art stood for growth, freedom, the individual, and the open future. As a young man, John Reed, who was later to report the Russian revolution, supposed that Futurism was the artistic corollary of Socialism; who could foresee then the Fascist ties of this Italian movement, which glorified action and violence as ends in themselves? But the Socialist leaders were most often conservative in art. Their minds fixed upon politics alone and expecting from artists works directly useful to their movement—easily legible images of misery, class struggle and the radiant Socialist future, or relaxing pictures of nature's beauty—they were repelled, like any conservative bourgeois, by what struck them as the "nihilism" of the new art.

V

From the account of the Show and the history of modern art, sketched here briefly, it is clear that the Show was no crisis for the American modernists, but a kind of triumphal entry. To have created these works, to have reached the public, to have gained supporters, was already an achievement. And with the example of victorious generations of modernists before them, these men were sure that their own work would be recognized before long. Their struggles and sufferings, the abuse to which they were subjected, rarely made them doubt their aims; they continued to work, and produced new forms; the external obstacles were no impasse.

In what sense then was the Armory Show a crisis in American art? Crises of culture, unlike those of economics, politics, and war, do not concern great multitudes. They have been until now the problems of a profession that for over a hundred years has lived in chronic uncertainty; and although they affect the spiritual life of the community, their issues are not urgent for the latter. Within the concerned group, however, the crisis may be an emergency in which the survival of the art itself or of some basic standard is in question.

It was mainly for those who attacked the new work as a monstrous degradation of art by lunatics and charlatans that the Armory Show was a crisis. Yet if their vehement criticisms were correct, the strange art should hardly have caused them concern. The exhibition of mad or insincere work is no challenge to a serious artist. Incompetent painting is quickly forgotten. A true crisis would have been the failure of the aggrieved artists to produce any good art at all. It would then have been not only a crisis in their own art, but a total crisis of art, since they believed that the fate of American art was in their hands alone.

Yet many artists were deeply disturbed. Not simply because the wild men were enjoying the stage for a few months, and might seduce the public into accepting their work, but because the conservatives felt, in spite of their condemnations, that this art of the charlatans and madmen did have meaning and was a possible alternative to their own. It was for them no unexpected irruption; they had sensed it on the horizon for some time, and they had observed its advance in Europe. Its growing strength was clear from the response of able artists, who had gone abroad to study and had been infected with the new ideas. The most talented young Americans were being drawn further in that direction. And these opponents of modernism were not unaware that they themselves had compromised with the modernism of an older generation, adopting some elements from it in their academic work. As defenders of tradition they knew also that their own art lacked the freshness and conviction they admired in the great painters of the past, and which these new men showed in an evident way, even if they broke all the rules. We suspect that to some more sensitive and intelligent conservative artists, the wildness of the new art, like the mysterious originality of the great masters who were beyond rules, seemed peculiarly demonic and inspired, even if crude.

If this new path was the right one, then the established American artists were on the wrong path. Their whole education seemed useless. For centuries the artist's training had been in the study of the nude figure, in drawing and painting from careful observation of the model, and in the copying of works of the old masters. All this severe preparation was now irrelevant. Of what good was the long practice in representation when the aim of the painter or sculptor was to create objects in which the human figure scarcely existed or was deformed at liberty? The new art was the negation of the basic values of their own art; it abandoned ideal forms, noble subject-matter, harmony, decorum, nature, the visible world.

The academic spokesman, Kenyon Cox, claimed for his side the example of the great artists of the past. But his familiarity with tradition did not help him to sense the quality of Cézanne, whom he characterized as "absolutely without talent and absolutely cut off from tradition. He could not learn to paint as others did, and he spent his life in the hopeless attempt to create a new art of painting for himself." The radical moderns, we have seen, also claimed tradition; but tradition meant to them what it meant to scientists—not the authority of a past result, but the example of an independent spiritual attitude that had created new forms. Not long after the Show, Cox, in a picture perhaps inspired by these polemics, symbolized Tradition as a maidenly figure carrying an oil lamp that had been lit at the everlasting torch of the beautiful, and Painting as a muse in ancient costume. It seemed to him that the rebels were about to spill the oil and extinguish the light, or to violate the beautiful muse. The history of art was for him a quiet succession of great masters—teachers and pupils—without conflicts or disturbing changes. For the academic artists, this new art meant a loss of certitude; relying on the past, they now saw themselves cut off from the future.

The style the conservatives were defending was not one they had themselves created. They were docile craftsmen who practiced with more or less skill a method that had never been for them a discovery, a torment, and a risk. Yet some of them were men of taste, with a reverent feeling for the excellences of old art. Their uncomprehending rejection of the new must not be compared with the negative attitude of masters like Cézanne and Renoir to younger art. To judge sympathetically the novel work of younger men is, in any case, exceedingly rare; but the academic critics of the new art condemned what now appears, even to the conservative, the best work of their own and the preceding generation. Their complaints were those of comfortable habit against the demands of life, of a dull, respectable, premature old age against the rowdiness of youth. They wanted for themselves a spiritual security that they had not earned. The young modernists could admire the older original artists of the Academy, Ryder,

Eakins and Twachtman, but not the pious, smooth imitators of French academic art. The plight of the conservative painters was hardly tragic, for nothing valuable had been lost; the academicians continued to enjoy wide prestige, many sales, and the control of the schools, while the victims of their attacks struggled against a hostile or indifferent taste.

The American artists of realistic tendency were also shaken, although their public criticism of the new art was more restrained. Vigorous in denouncing snobbery, conformism, and the backwardness of academic art, confident of the necessity of an art related to the movement of contemporary life, they were now faced by more radical conclusions drawn from their own appeal to freedom and modernity, conclusions they could not easily accept or even understand.

These reactions to the new art betray not only the limits of the conventional respect for the individual in a weak conservative culture, but also the precariousness of the liberal historical view of art. In the course of the nineteenth century, Classicism, romanticism, Realism, Impressionism, following each other rapidly, had destroyed or at least weakened the older notion of a supreme model of style. It was recognized that art can create many different forms, that each age has its own kind of art, and that masterpieces, although rare, are possible in all of them. In consequence, the art of the past was re-examined, exclusive norms were abandoned, and the history of art—once a schematic picture of a landscape with a culminating peak, with predestined rises and falls—became a marvelous evidence of varied human creativeness nourished by new conditions of life. But confronted by the newest art of all, even this liberal view, which could admire both Raphael and Rembrandt, began to falter; opposed to a privileged content or style in the past, it could not do without the faithful image, and reviled the new artists as "inept" and "epileptic." Tastes were not to be disputed, provided they observed certain minimal rules. These opponents of modern art were like political liberals who, having overcome absolutism in a long struggle for "human rights," draw the line of liberty and equality to stop a more radical demand. They felt themselves now to be the defenders of a threatened heritage and, in the name of all the past and sacred values, they opposed a new possibility of freedom in art.

The uncertainties that the new art introduced were to affect the modernists as well. Within a few years the creators of Cubism returned to representation, and Expressionism yielded in Germany and elsewhere to a dry veristic style. The history of the modern schools includes the renegades and penitents who abandoned the standpoint of the revolutionary art. But even where the search for new forms continued, the modern movement has provoked a perpetual uneasiness among its followers. In the past an artist of limited originality could rely on what he had learned and like a skilled artisan perfect for himself the style of his youth, confident that the public would find it valid. This is no longer true. The rapid changes of taste, the many competing forms, unsettle the young artist and disturb the mature one. It is necessary to take a stand, to respond to new ideas, to keep up with history. In the sea of modernism, the minor artists are tossed about dangerously by the waves of fashion created by the larger or swifter men. The new art of 1910–20 did not create this situation, which was already noted in Europe in the 1840's as a demoralizing peculiarity of modern art; but it has become more acute during the last decades. The original artist who holds to his personal method runs the risk of appearing uncreative. It seems a limitation of a great painter that his style has not changed appreciably in twenty years. The world-shaking art of the revolutionary period has become a norm; one expects a revolution in every decade. This strenuous ideal breeds in the artist a straining for modernity and a concern with the historical position of his work; it often prevents him from maturing slowly and from seeking depth and fullness as much as freshness and impact.

If the old school was bitterly opposed to the new, they had nevertheless a common ground in certain broad aims. By a slight turn in the accepted values of American art, one came upon the new European values, which seemed to contradict them. But the variable sense of these common values first became clear in the modern works to which they led. What was thought to be a universal language of colors and forms was unintelligible to many when certain conventions were changed. The means—for one thing—were very different; and since in art the means are a visible element of the whole, not easily distinguished from the ends, the latter also seemed irreconcilably opposed. What the Classicists hoped to achieve through the precise forms of idealized statuesque figures—lines that had been criticized in the nineteenth century as "abstract"—the moderns reached more convincingly through geometrical forms. The qualities of purity and rigor, of exactness in composition, of an impersonal order, are more evident to us today in the best Cubist paintings than in the work of any of the contemporary academic artists who fixed their eyes too long on Ingres and Greek sculpture. If there are eternal values in art, it seems they are preserved only by those who strive to realize them in a new content.

This conviction was the source of the vitality of the American Realists at the time of the Armory Show. These painters—Henri, Luks, Sloan, Shinn, Glackens, Bellows—loved the American scene, in particular the common types and the outwardness of city life. They approached their subjects with a rapid, sketchy, illustrator's style repugnant to the traditional draftsmen; often shallow, it was a frank style, adapted to the kind of perception their content required. Their awkward composition was less calculated than the composition of the schools, but more natural and with abrupt, surprising contrasts. This American art sprang from an ever growing sentiment of freedom, the joys of motion and the excitement of the city as an expanding world of gigantic creation and the ceaseless play of individual lives, which Whitman had celebrated and which now offered themes and a viewpoint to Dreiser's tragic novels.

These painters, affirming in retarded forms the living spectacle of modernity, made at least some part of the new European art accessible as a more radical interiorized manifestation of the same spirit. If Bellows, in defiance of the traditionalist's desire for beautiful models, painted the portrait of a cross-eyed boy, the same theme in the early work of the Frenchman, Rouault, appears immeasurably more searching and forthright. If they valued bright and deep color as more essential than delicate or sweet tones, Matisse offered them a palette of a hitherto unknown daring, with astonishing juxtapositions of intense colors and off-shades. If they adored the big city as an overwhelming spectacle of traffic and the dizzying rise of immense buildings in the sky, Delaunay's Eiffel Tower was a more striking expression of these qualities, which the American, John Marin, transposed to his views of the Woolworth Building. If they valued movement in itself as an attribute of vitality and as the metaphysical opposite of the static in tradition, Duchamp's *Nude Descending a Staircase* was an exciting assertion of a dynamic principle, much like the philosopher Bergson's, or like the moralist Nietzsche's call to perpetual self-transcending action.

What raised the best of the new Europeans above the American artists was their greater seriousness about the qualities of painting; they probed the medium more deeply and were more inventive in their means. Their feeling for the objects they represented was also more imaginative.

The American landscape painters, too, coming after the French Impressionists of the 1870's and '80's, had educated American eyes to a less formal art in which the charm and poetic character of the intimate aspects of the native scene were translated by a method of painting in fine free touches of color, rather shapeless, but harmonized through light, atmosphere, and paint texture, in a manner strange to the tight academic methods. Those who were touched by this art could approach more readily the art of a Cézanne, a Bonnard, a Vlaminck, a Marquet, as a development of similar methods towards greater constructive force or a deeper lyricism. Those who grasped the art of Ryder, one of the greatest of living American painters, a poetic solitary who saw nature in large mysterious patterns of light and dark, could be captivated by the French mystic Redon, and could approach those foreign artists who subdued details for the sake of strongly silhouetted forms. There was also in this country a heritage of contemplative idealism, religious and moral, which sparked in some a response to the spirituality of a Lehmbruck or a Brancusi.

The existing values of American life and art provided some ground, then, for this foreign art. But the number of hospitable minds, it must be said, was not large. For the great mass of people, good painting and sculpture were an exceptional, rarely accessible, experience. Living on the farms or in small towns and in tenements of crowded cities in recently formed, often unstable communities, they had little if any artistic heritage, even of folk arts. Today, nearly forty years after the Armory Show, when art has become widespread, an enormous span separates the interest of the serious forward-looking lovers of art from the taste of the average, educated man. Painting and sculpture mean little to him, and he observes with suspicion whatever in art comes from beyond his horizon. Although in his profession or business he is often keyed to the new, and respects originality, he is satisfied in art with the conventional and obvious, and still worse. The fact that he is at home with mechanical things and loves the calculated and precise does not mean that he will respond to a painting by Mondrian or Léger. Modern art in its graver, more poignant aspects is a disturbing challenge, offering a model of a desired inner freedom and emotional release that he does not venture within himself, or for which he is spiritually unprepared. He has not the habit of savoring the style of things, the more or less of a quality that makes up the magic and perfection of a work of art. This uneasiness or indifference before modern art is known in Europe too; it is striking to observe in America where individuality and freedom are advertised as national traits. Outside the cultural professions, some exceptional men who feel a kinship with the artists through their imaginativeness and independent spirit are attracted to novel contemporary work. But relatively few of the wealthy in this rich nation support new art. One should not be misled by the great collections of the dead moderns of the pre-Armory Show period; these are now well-established traditional values; they are the past of modernism and image another world, easier and more relaxing than our own. In the collecting of this older art, motives of investment, fashion, and snobbery often play a role. Of those who buy such works, few risk an independent judgment or show a live curiosity about more recent art. There is, of course, a genuine conservative taste that meditates its choice old objects as a pure spectacle in detachment from all problems of living art. It is mainly the young, intellectually active, freer personalities that are drawn to the uncertainties, surprises, and joys of the contemporary in art.

In the great crowds that came to see the Show, many were undoubtedly attracted not so much by the art as by the scandal it produced in the world of high culture. Art had meant the precious and solemn and costly, a fragile aristocratic beauty. The Armory Show suddenly exposed to view hundreds of framed and pedestaled works with oddly misshapen figures, raw paint, childlike drawing and noisy color—a bedlam or underground of the imagination. The nude figure, ordinarily forbidden to public view except as an object for refined æsthetic contemplation, dominated the Show in the puzzling guise of Duchamp's *Nude Descending a Staircase*—it was likened by a gay observer to an explosion in a slat factory. The same painter was to exhibit later a photograph of the Mona Lisa with a mustache, and to send the model of a urinal as a piece of sculpture to the Society of Independent Artists, which was formed soon after the Armory Show. Anticipating the ironic Duchamp, there was also in the popular response in 1913 a latent Dadaism, an assault on art as a highfalutin, pretentious cult. The caricatures of the Armory Show, the verse parodies and satires, betray a note of pleasure, an eagerness to participate in this crazy carnival of art in which the aristocratic muse had been dethroned. The explosive wrath of outraged academicians and arbiters of taste was not altogether disagreeable to the public. The press that lampooned the new art counted on the reader's enjoyment of distortion and violent expression. The caricaturists in ridiculing the Show by grotesque imitations of the exhibits produced drawings much more interesting and original than their ordinary work.

This public, not very attentive to art, came to accept certain of these strange forms some years later as a decorative and a comic style. They have become familiar to everyone through industry and trade. At first admitted in the factory, the airport, the office, and the window display of the store, they have entered the ordinary home, though piecemeal rather than as a consistently designed décor. Abstract painting and sculpture have directly or indirectly inspired the designers of autos, furniture, packaging, utensils, and clothes. The Expressionist and Surrealist currents provided models for caricature, comic illustration, and gay advertising. The building arts more than the others show the impact of the modern movement. The environment, where it has been remade, has a new look that would not exist but for modern art. Modern art, we may say, has at last been domesticated in universally accepted mass-produced forms. These are a language, often a kind of pidgin-modern, with its special banalities and clichés, rather than a style in the stronger sense of an individual master's art or the art of sincere craftsmen employed on a collective task. They retain the broad connotations of certain currents within modern art—particularly the constructive-abstract, which is inspired by modern technology and is the most impersonal of all—but they lack the force or finesse of the individual paintings and sculptures, and hardly affect the life attitudes of those who accept this mass-modernism. This popular taste is rarely a conviction and determines no active, discerning habit of the eye, open to original contemporary art. A new convention has been created, which is accepted most quickly where the content makes the least demand. Only the small change of modernity circulates everywhere through these cheap adaptations.

It should be said, however, that the new decorative forms have not replaced the old. With all its advances and the wider public interest, modern art has been unable to establish itself in this country as the style of our time with the same necessity, completeness, and self-evidence as did in their day the Gothic or the Renaissance styles. Manufacturers today offer both "modern" and traditional designs; the modern is only one among many historical styles available to the consumer's choice. The symbolic value of the older styles as signs of rank, culture, and heritage has still a powerful hold. Public buildings are most often designed in some past idiom of form, and the furnishings of an American home are only exceptionally homogeneous in style.

The public that buys the undecorated, abstract-looking, mass-modern objects, still prefers the photographic and trivial, sentimental picture, with little regard to quality. To many who are conscious of the modern, a slightly accented, stylized imagery has the strongest appeal. During the decades since the Armory Show, the academic art schools have continued to function, changing their methods very little; they have satisfied the demand for slick illustrators who impenitently produce debased versions of the styles of the later nineteenth century.

Although modern art appears to many a highbrow, exotic taste, foreign to American plain-spoken and practical ways, it has resolved to some degree the old antagonism of the popular and the elite in American culture.

The most advanced taste in the United States about 1900 had been self-consciously aristocratic, hostile to American customs, and deeply attached to the æsthetic as a superior way of life. Its representatives, Whistler and Sargent, preferred to live abroad. These two painters were not in the vanguard of the world art of their time; but in their concern with a refined style and technique they were closer to the new European art than to the American. They lacked however the originality and robustness of the European innovators, their great appetite for life. It is the latter quality that becomes important in American paintings as in literature just before the Armory Show, but it is carried by men who are not fastidious artists. As painters, the vigorous American Realists of that time, with all their zest, were unimaginative and often crude. The Armory Show introduced Americans to a tradition of European painting in which a vernacular directness is allied with a great and aristocratic seriousness about artistic problems. After 1913 we discover more often in this country a type of painter who is both an inventive, scrupulous artist and a tough. In literature still more clearly, the polarity Henry James-Mark Twain is replaced by the artist-type of Hemingway and Pound.

This change in the model personality of the painter corresponded to the actual life of the artist. He had become in the course of the nineteenth century, particularly in Europe, distinct from the artisan, the professional, and the man of affairs. Unless he was an academician who had status through privileged membership in a recognized society, he lived in a world apart, most often poor, struggling, uncertain of the future, and sustained by his devotion to ideal ends that were generally respected by the public in the great artists of the past (their established fame was a kind of success), but were not recommended in the present to the young of the middle class. His dress, his manners, his home, his outlook, were less conventional than those of the class from which he came. His reputation for irresponsibility and disorder extended to his morals. But in time this liberty became a model to others who could afford it. His bare studio with large windows and simple furniture, his informal ways and ready responsiveness to people and art, represented for many a better style of life. He was a leader in breaking down the rigidities and narrowness of older social customs, the stuffiness of Victorian life. He anticipated an ideal of openness and simplicity that became more general in the next decades, with the growth of the city and the greater mobility of individuals. It is easy to see that the new art was closer than the old to this condition of the artist. In America the introduction of modern art coincided with the prestige of Greenwich Village as an artistic Bohème. It was not necessary that a Cubist be radical in politics, libertine in morals, and simple or careless in dress; what was important was the general atmosphere of gaiety and spiritual independence, an atmosphere indispensable for an artist's life.

The Armory Show, held just before the first World War,

marked the end of an era. It took place at a high point of social idealism in America. Although much of this spirit lived on after the war, there was a notable shift in thinking to a more personal field and to faith in psychology. What may be called the idealistic individualism of the pre-1914 period was more keenly aware of institutions and of society as a whole, and was more confident of being able to shape them for humane ends. Faced by the great corporate powers, which had emerged from the smaller economic units of the nineteenth century and which now threatened the old liberties, democratic opinion in the first years of the century became more militantly radical. This active social sentiment waned after the first World War, at a time when freedom or at least mobility in personal life, in culture and recreation, decidedly increased. The advanced artist, in a corresponding way, reacted to the declining confidence in radical social aims or the social group by asserting more forcefully the value of the personal world and of art. (This attitude had already become prevalent among advanced European artists before the end of the nineteenth century, probably because of the acuter crises of European social life.) While the new art seems a fulfillment of an American dream of liberty, it is also in some ways a negation. In suggesting to the individual that he take account of himself above all, it also isolates him from activity in the world and confirms the growing separation of culture from work and ideal social aims. But not altogether, for at certain moments of prosperity this art, through its geometrized forms, celebrates the beauty of machines and the norms of industry and science as a promise of ultimate harmony and well-being. Yet it does this uncritically, almost childishly, without deep awareness, detaching the technical from the fuller context of subjection and suffering, and surrendering the spontaneity of the person for the sake of an impersonal outward strength that comes to look inhuman.

But if the new art is in some respects a retreat from a more critical and positive conception of culture, it should be observed that a trend toward an art of intimacy and sensation was already well advanced here before the Show, although it was thirty years behind the corresponding French art. The American Impressionists, like the Europeans before them, took as their chief objects smaller and smaller bits of landscape, interesting for some personally savored nuance of color, light, and air. The painting of several of the leading members of the group of the Eight, which is often described as popular, activist, and American, in contrast to the æstheticism and foreignness of the later art, represented the city streets and docks as a pure spectacle, without meaning beyond the sheer animation or phenomenon of movement; it loved the merry-go-round, the theater, the circus, the prize-fight, the crowds at the beach and the park; the favored subjects of portraiture were picturesque or exotic—the foreigner, the gipsy, the actor, the kids from the slums, who in their oddity of dress and appearance embodied a freedom from sober American conventions. It was no searching or epic realism of American life, but an enjoyment of impressions of vitality and movement.

The revival of political radicalism during the depression of the 1930's led to criticism of modern art as too narrow and as incapable of expressing deeper social values. Many artists hoped then to find a bridge between their æsthetic modernism and their new political sympathies; but the weakness of the radical movement, the eventual disillusionment with Communism, and the effects of war, re-employment, and the growing role of the state in the 1940's, reduced the appeal of this criticism. Artists today who would welcome the chance to paint works of broad human content for a larger audience, works comparable in scope to those of antiquity or the Middle Ages, find no sustained opportunities for such an art; they have no alternative but to cultivate in their art the only or surest realms of freedom—the interior world of their fancies, sensations, and feelings, and the medium itself.

Today, almost forty years after the Armory Show, modern art is still a recurring problem for the public, although so many more painters and sculptors practice this art. The hostile criticisms made in 1913 have been renewed with great virulence. We hear them now from officials of culture, from Congress and the president. The director of the Metropolitan Museum of Art has recently condemned modern art as "meaningless" and "pornographic," and as a sign of the decay of civilization in our time. These criticisms are sometimes linked in an unscrupulous way with attacks on Communism, foreign culture, and religious doubt. They have a parallel in the attempts of the totalitarian regimes in Europe to destroy modern art as an unpalatable model of personal freedom of expression and indifference to the state. The Nazis suppressed this art as "cultural Bolshevism"; the Russian government and its supporters in the West denounced it as an example of "cosmopolitanism" or "bourgeois decadence"; Catholic spokesmen have rejected it as a manifestation of godless individualism. But no serious alternative has arisen to replace it. Those who demand a traditional and consoling art, or an art useful to the State, have nothing to hold to in contemporary painting and sculpture, unless it be some survivals of the academicism of the last century, or hybrid imitations of the modern art of fifty years ago by mediocre conforming painters, works that the enemies of the modern can hardly support with enthusiasm.

X. *Woodrow Wilson's Tour*

What lay behind Woodrow Wilson's last desperate attempt to win public support for his League of Nations in the late summer of 1919? Professor Dexter Perkins tells the story of Wilson's ill-fated speaking-tour and the last arduous years of his Presidency. Out of touch with his constituents, he did not appreciate the spiritual deflation that had taken place after the war, or the ugly tensions—political, economic, and social—that made 1919 one of the most brutal and violent years in American history, nor could he overcome the opposition leaders who turned a serious question of foreign policy into a narrow partisan issue. Unfortunately for the country then (and future historians may say the same about 1952), the great questions at stake were subordinated to party conniving, personal antipathies, and the prejudices of ethnic minorities. The idea of collective security, dead in 1920, was revived during the next decade, however, and the positive American role in world affairs today is proof that the experience of 1919 was not forgotten.

X

Woodrow Wilson's Tour

Dexter Perkins

Professor of History, University of Rochester

In June of 1950, the forces of the United Nations, largely represented by the forces of the United States, engaged in battle in Korea. They took up their work there in behalf of an ideal, rather than for any material interest. So far as the United States was concerned, the argument, from the purely military and logistical point of view, ran rather against than in favor of the present enterprise. No important economic interests on the part of the American people were concerned. The leadership that the American government is exercising today is connected with a question of principle, and is one of the first great tests of the validity of that principle. What is involved is clear. It is whether or not aggressive warfare is to fall under not only the moral but the practical disapprobation of mankind. We cannot say what will be, in the future, the practical scope of so broad and all-inclusive a doctrine. But we can say that this doctrine has now, in a very large and significant way, entered the field of practical international politics, that it has gained the adhesion of most civilized states not bound to the chariot wheels of the Kremlin, and that it has secured wide acceptance among thoughtful people in the United States.

In the field of theory, the idea of collective action against a lawbreaking state cannot be said to be novel. It has been at the heart of many schemes for the preservation of world peace. But it entered the sphere of practical politics only a little more than thirty years ago. It was first incorporated in an international document in the Covenant of the League of Nations, an essential part of the treaty of Versailles. It owed its inclusion in this document in very large degree to the efforts of an American statesman, Woodrow Wilson. Its application at that time depended upon its ready acceptance by the people of the United States. Its rejection, in the Senate of the United States, and, by implication, by the American people in the election of 1920, was a landmark of substantial importance in the development of American diplomacy. That is why it is possible and desirable to include in this series on crises in American history some account of the events of the years 1918–20 and of the great struggle over the Covenant.

We need say only a little about the origins of the Covenant itself. The notion that there should be formed a League of Nations competent by collective action to maintain peace became current not very long after the outbreak of the first World War. That war itself, coming after a long period of peace, so far as the major states of Europe were concerned, brought with it a sense of profound shock. Thoughtful men began to ask if there were not some way to avoid the repetition of so great a catastrophe. In the United States there took shape in the fall of 1915 an organization known as the League to Enforce Peace, under the presidency of an ex-President of the United States, William Howard Taft. Already in the fall of 1915 Woodrow Wilson had begun to interest himself in the idea. On the 27th of May, 1916, he formally endorsed it. It found a place in the platform of the Democratic Party in the national nominating convention of 1916, and was more than once alluded to by the President in the course of the campaign. And in still more definite fashion, in his last desperate attempt to secure a peace by agreement between the belligerents, in his speech of January 22, 1917, Wilson definitely proposed American adherence to an international compact to prevent war. The matter had now come to occupy a foremost place in his mind.

Still more, the entry of the United States into the war gave new significance to the idea of a League to Enforce Peace. Once the Germans, by the resumption of the submarine warfare, had sharply challenged the position of the American government, and had brought this country into the world struggle, Wilson, like every leader of a democratic people in time of conflict, sought to sublimate and elevate the issues. What could justify the expenditure of so much blood and treasure as the American people were now bound to pour forth? Certainly not the mere vindication of the neutral rights of the United States on the high seas. Certainly not a victory over the Central Powers which was no more than a truce, and which might merely pave the way to a new struggle. Certainly nothing less than "such a concert of free peoples," to quote from the great speech of April 2, 1917, "as shall bring peace and safety to all nations and make the world itself at last free."

Because the President believed so deeply in this objective, he felt obliged, when the war came to an end, to go to Europe and fight for it. He put the drafting of the Covenant of the League of Nations in the forefront of his program in the peace negotiations in Paris. He saw to it that it was brought under early discussion. He gave his evenings, after wearisome day-long debates on other issues, to presiding over the commission that was to draft this charter for a free world. He made it clear that no other objective was so important and so vital. He made it clear that he would fight for it at home, as he fought for it abroad. At Paris he was successful. The Covenant was drafted, and incorporated into the treaty of Versailles. And in July Wilson sailed for the United States confident that the American people would approve his work. But now the difficulties began to multiply. In the elections of 1918 the Republicans had secured control of the Senate. The important Committee on Foreign Relations, which would have in charge the great treaty, was presided over by Henry Cabot Lodge of Massachusetts, a bitter personal enemy of the President and a convinced and narrow partisan. The committee itself was packed with those most disposed to contend against the President. After the submission of the treaty, there were weeks of delay, interminable hearings conducted in public, in which every grievance was ventilated, every criticism given multiplied force. The treaty stood in danger of amendment, or if not of amendment, of a more subtle form of emasculation, by what were known as reservations. To Wilson a great issue was being joined. He had always had a convinced faith in the wisdom of the people. He believed deeply in the validity of the democratic process. There was open to him only one course of action. That was, of course, to appeal directly to the electorate. On the 4th of September he set forth on a speaking-tour that was to carry him across the length and breadth of the United States. Great audiences came to hear him in his passionate and deeply felt pleas for the unqualified acceptance of the Covenant. He made this plea because he believed that the core of his program for a peaceful world was being menaced.

And on occasion he gave solemn warning that the failure of the United States to put its power behind the settlements of Versailles might well lead to another war, even more destructive than the war from which the country had just emerged. Thus, at the outset of his campaign, speaking at Omaha, the President declared: "For I tell you, my fellow citizens, I can predict with absolute certainty that within another generation there will be another world war if the nations of the world do not concert the method by which to prevent it." Again, at Coeur d'Alene, he reiterated this theme: "If you want to keep your boys at home, you will see that boys elsewhere are kept at home. Because America is not going to refuse, when the other catastrophe comes, again to attempt to save the world, and having given this proof once, I pray God that we may not be given occasion to prove it again." And once more at Cheyenne came the same solemn warning: "The upas tree is going to grow again; and I tell you, my fellow-countrymen, that if you do not cut it up now it will be harder to cut it up next time. The next time will come; it will come while this generation is living, and the children that crowd about our car as we move from station to station will be sacrificed upon the altar of that war." In words such as these Wilson pleaded for his cause with an intensity that was almost apocalyptic.

Then came the dramatic climax. The President found himself approaching mental and physical exhaustion. At Pueblo, Colorado, he collapsed. He was hurried back to Washington. There he suffered a paralytic stroke, which was to make him for the rest of his term an invalid, to insulate him from all but a few persons, to warp his political judgments, and to harden him in intense opposition to even mild modifications of his beloved Covenant. Meanwhile, the Senate proceeded to adopt reservations to the treaty, reservations the exact significance of which, and the acceptability of which, so far as other nations were concerned, it is difficult to judge. The President, however, had no difficulty in judging them. He advised his party followers to vote against the whole treaty, if these reservations were attached. They did so, and the treaty failed of ratification in November of 1919. The struggle was, however, not yet over. Attempts at compromise were set under way. But the President would have none of this. In January of 1920, he expressed himself as of the opinion that if there were any doubt as to the popular judgment, the issue of the ratification of the treaty must be thrown into the presidential campaign of 1920. Not all his followers were ready to go so far as that. A second vote on the Versailles compact saw more Democrats desert him, and vote for conditional ratification, but not enough to bring about acceptance. Wilson, stricken though he was, had his way. The issue went to the people in a great political campaign, and the American people elected Warren Harding to the Presidency. The League was repudiated by the new Chief Executive as soon as he entered office. In the immediate sense, the issue of collective security had been decided in the negative. Wilson had suffered a decisive defeat. The crisis had ended in what Harding so mellifluously described as a "return to normalcy." The United States was never formally to enter the League of Nations. In the period between two wars it was never to put its full weight behind the movement for collective security. The opportunity to participate in international action for the maintenance of peace was lost. We may well ask ourselves the question whether, if the principle had been supported by the United States in the twenties and early thirties, the rise of Hitler would have been as easy and as rapid, and his triumphs as complete, down to 1940, as was actually the case.

But this, of course, would be speculation, not historical narrative. What we must do is to analyze the implications of the events that we have just briefly sketched, to see why matters fell out as they did, and to sketch the consequences of the momentous struggle over the Covenant. What were the various factors involved in the defeat of the President? Was this defeat final and total? What did the American people feel in 1919 and 1920 with regard to the issue that we have briefly examined?

It is a melancholy reflection on the events we have just sketched that partisanship played a very large part in the problem. Probably it is fair to say that the foreign policy of no other great nation has been affected by such considerations to the same degree as has the foreign policy of the United States from the days of Washington to the days of Wilson, and perhaps even today. Singularly secure as we have been until the modern age, we have been able to enjoy the luxury of political debate even on foreign affairs; the urgent sense of the need for unity in the face of external peril has usually been lacking; even in our wars in 1812 and 1846 this was true to no small extent; there was a strongly political flavor to the debate on imperialism that followed the war with Spain; Wilson himself was frequently attacked on his conduct of foreign affairs in the course of his first term and in the election of 1916. Nor was he himself free from the partisan motive and the partisan point of view. In a sense, indeed, his theory of government was derived from it. He visualized the Presidency as an office of political leadership, and the Democratic members of Congress as the agents through which this leadership was to be translated into reality. A great admirer of the parliamentary form, he sought to translate it into reality in the United States. It was for the majority to make up an issue and carry it to fruition. If the issue were wisely chosen, the minority would come along. It is this way of looking at the problem that helps to explain, though it can hardly be said to justify, Wilson's appeal for a Democratic Congress in the fall of 1918. He was warned by his friends that this was a dangerous maneuver; that if the appeal failed his own loss of prestige might be substantial; and it was obvious, moreover, since a treaty requires a two-thirds vote in the Senate, that the peace pact at the end of the war could not be ratified without Republican support. But Wilson brushed aside the counsel of most of his advisers, and chose to ask for what he doubtless regarded as an endorsement of his administration. The nation did not heed his appeal; the Congress that came back to Washington in 1919 was, in both houses, though in the Senate narrowly, Republican.

Furthermore, the appeal of November 1918 was only one instance of Wilson's partisanship. He seemed to defy his enemies, rather than seek to conciliate them. He declared that he would so tie up the Covenant with the treaty of Versailles itself as to make it impossible to extricate one from the other; in his brief visit to the United States during the peace negotiations at Paris he landed at Boston in Senator Lodge's own bailiwick, and there issued a challenge to the foes of the League; in his great tour of the country, though always proclaiming that the issue was above party, he was in effect seeking to bring pressure to bear upon his partisan opponents, and his rather naïve conviction that the whole issue could best be settled in a Presidential political campaign was a disastrous example of the partisan cast of his mind.

Let us say once again that there was a theory behind this bent. But unfortunately the theory did not correspond with the realities of American politics, or with the facts of American constitutional life. In his zeal for his objective, Wilson forgot some of the essential factors in his problem.

This is not to say that the opposition to Wilson was swayed by high motives or was to pursue a course above reproach. Though Theodore Roosevelt was to die before the League struggle began in earnest, the venom with which he attacked the President betrays not a little political jealousy, and his rapier thrusts at the Chief Executive may have had something to do with the appeal of November 1918. Henry Cabot Lodge, who in the new dispensation was to become chairman of the Foreign Relations Committee of the Senate of the United States, was filled with personal and partisan animosity, as any reading of his account of the struggle over the League suggests. Plenty of other examples of this cast of mind might be cited. The very solidity of the Republican vote in the Senate in opposition to the unconditional ratification of the treaty suggests that not cool judgment but partisan calculation played a large part in the whole controversy. The inner logic of the situation also led to an emphasis on the partisan motive. For the adoption of the Covenant, as it stood, could hardly fail to be an impressive endorsement of the President himself; and by this very token could hardly fail to strengthen the Democratic Party in the elections that, by the time Wilson came back from Paris, were less than sixteen months away.

We can see the operation of partisanship in the play of public opinion as well as in the operations of politicians. As Professor Bailey has well pointed out, the greatest support for the unconditional ratification of the treaty came from the South; every other section was less enthusiastic. It was, perhaps, natural that those who were not the devoted followers of the President would view with some scepticism the compact that he had made; and that, even if they were in sympathy with its general objectives, they would not be willing to give it an unqualified endorsement.

From a very early period in the battle over the Covenant a substantial body of persons were in favor of some kind of reservations; and, indeed, there was in no section of the country except the South a majority who were ready to accept it as it stood. It is highly probable, as I have just stated, that partisanship, though not necessarily partisanship of a venomous kind, had something to do with this attitude.

There were other motives, too, that undeniably operated to qualify the enthusiasm with which Wilson's League was received in the United States. He himself had said that the acceptance of the League idea was inevitably tied up with the character of the peace itself. And many Americans, and indeed many Americans who in general viewed international politics from an idealistic point of view, were by no means convinced that the treaty of Versailles was such a document as they could highly approve.

The whole process of the peace conference itself had been disillusioning to these people. Paris, some naïve persons believed, was to see the rearrangement of the world on the basis of abstract ideas of justice. But in actual practice, the conference seemed to have degenerated into a kind of huckstering, in which these ideas were lost sight of. The Saar Valley, indubitably German, was detached from Germany and put under international control for a term of years. The union of Austria and Germany, both German-speaking countries, was made virtually impossible by a clause that required the assent of the Council of the League to such a step, and that gave to France and Italy by this provision a virtual veto on the so-called *Anschluss*. The Italian frontier accepted by Wilson at Paris was open to grave criticisms. The Japanese succeeded to the German economic rights in Shantung, despite the protests of the Chinese at Paris, and their eventual refusal to sign the treaty. On the economic side, staggering reparations were to be asked of Germany. There were many petty examples of vindictiveness in the economic section of the treaty. And the validity of criticism of the instrument, based upon such questions as these, was given force by the attitude of one of the heroes of the so-called "Liberals" at Paris, by General Smuts of South Africa, who put his signature to the momentous compact only after expressing profound dissatisfaction with much that was in it. To Wilson, the treaty seemed on the whole to conform to his own standards (perhaps he was a little blind on this score), but in any case he hoped, as his speeches on his tour show, that by the operation of the League, its defects were one by one to be eliminated. This was not necessarily an unreasonable view. But was a treaty such as that just outlined rightly to be guaranteed by the collective force of mankind? This was precisely what the President proposed. He set great store—the greatest store, in fact—by the famous Article 10 of the Covenant, which declared that "the nations of the League agree to respect and preserve as against external aggression the territorial integrity and existing political independence of the members of the League." Was such a guarantee of the status quo against forcible disturbance wise or just? Was it possible to set the seal of approval in this way on the arrangements that had been made at Versailles? To many persons, to many sincere and forward-looking persons, the answer to this question was: No.

But, if from the left there came criticism of this kind, from the right came doubts of another nature, doubts as to the desirability, in principle, of forsaking the traditional policies of the United States to participate in a worldwide guarantee of peace. For the greater part of its history the American people had abstained from interference in the affairs of the Old World. They had been warned by Washington himself to abstain from entangling alliances, to preserve a certain detachment with regard to the events that might take place on the other side of the Atlantic. For a century, and perhaps more and more consciously as time went on, they had been following that advice. True, the counsel of 1796 had proved inadequate to the circumstances of 1917. The country had been reluctantly involved in a great European war. But now that the war was over, now that the menace of German victory had been removed, was there not much to be said for withdrawing once again from the world scene, and leaving to the states of Europe the settlement of their peculiar problems? Especially in view of the cynicism and the selfishness that was so much in evidence at Versailles, was it not reasonable for the United States to draw back from the complexities of European politics, and cultivate its own garden for a while? What in any case, speaking practically, had the country to gain by acceptance of the League idea? Might not its own interests be jeopardized? True, Wilson had sought to answer this last possible criticism by inserting in the Covenant a provision that domestic questions were to be excluded from the purview of the world organization, and another provision that recognized the special place of the Monroe Doctrine in American diplomacy. But the language of these provisions was subject to possible criticism, and it was not difficult to argue that they insufficiently protected the rights and the interests of the United States.

On the conservative side, too, were those preoccupied with the internal problems that inevitably arose at the end of the war. To many persons these problems, the problems of demobilization and industrial readjustment, seemed more significant than the questions of international politics. The country had had a very large dose of Wilsonian idealism; was it not time to get down to brass tacks and to the more immediate questions that confronted the American people at home?

But it was not only the liberals of a certain stripe, and the conservatives of a certain stripe, who had their doubts about the Covenant and the treaty. It was also certain racial groups in the United States itself. The German-Americans, for example, were naturally disposed to believe that the treaty was unduly drastic in dealing with the Reich, and were not impressed with the argument that the pact's inequities could be cured in good time. Their dislike of the new arrangements could only have been increased by the humiliation put upon the Germans when they came to Paris, and by the acerbities of Clemenceau—and to a certain extent of Wilson himself—in dealing with them. The Italo-Americans could not fail to remember that the President had been the leader in denying to Italy the port of Fiume (to which, in fact, her right was doubtful), and in appealing to the Italian people over the head of their own government to sustain him. The Irish-Americans, with the spectacle of Irish revolt against the British oppressor before their eyes, found it hard to stomach a document that gave to Britain and her dominions six votes in the Assembly of the League, and that seemed to set the seal upon Britain's predominance in Europe. True, the Irish question in no way touched the Covenant, nor did the Covenant touch it in any precise sense. But the Gaelic mind is often more remarkable for intensity than for logic, and this fact had little weight with the more vociferous advocates of the defeat of the treaty. Taken altogether, these various elements constituted a formidable opposition to the pact, and undoubtedly exercised a powerful influence.

Taking all these points of view into account, it is easy to see why Woodrow Wilson could not expect an easy victory over his enemies in the battle of 1919 and 1920. It would have been strange, from the perspective of the historian, if the country had been willing to swallow without debate, and without question, the compact that the President had brought back from Paris. A great work of political education was necessary, and that work of education, if it could be accomplished at all, was bound to take time, much time, and perhaps an additional experience of the dangers of isolation as well.

But there is another aspect of the struggle over the Covenant, and of the President's attitude, which we must now examine in some detail. Was the President right in the position he assumed? Was his uncompromising opposition to the reservations proposed by the Republicans sound? Did he act wisely in urging his Democratic followers in Congress to vote against the treaty in the form in which it was submitted to the judgment of the Senate? This is a question of compelling interest, and deserves a careful analysis.

To begin with, it ought again to be made clear that the President did not oppose what he described as interpretative reservations, that is, reservations that required no action upon the part of other governments, but which were hardly more than a gloss upon the treaty itself. What he objected to in November when the treaty was first voted on, and objected to as of central importance, was a provision in the act of ratification that three out of four of the great powers, of the principal signatories of the pact, must signify in writing their acceptance of the reservations adopted by the Senate. And, in addition, he held extremely strong views about Article 10. Whether from pride of authorship, or from a more generalized conviction as to its significance, he believed that this article must be upheld in all its force. As he interpreted it (and the reader will remember that it involved a pledge to uphold the territorial integrity and political independence of the members of the League), the obligation assumed was not a legal but a moral one. But the moral pledge was the "heart of the Covenant," the core of the whole system that he had set up. Any action that weakened it, or destroyed it, would be, in Wilson's view, a deadly attack upon the League organization as a whole.

Now it is a common experience for a negotiator to attach very great importance to the work of his hands, and it is comprehensible that he should approach with reluctance the task of consulting all over again those with whom he had already come to an agreement, after long and sometimes painful discussion. The Senate reservations to the treaty, I repeat, required that three out of the four principal associated powers accept the reservations as a whole. Was the President right in believing that this provision was nullifying in its effect?

This is a question that cannot be answered dogmatically, or scientifically. We do not, as a matter of fact, know what the other powers would have done if they had had the chance. We can only speculate. Let us, however, put the case for the President as strongly as we can. In doing this, it will have to be conceded that some of the reservations were completely innocent, and that they would have caused no difficulty whatsoever. But there were others that might conceivably have been objectionable. The Japanese, to cite one case, would not have found it easy to accept that reservation by which the United States refused to recognize or be bound by the settlement arrived at in Paris with regard to the question of Shantung. The British might have found some difficulty in accepting, with the cordial support of their Dominions, that Senate provision which declared that the American government could not be obligated to follow any decision that had been arrived at. The French might conceivably have been irked to see the status quo set up at Versailles threatened by a Senate reservation that attenuated the importance of Article 10. In favor of the President's position one other fact may be added. The World Court protocol, when accepted by the Senate in 1926, was loaded down with reservations, as the Covenant had been before it. It took nine years to renegotiate the document, and then it was defeated in the Senate itself. These facts are at least interesting in connection with the problem we are examining.

But there is another side to the matter. The powers of Europe, at any rate (we say nothing of Japan), were extremely eager to see the United States play a part in the system that had been erected. Sir Edward Grey came to the United States in the winter of 1919 charged with a special mission, and intent upon breaking down Wilson's opposition to the action of the Senate. Long before this, Ambassador Jusserand had indicated that France

would accept reservations as the necessary price of American adhesion to the Covenant. The French press, including the semi-
official *Le Temps*, took the same view. We have no special information with regard to the Italians, but it seems unlikely that they
would have stood out against France and Britain. There is, therefore, some reason to believe that the steps prescribed in the
Senate resolution of ratification would not necessarily have prevented the acceptance of the treaty. And there is one other thing
to be said. Most moderate-minded men were convinced by 1919
that the experiment should at least be tried. To Senator Porter
McCumber, for example, the only Senator on the Republican side
who was in favor of unconditional ratification, and who stood
bravely with the administration through thick and thin, the action
of the President was nothing less than disastrous, the destruction
of a great work accomplished, an act of folly when victory was
within Wilson's grasp. Many historians have argued the same
way. It is not fair to say that in appealing to his partisans to reject
the treaty with reservations in the fall of 1919 Wilson kicked
over his own work, because we cannot assert dogmatically that
the reservations would have been accepted. But the whole episode
leaves an uneasy feeling in the mind, and the rigidity of the President's attitude is, I think, difficult for all but his thick-and-thin
admirers to approve.

In defense of the President, however, it is to be said that from
his point of view the Senate reservations eviscerated the Covenant
itself. He was, of course, particularly opposed to the reservation
on Article 10, which seemed to limit the action of the government
of the United States in supporting other members of the League
in collective action against an aggressor. "The United States as-
sumes no obligation," read this reservation, "to preserve the territorial integrity and political independence of any other country
or to interfere in controversies between other nations—whether
members of the League or not—under the provisions of Article 10,
or to employ the military and naval forces of the United States
under any article of the treaty for any purpose, unless in any
particular case the Congress, which, under the Constitution, has
the sole power to declare war or authorize the employment of
the military and naval forces of the United States, shall by act or
joint resolution so provide."

This reservation, as I construe it today, was indeed, as Wilson claimed, distinctly objectionable. It virtually nullified the obligation set up in the text. If Article 10 was the heart of the Covenant, then the damage done by the Senate was real. And one may indeed go further. Though I am not aware that the President ever raised the point, the reservation contains a distinct restriction on the freedom of action of the Executive. The statement that Congress has the *sole* right to authorize the employment of the military and naval forces of the United States is certainly open to serious challenge on constitutional grounds. Instance after instance could be cited in which American troops have been employed on the initiative of the President alone. And to come down to our time, if the Senate view had received general acceptance, there would have been no possibility of prompt action on the part of the President in the Korean business, or of the sending of reinforcements to Europe in such a situation as that which exists today. Would it have been wise in 1919 thus to tie the hands of the Executive? No doubt some of the Republican Senators in the present Congress would answer in the affirmative; but yet it still remains a question whether it accords with the true interests of the American people thus to limit, on the part of the President of the United States, the possibilities of strong and effective action in an emergency.

Here too, however, as with regard to the requirement of assent by other signatories, there is another side to the matter. Was Article 10 as central as Wilson thought it was? Was it worth while to take the risk of the total defeat of the Covenant, rather than submit to the elimination of this single article, or, actually, to the attenuation of the American obligation under it? The President himself at times seemed to provide a negative answer to this question. For in his tour he frequently stressed, as of the very first importance, the provisions of the Covenant requiring that all questions be submitted to arbitration, or conciliation, before resort to war, and he again and again pointed out the significance of Article 11, which authorized any nation to draw the attention of the League to any situation that threatened the peace of the world. He found time to praise, too, the mandatory clauses and the setting up in the treaty of the International Labor Office. Indeed, he made himself the champion of the whole instrument (save the provisions on Shantung) as making for a progressive and reasonable peace. How, then, could he feel that the principle of Article 10 was so vital? How, then, could he take the risk of seeing the treaty defeated in those November days of 1919 on any such ground? Was he judging realistically the situation that confronted him? Or had his mind hardened and his view contracted as a result of his own physical sufferings and of his own intense and burning conviction?

The questions raised as to the significance of Article 10 are of great importance. For, after the defeat in November, the treaty, it will be remembered, came up a second time, and on this second vote the requirement for written acceptance by three of the four great powers (which we have analyzed) had been eliminated. The opinion of the country, as a whole, was certainly not at this time in favor of repudiating the League. If there had been at no time a majority for unconditional ratification, neither was there ever less than a majority for conditional ratification. Wilson had at this time a second chance to secure a large part of what he had fought for at Paris. Professor Bailey, who has studied the question with care, believes that if the President had said the word the log jam would have been broken.

By this time, however, Wilson had gone too far to commit himself to another course. On the 8th of January, he had written the Jackson Day letter (already alluded to), hinting at the necessity for a great and solemn referendum. He gave no encouragement to the friends of compromise. Once more the treaty failed and, as we have seen, the immense issue of the League was thrown into a Presidential campaign.

In the course he followed the President was taking enormous risks, and, I think it may fairly be said, straying far indeed from reality. For American political campaigns are rarely conducted on clear-cut issues; and the debate that takes place in them is as often designed to confuse, to obfuscate, and to prejudice the mind of the voter, as to enlighten it. Furthermore, the atmosphere of passion that is generated is by no means conducive to the careful consideration of a great question of state. It is, on the contrary, just that atmosphere in which intelligent decision becomes impossible.

The events of the year 1920 amply sustain these generalizations. The Republican platform on the League question was a masterpiece of clever evasion. The speeches of the Republican candidate were no less ambiguous, first suggesting that something might be saved from the Covenant, and then implying that it must be rejected altogether. So successful was this ambiguity that a very considerable number of distinguished Republicans, Republicans apparently especially distinguished by their naïveté, and amongst whom were Herbert Hoover, Henry L. Stimson, and Abbott Lawrence Lowell, issued just before the election an appeal to the American voters to elect Senator Harding on the ground that this was the best way to get us into the League of Nations. There could have been, in my view, few more remarkable examples of wishful thinking than this, on the part of men who ought to have known better; but none the less the incident illustrates beautifully how difficult it is to define an issue sharply in a Presidential campaign, and how widely partisanship operates to limit and prejudice judgment in such a campaign.

There was another hazard in Wilson's course. There were at the end of the war all sorts of accumulated discontents that were bound to work against the party in power—discontents, as we have already seen, in the field of foreign policy, and discontents in the field of domestic affairs, inevitable after the strain of war. And these discontents contributed to one of the greatest election victories in the history of the nation. It is a fact not wholly free from irony that Warren Gamaliel Harding was in 1920 the choice of the nation by the largest proportion of the popular vote ever given to any candidate. The result of course was the repudiation of the treaty of Versailles, and of the Covenant, and the cold-shouldering of the League of Nations when it was set up at Geneva.

In contemplating the results of the election of 1920 and the final abandonment of the League by the incoming administration, we come to the end of the crisis that in the literal sense is the subject of this essay. But there is still a necessity for a more generalized appraisal of the ground that we have just traversed. If we look at the matter narrowly we shall, I think, concede that the President's own inflexibility, an inflexibility perhaps intensified by his illness, was one of the primary causes for the failure of the treaty. There was always the possibility of adoption of the treaty with reservations, and the possibility, also, that these reservations would have posed no obstacle to the entry of the United States into the world organization. But if we look at the matter in a broader perspective we will take a somewhat different view. The appeal of the enemies of the League was essentially to a narrow American nationalism, and the existence of this narrow nationalism might and would have hampered the United States in making the League an effective instrument of peace.

Something of the same thing can be said with regard to the attitude of the reservationists. The reservations did not of themselves prevent the League from functioning. But the spirit in which a large part of the Republican membership of the Senate discussed these reservations was frequently the spirit not of faith in a great project for the future but of concern for domestic interests. Word by word, we can analyze them away, if we will. But we cannot so easily exorcise the doubts they inevitably aroused, the egotism of which they were the expression. Looking back on 1920 from our own day, we can see that formal acceptance of the Covenant would not have been enough. There would have had to be strong and general conviction that the instrument would work, and a firm determination to support it. Perhaps, if the American people had had such a conviction and determination, they would, making all allowances for the rigidity of his view, have supported Woodrow Wilson. The fate of the treaty suggests that they were confused and disoriented, that they were by no means ready to pay the price of international co-operation on a significant scale. And this view of the matter is buttressed by what followed. The reversion to economic nationalism in the Harding administration, the ridiculous Fordney-McCumber tariff bill, the stiff attitude assumed on the war debts, the restriction of immigration, the reluctance to accept a role even in the World Court (an institution whose origins were in no small degree American)—all these things seem to show that the United States in 1920 was not ready for the large mission that Wilson wished to assign to it. And it is more important to realize this than it is to assess blame for the treaty's defeat.

The blow dealt to the idea of collective security in 1919 and 1920 might well have seemed to the exultant foes of Wilson to have been a mortal one. For a little while the Harding administration (to its shame be it said), refused to have any dealings with the League at all. Bit by bit the attitude was relaxed; but in 1924 and 1925 the government of the United States would give no assurances that it would acquiesce in the application of economic sanctions against an aggressor state, and this attitude on its part no doubt chilled the ardor of other governments in their efforts to extend and strengthen the Covenant. In the same way, in 1931, though the United States co-operated with the League in condemning the Japanese occupation of Manchuria, and though the American Secretary of State would have liked to go farther, the opposition of President Hoover to any thought of sanctions limited the effectiveness, or at any rate the scope, of League action. Difficulties again arose when the League attempted to act against Italy on the occasion of the Italian invasion of Ethiopia in 1935. In this case, economic sanctions were in some degree applied, but there was no evidence that the United States would co-operate in any such policy, and the shipments of oil to Italy from this country suggested that American co-operation in an embargo on that product would be difficult to secure.

Yet on the other hand the idea of collective security was to show a remarkable vitality. Take, for example, the case of the Kellogg Pact, that remarkable treaty promoted by the American government, and actually signed and ratified by virtually all the great governments of the world, by which the signatories agreed to renounce war as an instrument of national policy. At first blush a purely romantic document, an unimplemented promise to abstain from violence, the pact derived at least some of its support amongst intelligent people from the conviction that condemning aggressive war as immoral was only a step from taking positive action against it. Again, in 1933, the offer of the Roosevelt administration not to interfere with economic sanctions applied by the League illustrated a new emphasis in American opinion. Far more important than this, however, was the development of American policy towards the close of the thirties. For while undoubtedly to some persons the advance of Hitler represented very early a threat to the future safety of the United States, to many others sheer dislike of aggressive action was a factor in the formation of views. Sustained by this attitude, President Roosevelt at no time pretended to a genuine neutrality in the world struggle; the famous bases-destroyer deal of September 1940 was only one instance of a policy flagrantly discriminatory between the belligerents; and the enactment of lend-lease in 1941 was such a measure of aid to a belligerent as would have been unthinkable in the course of the nineteenth or early twentieth century under the tenets of international law. Moreover, in 1945 the idea of collective security was written once again into the great international instrument that emerged from the conference of San Francisco; and on paper, at any rate, it was carried further than ever before. For while the Covenant relied largely on economic sanctions for the prevention of war, the Charter stresses the significance of military power, and suggests the creation of an international force to be put at the disposal of the world organization. We have seen the Charter in practical operation in Korea. Moreover, the idea of collective security has been given specialized and regional, as well as generalized, interpretation. Well within the spirit of the Charter, and written indeed before the Charter was framed, is the convention of Chapultepec, calling for collective action amongst the states of the New World in case of hostile action against any one of them, and the prescriptions of the protocols adopted at Mexico City in 1945 have been strengthened by the prescriptions of the conference of Rio in 1949. Still more important is the North Atlantic Pact, which applies to a new area the principle of collective action for the maintenance of peace, and which is one of the cornerstones of American foreign policy today. The idea for which Wilson contended in 1919 and 1920 was thus only wounded, not destroyed, in the course of the struggle over the treaty of Versailles, and it has shown of recent years a remarkable and increasing vitality. The grim old Covenanter who bent so little in the struggle of thirty years ago would find today that he had been, at least in part, vindicated by the outbreak of the second World War, and justified in his faith in the future by the application of the Charter to the invasion of South Korea in 1950.

It would be rash to predict that the idea of collective security will dominate and direct either American or European foreign policy in the future. There are situations where the application of collective force will be very difficult, if indeed it can be applied at all. Even in the case where it *is* applied, it may not be possible to win a clean-cut victory over the forces of aggression. It is not easy to secure worldwide action against an aggressor on a worldwide scale. But to say this is by no means to say that the conception is without influence or effect, or that, as so often happens in human affairs, its existence does not have collateral effects that are of far-reaching importance. The growth of the collective-security principle explains in part why in 1945 the United States accepted a place in the world organization of the United Nations. It explains, therefore, as a necessary consequence, the increasingly significant role that this country is now playing in international affairs, and the growth of popular interest in these affairs. It explains why the people of this country, apparently indifferent to the growth of Hitlerian power in the thirties, have taken a very different attitude towards the expansion of the Soviet Union, and have, through the Atlantic Pact and through the recent actions of the Truman administration, made clear their purpose to resist aggression in Western Europe. The idea of collective security furnishes the context in which American diplomacy is likely to operate as time goes on, and is closely associated with the whole conception of a world forum, to which the nations of the world make appeal, and to the conception of a co-operative system in which the United States works with, and is influenced by, other like-minded nations in its formulation of policy. Once again, let us not talk of the apocalypse. When Lowell in the *Present Crisis* (and the word "crisis" is significant), wrote the famous lines: "Once to every man and nation comes the moment to decide," he was sinning against the laws of history, in which man has the opportunity to redeem himself, and to debase himself, again and again and yet again. No formula is enough; no formula is always true.

But when all this is said, it remains the case, as we look back on 1919 and 1920, that what Woodrow Wilson was pleading for was a larger view of American responsibility than the country was ready to accept; a conception of international organization that, had it been applied in time, might well have prevented the rise of National Socialism; a conception that plays its part in the great secular struggle of today. In 1919 and 1920 the American people were confused as to the nature of the choice before them; that they voted Harding in by such vast majorities, even making due allowance for the equivocations that lured many voters into the Republican camp, seems to show that the issue of the League was imperfectly understood, and certainly not too deeply felt. They were not ready for the role that was to await them. They turned their back on opportunity. In his tour across the country in the fall of 1919, Woodrow Wilson tried to rouse the people to see the issue with the same intensity with which he saw it; and it must be admitted that he failed, else, rigid as was his view, they would still have supported him. But in the longer perspective did he fail? That question will be asked again and again as the scroll of history unrolls.

XI. *When the Banks Closed*

The origins of the 1933 bank crisis are as deep and complex as the origins of the great depression out of which it came. Industrial concentration, the drift toward monopoly, marked disparity in the distribution of income, have been frequently mentioned as underlying causes, but the more immediate determinants appear to have been the loose and inadequate banking-system, the decline in the value of bank assets, and the series of European bank-failures. The bank moratorium instituted by President Roosevelt ended the crisis and the needed banking-reforms were soon enacted, but it is Professor Walton Hamilton's contention that the economic agencies responsible for the conditions that produced the inflexible price-structure, and ultimately the banking crisis itself, remained essentially untouched.

XI

When the Banks Closed

Walton Hamilton
Southmayd Professor Emeritus of Law, Yale Law School

An incident now and then reveals a crisis in a people's affairs. A provincial governor, marching an army across a stream almost too small to be noted on the map, thought the stream not worth noting. But the Rubicon marked the limit of Julius Cæsar's lawful authority, and in the tramp of his scanty legion was to be heard the passing of a Roman republic that no longer was able to meet the demands of statecraft. A hammering of a host of usages of old into the Ten Commandments, the emergence of pages marked by movable type from a crude press, the meeting of a gang of robber barons—old style—at Runnymede to set down on parchment rights that they loved to think of as ancient, the endowment of the prosaic names of dull villages like Shiloh, Gettysburg, and Appomattox with a glory that centuries of honest living could never have imparted: all of these, and scores of their kind, lose the limited significance that the sheer happenings in themselves bestow, and take on significance in their revelations of—and even in their capacity to create—crises in social orders that seem to be firmly established.

A series of events, seemingly unconnected, may betray not the eclipse of a culture but the crumbling of the order of society under which alone it seemed able to carry on. When the eighteenth century had run almost three quarters of its length, all seemed quiet on the surface. But in the single year 1776, signals that pointed to the end of an era made their appearance. A Scot named David Hume, in an essay that no contemporaries could understand, dared to explore understanding itself. Across the water, in Prussia, the descendant of a Scotch émigré was torturing his mind in a critique of pure reason—and reason not so pure. Another Scot, Adam Smith, in that same year was publishing a book on which he had long been engaged and which bore the pretentious—even the sensational—title of *An Inquiry into the Nature and Causes of the Wealth of Nations.* This constituted a devastating attack upon the established economic order. The treatise was a great brief, naming names and reciting cases, in condemnation of mercantilism in general and the old Colonial system in particular. At Philadelphia, the second city in the Empire, a bookish country squire named Thomas Jefferson scribbled a document, in "decent respect for the opinions of mankind," which in a list of concrete charges against the English king recited the iniquities of this same Colonial system, effected the first great breach in the rising British Empire, and supplied Adam Smith the documentary proof of the correctness of his thesis. Gibbon, at about the same time, in one of those magnificent attacks upon a stupendous subject which marked the age, sought to explain the greatness of Rome and the reasons for its fall; and one wonders if beneath the smoothness of his historical prose he is not disturbed by the plight of the empire about him.

But, if such things were straws in the wind which told of ominous things to come, they were all animated by a gospel of faith. The order of society, which the ruling classes loved to think of as established, was not to endure from everlasting to everlasting. Upon it rested definite human obligation, and if it did not measure up to its responsibilities, it was destined to be revised or even replaced by its better. An uncompromising belief was that human reason—if accorded its chance—became a mighty support to "progress"; and in the works of these latter eighteenth-century radicals "progress" was put forward as a candidate for the primacy long held in respectable thought by order. It was artifice, in the form of social arrangements, that was the villain in the drama of man's destiny. A better social order, which would respond more profitably and more completely to the human demands upon it, was to be had in return for courage, intelligence, and labor in creating it. The appeal was, as Mr. Jefferson originally put it, to "Nature and Nature's god," or as Adam Smith deftly phrased it, to allow "the invisible hand" to get in its work. The demand was for the release and development of human faculties, for exploiting to the full the potential plenty that lies about us. As a matter of fact, no matter how it came to pass, Adam Smith, Mr. Jefferson, and others of their ilk were allowed, at least to some extent, to have their way with history.

Thus a single event is not self-contained. The importance it contains on its own merits is as nothing beside the significance with which it comes to be endowed. It may, like Cæsar's crossing the Rubicon, reveal a political order ripe for change. It may, like Adam Smith's *Wealth of Nations* display an economic system struggling to be born. It may, like the Declaration of Independence, at once constitute an indictment of an imperial system that has forsaken its task and an invitation to create a political order in which the subject is replaced by the citizen. All events, of course, are not of equal importance. To understand what is, in terms of how it has come to be, events must be sorted by size. But even a few, if properly selected and endowed with the attributes their representative character gives them, will serve the purpose. For through the critical event the whole course of history flows; and, within its catholic bounds all that has been, rubs elbows with all that is to be.

II

Events are not alike; and the more they signify, the wider the difference between them. It is a far cry from the Rubicon and Runnymede, from the fragments on government and the exaltation of pure reason, to the crises of our own day. But, like a hundred significant events so long behind us as to become classical, the closing of the banks in 1933 stems from a long course of events and takes its meaning from the whole of the culture within which it is set.

The facts themselves—at least the superficial facts—occurred very near the time the current generation of college students was born. If the facts came too early for them to remember, they are still fresh in the memories of their fathers and mothers. The stark fact is that in the later days of February and the earlier days of March 1933, bank after bank the country over hung on its door the perplexing legend: "Closed for business." Although in recent months the number of bank failures had increased, a note of hope usually was given by the qualifying word: "Temporarily." As a result those who had checking accounts were unable to possess themselves of the purchasing power they had loaned. Those who had laid by surplus income for old age, a rainy day, or the purchase of a home, found that their monies had taken wings, and prayed that it was only for a visit and not for a farewell. The fortunate persons who had been wise enough to choose banks able, for the time being at least, to ride out the storm could take little comfort in the plight of their neighbors.

In a feudal society the closing of the goldsmiths' shops would scarcely have been remarked. For those who had gold and silver that demanded safekeeping were few in number; and, after all, the land was the thing, and the land was still there. In the United States of the mid-nineteenth century, such an event would have ranked rather as a misfortune than as a widespread disaster. For then the national economy was still firmly established upon the land, and the perils of finance could threaten only so far as industrial activity had been brought under the sway of purchase and sale. But a silent revolution was already transforming our ways of making our living. The growth of manufacture and commerce turned villages into towns and, filling the landscape with smokestacks, office buildings, and railroad switches, drew people and plants and houses together into great urban communities. The handicrafts of old that produced for local markets were converted into gigantic industries that from focal points of production sent their goods out to even the most remote neighborhood. The farm ceased to produce all that the family required; instead it, like the trades, was caught up into the intricate network of industry and turned its attention to cash crops. Anyone who had something to sell or to lend—sheer labor, developed skills, savings for investment, the products of farm or of factory—was forced to go to market, first to exchange what he had for purchasing power, and then to exchange that purchasing power for the goods and services that made up his standard of life. Thus the population was caught up into an intricate and sensitive industrial order, in which all activities were closely interlocked and a blow at any strategic point would carry far and wide. It was this sensitive far-flung economy of a myriad of interlocked activities that in late

February and early March, 1933, was faced with the closing of the banks.

The closing of the banks was not, like many another critical event, a mere symptom of a lack of health in the social order which as yet had not broken through the surface. On the contrary, it was a far from unexpected blow in a series of tragic events which was bringing the national economy to the verge of catastrophe. To herald the all-is-not-well when peace and prosperity were written all over the surface of things, this threat to arrest the flow of credit, without which it was impossible for the economy to operate, should have appeared far earlier. If it had come at the latest by September of 1929 it would, as truly as the Rubicon or the *Wealth of Nations*, have been prophetic in its import. For so long as God was in his heaven and common stocks were riding high, the future was not being sold short, and even if assets were not perfectly sound, confidence was enough to keep bank doors open. Few new years have ever been ushered in with the acclaim that greeted 1929. Devices that add together the conglomeration of necessities, comforts, and frivolities of the standard of life to give indices of production are treacherous things. But in general terms they speak the truth in finding the national income to have increased more in the decade following World War I than in the thirty years that had preceded it. The productivity of labor per man was found, by resort to the magic of statistics, to have doubled during the period. The new automobile industry, with the slabs of cement it had stretched across the countryside, had imparted a dynamic urge to the whole economy. Securities of all kinds had gone to heights never before attained by certificates of indebtedness. There had been a shift in interest and in values from gilt-edge securities to common stocks, and a modern priestcraft had substituted the prices of common stocks for the entrails of animals in the reading of the omens. When the index of industrials had passed the record figure of 300 and kept on rising, it was clear to all sensible men that we had moved to a new and far higher level—and that upon it business activity had been stabilized. An economist of high repute in big-business circles had been crying disaster for three years, but caught the vision of a new heaven and a greater economy in time to join the Hallelujah Chorus just before the crash.

Then on a fateful day in October of 1929 the crash came. The stock market, which the optimistic bulls had come to regard as their own property, rebelled against its masters. Even the strategy of the investment bankers, and plans cunningly devised to support the market, failed to prevent the most beautiful of graphs from taking a downward slant. Industrials that had been taking the grade with a stride that promised to carry them to the 400 figure began to slip, and in an unwilling toboggan ride fell back to less than half of that figure. As the price curves dipped, investments ran to cover, plans for business expansion were revised or withdrawn; a call to entrenchment—or even to retreat—crept into the counsels of executives; the demand for new employees was suspended and even old ones were laid off, and the whole industrial system came to take a slower pace.

The crisis was met by leaders of American business with a wisdom that seemed born of a genius for making matters worse. The policy of a single concern, whose business covers the whole country and reaches into almost every home, is so typical of corporations of its kind that it would be indiscreet to name it. It kept its old employees but as, for a variety of reasons, they left, it refused to replace them, so the new workers it would have taken were left without jobs. It reduced the wages of its employees just when they had no opportunity to better themselves by going elsewhere—thus decreasing their purchasing power and lowering their capacity to keep other industries going. As the incomes of the people fell, the corporation maintained the high prices of the period of prosperity; and although it was a necessity, hundreds of thousands of its customers had to give up its service. This in turn made for lessened employment, and lower wages to its employees, a further decrease in purchasing power, and another blow at the operation of the economy. But throughout the period the corporation kept up its customary dividends, even if it had to deplete its reserves to do so. Multiply this mistake many times over—and you sense the incapacity of managerial business to cope with the crisis of 1929.

It was evident, even from the first, that the business community, whether acting as individuals or in such concerts as it might form, could tamper and tinker only to the end of making matters worse. Although it was far too long delayed, there was at last a recognition that the government must come to the rescue. The Great

Engineer was in the White House, and he was looked to for a program that would set all the curves of falling business activity in reverse. Mr. Hoover could never have explained that there are no such things as natural resources; that nature does no more than store up stuffs of one sort and another; that it is only as arts are developed to put them to use that the resources are discovered within some of these stuffs; that with the development of the useful arts the whole catalogue of resources is remade; and that, in the last analysis, the promise of the standard of life rests upon the state of our knowledge. Mr. Hoover was not a prisoner of the manmade "iron laws" of classical economics, which in its assumption of man's insatiable wants and the scarcity put here by nature had set down its own revised version of the Garden of Eden story. And, in an intuitive sort of way, Mr. Hoover had come to feel that our productive output—and the resulting standard of life—could be made pretty much what we would have it be. Mr. Hoover was not without his weakness for a good fairy-story; but he was never more the realist than when he spoke about "two chickens in every pot and two cars in every garage."

The hitch was that he did not formulate—he could not have formulated—a program for attaining such an objective. His skills as an engineer were not matched by equal skills as a down-to-earth economist, and he could hardly be accounted a master of statecraft. He accepted prevailing business arrangements, which had been in existence for only the briefest moment in human history, as among the inevitables of a natural economic order. Although they were all about him, he had little conception of the host of restraints under which the business system operates, and of the vested interests, the vested structures of industries, the vested ways of thought, which were barriers to the realization of his prophetic utterances. So he took no steps to sweep away these barriers, to set free the creative forces of industry, or to effect the return of the economy to a system of free enterprise. As a materialist, he saw more clearly than any of our Presidents the promised land that lay ahead, but he was blind to the necessity of contriving ways and means of reaching it. Instead he put his faith in a laisser faire that had already flunked the job. As a concession, he was willing to use the government in the emergency to help a natural economic system over the hard places. But it never occurred to him to bend business to the job it is here to do. Instead he indulged in the comfortable and treacherous philosophy that, if you pour a lot of money in at the top, it will trickle down the industrial pyramid and in some mysterious way eventually raise the standard of life. Accordingly, Mr. Hoover attempted to bring the government to the rescue by a bit of verbal magic and the creation of a new federal agency. The agency had as its function the lending of public funds to corporations in distress. The magic lay in the fusion of three rather respectable words, reconstruction, finance, and corporation, to give a persuasive name to the new arm of government. Its task was the making of loans to concerns whose continued existence was essential to the operation of the economy and to whom the investment banks would not extend a line of credit.

In theory the idea—even though far from adequate as a way out of the depression—was a good one; but, as so often happens in business and government, it was spoiled in its execution. For in choosing a personnel he regarded as competent for the new venture, Mr. Hoover came up with a paradox. He chose persons whose skills were assured by long experience as commercial bankers—yet the success of the agency demanded a scheme of values transcending the limitations of private finance. As a consequence, from the very first its officials were unable to make the R.F.C. an instrument of public policy. With the R.F.C. limping along—or even deserting the cause that had brought it into being—matters went from bad to worse. It has been argued valiantly by Mr. Hoover that, when in November 1932, he was voted out of office, he had "the depression licked." But, if he did, the returns did not come in.

So Inauguration Day in March of 1933 came. The weather, however brightly the sun shone in parts of the country, was gloomy. For as F.D.R. came into office a host of banks scattered across the land had closed their doors. Nearly three years and a half had passed—the longest depression in the history of the country—and instead of getting out of the woods we were getting more deeply into them. It was at last obvious that business was unable to take care of itself. The federal government, whose traditional rule had been to keep out of the affairs of business, had to be called upon to devise ways and means to restore the economy as a going concern. The closing of the banks did not bespeak a crisis ahead; it was a solemn warning that the crisis, which had outlasted its appointed span, had to be ended at once or the industrial system would cease to function. It was an "or else" sort of signal, giving warning that the separation of state and economy must be ended.

III

No previous depression in the history of the country had ever been so protracted; none before had been devoid of capacity to liquidate itself. The steady beat of industrial change had transformed the economy and stripped business of the resilience that had enabled it to take the impact of time. The firms that make up an industry had become larger. A dozen oil companies had each reached a size larger than the old Standard, which in the first decade of the century had been called an octopus. In many areas a host of concerns, pretty much alike, had been succeeded by corporations so few in number as to be able to keep in lock-step. As size grew, personal decision came to be replaced by established ways of doing things. An entity of multiple activities demands routine; and the bureaucracy of big business came into being and flourished. The giants who came to tower above their fellows and set an example that smaller concerns were to follow lost their mobility.

The shift, in a word, was from the open market to the politics of industry. In the good old days, before brethren of a trade learned to dwell together in unity, each pretty largely looked to its own advantage. Few business units could afford to hold their products very long; the cost of storage and of carrying the investment would eat up the value. Nor, ignorant of what the competitor was about to do, did it pay the trader to destroy part of his stock to sell the rest at an enhanced price. Instead, the trader was forced to sell; and, if the market was not good, to cut prices in order to stimulate the goods to move. Wages, of course, were cut, and purchasing power fell; but, with prices dropping, an adjustment was effected on a lower level. The accommodation of prices to the new circumstances enabled factories to keep going and materially reduced, even if it did not eliminate, unemployment. In addition, the economy was still close enough to the land to enable the farm to absorb surplus labor that the mills might disgorge.

But with the concentration of wealth and power a new order came into being. If all the firms in an industry are acting in concert, price is no longer made by the free play of forces converging in the market. It is announced by a leader, fixed by a committee of an industry, or determined by some procedure that is political in character. Wages are assessed by a process of collective bargaining, in which the union shrewdly measures the corporate-employer's capacity to pay, and the corporate-employer attempts to effect a settlement that will not put dividends in jeopardy. The structure of a corporation, and the industry into which its corporate units were gathered, tended to become rigid. Trade practices came to replace individual judgments. Tradition came to rule where once there had been response to current fact. The corporation came to lose its capacity to deploy its resources to best advantage. Managerial judgment involved too many persons who had to be consulted, and took too long a time, for decision to keep up with the course of events. Businesses stiffly took blows where their predecessors of a generation or two ago had yielded before the strokes and had presently caught a new foothold. Above all, the salutary institution of bankruptcy—so merciless to the individual, so helpful to the health of the economy—had lost its power to get in its work in time.

We know, in general terms, that the incapacity of the 1929–33 economy to take the impact of circumstances was due to its greater immobility. And we know that this inflexibility was due to the decline of the market as an agency of contact, the substitution of a political process in the making of business decisions, and the trend towards economic concentration. But we have no measure of the growth of concentration, and you will look in vain for a book that tells you how it all came about. It is in magnitude and importance a grand story, made up of a large number of concrete stories. It bears an undertone of tragedy, since the whole movement has occurred in opposition to American ideals that go back to the founding of the Republic. Fragments of this story—accounts of what has happened in a number of industries—are to be found in the hearings and monographs of the Temporary National Economic Committee and in reports of other Congressional bodies. A host of materials not yet beaten into industrial patterns lives in the files of various government departments or reposes in archives. But the general treatises on economics are devoid of any account of the mighty trends that have laid their grip on our people. The outlines and elements, the principles and treatises, are more subtle and articulate than those of forty years ago. But from their pages you will get no inkling that an old economy has been succeeded by a new one utterly unlike it in kind. The good books are still written as if the free play of the horse-swap and the resilience of petty trade were still marks of big business.

The term "corporate empire" is coming into vogue to describe the type of business which has come to be strategic. It may be a single imperium with far-flung activities. Or it may be a concordium of large concerns acting as a unit. As the move towards concentration has gone along, resourceful attorneys have created an arsenal of legal inventions with which business units, as occasion demands, may clothe themselves. The most usual picture of a corporate empire is a parent corporation with a host of subsidiaries and affiliates. There are in the land a large number of corporations that own more property, have more employees, and exert more power than such a sizable state of the Union as Iowa, Connecticut, or Georgia. Such a corporation has a clear-cut structure, parades a tight hierarchy of functions, and moves with a precision to which no state government can aspire. But corporate structure is not an essential to corporate empire. The device of contract has long been known to the law; but to serve big business the priestcraft of lawyers has turned it into a new institution. The manufacturer of automobiles looks upon the corporate structure of United States Steel as primitive. He seeks to establish an equally far-flung dominion without investing the funds and incurring the risks of complete ownership. So for his "parts" he makes contracts with independents. And, although these are for a short period and are subject to cancellation by either party on short notice, the part-maker has no other market, cannot afford to cancel, and has lost his independence. In like manner, the automobile manufacturer uses independents as "outlets" through which to market his cars. So hard and fast is the captivity that the lord of the assembly line dictates the terms upon which the dealer carries on the dealer's own business. The forms are those of contract as known to the free enterprise system; but those forms have come to mean a system of compulsion feudal in character.

The creation of corporate empires has been too rich and varied in its inventions to allow statistical statement. The general patterns are not only numerous, but each in its reality presents variety. The oil industry presents a beautiful blending of corporate and contractual arrangements. The motion-picture producers supply their features to independents; but through the ownership of some among competing theaters, it comes about that they can dictate to the independent exhibitor terms upon which he can have their pictures. In milk it is the distributor who is in big business; he is able, within wide limits, to dictate prices to the independent dairies, whence he draws his supplies, and to his customers. It is a fascinating—and endless—task to set down all the devices by which an industry is regimented. Take up a business manual and pick out the interlocking directorships between companies. You cannot escape wondering how many impulses towards unity of action pass along this network of connections. The old conspiracy in restraint of trade, which left its tracks all over the place in documents government officials could read, is a thing of the past. If gentlemen come into agreement—as gentlemen of a trade are prone to do—and, if there are few enough of them, they can dispense with the documents. A dinner now and then, given for the professed purpose of discussing works of art, may be enough. Or the custom of following the leader may be established without even a word of understanding —orally or in writing—by men of honor who hold themselves bound to live up to it.

Nor has the state been without fault in this drive towards concentration. If there is a single source of supply for a raw material—or a single control over multiple sources—a dominion over an area of industry may be created. The owner of a copyright may dictate the terms upon which a book is sold; his power, however, falls far short of monopoly, for the book must compete with many others of its kind. The owner of a patent on an invention, however, stands in a different situation. If the invention —or a series of inventions—constitutes an industrial art, all are barred from the industry who do not come to terms with the patent owner. Accordingly, the patent license—or permission to use the invention—has come to be a dominant device of regimentation. In a domain of the economy—such as glass containers, synthetic metals, or ethical drugs—no one can enter the industry except by the license, or permission, of the patent owner. And such a person can enter it only to the extent and upon the terms that the patent owner decrees. Thus, in glass containers the Hartford-Empire Company, the owners of patents that covered the whole of the process of production, appointed to each its distinctive field, such as milk bottles, beer bottles, pharmaceutical bottles, and the like. It dictated the quantity to be produced, the territory within which sales were to be made, and the prices to be charged. At the T.N.E.C. hearing its attorney admitted that the sovereign company regulated the affairs of the whole industry with a fullness and a precision that the law did not accord to a sovereign state of the Union. He defended the system, however, by insisting that the Hartford-Empire Company did the job far better than could any state in the Union.

This is not the place—nor is there here space—to pass other trends in review and to appraise those trends in terms of public policy or social morality. But three facts stand out with such significance that they must be remarked.

The first is that the myriad of decisions that made up the trend towards immobility in the economy were prompted by the soundest business motives. One and all they were animated by the urge for gain. If the actors were to blame, it was because zeal in the business game was not tempered by a solicitude for the public interest and the law of the land.

The second is that, when the drive towards monopoly engaged too many actors, it became self-defeating. It was grand for a concern to liquidate competition, to dictate its own prices and terms of sale, and to fortify its corporate estate against the impact of a turbulent market. Nor is there any nicer oasis than a monopolistic holding set in an economy of free enterprise. But when all take a fling at the restraint of trade, the concern that has thus sought dominion and security becomes a victim of like practices on the part of its neighbors.

The third is that the regimented industries thus are out of harmony with the American tradition and with dominant aspects of our culture. A neatly organized industry has a current efficiency that the sprawling pattern of competitive enterprise cannot give.

But free enterprise gives full play to talent at a number of focal points, and sports a dynamic drive alien to anything that is established. It is this freedom to think afresh, to try the unknown enterprise, to ride into all the winds that blow, that is sacrificed to an order and efficiency produced by regimentation. The rigidities in the economy have to be relaxed, or the social order has to be remade to accord with them. The breach between has been a fault-line, to borrow a geological term, along which seething troubles are bound to break into the open.

The closing of the banks in 1933 was a last sharp warning that that trouble was here.

IV

It would be extravagant to say that the closing of the banks was causal to the New Deal, by which its crisis was met. It would be untrue, however, to insist that it did not have a dominant role in the creation of that program. The climate of opinion, of sheer tolerance and of stark, human need, fix the outward limits of any series of political measures. Change all of these, or even any one of them—and the result would have been different. If F.D.R. had taken office—as Presidents now do—on the 20th of January rather than the 4th of March, 1933, the key move that touched off the course of action would have been different. If the banks had been closed some three months earlier, we would have experienced the tragedy of a national economy unable to fulfill its task of supplying our people with their livings—and measures more drastic than were called for would have had to be taken.

But no event, however serious, alone touches off its consequences. The events that follow occur in a social matrix, are shaped by distinctive circumstances, and are limited by the capacities of those in power. It rarely, if ever, happens that all the best of the knowledge and wisdom that is available is called into play in a crisis; that is an achievement of which the political process has not yet shown itself capable. If F.D.R. had been of another temperament; if he had chosen advisers other than he did; if the Congress had been made up of men more broadly experienced in public policy; there would have been a different story. It was a political, not an economic or a social, enterprise to which the administration stood committed. Measures could not be accepted or rejected on their own merits; they had to be converted into political values to win acceptance. As the course of human events cannot rise above human reason, so the program to meet the crisis could not rise above the wisdom of the persons whose task it was to formulate and administer it.

It was not—in no sense could it be—radical. There was no drive to the roots of the matter, no probing to discover the ultimate sources of the troubles with which the American people were confronted. Instead, the New Deal was a series of expediencies designed to solve a series of problems as they became finally too insistent to be neglected. F.D.R. was a superb political artist; but his sensitiveness to political values stood in the way of the detachment essential to thinking problems of public policy through. An understanding of a realistic and dynamic economy was not among the greatest of his gifts. In this domain he was accustomed to play by ear; and although he did not shrink from decision, his choices were limited by plans laid before him by his advisers. His political insight enabled him to realize a feat to which few who were skilled in politics could rise—that he not only could, but must, meet problems boldly, and he must do things that had never been done before. But the crisis in the affairs of the nation was far more serious and the public's tolerance of innovation far greater than even he realized. Nor was his temperament that of the real reformer. So he met issue after issue, as it arose, with an expediency. There was no attempt to reshape the economy to serve human needs through giving full rein to the dynamic impulses of business enterprise. Instead, the insistence was upon the measures necessary to make the old economy a going concern again. In executing the New Deal Symphony, F.D.R., as was his wont, improvised as he went along.

Statecraft is not an exact science; in fact it is not a science at all. It must take account of more factors than any formula can hold. And as it drives into the unknown, you cannot tell before the event who is wise and who is foolish. Consistency and political experiment are not boon companions. If the New Deal exhibits more ventures that had to be tried a second time, or even abandoned, boldness rather than unsoundness must be written down as the cause. But it is the art of politics to make failure wear the mark of success; and F.D.R. had the knack of deserting failure in a fresh and glorious adventure. His first task was to bail out the banks, in order that credit might flow again and the economy become once more the instrument of welfare. Here there was immediate success; such failure as there was, came in the long-time view. The state of public opinion made it possible to create a truly national institution of credit which might have given an upward lift to the whole industrial system. But the opportunity was not at once seized, and presently it was gone. Next was the task of reviving—and accelerating—the flow of purchasing power in order that a half-stalled economy might again get into high gear. To this end, a number of devices were employed. A brilliant invention called "parity"—which was all but a sheer fiction—was used to endow farmers with higher receipts for their crops. A belated recognition of unionism increased the bargaining power of labor and helped to vitalize the demand for consumer goods. A business or even an industry could not, tangled as it was into the national economy, lift itself by its bootstraps. But if all should together go into full production, a demand for the products of each would be created by the purchasing power of wages paid in all the others. So F.D.R. in 1933 asked the firms that made up the industries of the national economy to sign the President's Reemployment Agreement. Out of this modest venture came the National Recovery Administration and the brief but spectacular flight of the Blue Eagle. In the wake of these came a flood of alphabetical agencies concerned with matters that business alone could not handle and that had become matters of state.

It was all a drive towards recovery, full employment, a higher standard of life, and things unknown. If it moved in many directions, it moved with the spirit of life. If farmers were given fatter purses, it was through an agricultural adjustment that put the government's blessing upon restriction of output. If the N.R.A. performed the useful service of arresting prices that seemed destined for a headlong toboggan ride, it was by allowing the gentlemen of the several industries to write their own codes of business conduct. They, of course, went in heavily for self-administered systems of price; and the economy was saved for another and greater venture into rigidity only by the refusal of the governing board of the N.R.A. to put the appropriate "cost formulas for price" into effect. The Agricultural Adjustment Act and likewise an act for the control of bituminous coal had to be written twice before they fell into forms the courts were willing to accept. In 1934 and 1935, public policy moved definitely towards a neat economy made up of regimented industries. By 1938 and 1939, the administration that had gone in for industrial codes was engaged in the greatest trust-busting campaigns the country had ever known. Yet even here inconsistency was not in the saddle. As recovery was effected, we could at last afford to think of the kind of economy we wanted ours to be.

In one dominant way, however, the mark of the closing of the banks was left upon the whole program. The memory of the years 1929 to 1933 was fresh; a return to that period was to be avoided whatever the cost; security came to be a dominant value among the people—a security to which acceptable public policy must conform. The Guffey Coal Act came because the market could not impose order and solvency upon "the most unruly of all industries." The "case of oil" proved that when each company acted for itself, even big business could not achieve security. An over-all government control was deemed better than allowing the giants of the industry to gang up. Industrialists generally sought security through codes that bore the imprimatur of the N.R.A. And when that body became obdurate, and the Supreme Court added the knockout blow, many of them by the use of devices deemed legal, or by silence and stealth, attempted to go on with collective provision against the hazards of the market. The Securities and Exchange Act was designed to insure a greater protection to investment. The growers of corn, wheat, tobacco, and other staple crops found a like security in parity and agricultural adjustment. Laborers sought and were accorded a like protection in the encouragement given to collective bargaining and in the provision of a social security against such outstanding hazards as industrial accident, unemployment, and dependency in old age. A paradox lies in the resort to the antitrust laws to secure to small business some protection against the hazards to survival created by big business. Thus security, so antithetical to the spirit of free enterprise, came into the position of primacy in the shaping of public policy.

Thus the closing of the banks left its mark on public policy and the economy. We have now passed out of the New Deal, through a World War, and into a defense economy. The great legacy from the first term of F.D.R. has been a commitment to public spending. If monies can be appropriated to further the welfare state, they can in far greater abundance be used to create and maintain a defense economy. It is easy to spend for national security. As yet we have not learned how to spend and still avoid the concentration of wealth and the regimentation of industrial activity that turned the years 1929–33 into an era of calamity. Unless and until we probe to the heart of the social malady with which F.D.R. and his associates were confronted, the lesson taught by the closing of the banks will not take its place in a statecraft that is practical and drives to the root of the matter.

XII. *The Black Blizzards*

Like the yellow fever epidemic, the dust storms in 1937
seemed to be acts of God, but as Professor Paul B. Sears
points out in this essay, "an apparent 'act of God' was
traceable to the fact that men had become a geological
agency, without accepting the responsibility for that role."
If American men did not make the dust storms, they must
share much of the blame for their disastrous consequences.
Irresponsible cultivation of semi-arid regions in the Great
Plains was unfortunately symptomatic of the spirit in
which Americans have ravaged their priceless domain for
well over a century. After fruitless years of agitation
against ruinous exploitation of the land, after a cycle of
costly floods, fires, and dust storms, the conservationists
are being listened to, and a prodigal people are beginning
to learn the principles of ecology.

XII

The Black Blizzards

Paul B. Sears

Professor of Conservation, Yale University

I. *The Disaster*

In the late winter of 1932 the air of Oklahoma, where I was then living, began to darken with an ominous, cloudless, impalpable shadow. This shadow grew daily in intensity, as I recall it, until it began to be a kind of dry, choking dusk at noonday. The shadow was a sea of powdered earth, miles high. We soon learned that it extended over many states west of the Mississippi, and that it was being lifted by winds from the high plains west of the 100th meridian. The phenomenon repeated itself in successive years, at first a regional, finally a national, calamity.

Stories of unbelievable distress were reported from the source of this dust. Fields were drifting into dunes, burying fences and machinery, and piling against farmhouses up to the window sill. There were days when visibility was limited to a few hundred feet. The bearings of engines were being cut, the health of livestock and human beings was being visibly affected.

Two reporters sent out to get first hand accounts wired back what they saw. Their editor could not or would not believe them and sent a sharp reprimand—so sharp that they agreed to "relax and give the old man what he wanted." From their watered-down accounts many readers gathered that the situation wasn't so serious after all. But the censorship failed—the dust itself was on the air and carried its own message throughout the nation—even to the Atlantic seaboard.

Most of the dust had its origin in some seventy-two counties of western Texas and Oklahoma, southwestern Kansas, northeastern New Mexico and southeastern Colorado. Between 1932 and 1936 these counties lost a third of their population, many drifting blindly westward towards California; and John Steinbeck wrote the *Grapes of Wrath*. True, he located the Dust Bowl some two hundred miles too far to the east, and stirred in too much Tobacco Road for seasoning, but he caught the essential tragedy to human lives and human hopes. So why quibble?

II. *The Natural History of Dust Storms*

As a botanist and ecologist it has been my business to observe the relationships between living organisms and their environment. In the course of this work I have spent some twenty years in the great grassland region west of the Mississippi. There I had learned that the great prairies and the short-grass vegetation of the western High Plains did not lack trees because of Indian fires or bison grazing, nor because of any peculiarity of soil, all explanations that had been advanced by scientists. My colleague, Dr. Weaver of Nebraska, and Professor Shimek of Iowa, had shown beyond doubt that lack of moisture was the answer—not necessarily lack of rainfall, but rather very high evaporation in relation to rainfall. You may gather something of the power of evaporation from testimony of the City Chemist of Fort Worth, who said that on a dry summer day the air removes more water from the city reservoir than is drawn out for use. Or from the studies of Dr. Thornthwaite you may learn that a dry mass of air moving diagonally across the continent towards Florida will carry more water out to sea than is delivered to the Gulf of Mexico below New Orleans in the same length of time.

At Nebraska I had learned to respect wind as a geological force. At Omaha and Council Bluffs the Missouri River has cut between high banks composed of windblown material that had drifted in during periods of abnormally dry climate thousands of years back. This loess had come from sources not held in place by a healing cover of vegetation—much of it doubtless from glacial flour in the dry river-bed itself.

And I had learned a profound respect for grass and its associated herbs—not only for their direct utility to man and beast but for their role in the grand strategy of nature. Against the ruinous effect of drouth and the wear of wind and water, this green cover was a persistent and effective protection, so long as we did not disturb it too greatly in areas of light soil exposed to especial hazards.

I had also—too slowly as I now see it—learned something of the habits of climate in this great midcontinent. My first lesson came from an old banker who drove me about the countryside, pointing out farm after farm that the bank had foreclosed from one owner then another—then to sell it again to someone who started out in hope, prospered for a few years, only to lose the land from a series of bad years. Today we speak glibly of "weather cycles." I do not like the term, for it gives a misleading idea of regularity—recurrence is a better word than cycle. Tree rings and weather records show us that dry years and wet years tend to succeed each other in groups. These groups may last from two to ten years—all we can be sure of during a moist period is that it will be followed by a dry one, with attendant crop failures. This is a basic fact in the economy of the western midcontinent, where moisture is the key to survival.

Actually Nebraska had been the scene of a drama exemplifying these elemental forces of which I speak, and the lesson was clear enough. The stage was some ten million acres of lush grassland known as the Sand Hills. The cast included a good many thousand farm families. As public domain the Sand Hills had furnished rich pasture, and so long as the sod was unbroken, the loose soil was held in place. The villain of this drama was a well-meaning politician—completely ignorant of natural science, as too many of our political leaders are—who thought this land should be colonized by farmers and persuaded Congress to open it up into homesteads of 640 acres each.

Families flocked in and broke the sod for crops. Where they left it for pasture they put far too many animals on it. The dry years of 1910–13 came along and certainly did not help, although the Sand Hills have considerable subsurface water. But the wind is unceasing, and with the native cover broken by plowing and too close grazing, the sand began to drift from great blow-outs. I saw some of the last survivors in the spring of 1920, desperately hanging on, without income and with scarcely enough to eat.

Now all are gone, cattlemen have purchased the land in large holdings, the grass is back, and the area once more productive. These things did not happen without warning. Three warnings deserve mention. In 1874 Samuel Perkins Marsh published a book that became famous too late. *The Earth is Modified by Human Action*, he called it, and in it he showed that Man had become a geological force, often changing the earth to his own detriment. During the next decade Major John Powell, a keen naturalist, whose loss of an arm in the Civil War did not keep him from being an intrepid explorer, reported to Congress on the arid lands of the West. He pointed out that here water was the deciding factor for all human enterprise. Land should be in large holdings with pattern and mode of use governed by the availability of water sources. The traditional farm size and practices of Western Europe and our Eastern states would be doomed to certain failure. His warning and that of Mr. Marsh went unheeded, and one of the most costly penalties is the subject of this essay.

The third warning drew fire. It came from a professor at the University of Nebraska—a geographer. Even before the Sand Hills had been opened up to homesteading, its eastern margin, near Norfolk, had felt the plow. The first results seemed good, and local boosters began to boost. Weather conditions were favorable for the time being, but Dr. Bengtson knew what hazards to expect, both from future drouth and the loose, light soil. He spoke his mind as a scientist. Immediately a politician-Congressman of great influence demanded in wrath that he be discharged from the university, and I am told that the issue was close. Remembering what happened later to the professor in a dairy state who spoke a good word for oleomargarine, and to another in the Lake States who protested the fraudulent settlement of farmers in the barren cut-over lands, the retention of Dr. Bengtson was a minor miracle. Perhaps his Swedish name helped—certainly the confidence of friends and former students in his scientific integrity did. It should be noted for the record—since professors are often disparaged as "long-haired theorists"—that he wore his own close-cropped, while his attacker's hair fell in long locks about his coat collar.

III. *The Economic Background*

So much for prelude—now back to the High Plains of the Southwest. Where irrigation was possible, it seems likely that arid regions have been the cradle of agriculture. Certainly this has been true in Mesopotamia, Egypt, and Mexico. But with irrigation goes another ancient art, that of dry farming—essentially a method of gambling on the possibility of years with sufficient rainfall to make a crop. Before the introduction of machinery this was generally on a small scale, without enough sod broken to constitute a serious problem in case of failure.

During World War I the years were reasonably moist, and they continued so for more than a decade. Wheat was a prime necessity and the government sustained a high price for it. Meanwhile farming was becoming mechanized and manufacturers were going in for large-scale power machinery, beautifully adapted to the wide-spreading flat or gently rolling lands of the West. Here was a chance for private enterprise and patriotism to do their stuff. Dry-climate soils are rich in nitrogen and other minerals needed by plants. Wheat land could be plowed and planted in the fall, the crop could ripen without further labor and be harvested mechanically the following summer, then be sold for a high price. This looked like a set-up if there ever was one.

In 1920 the government withdrew its support on wheat. The price tumbled, and for the Eastern farmer with his heavy investment in land, improvements, equipment and livestock, and his high taxes, a long era of distress set in. For him the depression began nine years early, and we rode on his back with cheap food and high prices for everything else until stockbrokers began to peddle apples or jump out of windows in 1930.

But the dry-land wheat farmer did beautifully during these nine years. He was a mass producer. I know one who had a modest three-hundred acres, somewhat east of the Dust Bowl. On it he had a machine shed, with tractor, disc, seeder, and combine kept cleaned, oiled, and ready. With a maximum of ten days' work a year he planted and harvested his crop. Even with low prices he made a handsome profit, and so did countless other suitcase farmers, as far west as the racket could be extended. For it became a racket. Men bought land and expensive machinery on credit and the business snowballed, with banks and machinery concerns in it up to their eyebrows.

I recall a conversation, toward the end of this period, with a jubilant chamber-of-commerce official who had flown in from the West. "Great stuff," he said. "I flew over hundreds of thousands of acres just plowed for wheat." I remember asking him if this wouldn't be very serious when the dry years came and the soil started to blow. I remember too how he laughed that one off, indulgently. Perhaps my comment wasn't wasted, however, for I have no cause to complain of the staunch support of the business groups he represented when in later days my casual words came home to roost.

The eventual tragedy came in steps. There was a surplus of wheat in 1930, but by that time people had no money to buy it at any price. Oil was down to thirty cents a barrel and men were standing in breadlines. Payments on land and farm machinery were slowing down, but the gamblers kept on into the autumn of 1931. That winter the drouth came on in earnest and the wheat failed to grow. There was no green cover through the winter, and when the winds of spring began their yearly carnival there was nothing to hold the bare soil against them. The era of the dust storms was under way, and four years of a special kind of hell were added to the nationwide depression. There had been drouths and failures, and emigrations in the Great Plains in 1885, in 1890–5, and 1910–13, but nothing like this. The fury of nature was intensified by the mindless fury of mechanized life and irresponsible financialism in revolt against their creators.

IV. *An Excursion into Morals*

There are, I suppose, two orders of disaster that overtake mankind. One is the apparent act of God—flood, eruption, earthquake, plague, famine, hurricane. The other is the moral failure of society or its leaders, leading to collapse, revolution, invasion, or enslavement. I use the word "moral" in a pretty broad sense here to include all great lapses in responsible conduct, so far as we can foresee consequences.

Men of spiritual insight, the prophets and the poets, have long

sensed that these two orders of disaster are not always as inseparable as we tend to make them. There is meaning in the story of
the Flood, for all of its absurdities. Modern technology has certainly transformed plague and famine into moral problems, solv-
able in terms of hygiene and transportation, respectively. Man's
responsibility to his fellow man in such relatively simple ways
seems clear enough. We have more difficulty with other types
of disaster, which we still like to think of as Heaven-sent or
beyond our control.

Western religion and morality are sufficiently explicit on man's
duty to God and man. Of duty to nature it has nothing to say.
Historically the Jews, in their revolt against the primitive and
corrupt nature-worship of their ancestors, went all the way and
ceased to identify nature with either God or man. It became an
instrument merely. To the Christian, with his spiritual exaltation
of the individual, it was often an obstacle, something to be cast
off, and certainly nothing to be revered. The Taoist of the Orient,
however, condemns not only violence toward fellow man, but
violence toward nature.

It is well, I think, to remember that modern science is directly
and necessarily a product of faith. No scientist would have the
courage to proceed with his task unless he were sustained by an
implicit belief in the orderliness of the universe as an expression
of law. And modern science has been precisely most fruitful in
explaining man to himself by revealing that, however unique he
may be, he is fundamentally a part of the great system and
process we call the world of nature. If I read the signs aright, our
system of ethics is due not for destruction at the hands of the
scientist but for an expansion through the insight he has given us.
I do not see how we can very well carry on with the Christian
concept of respect for man without a corresponding reverence
for nature, of which he is so noble an expression, so integral
a part.

That mankind has suffered because of his violence towards
nature we can now be reasonably sure. There are too many instances to leave the matter much in doubt. The destruction of
hillside vegetation by goats and other cattle in the Mediterranean
region has rendered sterile and unproductive much of that once
fruitful land. Enrico Martinez in 1606, just eighty-five years after
the conquest of Mexico, describes the uplands around Mexico

City as "*descarnado*"—stripped to the bone—by deforestation and overgrazing, and tells of mud washed down in consequence. These stories can be matched in every continent. We have had in the United States an increasing mass of evidence, especially since 1910, of the evil effects of our own folly in dealing with soil, water, and forests. Yet in 1910 an official statement of the Department of Agriculture referred to the soil as our one inexhaustible resource, and Hugh Bennett, present Chief of the Soil Conservation Service, had to labor for years against the inertia of which that statement is typical.

But he had the evidence on his side. And so when the dust storms came it was possible to recognize our own moral complicity in what, a few decades before, would have been piously laid to the door of the Almighty as an "act of God." *Here, it seems to me, is the peculiar significance of this disaster. It dramatized, as nothing before it had ever done, the need to expand our ethics to embody the sacred principle of Tao. Violence against the realm of nature is an evil thing, as is violence against our fellow man. Indeed it can be read as ultimate evil against ourselves.*

Here is stuff for the poets and prophets. Thus far Aldo Leopold in his "Land Ethic," and Frank Darling, the British ecologist, in his beautiful and sensitive writing, have given it the finest expression. Aldous Huxley understands it—indeed it was in a letter he had written to Fairfield Osborn that I first learned of the Taoist doctrine of reverence for nature as well as man. But it will take time and the creative touch of the artist to build these principles into our sacred values. So let us turn back to concrete actions resulting from the disaster.

V. *Extremity Becomes Opportunity*

We have spoken of the exodus occasioned by the storms. There were men who remained to fight and redeem the situation. Notable among them were groups in the extreme west of Texas, the Panhandle. These men were individualists, yet they sensed that only by concerted action could they be effective. They obtained authority from the legislature to organize districts for the control of wind erosion, and those who became members pledged themselves to adopt whatever measures were necessary. Technical advisers were furnished by government.

Meanwhile Hugh Bennett's long campaign against erosion had borne some fruit. He was placed in charge of a Soil Erosion Service in the Department of the Interior. The older bureaus of agriculture were not prepared to deal with the problem, perhaps not even too greatly concerned about it. But Bennett and his small group were ready when the emergency arose. And as the dust crisis gathered headway the storms providentially darkened the skies of Washington while Bennett was presenting his case before a Congressional committee. It was not long before he and an adequate staff were set up as the Soil Conservation Service in the Department of Agriculture. It was his body of experts, in co-operation with state employees, who helped the Texans level their drifts and stabilize the soil with vegetation. I shall never forget the transformation wrought in West Texas within three years, for I watched it happen. And by way of punctuation, here and there in the green expanse was the ranch of the inevitable objector, with his fields still barren and blowing. The law, I believe, was presently strengthened to allow the district to move in and stabilize such lands if they were a threat to others. Kansas soon followed suit.

In Washington Secretary Wallace secured the services of an able group of men to draft a model law that each state might adapt to its peculiar needs and beliefs. This law was aimed at both wind and water erosion—indeed at thorough conservation of soil and water—through districts organized by farmer vote. This law was sent to governors throughout the Union, and at first blessed or cursed by them as a New Deal measure according to their commitments. This was in 1936, as the drouth was nearing an end, with millions of acres still desolate.

The farmers of Oklahoma, sensing a new hope, descended upon Governor Marland, whose physical and political powers were waning and who was being driven hard by vigorous opponents of the New Deal. The pressure for relief from wind erosion had been terrific. The year before at the University of Oklahoma the president dispatched a courier to every department to see what it could contribute toward a solution. The courier came to the Department of Botany just as the idea of a book, to be called *Deserts on the March*, had come to me. I felt that the most direct contribution I could make was to explain what was happening. I offered, if given freedom from teaching for a few months, to do this; I began in April, had the manuscript ready by June, and the excellent University Press had it published in autumn of that year. Probably for this reason I was invited to join the farmers when they stated their case—in no gentle terms—to the governor. His Excellency, with the best will in the world, was obviously in trouble, when an alert young newspaperman, Frank McNaughton, now with the Luce staff, stepped up and spoke to him. The result was that I suddenly found myself chairman of a committee to do something, God help me! We had the model law to work on, but it had to be tailored to Oklahoma prejudices and conditions, then sold to a powerful legislative opposition. This opposition was headed by Frank Phillips, who has no nonsense in his make-up and who made me sweat blood before he was through. It is to his everlasting credit that as soon as he saw that our proposals were on the level he put them through without stooping to make political hay.

This more or less represents the process by which every state in the Union has come, some readily, others reluctantly, to pass a soil-conservation-district law. For the six hundred million acres of our country that are in farms and ranches the soil-conservation district represents a thoroughly democratic and substantial means of action. The alternative choices are, as Kent Leavitt, a leader in the district movement puts it, to bribe the farmer to conserve his soil, to force him to do it or, of course, to do nothing about the matter.

A soil-conservation district may be a county or a watershed. Usually it is a county. It is formed by majority vote of the farmers within the area, who then organize by electing a committee to represent them. The district then enters into a contract with the Soil Conservation Service, which assigns a technical expert to advise the district. The district decides what to do with this advice and how to go about applying it. The arrangement is a purely voluntary and co-operative one.

The accepted procedure has been to develop conservation plans farm by farm, the farmer paying for the actual work but the district assisting in securing necessary services, such as heavy machinery, when necessary. Larger projects involving groups of farms may be worked out by the district, always with consent of all concerned. Through the trained technician all of the latest and best procedures are made available.

Something of the magnitude of the task can be gained by noting that an average midwest county may have about two thousand farms, and that an industrious technician can work out some fifty farm plans a year, or about one a week. This would be a forty-year assignment, but actually it is moving faster than that. Flying over the South today we cannot help being impressed by the progress that has been made in some thirteen years since district legislation has been under way.

I think it fair to say that while we might in any case have developed the district plan for soil and water conservation, the vivid tragedy of the dust storms hastened that process by many years. And because this is true, it is appropriate to analyze the broader effects of the district plan in the American scene.

It is really not difficult to interest people in conservation. The problem has been to direct their energies into effective work. The district plan enables one to do this, regardless of whether he is dealing with rural or urban groups. Rural possibilities need no further explanation, but what of the city dwellers? A few illustrations will suffice.

One great harbor-city has been put to increasing expense to dredge clear the river channel that carries its vital commerce. Within the past four years the financial and industrial leaders of that city have learned what they did not know before—that the source of their costly trouble lies in the eroding farmlands upstream. They have further learned that the solution lies in encouragement of conservation districts in several counties, and the powerful resources at their command are now solidly behind that program.

Again, the sportsmen of the nation are a potent group, as many legislators well know. Their numbers continue to increase as fish and game supplies are being hard pressed. Annual fees for hunting and fishing licenses run into the scores of millions, while money spent for travel and equipment far exceeds that spent for licenses. Until recently, public agencies were frantic and too often ineffectual in attempting to meet the demands of sportsmen for more fish and game. Today sportsmen are beginning to learn that fish and game depend upon favorable habitat—clear water, fertile land, food and shelter. And since eighty per cent of land

in the United States is in private hands, the solution for the sportsman lies largely in better conservation on these lands. Sportsman
groups are now beginning to encourage the formation and operation of soil-conservation districts.

The rural banker of today can no longer afford, like my old
Nebraska friend, to make money through the failures in his
community. Their failure, ultimately, becomes his own, their
prosperity is his. We have plenty of proof now that sound conservation is sound business. The day may come when a rural
banker will insist, as some do today, that his clients, before they
can have credit, show their co-operation in practices adopted by
the local district. More than one such district owes its beginning,
in part, to banker encouragement.

Finally, there is the perennial problem of stream control, on
which the federal government has been spending some billion
dollars a year for many years, with even vaster expenditures in
the offing. It is always easy, when flood victims have buried their
dead, dried out, and finished shoveling mud, to secure appropria-
tions in the hope of preventing a recurrence of disaster. If the
offending river-basin is not too large, and the land draining into
it has a good cover of vegetation, fairly simple reservoirs to store
the surplus flood-water until danger is over will suffice. This was
the plan developed by Arthur Morgan for Governor Cox of
Ohio in the Miami Basin. It has worked beautifully and was,
moreover, financed entirely by the state.

But some of our most dangerous streams, for example the Missouri, cannot be so easily governed. They flow through many
states, drain vast and varied areas, and their flood-plains (significantly named) afford sites too valuable to be left unoccupied,
despite the hazard. And because of the very human tendency to
apply a remedy at the seat of pain, rather than the source of it,
much money has been spent on dikes and other downstream
works where the damage from flood is greatest.

The trouble with such measures is that they attempt to meet
the problem at a point where water and silt have gathered headway and become unmanageable. The effective place to begin the
control of water is where it falls—at the heads and margins of
valleys. We have much to learn about this complex problem, but
one thing is certain—proper land use is involved quite as much as
engineering. It is not enough to build reservoirs, even headwater

reservoirs, unless there is abundant plant-life and mellow soil to absorb the rain and retard run-off. Add to this the fact that we need far more efficient land-use than we now have, for the sake of what it will produce, and the general problem seems clear enough.

As a measure of our present emphasis, the following figures seem significant: I assume that four agencies of government are in a position to deal with the land upon which water falls.

Bureau	1950 Appropriation
Forest Service	$ 86,800,000
Soil Conservation Service	55,100,000
Bureau of Land Management	9,600,000
National Park Service	30,600,000
Total	182,100,000

Two agencies, on the other hand, deal with water after it has entered the stream-bed and has become difficult to manage.

Bureau	1950 Appropriation
Army Engineer Corps	$ 686,900,000
Bureau of Reclamation	393,800,000
Total	1,080,700,000

Granting that wise land-use must be supplemented by skillful engineering, and without making extravagant claims for what good land-use will do, the expenditure of more than five times as much for engineering as for better land-use seems somewhat out of proportion.

Actually the engineering costs are so stupendous that they cannot be charged against flood-control alone. Electric power, irrigation, and an often dubious benefit from navigation must be reckoned in to justify the expense. But reservoirs designed for flood-control are not always compatible with the most efficient generation of power. And as to irrigation, the cost per acre is seldom less than three hundred dollars, and may be as much as fifteen hundred. The cost of bringing farmland already settled and improved, representing a heavy investment, up to high standards of management should seldom exceed thirty dollars per acre. And it is the farmer already settled who is to be taxed to bring new irrigated land into production!

What is needed to harness the great rivers of the West is a more leisurely, thorough, and disinterested study of the entire problem than we have yet had. The temptation to spectacular action following a great disaster is almost irresistible, but it should be resisted until such study can be made.

In the meantime, we may safely proceed to approach these ungoverned streams at their sources and their valley margins. Generous reserves of wilderness and forest, of well-managed grazing lands should be set up and properly cared for. Among the ranches and farms where water falls, soil-conservation districts should be put into operation. As these districts develop, they should co-operate with each other, and ultimately with downstream areas, gradually working out, by consensus, a sound solution of the whole problem of control.

When we have done our best where the water falls, and all concerned have a more mature understanding than they now have, it will be time enough, except for rare and obvious emergency measures, to move downstream into the lower reaches and undertake operations there. For in the words of the President's Water Resources Commission, there is a "sobering finality" about great structures of concrete.

The trouble with such a proposal, I suppose, is that it is too reasonable to be adopted. It means that fat construction-contracts would have to wait their turn at the public till while far less costly and spectacular measures are being worked out. It means that the citizen, through his soil-conservation districts and the agencies that manage his public lands, would participate in the actual working out of river-basin plans, instead of merely signing the check as he does now.

VI. *Are We Backsliding?*

We have at some length described the aftermath of the dust storms, showing how they served to dramatize soil and water as every man's concern. We have given our judgment that these events hastened, if they did not create, the opportunity for effective and democratic action by means of soil-conservation districts. But every saver of souls knows the phenomenon of re-action and let-down that follows the high fervor of religious exaltation. That is when the devil returneth to find his former abode swept and garnished.

The Soil Conservation Service, though still young, has not been wholly able to escape the fate of older bureaus whose inertia made its establishment a necessity. There are simply not enough first-class conservation technicians to supply each present district with the quality of guidance it should have, any more than there are enough good teachers so that every child can be well taught during each of his several school years. The result is that some districts are badly run. Every third-rate district, every stupid error and failure, becomes a highly visible target. Some outside agency is needed, as Morris Cook has suggested, to rate each district and pronounce it A, B, C, or D, lest all fall into discredit.

Much more serious are certain elements in the larger picture of our national life. I have spoken of the protracted hardships of the farmer, beginning in 1920. True, there were farmers, prudent, thrifty, and industrious beyond the average, who did well enough in the worst of this period. For most others the distress was genuine and widespread, and so we came to the rescue with subsidies or benefit payments. After some juggling these were finally made legally palatable by hooking them up with the newly magic word "conservation." They had, however, precious little to do with the Soil Conservation Service until a recent decree, whose effect remains to be seen.

What concerns us here, however, is that subsidies have continued into an era of high prices for farm products. In the opinion of many, they have been a serious factor in the general increase of living costs. In any case, these subsidies have kept many inefficient, high-cost farmers in business. They have kept under the plow much land that ought to be in other uses, even though they have certainly stimulated pasture improvement. And they have done nothing to prevent, if indeed they have not encouraged, a renewal of the large-scale, mechanized, speculative growing of wheat in the old dust-storm area.

History has been repeating itself on the acres so painfully restored to grass after 1936. Wheat prices have been high, moisture relatively abundant. Driving through this area in 1948, I could not fail to recognize the familiar pattern of twenty years earlier. There was the same display of big shiny cars, the same offhand talk of one crop paying for the land, even the occasional:

"Don't give a damn what happens next year. We'll ride this one till she busts, and then take it easy."

Among those who do give a damn, there have been some anxious periods—threats of trouble, even sizable dust storms, relieved thus far by timely rain. Reports now are current that the past winter has been unusually dry and the harvests will be meager in much of the dry-farming area. Dust storms again? This year—ten or fifty years from now? Perhaps. Perhaps not. But one thing is clear. If private enterprise ever falls in this area or elsewhere it will be on its own dagger. No enemy can be so dangerous to it as its own folly.

I have given you my interpretation of the dust-storm crisis, its setting, and its consequences as they appear to me, with my training and experience as a naturalist. It is evident from the preceding paragraphs that many "practical" men do not see it as I do, or if they do, are willing to risk consequences.

But I would not be fair unless I pointed out that my viewpoint is not shared by a historian of the grasslands, Professor Malin of Kansas, for whom I entertain the greatest respect. In his view, dust storms are a normal phenomenon of the High Plains, to be taken as they come, and not especially the fault of man.

Be that as it may, and allowing for inevitable relapse, American attitudes toward the soil will never be what they were before the skies darkened at noon with dust from the dead wheatfields of seventy-two counties.

XIII. *Black Legions on the March*

The episode of the Black Legion has been very largely forgotten but, at the time, the story of the hooded men who operated in secrecy and who whipped and murdered their victims provided sensational material for the press. Democratic liberals saw the Legion as the incipient Fascist movement that it was. The Communist Party tried to link Legion activities with big business. That the contrary was true is made clear by Professor Morris Janowitz, but he demonstrates how the Black Legion and similar types of Fascist organizations can flourish in a sick society, and suggests the possibility of an even more dangerous repetition should similar conditions again obtain.

XIII

Black Legions on the March

Morris Janowitz
Department of Sociology, University of Michigan

I. *The Rise and Sudden Decline of the Black Legion*

When the final legal actions against the Black Legion were concluded in 1939, thirteen members had been given life sentences
for murder and thirty-seven more were serving prison terms up
to twenty years for terrorist activities. V. F. Effinger, the master
mind of the organization, remained free when charges of criminal
syndicalism were dropped, under circumstances in which the
law-enforcement agencies of the state of Michigan, where the
prosecutions took place, had become suspect because of their
connections with this nativist organization. Since the power of the
Black Legion had been broken, further legal action could serve
no purpose except to embarrass citizens caught up in its ramifica-
tions.

The origins of the Black Legion are difficult to reconstruct.
Clearly, however, a strong impetus for its growth came from
the social disorganization created by the Great Depression. The
most generally accepted account is that the Black Legion originated in Ohio in 1931 when several hundred men who had violated
the rules of the Ku Klux Klan dyed their robes black and formed
a separate organization. Between its inception and 1933 its activities attracted little attention except in the industrial suburbs of
Detroit, where the organization experienced its most extensive
growth. In 1935 the Black Legion began to receive newspaper
publicity when its members were involved in repeated floggings.

But it was in May of the following year, 1936, that the organization created a storm when seven of its members were involved in a murder the motive for which was indeed strange. The murder was termed a "ritual slaying," its purpose being to enforce organizational discipline.

In the police investigations that followed, a Fascist-type organization was uncovered that had grown to widespread proportions in the Detroit area and that had spread its tentacles throughout the industrial concentrations of lower Michigan, and into Ohio and Indiana. Small nuclei had sprung up in many other states. The exposure of its activities brought to light a weird record of intimidation, violence, racist agitation, and political intrigue. Before the organization collapsed in 1939, the list of its terroristic activities was extensive, for in its fight against the law-enforcement agencies it resorted to threat, murder, and violence to maintain discipline over its members.

In its formalities, rituals, and practices, it displayed many of the characteristics of European Fascist parties, with particular adaptations to American customs. The Black Legion was organized along military, authoritarian, and hierarchical lines from its constituent cells, each of which remained relatively isolated from the others. Officers held military titles equivalent to army ranks, and enforced Fascist discipline. Members were inducted only after being invited to join, and at the point of a gun as a symbol that treachery to the organization would mean death. When the police raided the Black Legion headquarters they found an arsenal of pistols, rifles, whips, and knives. Among the captured documents of General Effinger, commander-in-chief, was the declaration that the Black Legion was "a guerrilla army designed to fight the Republican and Democratic parties."

How many members joined is impossible to estimate, for various sources describe the Black Legion as having anywhere from three thousand to over one hundred thousand followers. It is probable that some forty thousand individuals were involved at one time or another. Southern workers from Tennessee, Kentucky, and Mississippi who migrated to the industrial centers of the Midwest were especially attracted to the organization. One journalistic report described the typical member as a man in his middle thirties, born in the South, of Anglo-Saxon descent. Most likely he would be a man with two children who, together with his wife, was living in some industrial suburb and had never quite got used to his unskilled job. Getting and maintaining a job was his main preoccupation, for these workers had a sense of self-respect that led them to look down and stereotype as lazy the men who were employed on W.P.A. Although a devout churchgoer, he was likely to feel that the Black Legion offered him the necessary protection against Jews, Communists, and Negroes. He was unaware of the extent of the Black Legion, yet to him it was an extensive, ritualized movement of which he was a part and which gave him a sense of solidarity and belongingness.

Police records show in addition that many respectable middle-class individuals joined or were intimidated into joining the organization. Politicians signed up in order to be on the right side, and because they were not sure of the actual extent of the organization's political influence. In fact, local police departments, particularly in the Detroit area, were not immune to Black Legion membership. All available data underline the middle-class origin of the top leaders; they included many men whom the depression had forced on the W.P.A. rolls or into factory work. Thus, in organizational character the Black Legion was a group that succeeded, if only temporarily, in recruiting and uniting a working-class and middle-class membership.

Despite quasi-military organization, the movement developed factionalism, which the leaders tried to control by the most authoritarian methods. Other organizations of similar character and aim sprang up (e.g., the Black Guards and the United Brotherhood of America), all of which added indirectly to the power of the Black Legion, since it was not clear whether these organizations were truly independent or were front organizations. In certain areas the Black Legion had premeditatedly organized under alternative names.

In ideology, the Black Legion was overtly anti-Negro and anti-Semitic, as well as anti-Catholic. But its appeal went beyond an appeal to racial intolerance. The Black Legion set up a front organization in the Michigan Relief Association, which extended welfare benefits to prospective members, established an informal employment agency by terrorizing minor executives in the automobile industry, and became an influence in allotting W.P.A. jobs. To achieve its political ends, which were hardly explicitly promulgated, the Black Legion at election time sought to infiltrate its members into the ranks of both parties. It followed the policy of circulating literature on the racial and ethnic background of the candidates involved, in order to prevent the election of Catholics and Jews. In true Fascist style, the Black Legionnaires were less interested in program and more interested in "men of action"—which for them implied the appropriate ethnic and racial background.

Religious symbolism pervaded the organization, as well as did a sense of mission to correct degenerate morals in the community. With gruesome paradoxy, they applied the most authoritarian methods in their efforts to create a moral regeneration. The Black Legion's totalitarian character extended to the point where supervision of the morals of its members entitled the leaders to enter freely into the homes and domestic lives of its members. In fact, they sought to supervise personal contacts not only in the name of morality but also as a means of enforcing discipline and secrecy.

Like other Fascist organizations the Black Legion became a source of revenue to its top leaders. For example, the commander-in-chief was entitled to ten cents each month from each member's dues. When the newspapers exposed the Black Legion, much was made of such petty rackets. But there is no evidence to indicate that the members resented these arrangements or that the arrangements in any way interfered with the growth of the organization.

The Legion collapsed suddenly after legal investigations and prosecution. No doubt the police intervention destroyed the records and removed most of the top leaders, while newspaper publicity frightened away many of the members. Nevertheless, the sudden demise of the Black Legion is reflective of an organization in which loyalty was exacted only partly by common consent and more by violence. Some of the members withdrew only temporarily and reappeared in other similar organizations, which were already active or which sprang up in the areas where the Black Legion had operated.

II. *The Dimensions of American Nativism*

The Black Legion was the prototype, in most respects, of the agitators and organized intolerance-groups that came into existence in the United States during the depression years. No doubt its emphasis on terror was greater and its formal organization rather unique. Yet its preoccupation with ethnic intolerance as a basis for social politics rendered it typical of the activities and agitation of those racist organizations which have been characterized as America's "native Fascist movement." Since American history has been marked by repeated outbursts against foreigners, immigrants, and Negroes, the question arises whether the newer forms of nativism which manifested themselves in the period from the onset of the Great Depression to the outbreak of World War II were essentially different and can justifiably be called Fascist in orientation.

Patterns of ethnic hostility in America have been so uniform as to make it almost possible to speak of a hostility cycle. For example, at one point in American history Irish Catholics—the most recent immigrants at that time—found themselves the object of native Protestant aggression; later they took an active role in hostility against lower-status and more recent minority groups. Native white Protestants have typically attacked the foreign born, Catholic, and Negroes. The North and West European stocks, who arrived in America earlier, attacked the South and Eastern Europeans, who in the main arrived later. More recently the Catholics, so long the objects of attack, themselves have attacked—either independently or in combination with Protestants—the Jews and the Negroes. They do this as Christians and as Whites. These nativist agitations have been continuously present on or near the surface, and periodically have burst out in waves of frantic intensity; e.g., the agitations of the 1830's, Know Nothingism, and the Ku Klux Klan movements after the Civil War and after World War I.

In each case particular religious and ethnic groups were attacked, but leaders of these movements did not pretend to criticize or attempt to modify the basis of the American economic or political system. Nor did they reject the social system as such, except with respect to the toleration of particular religious and ethnic groups. However, during the Great Depression, such organized intolerance movements as the Black Legion began to assume a new character. They began to agitate against the existing political and economic *system* as such, and sought an alternative system, albeit not a clearly defined one.

The successful Fascist revolutions in Europe gave nativists not only a model for directing their hostility against the existing order, but also in varying degrees some self-consciousness and confidence in their goals. These Fascist revolutions and the demagogical leaders they brought into being in Europe could be linked with the long-term development of industrial capitalism and the breakdown of mass democracy. Industrial capitalism brought a spread of literacy, the means for a higher standard of living, and working-class pressure for democratization of political power. Industrialism also brought economic instability and nationalistic wars of ever increasing intensity. Germany emerged as the foremost example of the breakdown of institutions and the clash of values, which paralyzed the social order and made possible the popular appeal of Fascism as a device by which to mobilize the nation to unified action.

Germany was a country of high literacy, extensive industrialization, and a well developed and powerful trade-union movement. Yet National Socialism, which blamed the ills of the nation on the Jews, the international bankers, and the international Communists, was able to seize power, institute an authoritarian form of government, and radically alter the entire complexion of German society. National Socialism, as a political movement of middle-class leadership, combined revolutionary and traditional appeals to achieve its political objects. To the working class it offered security, to the middle class it pledged self-respect and a nationalistic revival. To all it pledged racial purity. The result was a new type of revolution, which emphasized obedience and which by its very nature was dedicated to war. Thus in Europe the Fascist movements employed racial intolerance as a propaganda appeal, a political slogan, and a program for action in a conscious effort to modify democratic institutions, which could not cope with the internal problems of economic insecurity and social disorganization.

In the United States, such was precisely the character of wide segments of the groups and agitators organized consciously to promote intolerance after the outset of the Great Depression. It was precisely these political overtones that distinguished the newer forms of nativism from the widespread ethnic intolerance found throughout the population. In particular, for the nativists, the Jew became the central object of attack. Their hostility against the New Deal as the "Jew Deal" intermeshed with Nazi propaganda about the United States and helped them to feel a closer kinship with German National Socialism. (With Hitler's rise to power, which coincided with the recrudescence of nativism, the leaders of German-American Nazism paid very close personal attention to the leaders of certain native American groups.)

Nativists came to believe that the Axis powers constituted no real danger to the national security of the United States, and that indeed their success was to be desired. American foreign policy, in their view, was a deliberate attempt to force the Axis powers to wage war on us. For the first time in the history of American nativism, it was possible for "Americans" of the nativist variety to support foreign-born groups involved in foreign politics. More and more the nativist propaganda-themes converged with the central propaganda-themes of the German Nazis, to the effect that the Jews, Communists, and the International Banker were more of a threat to the United States than were the Axis powers.

Such a definition enables a distinction to be drawn between Fascist nationalism and the broad mass of the American people, together with many of their leaders, who were indifferent to the war in Europe or who merely hoped to be able to avoid involvement—those who could be called genuine isolationists.

Despite the similarity of the economic insecurity and social dislocation of the Great Depression in Europe and in the United States, the nativism movement at home—if we are justified in labeling it a movement—never developed the proportions required to assume power. Economic insecurities, it can be argued, were not deep enough, while the prospects of economic revival were never fundamentally shaken. The hold of the ideology of America as a land of personal mobility was too strong to permit the development of an authoritarian solution and a politics of intolerance.

Of great importance was the fact that American big-business leaders, partly for religious reasons, had a strongly developed social consciousness, at least as compared with many in Europe. Many stood ready for political compromise that might make it possible to alleviate the impact of the depression, as witnessed by the involvement of certain business-groups in the ranks of the New Deal. Likewise the big-business class, with only few exceptions, refused to place large amounts of funds at the disposal of Fascist agitators, in contrast to the frequent case in Europe. Most of the financing of Fascist organizations came from small contributors.

Moreover, the European historical context in which the Great Depression took place differed from that of the United States, where feudal traditions operated less effectively as barriers to the development of political democracy. The roots of equalitarianism and the distrust of authoritarian solution were indeed deep. Even more significant perhaps, was the great religious and ethnic heterogeneity of the United States. Religious and ethnic heterogeneity is the stuff out of which Fascism is constructed. But in a nation where religious and ethnic heterogeneity is so great that it is difficult to define the majority group, it is difficult in turn to develop a consensus as to which group is really the "dangerous" minority.

III. *The Scope and Structure of the Nativist Movement*

As crucial as these factors may be in accounting for American resistance to the political aspirations of native Fascism, the lack of an audience is not a complete explanation. Favorable as the economic conditions of American life were, there is sufficient evidence to conclude that latent and manifest attitudes were widespread enough to support a mass movement of some proportions.[1] The hypothesis emerges that the *native Fascist movement in this country during the 1930's failed to organize*

---

[1] Systematic research into native Fascism is almost nonexistent. The covert nature of many activities is a barrier to research. Nevertheless, possibilities for social scientific research have hardly been exploited, and even documentary materials have never been fully analyzed. The observations and hypotheses of this essay are based upon an examination of available published materials, the files of voluntary associations engaged in combating native Fascism, as well as upon personal observation and interviews, but they await further research. A critical bibliography of available research is presented on p. 360.

and exploit politically more than a small fraction of the sentiments that were in sympathy with its activities and goals. An analysis of the weak internal structure and lack of organizational unity, the instabilities and lack of administrative skill of its leaders, as well as a failure to develop a comprehensive and effective positive ideology, are elements in the defective character of the nativist movement which help to explain its failures. All of these elements indicate that the potential for native Fascism during the Great Depression was greater in scope than that which was effectively organized.

Public-opinion polls, although subject to scientific and technical limitations, supply crude indicators of the extent of the Fascist potential during the period. If extreme anti-Semitism with political restrictive implications can be taken as a measure of Fascism, polls since 1936 have shown that somewhat less than ten per cent of the nation's population fall into this category. That percentage gave anti-Semitic responses to certain types of political questions, which did not refer to Jews. Moreover, as late as 1939, fifteen per cent of national samples stated that they approved of Father Coughlin, with almost half of the respondents in the "don't know" or "no answer" categories.

More direct evidence on potential followers can be inferred from temporarily successful attempts at forming regional nativist organizations of rather extensive scope.

1. *Mississippi Valley: The Huey Long "Share Our Wealth Clubs."* In 1935, Huey Long's files showed a total of over twenty-seven thousand clubs, with seven million interested individuals scattered throughout the United States, although concentrated most heavily in the Mississippi Valley.[2] A full-time staff of thirty-five people were assigned to handling mail inquiries. *The American Progress*, Long's weekly publication, had a paid circulation of three hundred thousand while he, at that time, was beginning regular radio broadcasts. At the time of his assassination he firmly controlled his own state from Washington with outright dictatorial ruthlessness, and his ambition to dominate regional power-politics in the South was openly acknowledged.

2. *North Central: Coughlin's Radio Audience.* In 1938, the American Institute of Public Opinion reported that Coughlin had

[2] Jay Franklin: *The American Messiahs* (1935), pp. 22–7.

five and a half million listeners, with the heaviest concentration in the North Central states. In the landslide election of 1936, his Third Party, which supported William Lemke, managed to get nine hundred thousand votes despite Roosevelt's popularity and the even greater reluctance of Americans to vote for a candidate who offered little hope of victory. Coughlin's files contain the names of over five million people who have written to him and who have purchased his publications.

3. *New York City: The Christian Front.* The Christian Front, Father Coughlin's organizational arm, achieved its greatest success during the summer of 1939. During that period the Front held over sixty street-meetings per week. At the end of the year the New York City Police Department reported that a total of 238 persons had been arrested in New York City during the preceding six months for inflammatory Christian Front street-speeches, and of their number, 112 had been convicted and fined or sent to prison. The Police Department itself was not free of Christian Front penetration. Over four hundred of its members had at one time or another applied for membership to the Christian Front.[3] The following year the FBI seized seventeen Brooklyn Christian Fronters, with a formidable arsenal and the plans for a bizarre plot to organize an armed coup.

4. *The "Bible Belt": Gerald B. Winrod.* Religious fundamentalism has grown in intensity in certain groups in the American population during the last twenty-five years. On the extreme right wing of fundamentalist religious activities are a substantial number of preachers who express nativist political views. One of the most successful is Gerald B. Winrod of Kansas, whose influence outgrew the limits of his parish, through his publishing and radio-broadcasting ventures. In 1937, his monthly publication had a circulation of over one hundred thousand, and his annual budget was in the neighborhood of seventy thousand dollars.

Because of the covert nature of its activities, over-all estimates of the magnitude of the movement are difficult to make. Nevertheless, in addition to these regional activities, over 120 separate organizations disseminating anti-Semitic propaganda were identified during the latter half of the 1930's.[4] The number of individ-

[3] The American Jewish Yearbook (1940), p. 289.
[4] Donald Strong: *Organized Anti-Semitism in America* (Washington, D. C.: American Council on Public Affairs; 1941).

ual self-appointed agitators who were active for longer or shorter periods without benefit of any organizational connection, although difficult to estimate, would swell the ranks of the activists in the movement.

During this period the nativist movement was characterized by a peculiar organizational structure. The movement consisted of a series of independent groups and organizations, each representing local or regional conditions, and each dominated by a local or regional leadership. Formalized unity between the groups never emerged. Nevertheless, the nativist organizations during the 1930's—and even since that period—have been characterized by recurrent efforts to form a unified, consolidated organization. These attempts at unification have always been the work of the top leadership and have left their constituent organizations almost entirely unaffected.

In 1934, under the sponsorship of a German agent, Peter Gissibl, who worked through the German-American Bund, a group of anti-Semitic leaders met in Chicago to co-ordinate their activities. The same pattern was repeated in Asheville, North Carolina, in August, 1936, at a conference "for Americanism and against Communism," called by Reverend Ralph E. Nollner of the American Forward Movement. A split developed; forty-five of the delegates, led by Dr. Gerald B. Winrod, bolted and formed the National Conference of Christian Churchmen and Laymen, which was openly anti-Semitic and nativist. The list of "national" delegates was impressively headed by Congressman McFadden from Pennsylvania, and included most of the notorious nativist leaders.

A third effort was made the following year in Kansas City when a meeting was called by George Deatherage, who described the affair as a "coalition of Christian Anti-Communist Organizations." As a result of these "conventions" and many other strategy meetings, informal contacts were strengthened but concerted action was not promoted nor was a permanent organization created. After the Kansas City assemblage and until Pearl Harbor most of the "nationalist" leaders temporarily became less interested in the problem of unification and instead many devoted energy to infiltrating local chapters of the America First Committee as it became active on a nationwide scale.

Initially, the America First Committee constituted the main vehicle of genuine isolationist sentiment in the United States.

Particularly after January 1941, Christian Front members and other nativist groups began infiltrating the local chapters of the America First Committee, especially in New York, Boston, Chicago, and other metropolitan centers. Although some notable attempts were made to keep them out, the task was by the very nature of the circumstances impossible. Lindbergh's Des Moines speech in the fall of 1941, in which he claimed that the British, the Jews, and the Roosevelt administration were dragging the United States into war, increased the attractiveness of the America First Committee to the nativists. During this period the principal contribution to America First activities made by many of the local nativist leadership and their followers was their time and energy in distributing the official America First Committee isolationist literature, and in getting out audiences for mass meetings organized and financed by the America First Committee.

Pearl Harbor paralyzed nativist activities. Ideologically, their position was rendered unacceptable to the mass of the population, in whom a resurgent patriotism formed the basis for an increased amount of national consensus. The high level of employment and the improvement of standards of living reduced the potential audience for Fascist agitators, who were at the same time inhibited by fear of governmental repression in the name of internal security.

Although the conscious efforts at unity failed, the nativist movement had developed a complicated system of informal communication and co-ordination of effort, much of the complexity being due to the informality. Even a superficial examination of their publications revealed a pattern of group co-operation that consisted of a network of mutual endorsements, exchange and distribution of propaganda materials and speakers, and mutual assistance in fund raising.[5] Common use of German propaganda-

---

[5] It remained for the mass sedition-trial of thirty-one nativists (*U.S. v. McWilliams et al*) to bring into perspective the entire pattern of group organization. In this case, the federal government sought to convict the most outspoken and active American Fascists under the peacetime sedition statutes, by proving that these people were engaged in a conspiracy the intention of which was to undermine the will of the armed forces to resist. To prove this, the government had to establish: (1) that there was a Nazi conspiracy for world domination which included deliberate attempts to undermine the American morale through the use and support of native Fascist groups in the United States; (2) that the defendants knowingly entered into this conspiracy; and (3) that the defendants conspired and collaborated among themselves to this end. The federal prosecution sought

materials and themes contributed to this form of co-ordination. An examination of these interrelations revealed strikingly that, despite the frequency of contact, these interrelationships remained informal, fluid, and highly personalized. Groups never or seldom developed to the point of having fixed and formal liaison with other groups or individuals, with the result that singleness of purpose was drastically hindered.

IV. *Leadership and Symbolism:*
Factors Hindering Unification and Growth

The disorganized character of the nativist movement constitutes a sharp reflection of the type of leadership that it attracted and that attained power. Not only were the interconnections between individual groups extremely loose but internal group-organization was extremely haphazard. In the main, the leaders of intolerance were messianic personality types who were driven into their "vocation" by elements of paranoia and megalomania. The impulsiveness that drove these men into extremely aggressive behavior and speech likewise prevented them from developing the administrative skills required to build stable organizations. They were men driven by immediate pressures to take instantaneous action. They believed themselves to be constantly on the verge of success and therefore they de-emphasized those techniques necessary to consolidate their positions.

---

to establish point one by various forms of documentary evidence. Point two was a matter of legal interpretation, varying for each defendant involved. However, the data gathered under the third point by the government threw light on the full depth of the group organization of the American intolerance-agitators. Behind the obvious and manifest propaganda tie-ups were a mass of personalized contacts that disseminated ideas and gave direction to their efforts. Correspondence between the leading individuals was voluminous, and it revealed a pattern of routine informal meetings and sessions between small groups of leaders. To summarize and document the main contacts of the defendants (not of the movement's leaders as a whole, for only a number of the most active ones were tried) the government prepared an index volume of some 285 pages. The case, which rested in large part on these interconnections, became so complicated that, in order to guide the thinking of the legal experts, a group of social scientists prepared a series of sociometric-like charts, which summarized the various types of group relations that existed between the defendants, as well as their frequency and the degree to which they had become formalized. The death of the presiding judge, plus the unwieldy nature of such a large-scale legal proceeding, prevented the completion of the case.

As a result, almost without exception, they were marked by their inability to organize their administrative apparatus effectively, or to hire others to do so. An examination of the physical condition of their offices and their files, even those of the more successful leaders, reveals hopeless confusion, impatience, and fortunately, misuse of resources. Although some of them were quite facile verbally, they were, by and large, men for whom the normal modes of social mobility were closed. In the United States, the skillful organizer was likely to find more socially acceptable and more rewarding outlets for his talents.

Although adequate data are not available, some tentative generalizations about the psychological motivation of nativist agitators can be drawn from a reconstruction of the life histories of over sixty vigorous nativist leaders active during this period. The few successful top leaders, although they could be characterized as strongly motivated by internal pressures of paranoia, delusions of grandeur, and megalomania, seldom could be classified as grossly disturbed from a psychopathological point of view. In this regard, they seemed to differ little from other individuals seeking leadership. Among the less successful leaders, grosser psychopathology was much more frequent.

The social careers of nativist leaders present interesting uniformities, since many of the group were born on farms or in small towns and during late adolescence drifted into large urban centers. In Europe, the modern dictator and demagogue who claimed to be the self-expression and exclusive representation of his nation was frequently born either outside of his country or along its frontiers, and frequently spent his most receptive years outside of the fatherland. In America the agitator who seeks to address and unite the urban middle-class and working class seems to be either of small-town origin or an alien in the metropolitan center in which he chooses to propagandize. He comes to hate the city and to dedicate his life to preaching against what he believes to be its evils.

These leaders are mainly lower middle-class in social origin; their fathers small businessmen, preachers or, occasionally, professional men. Over half of the group were first reported to have undertaken active propaganda-work during the depths of the depression. Their lives were marked by constant occupational difficulties—they were always losing their jobs and never getting ahead—and by constant financial difficulties. Criminal records arising out of financial fraud appear among the group. Many of the nativist leaders active on the current scene display these same characteristics.

Such leaders developed their local followings almost exclusively on the basis of a direct personal relationship between themselves and their audiences. There was no hierarchical structure, which would be necessary if large numbers of people were to be organized. Public meetings were often conducted in the informal "you and me" fashion, without any of the awe-inspiring techniques employed so successfully by the Nazis in developing both respect and fear among their adherents. Nativist speakers were too informal to develop any discipline among their followers, and the movement gave the appearance of being limited by the number of people with whom the leaders could personally be acquainted.

Where organizational success had been achieved by the "Christian nationalists," it was due in part to the ready existence of some administrative machinery. Charismatic leaders cannot become politically effective without an integrated and effectively functioning party bureaucracy. New political movements in the United States, when deprived of political patronage, have faced notorious obstacles in their efforts to organize. Huey Long, the propagandist, seized control of the already existent Democratic machine of Louisiana, but he did not create it. In New York City and Boston, the Christian Front achieved success because in part it was able to learn from and to utilize the existing Catholic Church functionaries, institutions, and propaganda outlets. Father Coughlin's audience was built up largely by radio and by *Social Justice,* but it never was transformed into a continuously organized group, except in those areas of the Eastern seaboard where the Christian Front was active.

Moreover, when it came to unifying the various factions, the nationalist "cause," because it was built on informal relations, suffered disproportionately from the personal rivalries displayed by its leaders. Not only was there great personal antagonism in financial matters or in the struggle for loyal followers, but the suspiciousness of the leaders, who were projecting their personal inadequacies onto scapegoats, prevented them from co-operating freely with other leaders. In the nativist Fascist associations, aggressive, hypersensitive, and suspicious personalities were not held in check by organizational procedures and thus personal rivalries reigned unrestrained.

The diffuse leadership of American nativism determined the character of the followers who were actually activated into loyal and continuous participation. Of those who were in social protest against the economic system, and who because of inner psychological pressures would be prone to accept the racial and demagogical appeals of nativist leaders, the most alienated actually took the steps personally involving themselves in the agitation. These followers revealed a style of life characterized by personal and social disorganization; they were the victims of the various anomalies American civilization produced in the thirties.

An eyewitness account of a typical meeting of the period in the Midwest furnishes an interesting illustration of the character of the followers:

> The audience was predominantly middle-aged, although there were a goodly number of young people in attendance. They were a sad lot; the men were without any visible esprit de corps and the women, although talkative, had the most empty facial expressions. A few smartly dressed young girls sat in the balcony and seemed to enjoy themselves and their boy friends who were in attendance with the hope of finding some possibilities for expressing their political ambitions. These young men were of a different character than the young rowdies who sat downstairs and mingled with the crowd and who had all the earmarks of would-be storm troopers. When Y—— and his henchmen entered the hall the audience lit up; someone had come into their awful dull and impersonal lives. They shouted and clapped with a sense of conviction that was downright frightening.

Huey Long's initial support came from the marginal upstate Louisiana farmers whose eroded land was forcing them into social disgrace and bankruptcy. Among the leaders of the Christian Front were second-generation immigrant youths of New York and Boston, in whose disorganized family backgrounds old world and new world traits clashed. An analysis of the New York City police department records revealed that the overwhelming majority of juvenile offenders apprehended for violent anti-Semitic outbursts came from broken homes or homes where parental adjustment was low. Many of Gerald L. K. Smith's followers were men and women over fifty who found themselves psychologically displaced in a society that accents youth and youthfulness.

The defects and limitations in leadership were matched by the inadequacy of native Fascist symbolism. Native Fascist groups had the Jews, the Communists, and the International Bankers as the main targets of aggression, and it was natural that a protest movement should be characterized by hostilities flowing out against the imagined enemies. But hostilities have to be managed and co-ordinated to contribute to the development of unification and solidarity within the movement. Here symbols of identification and the symbols in the name of which the movement acts are crucial. The two main symbols of identification they employed were "national," or some equivalent, and "Christian." These symbols seem to have been hardly adequate to contain much of the internal factionalism. In addition to personal factionalism, there was the ethnic heterogeneity of the United States, which reflected itself in a sharp cleavage between Protestant nativism and Catholic nativism. "We don't want any damn Catholics telling us how to get rid of the lousy Jews." Such was the ideology of factions of urban nativists before the second World War. In particular, fundamentalist preachers who espoused the attack on modernism and on the Jewish-Communist conspiracy were also strongly anti-Catholic. This split, for example, prevented Coughlin and Long, among other reasons, from effecting any political compromise even though they flirted with one another.

Moreover, an overwhelming negativism and lack of clarity as to political method characterized their ideology. Examination of the nativist propaganda during the last decade reveals clearly that it is predominantly "anti-other," rather than "pro-self." It has been estimated that the "anti-other" propaganda outnumbers the "pro-self" symbols in a ratio of ten to one among the anti-Semitic organizations of America.[6] As for specific promises and platforms, a great deal of negativism was apparent.

The leading theoretical American Fascist, Lawrence Dennis, wrote two books that display some realistic insight into American

[6] Donald Strong: *Organized Anti-Semitism in America*, p. 163.

political and economic problems, and are guideposts to action.[7] Yet neither of these books became the *Mein Kampf* of the American scene. Partly this is due to the fact that Dennis personally has done little to disseminate his ideas actively among practicing agitators. More important, however, is the fact that positive goals do not clearly emerge from his analysis, although the "revolutionary" implications of his conclusions are obvious to experienced readers of political literature.

In general, American nativists have not been able to formulate clear conceptions as to the form that their political action should take. Like all revolutionary parties they have to decide whether they should participate in the legal political process, and if they do, whether they should build a third party or attempt to seize the existing parties. Some of the more intelligent native Fascists in private circles held to Huey Long's motto that Fascism, if it comes to the United States, will come in the name of Americanism. Therefore, the existing parties should be exploited, infiltrated, and democratic procedures employed until a strong nucleus has at least been developed. With the exception of Huey Long, the efforts of nativists of the more extreme variety to infiltrate the two major parties have resulted universally in failure.

However, the more messianic leadership of intolerance has often tended to avoid the politics of the two-party system or even to think in terms of a third party. Avoiding the conventional political process was also a function of the urge to take power directly. It was an expression of their violent rejection of existing institutions, although if they were to take power by such tactics they might suddenly become preoccupied with legalizing their status.

The relative infrequency of "pro-self" symbols as compared with "anti-other" symbols, and the low sense of common identification among the nativist Fascists, are all related to the inability to attract large and stable followings. Although there is a great short-term political advantage in limiting political propaganda to an attack on others, such a technique can hardly suffice for a revolutionary mass-movement in a society that is very predominantly individualistic and self-centered. It provides no answer to the great American question: "What's in it for me?"

[7] *The Coming American Fascism* (New York: 1935), and *The Dynamics of War and Revolution* (New York: 1940).

There have been variations in this pattern, which usually have centered about economic promises. Huey Long, in his "Share Our Wealth Plan" most skillfully gave positive appeals to his propaganda approach. Other native Fascists have at times stepped up their positive economic appeals—but too often such appeals are limited to some single subsidy for particular groups. The Townsendite movement is an example of such an outlook. In general they did not develop a full theory of economic and social totalitarianism, although the beginning of such an ideology could be clearly seen. They did not have at hand the formula of the Nazis, which appealed both to the working-class population and to the higher-income groups in the community. They seemed to be fearful of developing more explicitly the antiplutocratic overtones that were so effective in Germany. For them, in Fascism lies an outlook rather than the blueprint of a future state to which they look forward. Nativists could have used the Nazi critique of present society because it corresponded to their aggressiveness and anti-authoritarianism; but Nazi doctrine was too positive for their state of mind and too disciplined for their disordered individualism.

V. *Response to the Nativist Movement*

The enactment of New Deal legislation and programs represented the major response to the popular demand for alleviating the economic insecurities that underlay the recrudescense of the new forms of nativism. The conditions for economic security nevertheless had not yet been achieved by the New Deal when the Japanese attacked Pearl Harbor. While the issues of economic recovery received widespread and continuous public attention throughout the decade, with the exception of such spectacular episodes as that of the Black Legion, the public response to the threat of native Fascism displayed considerable avoidance and indifference. There was a tendency on the part of the press to label nativist efforts as the work of a "lunatic fringe." Although such a label was highly inaccurate in many respects, it did have the effect of creating resistance among certain individuals who might have otherwise become personally committed.

It would be naïve to think that economic measures alone could undo the social disorganization and psychological insecurity that the ten years of depression had created. Efforts to eliminate or reduce the race-prejudice aspects of nativism in terms of its social and psychological components had to wait until the end of World War II, when high levels of employment failed to reduce inter-group hostility and stimulated awareness in certain quarters that a broader program was required. The result has been the rise of the so-called "intercultural" education movement on a broad scale, and major efforts to enact civil-rights legislation involving especially the federal government in an effort to deal with the noneconomic sources of interethnic hostility.

But the task of attempting to engage and contain the day-to-day political manifestations of the nativist Fascist organizations during the Great Depression was taken up by the two major political parties, the radical movements, and certain middle-class minority-defense organizations. For the leftists, nativist agitation supplied an excellent foil for countervituperation and counterthreats. When the two extremist factions engaged each other with picket lines and public demonstrations, the result was to increase confusion and to permit the leftists to claim that they were militantly defending democracy. Such tactics only exacerbated the nativists, who now had "concrete proof" of the correctness of their propaganda claims that the "Communists were taking over."

However, in the major Northern urban centers it fell to the local organizations of the traditional major political parties—both Democratic and Republican—to oppose more realistically the Fascist groups and agitators because of the threat they posed to organized status quo politics. This was especially the case when Fascist agitators tried to run for election. Party machines responded effectively in crushing upstarts who threatened the political equilibrium. Extremist agitators frequently incurred the wrath of the political parties (especially the Democratic Party) since the political parties were committed to defending the minorities who were being attacked by these agitators. Constant and subtle pressure was the order of the day, although certain local political organizations displayed traces of nativist infiltration and in individual cases, such as the Black Legion, fell prey to its influence.

The role of civil-liberties and minority-defense groups was to supply documentation for the exposure of Fascist groups in the press and for educating the community to the inherent dangers of these groups. They organized strategy among the democrat-ically oriented voluntary associations, and, although their role is difficult to assess precisely, their contributions were significant. At times, in their ardor to defend democracy, they were subject to excesses of zeal, but generally they sought to operate within a philosophy that would guarantee freedom of speech, short of in-citement to riot, even to the Fascists.

An analysis of America's native Fascists during the Great De-pression supplies the basis for speculating about future potentials in the United States. The leaders who managed nativist agitation in the thirties appear somewhat limited and ineffective, although they made their contributions towards weakening democratic institutions. They seem never to have exploited or organized any considerable portion of their potential following, which under conditions of similar mass insecurities is likely to reach the same or higher levels. The history of native Fascism during the Great Depression, if it proves anything, indicates that a more prominent and effective leadership as well as a more positive ideology are required if the latent insecurities are to be mobilized on behalf of politics of irrationality. The history of native Fascism in the thirties indicates, moreover, that international relations play a decisive role in conditioning the domestic policies of Fascist groups. Thus, today economic insecurity is supplanted by the threat of the insecurities of intercontinental warfare, and greatly alters the possibilities.

It does not seem likely that Fascism could be the effort of a small handful of men seeking to cope with the economic and strategic insecurities of America in an authoritarian fashion. It requires a cadre of skillful organizers and propagandists to lead wide sections of the population to reject our democratic institu-tions. Probably no other group constitutes as large a potential source of such subleaders as the strongly motivated individuals who today are acquiring higher education or parts of a higher education, should they not find appropriate rewards and recogni-tion for their efforts and skills, or should they believe that there is a contraction in the expected possibilities of social ascent tradi-tional in the United States.

XIV. *The Nazi-Soviet Pact and the End of a Dream*

The non-aggression treaty between the U.S.S.R. and Nazi Germany did not come as a great surprise to those already accustomed to sudden shifts in Soviet foreign policy. For American writers and intellectuals, however, who had believed in the Communist experiment and who had managed to stomach disillusioning episodes like the Moscow trials, the Nazi-Soviet pact was the final disenchantment. In this essay, Professor Norman Pearson asks the question: why did intelligent and sensitive people during the thirties make a commitment that seems so inexcusable today? In order to answer it, he turns his attention to the spiritual as well as to the economic crisis of the depression decade and analyzes the impulse of an idealistic generation, alarmed by the unchecked expansion of Fascism, who made the mistake of ascribing their own humanitarian values to a repressive totalitarian state.

XIV

The Nazi-Soviet Pact and the End of a Dream

Norman Holmes Pearson

Associate Professor, Department of English
Yale University

To look back upon history is inevitably to distort it. As Ambrose Bierce morosely snarled: "God alone knows the future, but only an historian can alter the past." Bierce may have regarded historians as bumblers of facts. We may view them simply as contrivers of necessary fictions that are the only approximate means we have for understanding yesterdays. The data historians choose from the web of events are usually those which lead directly to outcomes they already know. The tone they give is the tone they wish. The nearer we are to the present, the more difficult is the choice of material, since the less we can be sure that there are any true or discernible conclusions to form structures against. There are only steps (and many false ones) along the way to the uncertainties of an indeterminate future. The present is at least as difficult to assess as either the past or the future. It is as difficult to understand and to plan. That is why there are crises in the present, have been crises in the past, and unquestionably will continue to be crises in the future. They are the results of general failures of assessment. Yet in the necessity for making assessments, each of us is always a practicing fictionalist, whether or not we indite. We share in the process, and if we learn nothing else from the history of crises we may perhaps learn a decent humility in regarding them.

Such a crisis was the Nazi-Soviet Non-Aggression Pact of August 1939, which brought an end to the decade that had begun with the depression, and joined enemy to apparent friend in a confusion of loyalties that shattered the confidence of many writers. Today, the strong friendship with Russia in the 1930's seems somehow inexplicable to a generation whose mature life is a matter of the years since World War II. Other factors have intervened to create a new situation, altered allegiances, and even new crises. What occurred then took place in a different scene. Regarded solely from the present, the affinities of the thirties appear in a sometimes dismal light; when they are looked at in terms of what had preceded them, a different tone prevails. For the writers of the thirties had a special conditioning and worked by values that first led them into such sympathies and then away. The values remained. What is now needed is an understanding of the impulsions.

Behind most writers lies their tradition, and there is much about the American tradition which is ambiguous, even paradoxical. It is a remarkable characteristic of the American psyche that, no matter how externally confident we may appear, we are always examining ourselves before mirrors, and our self-chosen classics of American writing are chiefly self-critical. Just as we are constantly discontented with our mechanical technologies and seek to improve upon them even at the cost of retooling, so we seek the same opportunity and find the same necessity with our nation and with our egos. Just as we seek for the truth of process so we seek for the truth of self.

Something of this self-consciousness may be charged to a persistent psychology of national and personal adolescence. We are told, and tell ourselves, that we are a young nation. We live in a constant puberty, with our voices changing. We grope our way, like adolescents, without any easy confidence of acceptance as equals in a mature world. Such behavior may appear gauche, but it is also a source of strength, since our awareness of our youth encourages change and the possibility of change, and keeps us from an easy acceptance of things as they are simply because they are as they are. Progress for us is a continued disruption of the status quo, and our sense of innate youth gives us the energy, the daring, and the freedom for progress.

Yet the malaise goes deeper than mere awkwardness, and does not altogether find its compensation in the fact of achievement. The achievement always seems partial. There is an exhilaration in the process of "becoming," but there is a definable tension that comes from never arriving at the ideal stage that we envision. Americans are a race of sad young men because they dream of ideals without being able to achieve them in any absolute sense. Any momentary achievement is always overclouded by the further possibilities. Satisfaction is blended with unrest. The history of the American race shows how much has been altered for good; but when so much remains still to be done, the failure to accomplish it nourishes' anguish. Such frustration accompanying such hope is a paradox of youth and Americans.

We have only to look briefly at American literary classics to see how dominant self-criticism has been. A substantial shelf of Cooper's books exist that scold Americans and American ways as severely as Sinclair Lewis was ever to do. Even Cooper's Natty Bumppo turned his primitive back on the increasingly dominant culture-patterns. Cooper felt such criticism to be his responsibility and a proper function of fiction. He was, as his literary ancestor Cotton Mather had put it, his brother's keeper as well as his own; and Cooper's books like Mather's were meant to do good. A cliché of consolation for us in many circumstances comes from a conviction that bitter medicine is administered for our own good. The criticisms of our materialistic way of life which Thoreau made in *Walden* are obvious, and still, we feel, pertinent. Mark Twain's Huckleberry Finn took to the river rather than the shores of the Mississippi, as Thoreau had taken to the pond. Huck hit out even farther at the end. "I reckon I got to light out for the Territory ahead of the rest, because Aunt Sally she's going to adopt me and civilize me, and I can't stand it. I been there before." The conclusion was more than comic; the book involved more than the ways of juveniles. Hawthorne's novel, *The House of the Seven Gables*, was an attack on the greed for property; and *The Marble Faun* a discussion of aspects of American immaturity. One does not have to read far in Melville to find characterizations of distrust. The preoccupation of Henry James with American cultural deficiencies was constant. Even Whitman pleaded for what was still latent rather than altogether realized. Yet none of these writers could be said not to have loved America; they were goading her toward the achievement of an ideal.

The writers of the 1930's were essentially the group who had been writing in the decade after World War I. One understands them as well by what they read as by what they wrote. An aspect of the 1920's was its awareness of such a literary tradition of self-criticism, and a certain dignity accompanied the writer who was willing to stand up against public criticism and complacency in order to point out the truths. Into the family of American classics, the intellectuals of the twenties adopted two books; and the adoption showed characteristics of the decade. One was *The Education of Henry Adams;* the other was Melville's *Moby Dick.*

The *Education of Henry Adams* was a depiction of shared plight, of isolation, of man's uneasiness and uncertainty, and of his agonized effort to understand himself, his heritage, and his age. The figure of Adams himself emerged as a Hamlet *de nos jours:* the prince who had been deprived of succession to kingship, who is in danger of being overcome by too much intellectualization and unable to adjust himself to a decayed court, yet persists in his education as though, even were the conclusions intolerable, the very achievement of them were an act of moral rectitude. One can hardly understand the tone of Adams's autobiography unless one reads it in the light of the implicit belief of Americans in the value of education. From the beginnings of the country there has been this reliance. From education comes the possibility of an enlightened electorate, the enlightened technologist, and the enlightened son of God. Henry Adams equates education with its goal, which is understanding. If there is no final understanding there has been, on these terms, no education. But this is really little more than to say that one has not been graduated; and for Americans the final examinations come only, if ever, at death. Yet Adams, in actual fact, was like most Americans and did believe in education as a process as well as an end. He uses the word in the sense both of attaining and of attainment. He relinquished neither meaning. He was always educating himself, and the goal was knowledge, not simply as a trophy but as an applicable science of history, which would serve as a technology of truth. "Any science of history must be absolute," he said, "and must fix with mathematical certainty the path which human society has got to follow." When Adams says "the path which human society has got to follow," he means it as an imperative only because it is the path of truth, which to the educated will be irresistible because it can be recognized through reasonable demonstration. Truth as a goal, and reason as a method, have been American tenets. If for Adams truth was in the world's decline, he was dignifying his countrymen by deeming them capable of being trained to a maturity that could bear the burden of pessimism.

In the literary myth, the figure of Adams was blended by T. S. Eliot into the Gerontion of "a dry month, being read to by a boy, waiting for rain." "After such knowledge, what forgiveness?" Eliot said of the situation. A Gerontion was incapable of action. "What will the spider do, suspend its operations, will the weevil delay?"

If [Adams had said in 1894 in speaking of his construction of history] an hypothesis is advanced

> that obviously brings into a direct sequence of cause and effect all the phenomena of human history, we must accept it, and if we accept it we must teach it. The mere fact that it overthrows social organization cannot affect our attitude. The rest of society can reject or ignore, but we must follow the new light no matter where it leads.

Such a light might seem to lead underground.

But Gerontion was only a facet of the psyche rather than the whole of it. Too much has been made of the "lostness" of the twenties, and too little of the spiritual daring, which was equally characteristic. The decade supplied a complementary answer to despondency by its admiration of Melville's Captain Ahab, whom it saw as a man of indomitable will, going gallantly even to death in his attempt to harpoon evil in the destructive body of the whale itself.

One way of expressing the indomitable will was through a reliance on youth, and the romantic powers of natural man. There was a freshening of the value of the romantic ego. The "mimic hootings" of Wordsworth's nature boy of Winander were being given new and blatant tones in the blare of the saxophone. The more "natural" one could become by casting aside encrusted hides of convention (tonal or otherwise) the closer one came to a modern adaptation of the state of Rousseau's primitive hero. Harlem became a convenient jungle in which inhibitions could be cast aside. To violate Prohibition was to assert one's natural freedom from legislation, and the recovered cocktail took on a sacramental glow. Sexual liberty became an asset, if for no other reason than that whatever was instinctive was right. Conventions were clichés of behavior, whose truth investigation denied. One of the characters in Dos Passos's *Manhattan Transfer* put the social case for the truth of reality:

> Everything would be so much better if suddenly a bell rang and everybody told everybody else honestly what they did about it, how they lived, how they loved. It's hiding things makes them putrefy.

Suddenly the bell had rung, and writers became bell-ringers. But it was not simply for the hullabaloo of clanging, though different ears heard it differently. It was a moral summons for the individuals to take out papers of naturalization.

Such a spiritual daring might lead to initial martyrdom at the hands of Philistines, who like whales took vengeance; but in the attempt lay the only hope for the destruction of sham, which by its deceitful nature was an evil. All this was in the sense of a dedication to the discovery of truth, based on the knowledge that even "whiteness" could not be accepted at surface appearance. Surface appearances had been profoundly altered since the previous century, though the public was not always quick to see what had happened. The scientific method, applied in various fields of knowledge, had toppled hitherto accepted definitions in physics, economics, politics, law, society, and religion. Secrets of the consciousness and subconsciousness of man had been laid bare. Writers, following this impulse and sharing in the dignity of scientists, were equally concerned with redefinitions in their attempts to deal with the description and analysis of life. Craftsmanship as a goal in writing was another aspect of the necessity for scientists to describe accurately the material they were dealing with. Truly accurate description in writing might, as Gertrude Stein had discovered in her portrayals of consciousness, lead to a rejection of established syntax. As science brought all data into the open as worthy of analysis, so writers broke down the barriers of censorship that inhibited subject-matter. The public's objections had nothing to do with the writer's necessity for presenting truth. Eventually, as writers knew, the public would come to accept it; because the public too, though more slowly than scientists or writers, believed as essentially in truth. Like Mather and

Cooper, these moderns also were writing essays to do good. When a Hemingway character "was embarrassed by the words sacred, glorious, and sacrifice and the expression in vain," as he famously put it, and was out after the "concrete names of villages, the numbers of roads, the names of rivers, the numbers of regiments and the dates," he was acting in the scientific spirit that pursued truth. What Hemingway was not doing—though many asserted that he was—was carelessly tossing aside the concept of values. He was simply examining, as though the world were his laboratory, the silken or iron curtains of slick words that halted the vision of reality. He was also following a principle of free inquiry that gave him a right to express his conclusions. By his actions he was himself exemplifying a value.

On every side the privilege of free inquiry was maintained, with those unabashed questionings after what is really true which are characteristic of more than Congressional committees. Congressmen, after all, act for their constituents. An at least quasi-scientific method had gone into a general examination of such an overwhelming phenomenon as World War I. By one investigator after another, unrecognized economic factors were shown to exist alongside the urgencies of such idealistic slogans as H. G. Wells's phrase "the war to end war." Events during and after the war made such slogans seem little more than sham. But behind the irony that in histories, novels, and poems attacked the factual validity of the slogans lay a yearning belief in their ambitions. Irony, as Ezra Pound remarked, is never negative, because it always posits an ideal which has been corrupted. Pragmatic concepts notwithstanding, idealism has played a dramatic role, either as protagonist or antagonist, in the American drama of contradictions. Relief could have been found for the tensions. All that was required of American writers was that they relinquish their values. This would have brought a lethargic and blinded contentment. But the values were too deeply ingrained, and the greatest enemy was inertia.

Something of the temper of the postwar years is to be found in an excerpt from an unpublished letter from William Rose Benét to his younger brother, written in November of 1919. Benét was working for a Washington journal known as *The Nation's Business*. "Dear Steve," he wrote:

This industrial situation makes me alternately feel Bolshevik and then just oh-what-the-hell's-the-use. This job is a good money-making job, but every once in so often I want to take the boat to Russia. I hate the way most things are going in this country and I am so damned tired of all this Americanization stuff I can hardly see straight. I have no illusions about the white purity of the working man, but the way these conferences have gone, and the attitude of the coal barons, and the [Versailles] Treaty all bitched to hell, and the League [of Nations] not even a ghost of itself—well, it seems to me as if all the world were ruled by mere stupid standpatness that just sits and sits and merely grunts when an idea comes along.[1]

Here were the uneasinesses that the 1930's were to heighten for so many writers.

The bell that *Manhattan Transfer* had called for as a summons to truth began to toll like a tocsin in late October of 1929, when the stock market crashed. Before the month was over fifteen billion dollars in market value had been lost. By the end of the year, the total was "an estimated forty billion." It was not too long afterwards, as history goes in time, when on the 6th of March, 1933, the "bank holiday" was declared, and with it the inviolability of economic clichés was shattered. Whatever else happened, it was now obvious that the old reliances no longer obtained, and that more and more people were beginning to realize this. What had seemed chiefly an ideological dilemma now became a dilemma in fact.

The succession of shocks was overwhelming. It was not simply an American situation that was witnessed. In England had come the "dole"; in Germany, such a dislocation of economy that youth having finished college had chiefly the choice between learning to play in the band of a cheap café or drinking vermouth and plotting to migrate. In Germany there was at least action. The Nazi Party began to emerge, following the Italian precedent; and the same emotionally and physically hungry ones went to its rallies as attended the meetings of the Communists. Over the speakers' stands at both, the same appealing banner hung: *Arbeit und Brot* (Work and Bread). But Hitler's stentorian nationalism was louder, and the roll of kettledrums boomed a more intoxicat-

[1] This passage, and the quotation on p. 347, are used with the kind permission of Mrs. William Rose Benét.

ing rhythm when the Führer strode, arms folded across his brown-shirted breast, through public halls filled with men whose palms were outstretched to touch a swastika'd savior.

Something was needed. As the troubled memory of writers played back over the episodes from the first World War to the Great Depression and afterwards, they could not help but be impressed by the ·absence of order and the lack of any binding ethics. There was only confusion. By 1932 at the Conference of Lausanne a despairing end was made to the frenzied financing by which American capital, depending upon a complacent view of its own powers, had lent money to Germany. By means of it, and while American capital winked, Germany had partly built up a new war potential and partly repaid reparations to countries that continued, by its means, to float their own American loans. By the summer of 1933 the flags flew at half-mast over the University of Berlin in mourning for the Versailles Treaty. Circles of young Nazis replaced the clustered *Studentenkorps* before the doors of learning. By now Germany was receiving apologies, and reviving young Germans were saying sometimes that the war had been lost by bad generalship, and anyhow that it was nothing for which their generation was responsible. Yet there was still little but sitting and grunting on the part of those others to whom the dangers of such a situation should have been obvious. No one seemed to listen to warnings. Japan, taking advantage of European confusion, had already in 1931 commenced her series of aggressions in Manchuria, but economic sanctions under the League Covenant were withheld because of the danger to British investments in Shanghai. No lessons had been learned from the first war. When it came time in 1935–6 for Mussolini to strike his fasces into Ethiopia, the same lack of principles prevented opposition. By the time of the Spanish War in 1936–9, the League of Nations was dead, not only because America had never joined in its initial idealism but also because Europe and Great Britain apparently did not want it either. From the moment in 1934 when Mussolini had marched his troops to the Brenner Pass to prevent Hitler from annexing Austria, and thousands waited at European radios for the news that war had been declared, it was only a question of time before, somewhere in the confusion, absolute calamity would break out. It did break out in Spain, when Germany and Italy ostentatiously used the peninsula as a practice ground. But even their bombings of civilians at Guernica and Barcelona could not overcome economic timidity. The word "time" had never seemed so important to those who desired to take measures against disorder.

Had there been anything like mutual good-will among nations in trying to work out on a truly rational basis any technologies for remedying situations, some progress towards order might have been made. A new force, however, had emerged, for which most American writers were ill prepared, but which they recognized for what it truly was long before its full significance was generally felt. This was Hitlerism as a positive force of deceit and evil. It had its testament in *Mein Kampf* and its affidavits in the slaughter of the Jews. To writers who believed not in the essential depravity of man but in his innate goodness, Nazi brutalities on street corners and in concentration camps acted not so much to change their belief as to rally them together against what was for the first time a common antagonist. Alongside such a foe, the earlier skirmishes of American writers in the twenties against Philistinism became trivial. But unless the values that had prompted them before were to be now relinquished, then they served as a basis for resistance against this more formidable opponent. The importance of demonstrating truths about a narrow range of local society became even greater in terms of the ubiquitous nature of Fascism. Echoes of Fascist-mindedness in America itself made Europe's problem one to be shared by us if we were not to be touched by the same cancer. That there was an indifference to the reception of truth was only an aspect of history repeating itself. Writers followed a moral imperative.

More and more the temper of writers had been altered. A dominantly personal ethic, as James Farrell was to point out, had shifted to a dominantly social ethic. Today when we wish to praise a book or insinuate unsuspected virtues in it, we say that it is basically religious. In the 1920's critical praise was reserved chiefly for originality and vitality and craftsmanship, with a premium for telling the truth. This was an expression of the morality of individualism. It was the individual who must be saved, and through his regeneration might come the regeneration of society. But in the 1930's the praise increasingly came for a book's social awareness or relevance, as though society could be directly manipulated and controlled. This was an expression of a developing sense of group involvement, and of the state as something separate from man. Under these circumstances the state was still man's servant. It was only later in America that the state began to be thought of as man's master or at least superior, and one could refer to such concept as that of the state's duty to man. More and more as the 1930's developed, the role that a book can play in terms of social influence was recognized. Through his books, the writer could become a kind of social engineer, molding and reforming. This possibility of playing an active part in society gave writers and their books a new dignity, for they were now more than critical observers.

Against such forces of evil as the Spanish War, presented both actually and representationally, there was a sense of a literary crusade with a tangible objective. The Spanish War seemed to represent a moment in history which drew together the disturbing strands of tendencies that writers opposed. To join forces, whether by actual enlistment in such a group as the Abraham Lincoln Brigade, or by writing as social engineers, was to oppose moral inertia. Expressed in Hemingway's highest rhetoric in *For Whom the Bell Tolls*, the Spanish War offered

> a part in something which you could believe in wholly and completely and in which you felt an absolute brotherhood with the others who were engaged in it. . . . Your own death seemed of complete unimportance; only a thing to be avoided because it would interfere with the performance of your duty. But the best thing was that here was something you could do about this feeling and this necessity too. You could fight.

There were various ways of fighting and feeling, and most writers used words, which were their special weapons. They were working for peace, or at least for the achievement of an equilibrium on which organized peace could be maintained not by any balance of power but by the eventual coming together of rational minds, working in terms of common values and dedicated to truth and freedom. What they had learned was that nothing could be accomplished by doing nothing. They had come to know that active forces of evil must be actively opposed. "The point is clear enough," Archibald MacLeish said in an address:

Those who fight against fascism are not fomenting war for the simple reason that the war is already fomented. The war is already made. Not a preliminary war. Not a local conflict. *The* war: the actual war: the war between the fascist powers and the things they could not destroy. Spain is no political allegory. Spain is not, as some would have us think, a dramatic spectacle in which the conflict of our time is acted out. These actors are not actors. They truly die. These cities are not stage sets. They burn with fire. These battles are not symbols of other battles to be fought elsewhere at some other time. They are the actual war itself. And in that war, that Spanish war on Spanish earth, we, writers who contend for freedom, are ourselves, and whether we so wish or not, engaged.

What was important was the objective, which was the crushing of the evil of Fascism. Mr. MacLeish's speech was made at the second Congress of American Writers in the summer of 1937. The first Congress had been held in 1935. As a chapter in American literary history, such gatherings, sponsored by names like those of Hemingway, Erskine Caldwell, Kenneth Burke, Malcolm Cowley, Theodore Dreiser, James T. Farrell, Horace Gregory, Lewis Mumford, and John Dos Passos, to name only an important few, were the first times when a substantial body of serious, though diversified, writers had come together with a sense of unity. Such gatherings were startling substitutions for those of the 1920's at the tables of the Dôme Café in Paris, but the functions of the two locales were not entirely unlike in serving the satisfaction for writers of being together with something in common. An un-Philistine idealism played a part at both meeting-houses. The sense of the importance of freedom of inquiry and a desire to reach toward truth were part of both. Only now the enemy was not intangible bigotry but tangible evil.

The political collapse of Europe, as Professor Hajo Holborn has called his newly published history of events, continued with increasing momentum. No matter what ennobling idealism the League of Nations may originally have represented, the League itself came tumbling down. The Spanish Civil War kept Europe busy from 1936 to 1939, while Hitler grew strong. In 1936 the Rhineland was remilitarized. In the same year the Rome-Berlin

Axis was established. By 1938 the annexation of Austria was achieved. Mussolini hurried this time only to be photographed at Hitler's side. In September of the same year came the pivotal Treaty of Munich, which, through Chamberlain's efforts at appeasement, gave Hitler the Sudetenland of Czechoslovakia, and eventually Czechoslovakia itself. Not even the United States, which through Wilson had helped to establish Czechoslovakia, made any tangible protest, though there were shudderings of nausea. Poland, which had once been freed like Czechoslovakia, put in a stained thumb for plums of territory, as though unaware of what greed would do against herself as the power of evil grew. The Spanish War ended as a failure for democratic values; the evils of Hitlerism had continued to flourish. The fiber of Europe was disintegrating.

But if during these years of the 1930's there was to be no effective formal association of nations to oppose what was increasingly evil, then at least there could be an informal association of right-minded peoples within nations, who could act together as a coercive force. They could form a protesting, if unauthorized, united front against a common enemy. As writers, when such was their skill, the people could continue to push aside the shams and false words and expose truth for truth. This was a goal; for American writers, joining such a movement, still retained their belief that truth, once revealed, would eventually triumph. That was perhaps their chief morality. So great was the force of the enemy that to join in opposition seemed in itself to be an affidavit of integrity.

The United Front as a name as well as an idea had been established in the summer of 1935, when the Third International decided that the U.S.S.R. would support democracies against the common Nazi enemy, and that Communists in countries other than Russia should support even bourgeois local governments. The role of the Communist Party in the United States, which had been established in 1919, took on aspects of third-party protests that had long been a part of American politics, and whose strength came not so much through their own electoral victories as through their pressure on more established parties.

It was in the name of a united effort that the first American Writers' Congress was called together in 1935. Few who attended had any illusions about whether or not the American Communist

Party, acting in the spirit of the Third International, was sponsoring the Congress. Many realized that the Congress had been developed at least partly to replace the John Reed clubs, which had been taken over by the Trotskyites. But the prevalent attitude of writers, not actually themselves involved in frictions within the Party, was that which MacLeish was to express for the laymen at the second Congress in 1937 in relation to the Spanish War. He was talking about those who felt "that the fascist issue is in actual fact nothing but a private squabble between fascism and communism, of no concern to anyone but the partisans, and of ulterior and purely factional concern to them." "The answer is, of course," Mr. MacLeish went on:

> that the man who refuses to defend his convictions for fear he may defend them in the wrong company, has no convictions. The further answer is that this fear of being used, this phobia of being maneuvered is itself a very curious thing. There is, to my mind, something about it unpleasantly squeamish and virginal—something indecently coy. Even if the danger of rape exists the tender spirit need not necessarily submit. Why *should* a man be "used" unless he pleases? Why should he not himself become the "user"? If a liberal really believes in the freedom of the mind and person which he protests, he will defend them against all comers and in any company and he will himself make the greatest possible *use* of those whom he finds at his side. All the great forays of the human spirit, whether by Marx or Rousseau, were originally one-man expeditions which gathered company from the bystanders as they moved. No writer worthy the name ever refused to make his position clear for fear that position might advantage others than himself—even others whom he had no wish to help.

Earl Browder, the head of the American Communist Party, welcomed the nondenominational writers to the first Congress of 1935, speaking of the struggle which writers had been engaged in from the beginning of the century, long before the name of Russia entered as a symbol either of admiration or suspicion. This, as Browder put it, was

> the struggle for a literature capable of satisfying the cultural needs of humanity in the period of break-up of the old social

economic system, the period of chaos and readjustment, the period of searching for the values of the new society. This new society is not yet in existence in America, although we are powerfully affected by its glorious rise in the Soviet Union. The new literature must help to create a new society in America—that is its main function—giving it firm roots in our own traditional cultural life, holding fast to all that is of value in the old, saving it from the destruction threatened by the modern vandals brought forth by a rotting capitalism, the fascists, combining the new with the best of the old world heritage.

To such words of idealism few writers could be cold. A traditional role of American writers, when they wished to be more than entertainers, stood behind them as precept. Their own earlier efforts in the 1920's gave the validity of personal experience. It would be impossible to say precisely how many writers were actually to take out membership cards in the Party, but of those who lent their support to the United Front there were few who felt that they should turn their backs on a country like the Union of Soviet Socialist Republics, which the United States of America had officially recognized in 1933, and which more than any other nation seemed to be taking action in a time that needed it, an action apparently firm in its opposition to that form of action which Fascism had developed.

From the time when the Russian Czars had been overthrown, the revolutionary movement in that country seemed, in its youthful disdain of an intolerable status quo, congenial to the American youthful impatience with situations that could be bettered. Such a quality gave the appeal that men like Benét felt. The political opposition to the Russian revolutionists, on the part of other countries, appeared to be little more than a customary reluctance against progress, which in time would be overcome. Recognition of Russia did, to an extent, overcome the reluctance. What came to be said in opposition to Soviet idealism was often simply technological in tone: that the experiment would not work out. But whereas other nations seemed to be more or less content with themselves in the postwar period, Russia had already in 1928 made the beginnings of its much publicized first Five-Year Plan. This was societal and industrial planning in which technologically minded Americans could not help but be interested. America's own course in the crisis of economic depression or in catastrophes was not completely dissimilar. Whereas the Soviet Union had been held up before the general public as a bogy, increasingly in the 1930's her international actions seemed to be toward peace and working agreements between nations. In July of 1932 the U.S.S.R. signed non-aggression pacts with Poland, Estonia, Latvia, and Finland; and in November of the same year a similar pact was made with France. In 1934, as though bowing to the justice of international reason, she recognized the loss of Bessarabia and joined the League of Nations. In 1935 a Franco-Russian agreement of defensive alliance was concluded. Both internally and externally the pattern of Soviet movements was towards order. Western-Christian-Democratic values were ostensibly dominant, and the policy of the Third International for a United Front appeared to signify an ideological readiness for democratic action in a world that seemed otherwise morally inert.

The Soviet Union was excluded by the other powers from the negotiations at Munich, and so did not share in that symbol of culpability; she even seemed to gain in moral prestige by the fact of her absence. As "the war of nerves" between Germany and western Europe drew inevitably nearer to a war of weapons, Soviet spokesmen began to urge a hands-off. "Do you really believe that this is an ideological war?" a poet like Kenneth Rexroth, following the line, was to protest even after later events. "The only way this war can be stopped is by starving it to death." There had been many who, during these moments, were ready to follow such a path of rigid non-intervention, despite their criticism of similar policies at the time of the Spanish War. Too many broken treaties, too much appeasement now stood in the way. "A plague o' both your houses!" was reborn from the grave of Shakespeare to the stage of the modern world.

Then suddenly, for many, the top blew off! On August 23, 1939, non-aggression and trade pacts were concluded between Germany and the Soviet Union. Variously the former was to be known as the Nazi-Soviet Pact, the Russo-German Pact, or the Molotov-Ribbentrop Pact. The last two titles only added diplomatic dignity to the description of a startling alliance for which there was no preparation in the minds or sensibilities of American writers. By it, Russia, although not actively entering the war on the side of the Nazis, gave them the green light for their entry into Poland. The food to be shipped proffered sustenance, not starvation. German Fascism, which had been painted as Hell, with Hitler as Satan, now was said by the facts of the Pact to be less culpable than the stand of those who were to be known as the Allies. For American writers remembered what had been said ideologically at the time of the Spanish War, when only active participation against evil counted, and when non-intervention of this kind was said to be in reality sponsorship of Germany and Italy. Whatever weaknesses of policy or even of motives could be laid at the door of the Allies, the truth about Fascism far more than counterbalanced them. Without actively opposing Hitlerism it was obvious that there would be no opportunity to accomplish good. Russia was no longer in active opposition.

What the Nazi-Soviet Pact represented, diplomatically speaking, was *Realpolitik;* but what it represented ideologically was the denial of the primacy of morality in politics, which as a goal represented a significant aspect of American aspiration. To the sophisticated historian educated in the diplomatic history of Russia and western Europe, such an agreement as had now been completed was simply a continuation of the traditional manipulation of balance of power. The Czars had negotiated variously on such a basis; the French and Germans and British had all done it. Most recently in 1926, Germany and the U.S.S.R. had concluded a Treaty of Berlin, which had established neutrality in the event of an unprovoked attack on either. The Franco-Russian defensive agreement of 1935 had not been dissimilar. The exclusion of Russia from the conversations at Munich had left her outside the group of western European powers, and, from the standpoint of traditional European diplomacy, pushed her toward the alternatives of either the throat or the arms of Germany. But such *Realpolitik,* though explainable on practical grounds of national expediency, has nothing to do with the defense of idealism or the supremacy of ethics. It had been on precisely these issues that American writers had listened to Russia. The absence of morality in politics was what they had tried to oppose. The value they placed on morality was a value they still clung to.

There were other values whose violation on the part of the Soviet Union they now saw more clearly. Past policies by Russia seemed more than possibly to have been framed in terms of expediency rather than courageous belief. Not unity so much as a shattering disunity had been sponsored, not order but disorder. The Nazi-Soviet Pact was to a very real degree a climax of smaller but cumulative crises. In meeting them, even before the Pact, more and more writers had slipped away from a belief in the "Bolshevik" alternative, which had once seemed so rosy. The Spanish War itself had demonstrated to many who participated in it, or knew it through less than a mist, that Russia had been as interested in fomenting dissension in Barcelona as in working for a speedy victory and peace. She herself had used Spain as a testing ground. Most significant of all these earlier repudiations of an ostensible idealism had been the long series of trials within Russia against internal dissidents. From 1927 on, when Trotsky and others were expelled from the Party and banished to the provinces, there was an increasing certainty that Russia herself would not permit the same encouragement of criticism she advocated abroad. Freedom of opinion, and the right of every man to search for and expose truth, could not be said to obtain under such circumstances. Education, in the American sense, was impossible unless man actually had the liberty for investigation which was promised him. In 1935, Zinoviev, Kamenev, and others were convicted and sentenced to prison; in 1936 some sixteen "self-reliants" were executed. In 1937 there were more trials, and in 1938 still others. The material achievements of which Russia boasted meant, if they existed, little more than Philistine achievements if idealism did not accompany them. Artists and writers began disconsolately watching the penned-in lot of their Soviet colleagues, with the feeling that Russia did not really respect intellectuals but found them only temporarily useful as pawns. Soviet Russia represented an orthodoxy more terrifying and oppressive than anything which American writers had termed as "Puritanism" or "Philistinism." What all these uneasinesses had begun, the Nazi-Soviet Pact brought to a climax. It was not a single crisis that had to be met, but a peak that was more than a monadnock.

The crisis that the Nazi-Soviet Pact represented for the American writer was spiritual, intellectual, and moral. He had been led by his training in the importance of truth; he was now met with a technique of deception. He believed in the primacy of the spirit, and was faced with the tactics of expediency. He had been instilled with a hatred of immorality, and was now asked to tolerate it. The very values that he had relied on, and been pledged to, were being betrayed. He had been tricked, led astray, and manipulated; and by these attitudes of distrust even his dignity as an individual had been shattered. Much more, however, than his self-respect and pride were involved, though these matters obviously came into play. The American writer had been trained too long in an American way. He had been educated in terms of a traditional role and responsibility of the writer. One of the responsibilities was the necessity of admitting errors of assessment when the truths of education pointed them out as false. It was not the least of the triumphs of the values impelling them that so many writers had the humility to admit the error of their assessment.

Not every writer did so immediately. Some were still learning and, even after the Pact, still clung to that which the United Front had promised. A public letter, in which the achievements and claims of Russia were still held forth, was published in *The Nation* in 1939, with some four hundred signatures of writers and intellectuals. The ten points of its argument were:

1. The Soviet Union continues as always to be a bulwark against war and aggression, and works unceasingly for a peaceful international order.

2. It has eliminated racial and national prejudices within its borders, freed the minority peoples enslaved under the czars, stimulated the culture and economic welfare of these peoples, and made the expression of anti-Semitism or any racial animosity a criminal offense.

3. It has socialized the means of production and distribution through the public ownership of industry and the collectivization of agriculture.

4. It has established nation-wide socialistic planning, resulting in increasingly higher living standards and the abolishment of unemployment.

5. It has built the trade unions, in which almost 24,000,000 workers are organized, into the very fabric of its society.

6. The Soviet Union has emancipated woman and the family, and has developed an advanced system of child care.

7. From the viewpoint of cultural freedom, the difference between the Soviet Union and the fascist countries is most striking. The Soviet Union has effected one of the most far-reaching cultural and educational advances in all history and among a population which at the start was almost three-fourths illiterate. Those writers and thinkers whose books have been burned by the Nazis are published in the Soviet Union. The best literature from Homer to Thomas Mann, the best thought from Aristotle to Lenin, are available to the masses of the Soviet people. . . .

8. It has replaced the myths and superstitions of old Russia with the truths and techniques of experimental science, extending scientific procedures to every field, from economics to public health.

9. The Soviet Union considers political dictatorship a transitional form and has shown a steadily expanding democracy in every sphere. Its epoch-making new constitution guarantees Soviet citizens universal suffrage, civil liberties, the right to employment, to leisure, to free education, to free medical care, to material security in sickness and old age, to equality of the sexes in all fields of activity, and to equality of all races and nationalities.

10. In relation to Russia's past, the country has been advancing rapidly along the road of material and cultural progress in ways that the American people can understand and appreciate.

This was a picture of the Soviet Union filled with appeals to the traditional American values, and by the nature of its appeal showed how strongly the values persisted as a judicial force. The assertions of the ten points did not coincide with whatever points would have clarified Fascism. Only the facts of the Soviet Union and its actions no longer seemed to fit the assertions either. Certainly they did not when Russia marched into Poland and the Baltic States, and invaded Finland. It was necessary to repeat once more the value-process of Hemingway's hero, who found abstract terms to be obscene when they did not jibe with what was actual and concrete. The error of American writers in the 1930's had not been so much that their method or values were fallacious as that putting them into effect had been only partial. Examining the abstract terms that had clouded the realities on one side, they had not pursued their method sufficiently to examine them on the other. They had for the moment drifted into a position where they were themselves properly suspect in thoroughness. But the vitality that had originally prompted them was maintained. They had demonstrated the possibility of error, but in their shift of position they showed the value of values. It was a better preservation of values to have used them than simply to have stood pat.

Nothing has restored Soviet Russia to the dream she once represented. Of his book, *I Like America*, published in 1938 when he was still a Party member, Granville Hicks could say after he had left the Party because of the Pact: "[It] contains only two or three pages, those dealing with the Soviet Union and the Party itself, that I could wish expunged." In 1950, William Rose Benét looked back on history, in a letter written little more than a week before his death. He himself had gone through many of the experiences which have been described in general terms. Now he could only say sadly:

> The situation abroad from what I can make out is pretty grim, though not to (apparently) the Daily Worker. What appalls me is that so many evil things are being done in the name of all we used to hold high-minded, for all of us at some time along the way have been taken by the dream of socialism. As poets when we were young we often inveighed against capitalism as a prison camp, and I was at first indignant at Hilaire Belloc's title for his book "The Slave State." Unfortunately he was right as rain.

What was importantly true for literary figures like Benét, and like Hicks, was not that any of their values had been proved wrong, but only the disheartening correlation of facts to them. To the values, they and others like them had stuck. It was not that being educated to truth, as Adams had put it, was incorrect, but only that their education had been incomplete. What was to be learned was—is—the true capacity to bear the burden of truth. If those writers were now old, there were others who were young and could learn from them and from history. But the endurance for both is inseparable from the iron help of the values themselves as a reliance. There is still the need for the values, and the values were not lost.

Descriptive Bibliography

1 *Jonathan Edwards and the Great Awakening*

Not only is there no single volume treating the Great Awakening in all its phases, but there is not yet one that studies the New England segment in comprehensive detail. Joseph Tracy, *The Great Awakening* (Boston: 1841), is still a valuable book, unfortunately long out of print and become a collector's item, because it reprints the major texts. For areas outside of New England three splendid studies exist, each of which is a model of its kind: Wesley M. Gewehr, *The Great Awakening in Virginia* (1930); Charles H. Maxson, *The Great Awakening in the Middle Colonies* (1920); and L. J. Trinterud, *The Forming of an American Tradition* (1949). W. W. Sweet, *Revivalism in America* (1944), treats the outburst in the perspective of the entire revivalistic tradition. A valuable study is M. W. Armstrong, "Religious Enthusiasm and Separatism in Colonial New England," *Harvard Theological Review*, Vol. XXXVIII (1945), pp. 111–40.

The intellectual issues of the period are best set forth in the relevant portions of H. W. Schneider, *The Puritan Mind* (1930): Joseph Haroutunian, *Piety versus Moralism* (1932); Alice F. Tyler, *Freedom's Ferment* (1944); F. M. Davenport, *Primitive Traits in Religious Revivals* (1905); and above all in H. R. Niebuhr's invaluable examinations, *The Social Sources of Denominationalism* (1929) and *The Kingdom of God in America* (1937).

For Edwards himself, an excellent selection for the general reader, with explanatory introductions and notes, has been published by C. H. Faust and T. H. Johnson, *Jonathan Edwards* in the American Writers Series (1935). The complicated question of the relation of the Awakening to the economic crisis of the period has been tentatively explored by J. C. Miller, "Religion, Finance and Democracy," *New England Quarterly*, Vol. VI (1933), pp. 25–58. The best biographical narrative is Ola E. Winslow, *Jonathan Edwards* (1940).

Perry Miller's book, *Jonathan Edwards*, in the American Men of Letters Series (1949) analyzes Edwards's ideas rather than his career. Three selections from his sermons during the Awakening were published as "Jonathan Edwards' Sociology of the Great Awakening," *New England Quarterly*, Vol. XXI (1948), pp. 50–78. Mr. Miller's edition of a hitherto unpublished manuscript, *Images or Shadows of Divine Things* (1948), casts light on some neglected aspects of Edwards's thinking.

2 *Insurrection in Massachusetts*

Critical but detailed accounts are provided by George R. Minot, *The History of the Insurrections in Massachusetts in the Year 1786* (Worcester: 1788; 2d ed., Boston: 1810), and Joseph G. Holland, *History of Western Massachusetts* (Springfield: 1855, 2 vols.), Vol. I, pp. 230–302. A briefer resume, in much the same spirit, is furnished by John Fiske's classic, *The Critical Period* (New York: 1888). Fiske's views of anarchy and collapse in the Confederation period have been challenged recently by Merrill Jensen, *The New Nation* (New York: 1950), but the rebellion is treated casually. A far more sympathetic handling of the incident than Fiske's is given by James T. Adams, *New England in the Republic* (Boston: 1926), and an imaginative pro-Shaysite reconstruction of the episode appears in Edward Bellamy's novel, *The Duke of Stockbridge* (1900).

For an understanding of the Massachusetts conservatives in this period, the reader is referred to Anson E. Morse, *The Federalist Party in Massachusetts to the Year 1800* (Princeton: 1909), chaps. i–iii, and, more recently, Robert A. East, "The Massachusetts Conservatives in the Critical Period," in R. B. Morris, ed., *The Era of the American Revolution* (New York: 1939). Samuel E. Morison's *Sources and Documents Illustrating the American Revolution and the Formation of the Constitution* (Oxford: 1929), pp. 208–26, offers a few choice documents on the crisis.

Certain aspects of the rebellion have been highlighted by twentieth-century investigators. Joseph P. Warren, whose unpublished doctoral thesis on Shays' Rebellion is in the Harvard University Library, has thoroughly documented the role of the federal government in the crisis in an article in the *American Historical Review*, Vol. XI (October 1905), pp. 42–67. Jonathan Smith has presented data on the debtor situation: "Features of Shays' Rebellion," *William and Mary Quarterly*, 3rd ser., Vol. V (January 1948). Aspects of Shays's career are considered by W. A. Dyer: "Embattled Farmers," *New England Quarterly* (July 1931), and R. E. Moody has furnished a portrait of Samuel Ely, Shays's precursor: *New England Quarterly* (January 1932). Sidney Kaplan has explored a number of facets of the problem, including the popular opposition to the legal profession (*South Atlantic Quarterly*, July 1949), the role of the Negroes in the movement (*Journal of Negro History*, April 1948), and the rise of a military caste in Massachusetts (*American Historical Review*, January 1951).

3 *The Yellow Fever Epidemics, 1793–1905*

The relationships of disease and human society are clearly presented in Henry E. Sigerist, *Civilization and Disease* (Ithaca, N. Y.: 1943); and a more specific discussion of the role of disease in modern European and American history is given in Richard H. Shryock, *Development of Modern Medicine* (New York: 1947, rev. ed.), chaps. v and xii. An able history of medical theory and practice concerning epidemics is C. E. A. Winslow's *Conquest of Epidemic Disease* (Princeton: 1943), see especially chap. xii. Such works provide the background, medical and social, for the story of the yellow fever epidemics in the United States.

The most dramatic of the American epidemics, that of 1793 in Philadelphia, is the subject of an extensive literature. Outstanding is the recent account by John Powell, *Bring Out Your Dead* (Philadelphia: 1949), which is vivid and at the same time critical and authentic. The part played by Dr. Rush is also analyzed, sympathetically, in Nathan Goodman, *Benjamin Rush* (Philadelphia: 1934), chaps. viii and ix; and the comments of Rush himself are given in George W. Corner, ed., *Autobiography of Benjamin Rush* (Princeton: 1948), pp. 95–102. Rush's contemporary accounts of the epidemic are listed in the Index Catalogue of the U.S.A. Surgeon General's Library (Army Medical Library), first series. Also listed there (under "Yellow Fever") and in Powell are accounts by observers who were critical of Rush. So catastrophic was this epidemic that the story has been told by literary as well as by medical men. Two Philadelphia novelists have featured it, Charles Brockden Brown in his *Arthur Mervyn* (Philadelphia: 1799), and S. Weir Mitchell in his *Red City* (New York: 1907).

Accounts of other yellow fever epidemics in the United States, both before and after 1793; can be located through the *Index Catalogue*. Scientific confusion about this disease continued throughout the nineteenth century, and is well reflected in the seventy-five pages of debate in the *Proceedings* of the Third National Sanitary Convention (New York: 1859), pp. 124–200. The final solution of the scientific problem, and something of the social implications, are well told in H. A. Kelly, *Walter Reed and Yellow Fever* (New York: 1923, 3rd ed.), and in Paul de Kruif, *The Microbe Hunters* (New York: 1926), chap. xi.

4 *South Carolina vs. the United States*

Among basic primary references for the nullification argument are Calhoun's *Disquisition on Government* and Webster's speeches in his *Works* (1853), Vol. III. A. C. McLaughlin's *A Constitutional History of the United*

States (New York: 1935) provides one of the best discussions of the legal side of the issue. C. M. Wiltse's *John C. Calhoun, Nullifier, 1829–39* (New York: 1949) is an excellent background study, and so is Charles Sydnor's *The Development of Southern Sectionalism, 1819–1848* (Baton Rouge: 1949). *A Critical Discussion of Nullification in South Carolina* by David Houston, though published in 1896 (New York), is still a standard work on the record of events in South Carolina. Peter Drucker's "A Key to American Politics: Calhoun's Pluralism," *Review of Politics* (October 1948), should be coupled with Richard Current's "John C. Calhoun, Philosopher of Reaction," *Antioch Review* (Summer 1934). Both are stimulating short treatments of Calhoun's political theory.

Other useful studies are: Marquis James, *The Life of Andrew Jackson* (New York: 1938); J. T. Carpenter, *The South as a Conscious Minority* (New York: 1930); F. B. Friedel, *Francis Lieber: Nineteenth Century Liberal* (New York: 1948); Laura A. White, *Robert Barnwell Rhett: Father of Secession* (New York: 1931); Frederick Bancroft, *Calhoun and the South Carolina Nullification* (Baltimore: 1928); C. S. Boucher, *The Nullification Controversy in South Carolina* (Chicago: 1916); William Dodd, *Statesmen of the Old South* (New York: 1929); Richard Hofstadter, *The American Political Tradition* (New York: 1949); A. M. Schlesinger, Jr., *The Age of Jackson* (Boston: 1945).

5 Horace Mann's Crusade

Manuscript materials by and about Horace Mann are to be found, naturally enough, in the great manuscript collections of Greater Boston. The so-called *Life and Works of Horace Mann,* edited by Mrs. Mann in three volumes (1865–8), and enlarged to five volumes by G. C. Mann in 1891, is sufficient for most purposes, albeit the life is uncritical. Horace Mann's reports, especially the famous Tenth Annual Report, are included. Old-fashioned but good are B. A. Hinsdale, *Horace Mann and the Common School Revival in the United States* (1898; reprinted 1911); and G. Compayré, *Horace Mann and the Public School in the United States* (translated, New York: 1907). With these should be read George H. Martin, *The Evolution of the Massachusetts Public School System* (New York: 1894, 1904). The two best interpretations of Mann's special difficulties and his special value are undoubtedly Raymond B. Culver, *Horace Mann and Religion in the Massachusetts Public Schools* (New Haven: 1929); and the discussion of Mann in Merle Curti's admirable *The Social Ideas of American Educators* (New York: 1935).

Background studies and useful books include Paul Monroe, *The Founding of the American Public School System* (New York: 1940); S. L. Jackson, *America's Struggle for Free Schools* (Washington, D. C.: 1941); F. T. Carlton, *Economic Influences upon Educational Progress in the United States*, Bulletin of the University of Wisconsin, No. 221; Edgar W. Knight, *Education in the United States* (Boston: 1934); Philip R. V. Curoe, *Educational Attitudes and Policies of Organized Labor in the United States* (New York: 1926); Emit D. Grizzell, *Origin and Development of the High School in New England before 1865* (New York: 1923); Edward H. Reisner, *The Evolution of the Common School* (New York: 1930). Books on American social history in the period are legion; perhaps as good an introduction as any is Alice F. Tyler, *Freedom's Ferment: Phases of American Social History to 1860* (Minneapolis: 1944). Appropriate volumes of the History of American Life series may also be usefully consulted. But in truth a new critical study of Horace Mann is needed and is not available.

6 *John Brown's Private War*

The starting-point in all John Brown bibliography is James C. Malin, *John Brown and the Legend of Fifty-six* (Philadelphia: 1942). More than half of this monumental work is devoted to an analysis and critique of the bibliography and historiography of the subject. None of the numerous Brown biographies approaches Malin's work in quality of scholarship. Two of them, written from opposite points of view, are of especial interest. They are Oswald Garrison Villard, *John Brown: A Biography Fifty Years After* (Boston: 1910), and Robert Penn Warren, *John Brown: the Making of a Martyr* (New York: 1929).

Of the legend-makers, two prominent examples are James Redpath, *The Public Life of Captain John Brown* (Boston: 1860), and Franklin B. Sanborn, *The Life and Letters of John Brown* (Boston: 1885). A scholarly analysis of the literature of the legend—which includes 255 poems, 31 plays, 58 novels, and 14 biographies—is Joy K. Talbert, "John Brown in American Literature," Ph.D. dissertation (University of Kansas; 1941, 2 vols.).

The most important published source material on Harper's Ferry is the result of a Congressional investigation of the raid, usually called the "Mason Report." It contains Brown's "Provisional Constitution," among other documents, and will be found in U.S. Senate Reports, 36th Cong., 1st Sess., No. 278. The unpublished documents are scattered in several collections. After the fall of Richmond in 1865 many of the Brown papers captured at Harper's Ferry were stolen and dispersed, but the largest and most illuminating part of them is still to be found in the Virginia State Library in Richmond. Another part, including the affidavits concerning insanity in the Brown family, are in the John Brown Papers in the Library of Congress. The Boston Public Library and the Massachusetts Historical Society contain a large number of manuscripts bearing on the raid. A convenient collection of the first public tributes to the martyr is James Redpath, *Echoes of Harper's Ferry* (Boston: 1860).

The most interesting recent study of the period of Harper's Ferry is Allan Nevins, *The Emergence of Lincoln* (New York: 1950), especially Volume II. The Ohio background of Brown is pictured in Mary Land, "John Brown's Ohio Environment," *Ohio State Archæological and Historical Quarterly*, LVII (1948), 24–47. The best biography of one of the Harper's Ferry conspirators is Ralph V. Harlow, *Gerrit Smith: Philanthropist and Reformer* (New York: 1939). On abolitionism see Gilbert H. Barnes, *The Antislavery Impulse, 1830–1844* (New York: 1933), and Dwight L. Dumond, *Antislavery Origins of the Civil War in the United States* (Ann Arbor, Mich.: 1939). On the Southern background Ollinger Crenshaw, *Slave States in the Presidential Election of 1860* (Baltimore: 1945), and Clement Eaton, *Freedom of Thought in the Old South* (Durham, N. C.: 1940), are of value. For the psychology and politics of the national setting of the crisis, Avery Craven, *The Coming of the Civil War* (New York: 1942), and Roy Nichols, *The Disruption of American Democracy* (New York: 1949), are recommended.

7 Upheaval at Homestead

There is no full-length scholarly study of the Homestead Strike. Recommended brief treatments of varying length and competency are in Samuel Yellen, *American Labor Struggles* (New York: 1936), and John R. Commons and Associates, *History of Labour in the United States* (New York: 1918), Vol. II. The first of these is preferred.

The fullest treatment of the entire Homestead episode, sympathetic to labor, and the basis for most later treatments, is Arthur G. Burgoyne, *Homestead. A Complete History of the Struggle of July, 1892, between the Carnegie Steel Company, Limited, and the Amalgamated Association of Iron and Steel Workers* (Pittsburgh: 1893). Also of value is another prolabor early account, M. R. Stowell, *Fort Frick* (1893).

Significant documentary sources are U.S. House of Representatives, *Employment of Pinkerton Detectives*, 52nd Cong., 2nd Sess., Report No. 2447 (Washington, D. C.: 1893); U.S. Senate, *Investigation of Labor Troubles*, 52nd Cong., 2nd Sess., Report No. 1280 (Washington, D. C.: 1893). The first contains much richer information than the second. Testimony presented before the House and Senate Committees, bearing on the role of the Pinkertons in the Homestead Strike, is reprinted, together with other material, in *Pinkerton's National Detective Agency and Its Connections with the Labor Troubles at Homestead, Penn., July 6th, 1892* (New York: 1892).

Some sense of the shape of contemporary opinion can be derived from three articles in the *North American Review*, Vol. CLV (September 1892): W. C. Oates, "The Homestead Strike. I. A. Congressional View"; G. T. Curtis, "The Homestead Strike. II. A Constitutional View"; T. V. Powderly, "The Homestead Strike. III. A Knight of Labor's View." For the effect of the episode on the churches, consult Henry F. May, *Protestant Churches and Industrial America* (New York: 1949). The role of the American Federation of Labor is indicated in Samuel Gompers, *Seventy Years of Life and Labor* (New York: 1925), Vol. I.

Two volumes in *The Pittsburgh Survey* are very helpful on the setting and the labor force at Homestead: Margaret F. Byington, *Homestead: The Households of a Mill Town* (New York: 1910) and John A. Fitch, *The Steel Workers* (New York: 1910). The second is excellent for the Amalgamated Association of Iron and Steel Workers. For the Carnegie Steel Company and Andrew Carnegie's role in connection with the strike, see James H. Bridge, *The Inside History of the Carnegie Steel Company* (New York: 1903). The Carnegie enterprise and the strike receive extended treatments in J. K. Winkler, *Incredible Carnegie* (New York: 1931); Burton J. Hendrick, *The Life of Andrew Carnegie* (New York: 1932); George Harvey, *Henry Clay Frick the Man* (New York and London: 1928); and *The Autobiography of Andrew Carnegie* (Boston and New York: 1920).

Alexander Berkman, *Memoirs* (New York: 1912), and Emma Goldman, *Living My Life* (New York: 1931), Vol. I, deal with Berkman's attempt on H. C. Frick's life.

8 *Manifest Destiny and the Philippines*

The best study of the ideology and psychology of American expansionism is Albert Weinberg's *Manifest Destiny* (Baltimore: 1935). Julius W. Pratt, *Expansionists of 1898*, is classic on the origins of the Spanish War and imperialism; see also his essay, "The Ideology of American Expansion," in *Essays in Honor of William S. Dodd* (Chicago: 1935), and for a general survey of American empire his *America's Colonial Experiment* (New York: 1950). Walter Millis, *The Martial Spirit* (Boston: 1931), is still excellent on the general climate of the 1890's, as on the war itself. The best interpretation of the imperialist politicians, in their larger social setting, is that of Matthew Josephson in the opening chapters of *The President Makers* (New York: 1940); there is also a mine of information at various points in Alfred Vagts's magnificent study, *Deutschland und die Vereinigten Staaten in der Weltpolitik* (New York: 1935, 2 vols.). On the role of the press, Joseph E. Wisan, *The Cuban Crisis as Reflected in the New York Press* (New York: 1934), goes beyond the modest claims of its title; Marcus M.

Wilkerson, *Public Opinion and the Spanish American War* (Baton Rouge: 1932), is also helpful. Thomas A. Bailey, *A Diplomatic History of the American People* (New York: 1950), is particularly suggestive about the domestic roots and repercussions of foreign policy.

The following are also of special value: Harold and Margaret Sprout, *The Rise of American Naval Power* (Princeton: 1939); Tyler Dennett, *Americans in Eastern Asia* (New York: 1941); F. R. Dulles, *America in the Pacific* (Boston: 1932); A. L. P. Dennis, *Adventures in American Diplomacy, 1896–1906* (New York: 1928); A. Whitney Griswold, *Far Eastern Policy of the United States* (New York: 1938); Grayson L. Kirk, *Philippine Independence* (New York: 1936), Moorfield Storey and H. P. Lichauco, *The Conquest of the Philippines by the United States* (New York: 1926).

9 Rebellion in Art

The catalogue of the Armory Show, which lists about 1,100 works by over 300 exhibitors, of whom more than 100 were Europeans, is incomplete. Many works added in the course of the exhibition were not catalogued, and groups of drawings and prints by the same artist were listed as single works. Mr. Walter Pach estimates that there were altogether about 1,600 objects in the Show. (Association of American Painters and Sculptors, Inc., New York. International Exhibition of Modern Art, February 17–March 15, 1913. A second edition with a supplement was published for the exhibition to the Chicago Art Institute, March 24–April 16, 1913, and reprinted for the Boston showing, April 28–May 19, 1913.) An attempt to recatalogue all these works and to trace their later history was made by Miss Chloe Hamilton in a master's thesis, unpublished, at Oberlin College ("The Armory Show: Its History and Significance," 1950), an excellent study that I was able to consult through the kindness of the library of the college. The late Walt Kuhn, one of the organizers of the Show, has recalled its history in an anniversary pamphlet: "Twenty-Fve Years After: The Story of the Armory Show" (New York: 1938), and another of the participants, Mr. Walter Pach, who was especially active in recommending and borrowing European works for the Show, has written about it in *Queer Thing, Painting* (New York: 1938), ch. xvii. For accounts of the Show by later writers, see Jerome Mellquist, *The Emergence of an American Art* (1942), and Oliver W. Larkin, *Life and Art in America* (1949). For contemporary opinions and criticisms, see the pamphlet edited by James Gregg, "For and Against" (1913), and the March 1913 issue of *Arts and Decoration*, III, pp. 149–84; *The Nation*, Vols. XCVI–VII (1913), pp. 174, 240–3, 281 (including the review by Frank Jewett Mather); *Life*, Vol. LXI (1913), pp. 531, 572, 577, 675, 680, 688, 740, 827, 838; *Century Magazine*, Vol. LXV

(1913–14), pp. 825 ff.; *Current Opinion*, Vol. LIV (1913), pp. 316 ff. Collections of clippings about the Show from newspapers and magazines are preserved at the Museum of Modern Art in New York, and at the New York Public Library.

For the ideas about modern art at the time of the Show, see Willard Huntington Wright, *Modern Painting* (New York: 1915), and, on a lower level, Arthur J. Eddy, *Cubists and Post-Impressionists* (Chicago: 1914); Roger Fry, preface to the Catalogue of the Second French Post-Impressionists Exhibition at the Grafton Galleries (London: 1912), reprinted in *Vision and Design* (London: 1920); Clive Bell, *Art* (London: 1914); *Blast*, edited by Wyndham Lewis, Review of the Great English Vortex, No. 1 (London, New York, and Toronto: June 20, 1914). Influential writings by European artists, translated into English, were Wassily Kandinsky, *Concerning Spiritual Harmony* (London: 1913); Albert Gleizes and Jean Metzinger, *Cubism* (London: 1913); Guillaume Apollinaire, *The Cubist Painters* (New York: 1944). Very important as an organ of American modernist taste was the periodical of photography, *Camera Work* (New York: 1902–17), inspired mainly by Alfred Stieglitz. On his personality and work, see Waldo Frank and others, *America and Alfred Stieglitz: A Collective Portrait* (New York: 1934). The great collection of Jchn Quinn, who was closely associated with the history of the Show, has been catalogued: "John Quinn, 1870–1925, Collection of Paintings, Water Colors, Drawings and Sculpture" (Huntington, New York: 1926).

10 *Woodrow Wilson's Tour*

The best source-material for the great battle over the League is to be found in the speeches of Woodrow Wilson, and the best edition of these speeches is *Woodrow Wilson, War and Peace: Presidential Messages, Addresses and Public Papers* (1917–24), Ray Stannard Baker and Willian E. Dodd, eds. (New York: 1927, 2 vols.). Of substantial importance is Edith Bolling Wilson, *My Memoir* (Indianapolis: 1939). Of less significance are J. P. Tumulty, *Woodrow Wilson as I Know Him* (Garden City, N. Y.: 1921), David F. Houston, *Eight Years with Wilson's Cabinet* (Garden City, N. Y.: 1926), and David Lawrence, *The True Story of Woodrow Wilson* (New York: 1924). Senator Lodge wrote an interesting account of the League fight from his own point of view, *The Senate and the League of Nations* (New York: 1925). Of great significance, as giving a contemporary view, though not so readily accessible, is David Hunter Miller, *My Diary at the Conference of Paris* (New York: 1924–6, 21 vols.). *The Intimate Papers of Colonel House*, edited by Charles Seymour (Boston: 1928), is of value. The robust student will, of course, find large bodies of material in the

Congressional Record for the session of 1919–20 (66th Cong., 1st Sess.) and in the hearings of the Senate Committee on Foreign Relations on the Treaty of Versailles (*Sen. Docs.*, 66th Cong., 1st Sess., No. 106). For press views of the struggle, and the movement of public opinion, it is necessary to consult the *Literary Digest* and the very full accounts of the struggle in the *New York Times*, made readily accessible by the Index. There is, of course, a voluminous periodical literature on the whole problem, but the reaction against the treaty is well studied in the files of *The Nation* and *The New Republic*, while a fairer view is to be found in *Review of Reviews* and *Outlook*.

Of secondary works, by far the best is Thomas A. Bailey, *Woodrow Wilson and the Great Betrayal* (New York: 1945). An account, extremely favorable to the President, of the party struggle is that by D. F. Fleming, *The United States and the League of Nations, 1918–1920* (New York: 1932), and another interesting discussion is that in Ruhl J. Bartlett, *The League to Enforce Peace* (Chapel Hill, N. C.: 1944). An excellent objective account is to be found in W. S. Holt, *Treaties Defeated by the Senate* (Baltimore: 1933). There are, of course, many biographies of Wilson, none of the very first order, but to the ones already mentioned for their value as sources there should be added, on the laudatory side, the one by William E. Dodd (Garden City, N. Y.: 1921), and, on the critical side, Robert E. Annin (New York: 1924). There are two biographies of Lodge, one by William Lawrence (Boston: 1925), favorable in tone, and one by Karl Schriftgiesser (Boston: 1944), extremely critical. One should also consult Claudius O. Johnson, *Borah of Idaho* (New York: 1936), and Philip C. Jessup, *Elihu Root* (New York: 1938, 2 vols.). Some interesting commentary is to be found in Stephen Bonsal, *Unfinished Business* (New York: 1944). See also Allan Nevins, *Henry White* (New York: 1930). For additional materials see the bibliography in Bailey, *Woodrow Wilson and the Great Betrayal*.

11 *When the Banks Closed*

For the period leading to the banking crisis there is no better narrative than Frederick Lewis Allen, *The Lords of Creation* (New York: 1935), especially chapters xiii–xiv, or the same author's *Since Yesterday* (New York: 1940), pp. 1–128. C. C. Nolt, *28 Days: A History of the Banking Crisis* (New York: 1933), is a contemporary chronological account. Reminiscences of an early New Deal "brain-truster" who had the advantage of intimate knowledge of government policy, colored by the circumstances of his own participation, are contained in Raymond Moley, *After Seven Years* (New York: 1939), pp. 138–95 and 366–7.

A general history of the New Deal decade is Dixon Wecter, *The Age of the Great Depression, 1929–1941* (New York: 1949). Broadus Mitchell, *Depression Decade* (New York: 1947), presents an economic history, chapters iv and v of which deal with the banking crisis. An analysis of the economic difficulties that produced the crisis, written shortly after the event and expounding the belief that fundamental change was required, is George Soule, *The Coming American Revolution* (New York: 1936). Official documents covering the banking crisis and the action taken by the President are contained in Samuel I. Rosenman (ed.), *The Public Papers and Addresses of Franklin D. Roosevelt*, Vol. II, pp. 3–47.

A hostile analysis of President Hoover's attack on the depression, in a contemporary pamphlet by one of Franklin D. Roosevelt's advisers, is Rexford G. Tugwell, *Mr. Hoover's Economic Policy* (New York: 1932). W. S. Myers and W. H. Newton, *The Hoover Administration* (New York: 1936), presents a documented history by adherents of Mr. Hoover.

News accounts of the crisis may be found in *New York Times,* March 8, 9 and 10, 1933, and in *The Analyst,* Vol. XLI, pp. 288–9, 361–2, 392–3, 456–7. Editorial comment and interpretation suggesting more fundamental reforms than occurred are in *The New Republic,* Vol. LXXIV, pp. 87, 88–91, 112, 116–18, 157–9, 176–8. See also *The Nation,* Vol. CXXXVI, pp. 247–8, 252, 276–7, 278.

12 *The Black Blizzards*

Basic materials for this essay include C. W. Thornthwaite's discussion of fundamental environmental patterns as they affect human activity and welfare in the great plains—see Carter Goodrich *et al., Migration and Economic Opportunity* (University of Pennsylvania; 1936), pp. 202–50, and Hugh Bennett, *Soil Conservation* (New York: McGraw-Hill; 1939), pp. 2–15 and 726–70, a general reference work containing a general study of erosion problems in the United States and a detailed consideration of conditions in the great plains. *Climate and Man,* edited by Gove Hambidge (Yearbook, U.S. Department of Agriculture, Washington, D. C.: 1941) is also a valuable source that contains, besides pertinent general articles, abundant reference-tables on climatic characteristics in all parts of the United States.

For more particularized books and essays on the problem, the following are recommended. James C. Malin, *The Grassland of North America* (Lawrence, Kans.: 1947), pp. 120–55, is a notable effort by a historian to review the entire ecological background of the region in which he is interested. Professor Malin is, however, highly critical of the judgment of ecologists who attribute heightened severity of the effect of drouth and dust storm to human interference. For a less technical analysis of the impact of man on nature, especially in North America, Paul B. Sears, *Deserts on the March* (Norman, Okla.: 1935, 2nd ed.), should be consulted. "Dust in the Eyes of Science," in Russell Lord, *Forever the Land* (Harpers; 1950), pp. 273-9, is a discussion of dust storms and their causes, particularly in the Basin of Mexico.

Readers looking for graphic personal accounts of the dust storms and their consequences will find the following titles relevant. Lawrence Svobida, *An Empire of Dust* (Caldwell, Ida.: Caxton Printers; 1940), is a description of what it means to the individual farm-operator to be overtaken by drouth and dust. Two other accounts that ought to be read in conjunction are George S. Reeves, *A Man from South Dakota* (New York: 1950), and Mari Sandoz, *Old Jules* (Boston: 1935). The first is a personal account of struggles, failures, and adjustments on subhumid land while the second is the biography of a rugged immigrant who attempts to impose old patterns of land use on a new and difficult environment. John Steinbeck's well-known novel, *The Grapes of Wrath* (New York: Viking; 1939), the dramatic experience of a family "tractored out" and forced to migrate from Oklahoma to California, is also relevant. Steinbeck places the Dust Bowl too far east, and his book has probably had more effect on treatment of California immigrants than on land use in Oklahoma, but it remains a powerful and important work of fiction.

13 *Black Legions on the March*

Social scientific literature on native American Fascism in the nineteen thirties is indeed limited. The concluding chapters of Gustavus Myers's *History of Bigotry in the United States* (New York: Random House; 1943) supplies a historical account of the main activities of nativist groups during the period. Donald Strong in *Organized Anti-Semitism in America: The Rise of Group Prejudice during the Decade, 1930–1940* (Washington, D. C.: American Council on Public Affairs; 1940) gives another descriptive account of those organizations which were predominantly anti-Semitic during the period.

Leo Lowenthal and Norman Guterman have undertaken an analysis of the propaganda themes of Fascist agitators as a method of understanding American Fascism: *Prophets of Deceit* (New York: Harpers; 1950). Their volume, which is psychologically oriented, is an insightful study of one phase of the problem. Around the period of Pearl Harbor, the Department of Justice prepared a number of systematic propaganda-studies that were used in court cases against seditious native Fascists. An excellent sum-mary of this work is contained in *The Language of Politics* by Harold D. Lasswell and others, chap. ix, "Propaganda Detection and the Courts." (New York: Stewart; 1949). An interesting attempt to trace some of the intellectual aspects of antidemocratic political thinking in the United States is contained in David Spitz's *Patterns of Anti-Democratic Thought* (New York: 1949).

Two journalists, Raymond Gram Swing in *Forerunners of Fascism* (New York: Julian Messner; 1935) and Jay Franklin in *American Messiahs* (New York: Simon and Schuster; 1935) have written with much concrete insight on the political 'skills of a number of leading contenders for nativist leadership in the Great Depression. Harnett Kane in *Louisiana Hayride* (New York: Morrow; 1941) presents a detailed and accurate account of the career of Huey Long. Further evaluations of Huey Long are contained in an exchange of viewpoints between Gerald L. K. Smith, a follower of Huey Long, and Hodding Canter, Southern journalist, published under the title, "How Come Huey Long?" *The New Republic* (February 19, 1935). Long's early program for action is contained in his book entitled *Every Man a King* (New Orleans: 1933).

A number of private investigators have written books of varying merit, which in the main are characterized by an exposé outlook. They are much richer in concrete personal details than they are descriptive of the processes of these organizations. The most popular and richest in detail of all these books is John Roy Carlson, *Undercover* (New York: Dutton; 1943). John L. Spivak in *Shrine of the Silver Dollar* (New York: 1940) has written about Father Coughlin with special reference to his alleged financial transactions and interests.

Considerable research has been done on the social psychology of Fascist predispositions and personality among various strata of the population. One of the most ambitious efforts in this regard is the Studies in Prejudice Series, of which *The Authoritarian Personality by Theodore Adorno* (New York: Harpers; 1950) and *The Dynamics of Prejudice* by Bruno Bettelheim and Morris Janowitz (New York; Harpers; 1950) can be mentioned. Both deal explicitly with the interrelations of personality, prejudice, and the politics of persecution. Two commentaries on these works are contained in Nathan Glazer, "The Authoritarian Personality," *Commentary* (June 1950), pp. 573–83, and Paul Kecskemeti, "Prejudice in the Catastrophic Perspective," *Commentary* (March 1951), pp. 286–92.

Finally, Sinclair Lewis's novel *It Can't Happen Here* (New York: 1935), which projects a portrait of the United States under native Fascism, still stands as a relevant and insightful piece of writing.

14 *The Nazi-Soviet Pact and the End of a Dream*

No single intellectual or emotional career of an American writer can be said to have followed consistently, or at each step, the pattern that has been sketched in the essay on this subject. But a background to the general quandary of writers in the twentieth century can be found in the personal narratives of *The Education of Henry Adams* (Washington: 1907), Jack London's *Martin Eden* (New York: 1909), and *The Autobiography of Lincoln Steffens* (New York: 1931). Also useful is Henry Adams's *The Degradation of the Democratic Dogma* (New York: 1919), which contains "The Tendency of History" and "A Letter to American Teachers of History." Hajo Holborn's *The Political Collapse of Europe* (New York: 1951) will be valuable for refreshing the knowledge of the European political correlatives, while Dixon Wecter's *The Age of the Great Depression* (New York: 1948) is important for the American scene during the thirties. The strain of American self-criticism, in the novel, can be found at every hand. Useful reading, with particular reference to this essay, will be found in Robert Cantwell's *The Land of Plenty* (New York: 1934); John Dos Passos's *Manhattan Transfer* (New York: 1925) and *U.S.A.* (New York: 1937); Ernest Hemingway's *A Farewell to Arms* (New York: 1929) and *For Whom the Bell Tolls* (New York: 1940); and James T. Farrell's *Studs Lonigan* (New York: 1938). Of particular importance are the two volumes of public addresses contained in *American Writers' Congress* (New York: 1935) and *The Writer in a Changing World* (New York: 1937), both edited by Henry Hart. Of parallel interest will be *Proletarian Literature in the United States* (New York: 1935), an anthology of fiction and poetry, edited by Granville Hicks and others; and "The Situation in American Writing," *Partisan Review*, Vol. VI (Summer 1939), pp. 25–51, and (Fall 1939), pp. 103–23, which consists of responses to a questionnaire by leading American writers. Similarly useful are Granville Hicks's *I Like America* (New York: 1938), a statement of values and intentions; the open letter from Jay Allen and others, "To All Active Supporters of Democracy and Peace," *The Nation*, Vol. CXLIX (August 26, 1939), p. 228; and Kenneth Rexroth, "Fighting Words for Peace," *The New Republic*, Vol. XC (October 4, 1939), pp. 245–6. The shift in position on the part of writers is to be found in many sources. Characteristic statements are to be found in John Dos Passos's novel, *Adventures of a Young Man* (New York: 1939), and in *The Ground We Stand On* (New York: 1941), a series of essays on the traditional democratic faith; in I. DeWitt Talmadge, ed., *Whose Revolution?* (New York: 1941), statements by Cowley, Hicks, and others on the post-Pact situation of the Liberal; in Archibald MacLeish's *A Time to Speak* (Boston: 1941), selected prose; and in R. H. S. Crossman, ed. *The God that Failed* (New York: 1950), which contains accounts of their abandonment of Communism by Gide, Koestler, Silone, Richard Wright, Louis Fischer, and Spender. Sidney Hook's "Communism and the Intellectuals," *American Mercury*, Vol. LXVIII (February 1949), pp. 133–44, is a biting analysis of the situation. In conclusion the reader will do well to examine the admirable statements contained in Ralph Barton Perry's *Shall Not Perish from the Earth* (New York: 1940), an essay on American values; and in Carl Becker's *How New Will the Better World Be?* (New York: 1944), a discussion of postwar reconstruction.